D1328312

THE SOVEREIGNTY
OF GRACE

THE SOVEREIGNTY
OF GRACE

Arthur C. Custance

Presbyterian and Reformed Publishing Company
Phillipsburg, New Jersey

To

An irrepressible and wholly dedicated secretary,
Evelyn May White. Never did any writer have
such a loyal and enthusiastic co-worker, nor such
a faithful critic.

ACKNOWLEDGMENTS

I wish to express my thanks to two of the Lord's people who helped in the preparation of this volume.

To **Hal Lochrie** who read the manuscript in an earlier stage with great care and perceptiveness and made a number of valuable suggestions.

To **Ruth Lochrie** who provided invaluable help in making the Index of Biblical References.

And to **Marie Schaub** who, in a busy life, found time to do a splendid job of typing the greater part of the original manuscript.

CONTENTS

PART TWO

THE CRYSTALLIZATION OF THE
THEOLOGY OF GRACE

Section One
Definition of *Total*

Section Two
Definition of *Depravity*

PART THREE

THE IMPLICATIONS FOR DAILY LIFE

PART FOUR

ELECTION AND EVANGELISM

PART FIVE

THE FUTURE OF THE NON-ELECT

INTRODUCTION

In the very worst period of the great depression in Canada, I found myself in the fall of 1933 in the province of Saskatchewan, which was perhaps the hardest hit of all the provinces. And I found myself in the worst possible position in terms of survival, since I had no resources and no job, and at that time there was no such thing as relief or welfare for transients. I was some miles north of Prince Albert, facing the winter months in a tiny little shack about twelve by sixteen feet in an area where coal was not available and wood was scarce. The temperature in this part of Canada can be bitterly cold, so cold in fact that the tiny stove I had would not keep itself going much of the time, and the temperature would drop to about -25°F. *inside*. On one occasion a hot water bottle froze in the bed during the night!

Yet it was marvellously quiet, and, since I had come to know the Lord only about a year before, the Bible was largely an unknown book to me and I had a wonderful opportunity to study it. That winter I went eight times through the entire Bible and worked out, almost entirely on my own, a personal systematic theology. I shall never regret the cold or the isolation. It was a golden period of my life in many ways, and an enormous privilege.

One afternoon that stands out in my memory as a time of glorious apprehension, I knelt down on a small rug which a friend had made for me out of overcoat samples, and I opened my Bible that lay on the bed before me at John 15. I have always loved to study on my knees. I still have my bed lighted specifically for this purpose—and what better attitude could there be for studying the Word of God? I read meditatively with pencil in hand, marking things as I went, and in due time I came to John 15:16: "Ye have not chosen Me, but I have chosen you." The words seemed to stand out from the page and this tremendous truth flooded my soul. I seemed to be kneeling in the silence of an eternity and hearing the words inwardly for the first time, though it was by no means the first time I had read them. I was quite simply overwhelmed. He, the Lord Jesus Christ, had chosen me; not I Him! I had always assumed myself to be the one who had acted. It was I who for some reason had felt a need and sought the Lord to fulfill it. I was the one who had taken the initiative.

In the youthful enthusiasm of my Christian experience (I was then twenty-three) I had often preached to small groups and spoken to individuals about their need of a Saviour. It had seemed proper to argue with them, or plead with them, or in one way or another try to persuade them to "make their decision for the Lord," as I supposed I had made my decision for the Lord. It seemed to me to be my privilege and responsibility to persuade men by the zeal of my missionary activity. But here, suddenly, I was jolted into the realization that it was not I who had decided for the Lord; the Lord had decided for me! I have had the joy since of leading not a few to the Lord over the years and, what is perhaps every bit as important, of seeing many of these new bairns go on and grow into mature and fruitful children of God. And I know that at times it must have seemed to anyone watching my activities that I really did believe my powers of persuasion can be critical in the moment of decision. Yet I know this is not so.

I know with my heart and my mind that in the final analysis it is the Lord's work to draw men unto Himself and ours only to "lift Him up" (John 3:14). Men are not born again by human will, nor because of blood relationships, nor even because out of their own inner being they desire to be saved (John 1:12, 13). It is perfectly true that whosoever will may come, but it is also true that whosoever *may, will* come. We will to come only because God has graciously worked upon our wills to turn them about. We may come only because He has opened the way for us and in us, making it possible. Whosoever will, may come; and whosoever may, will come. When God makes it possible by converting our wills to seek his face, then we may come, and only then. At the same time, because of his sovereignty, once this turnabout has been wrought in us by his Holy Spirit, then the rest is certain, no matter how long it takes. We *shall* come.

As I knelt before the Lord after hearing these wonderful words, in a manner of speaking, for the first time, there was instantly born in my mind a first real intimation of man's true nature and of the sovereignty of God's grace. And I spent the remainder of those winter months reading nothing but the Word of God and constantly finding in it reflections of the wonderful truth of his sovereignty in our salvation. This became the rock upon which over a period of some forty years I thereafter built the edifice of my theology.

During the winter months of 1970-1976, after retirement, I lectured or gave seminars to varying numbers of people from fifteen to two hundred in this quiet little town and always the ultimate emphasis has been upon the sovereignty of grace. Finally it seemed good to try to set down something of the substance of these lectures and seminars in the hope that their usefulness might in the Lord's goodness be extended to a larger audience.

Due to the circumstances under which my theological development took place, without formal training in the subject and usually far away from the kind of library facilities that are considered normal to such a training, surprisingly little was owed in my development to the great writers on these themes like Augustine, Calvin, Owen, Spurgeon, Hodge, Strong, Warfield and a host of others. All of these I read now with delight, and it never ceases to amaze me how a deep study of these great fundamental truths in the Word of God leads to a meeting of minds. Those winter months nearly forty-five years ago established a pattern of thinking which subsequently worked itself out until the agreement with these great men of God was very nearly complete. What they contributed above all was refinement and certain modes of expression which are beautifully apt. When I began to read them for the first time about fifteen years ago, I found their powers of expression when dealing with matters that I had struggled to put into words by myself were like a great liberating force, setting my mind free in wonderful new ways. But this circumstance may explain in part why I have not always followed the lines of reasoning which are customarily followed by those whose training and background has been more formal and routine. This is why I have sometimes used different passages of Scripture to support the same basic conclusions. And this is why I have coined some phrases and developed some lines of argument that they did not employ. But my agreement with them is well-nigh complete.

I'm not sure that Calvin was always wholly logical in his conclusions, but then I am sure I am not either. I do not agree with him, for example, in his view regarding Double Predestination, not for philosophical reasons, but because I do not believe either Scripture or logic demands it. And I suspect Calvin himself may have had second thoughts on the matter.

As to the great Confessions—the *Westminster Confession*, the *Thirty-Nine Articles*, the *Heidelberg Confession*, the *Canons of Dort*, and so forth—I rejoice in them. Surely here the human mind has been exercised with the deepest and most profound aspects of truth, finding a peculiarly appropriate eloquence for the task in the choice of words. What feasts these statements are, and how poor is the man who has never reflected upon them! Surely there is no meatier food for the human intellect than is here displayed in an ordered form.

And so with these words of explanation, I commend to the Lord this study of his gracious sovereignty in salvation, without which no man would be saved, but all would remain dead and lost. I cannot but rejoice in the wonderful words of a hymn which expresses so profoundly, yet so succinctly, the great truth which I have struggled to elaborate in the chapters which follow.

> I sought the Lord, and afterward I knew
> He moved my soul to seek Him, seeking me;

It was not I that found, O Saviour true;
No! I was found of Thee.

Thou didst reach forth thy hand and mine enfold;
I walked and sank not on the storm-vexed sea;
'Twas not so much that I on Thee took hold,
As Thou, dear Lord, on me.

I find, I walk, I love; but O the whole
Of love is but my answer, Lord, to Thee!
For Thou wert long beforehand with my soul;
Always Thou lovedst me.

(Anonymous)

Arthur C. Custance
"The Terraces"
Butternut Bay Road
Brockville, Ontario,
Canada

PART ONE

From the New Testament
to the Reformation:
A Historical Survey

1

THE BIBLICAL BACKGROUND

This is by no means a *history* of the doctrine of Election. It is an attempt to provide the reader with some sense of continuity. For the doctrine of Predestination and Election is not a new thing that began with Calvin and has since gradually lost favour with the passing of the years until today it is believed by only a few and understood by even fewer. It is synonymous with the Gospel of salvation by grace. It *is* the Gospel, in fact.

Every departure from the doctrine of Election in any degree has been a departure from the Gospel, for such departure always involves the introduction of some obligation on man's part to make a contribution towards his own salvation, a contribution he simply cannot make. This is unrealistic with respect to man and dishonouring with respect to God. There are no shades of truth here. This is an all-or-nothing doctrine. Election and the Gospel are alike in this. There are no halfway positions that are not a total betrayal of the truth of God. Paul is very explicit and completely logical when he says regarding the method by which man is to be saved, "If [it is] by grace, then it is no more works: otherwise grace is no more grace. But if it be works, then it is no more grace: otherwise work is no more work" (Rom. 11:6). There simply is no way out of this equation. If man contributes anything whatever to his salvation, even his own responsiveness of heart or the exercise of his own faith, then salvation is no longer by grace. For it becomes a co-operative effort between man and God in which the decision of man and not of God determines the issue.

Mention of the words *Election* or *Predestination* today, in any but a theological environment, almost inevitably brings to people's minds the name of Calvin as though it all began with him and was an unheard-of doctrine before his time. Very few are aware of the continuity of the tradition during the centuries following the close of the New Testament. Even fewer people are aware of the fact that John's Gospel probably contains the most explicit and most frequent statements on the subject to be found in the Bible. And perhaps almost no one who has not studied the subject in depth will be aware that the Old Testament is also full of it. It is, in very truth, the kernel of the Gospel and thus is common to the whole of Scripture in symbol, parable, and plain declaration.

It is not my intention to trace the history of the doctrine in detail as it was subsequently developed in Christian theology since apostolic times. But it may be helpful to establish a kind of framework in order that the serious but historically uninformed reader will be able to see the various nuances of interpretation as they were developed by succeeding generations. Calvin by no means stands alone except perhaps in the thoroughness with which he worked out the implications, and in the lucidity of his reasoning. John Owen, among others who followed Calvin, wrote almost as much on the subject; but Owen seems to have felt that the use of any kind of literary device (even simple eloquence!) for the communicating of such truths was unworthy of the subject. His writing is somewhat stilted as a consequence and requires considerable dedication on the part of the reader to pursue his reasoning to the end. He is as exhausting to read, in many places, as his argument is exhaustive. He has accordingly suffered the penalty of too much erudition by being less well known.

But let us make a quick survey of the evidence in the Old Testament, and the New, in order to establish just for the moment the fact that Calvin was indeed continuing a very scriptural tradition by his insistence on the absolute sovereignty of God in the matter of man's salvation. What I propose to do first of all is to draw attention to passages of Scripture which are unequivocal and which need few words of explanation. They represent the tips of icebergs. Just below the surface is a mass of evidence that only the perceptive reader will be likely to recognize for himself. For most of us, much of the supporting evidence has to be drawn to our attention. Once it has been, we may wonder how we could have been reading the Word of God for so many years without becoming aware of the true nature of its message.

In the Old Testament there are numerous references to the basic doctrines of the Reformers, to the Total Depravity of man, to the absolute sovereignty of God in the life of the individual even as God is sovereign in the history of the human race, and to the necessity of divine initiative in salvation as an act of pure grace on the part of God. Frequently these statements are categorical. Sometimes they are veiled in language appropriate to the spirit of the Old Testament Scriptures in which theology remains largely unstructured, the basic objective being the elucidation of religious (it would perhaps be appropriate and better to use the term *Christian*) experience. For the Old Testament is experience spelled out within the framework of history at large. It is not until we reach the Epistles that we enter the arena of Christian theology in the reasoned, step-by-step, formal sense of the term, characteristic of Paul's letters.

Consider, then, the following passages from the Old Testament. First, those which underscore the total sinfulness of human nature:

And God saw that the wickedness of man was great in the earth, and that every imagination of the thoughts of his heart was only evil continually (Gen. 6:5).

Who can bring a clean thing out of an unclean? (Job 14:4).

What is man, that he should be clean? And he who is born of a woman, that he should be righteous? . . . How much more abominable and filthy is man, who drinketh iniquity like water? (Job 15:14, 16).

The Lord looked down from heaven upon the children of men, to see if there were any that did understand, and seek God. They are all gone aside, they are all together become filthy; there is none that doeth good, no, not one (Ps. 14:2, 3).

Behold, I was shaped in iniquity; in sin did my mother conceive me (Ps. 51:5).

God looked down from heaven upon the children of men, to see if there were any that did understand, that did seek God. Every one of them is gone back; they are altogether become filthy. There is none that doeth good, no, not one (Ps. 53:2, 3).

Because sentence against an evil work is not executed speedily, therefore the heart of the sons of men is fully set in them to do evil (Eccles. 8:11).

Why should ye be stricken any more? Ye will revolt more and more: the whole head is sick, and the whole heart faint. From the sole of the foot even unto the head there is no soundness in it, but wounds and bruises, and putrifying sores. They have not been closed, nor bound up, neither mollified with ointment (Isa. 1:5, 6).

All we like sheep have gone astray; we have turned every one to his own way, and the Lord hath laid on Him the iniquity of us all (Isa. 53:6).

But we are all as an unclean thing, and all our righteousnesses are as filthy rags, and we do all fade as a leaf; and our iniquities, like the wind, have taken us away (Isa. 64:6).

The heart is deceitful above all things, and desperately wicked; who can know it? (Jer. 17:9).

The good man perisheth out of the earth, and there is none upright among men; they all lie in wait for blood; they hunt every man his brother with a net.

That they may do evil with both hands earnestly, the prince asketh, and the judge asketh for a reward; and the great man, he uttereth his mischievous desires, so they weave it together.

The best of them is like a brier; the most upright is sharper than a thorn hedge . . . (Mic. 7:2-4).

Then we have those passages which declare the sovereignty of God not only in the general sweep of history but in the particulars of individual lives:

> The kingdom is the Lord's: and He is governor among the nations (Ps. 22:28).

> For promotion cometh neither from the east, nor from the west, nor from the south. But God is the judge: He putteth down one and setteth up another (Ps. 75:6, 7).

> Surely the wrath of man shall praise Thee: the remainder of wrath shalt Thou restrain (Ps. 76:10).

> The Lord hath prepared his throne in the heavens; and his kingdom ruleth over all (Ps. 103:19).

> Our God is in the heavens; He hath done whatsoever He hath pleased (Ps. 115:3).

> Whatsoever the Lord pleased, that He did in heaven, and in the earth, in the seas, and all deep places (Ps. 135:6).

> A man's heart deviseth his way: but the Lord directeth his steps (Prov. 16:9).

> There are many devices in a man's heart; nevertheless the counsel of the Lord, that shall stand (Prov. 19:21).

> Man's goings are of the Lord; how can a man then understand his own way? (Prov. 20:24).

> The king's heart is in the hand of the Lord, as the rivers of water: He turneth it whithersoever He will (Prov. 21:1).

> There is none that can deliver out of my hand: I will work and who shall hinder it? Thus saith the Lord (Isa. 43:13).

> Who is he that saith, and it cometh to pass, when the Lord commanded it not? (Lam. 3:37).

> Son of man, Nebuchadrezzar, king of Babylon, caused his army to serve a great service against Tyre; and every head was made bald, and every shoulder was peeled: yet had he no wages, nor his army, for Tyre, for the service that he had served against it: Therefore, thus saith the Lord GOD; Behold, I will give the land of Egypt unto Nebuchadrezzar, king of Babylon; and he shall take her multitude, and take her spoil and take her prey; and it shall be wages for his army. I have given him the land of Egypt for his labour wherewith he served against it, because they wrought for Me, saith the Lord God (Ezek. 29:18-20).

> Daniel said, Blessed be the name of God, for ever and ever, for wisdom and might are his. And He changeth the times and seasons; He removeth kings and setteth up kings (Dan. 2:20, 21).

. . . to the intent that the living may know that the Most High ruleth in the kingdom of men and giveth it to whomsoever He will and setteth up over it the basest of men (Dan. 4:17).

[Nebuchadrezzar blessed and honoured Him] whose dominion is an everlasting dominion, and [whose] kingdom is from generation to generation. And all the inhabitants of the earth are reputed as nothing: and He doeth according to his will in the army of heaven and among the inhabitants of the earth, and none can stay his hand, or say unto Him, What doest Thou? (Dan. 4:34, 35).

The Most High God ruleth in the kingdom of men, and He appointeth over it whomsoever He will (Dan. 5:21).

These verses are not selective in their application but seem clearly to apply to saved and unsaved alike. Turning more specifically to the matter of Election to salvation, consider the following:

. . . the Lord will show who are his, and who is holy; and will cause him to come near unto Him: even him whom He hath chosen will He cause to come near unto Him (Num. 16:5).

I have reserved to Myself seven thousand which have not bowed the knee to Baal (1 Kings 19:18).

Blessed is the man whom Thou choosest, and causest to approach unto Thee (Ps. 65:4).

Quicken us and we will call upon thy name. Turn us again, O LORD God of hosts . . . and we shall be saved (Ps. 80:18, 19).

Thy people shall be willing in the day of thy power (Ps. 110:3).

The preparation of the heart in man, and the response [answer] of the tongue, is from the Lord (Prov. 16:1).

Lord, Thou wilt ordain peace for us: for Thou hast wrought all our works in us (Isa. 26:12).

Oh Lord, I know that the way of a man is not in himself: it is not in man that walketh to direct his steps (Jer. 10:23).

Turn Thou me, and I shall be turned; for Thou art the Lord my God. Surely after that I was turned, I repented. . . (Jer. 31:18, 19).

I will pardon whom I reserve (Jer. 50:20).

Turn Thou us unto Thee, O Lord, and we shall be turned (Lam. 5:21).

A new heart also will I give you, and a new spirit will I put within you: and I will take away the stony heart out of your flesh, and I will give you an heart of flesh. And I will put my spirit within you, and cause you to walk in my statutes, and ye shall keep my judgments, and do them (Ezek. 36:26, 27).

It should not be too surprising, in the light of such passages as these that the Gospels should reflect the same truth. When man approaches God in search of salvation *in God's way*, it is only because he has first been called of God and inclined towards Him in his search. What is perhaps more surprising is that the clearest of all of the Gospels in this respect is John's, which is pre-eminently the Gospel of love in most people's eyes. In view of the fact that popular opinion holds Election to be a cold if not actually a repugnant doctrine, reflecting the harshness and unfairness of God rather than his love and graciousness, a great many Christian readers never even look for evidences of Election in John. But the doctrine is more firmly established here than in any one of the synoptic Gospels, and it is for the most part by reference to the words of our Lord Himself rather than to the descriptive matter supplied by the evangelist that the truth is best established.

We shall have occasion later to examine this evidence much more fully, but consider only what the Lord said as revealed in John 6. Putting together the words of verses 37, 39, 40, 44, and 65, we have this clear enunciation of Election to salvation by grace initiated entirely by the Father:

> All that the Father giveth Me shall come to Me. . . . And this is the Father's will which hath sent Me, that of all which He hath given Me, I shall lose nothing. . . . This is the will of Him that sent Me, that every one which seeth the Son, and believeth on Him, may have everlasting life. . . . No man can come to Me, except the Father which hath sent Me draw him: and I will raise him up at the last day.

The result of these statements made with such force and repetition by the Lord was that many of his disciples were highly offended. And why not? These statements simply reduced the disciples' pride to zero, for if they were to be saved it was to be in no sense to their personal credit. But how did Jesus respond to their protestations of offence? He reiterated his words, in no uncertain terms: "Therefore said I unto you, that no man *can* come unto Me, except it were given unto him of my Father." How this must have humbled them when it dawned upon them that He really meant it. We are told, in fact, that "from that time many of his disciples went back and walked no more with Him" (v. 66).

There is no doubt about it. The chapters which precede bear out the implications of this pronouncement. We are not born again by the will of man, nor by the will of the flesh, nor by blood relationship—but of God. It is God, and God alone who gives us power to become his children (John 1:12, 13).

Equally clear is the Lord's statement in John 15:16: "Ye have not chosen Me, but I have chosen you."

Peter is no less positive in his first sermon when he says in Acts 2:38, 39: "Repent and be baptized every one of you in the name of Jesus Christ for the remission of sins and ye shall receive the gift of the Holy Ghost. For the promise is unto you and to your children and to all that are afar off, even as many as the Lord, our God, shall call." These words were spoken in the spirit of Numbers 16:5 ("The Lord will show who are his, and who is holy: and will cause him to come near unto Him: even him whom He hath chosen will He cause to come near unto Him") and in the spirit of Jeremiah 50:20 ("I will pardon whom I reserve").

It is Paul who not merely proclaims the sovereignty of God in this matter of Election unto salvation but who formalizes and structures the doctrine, giving us by revelation most of the light we have on other aspects of God's elective grace such as, for example, why one is chosen and another is not. It is Paul whose whole theology of salvation by grace is presented as an e-quivalent to the Gospel itself by showing that if man is saved entirely without making any contribution himself, he must be saved by sovereign grace. For if man contributes anything whatsoever, and that contribution is essential to his salvation, he is in the final analysis saved by his contribu-tion. If we are saved by any kind of co-operative effort between man and God, no matter how little is man's contribution and how much is God's, then grace is no more grace (Rom. 11:6). It is an all-or-nothing situation.

But man's contribution need not be in the form of actual deeds to his credit; it could be merely that he decides to respond favourably to the mov-ing of the Holy Spirit in his heart. Others don't, and they are lost. He does, and he is saved. The decision is his. His responsiveness is his contribution. But Paul is clear on this, for it too would at once become the key, as indeed it is often said to be from the pulpit today. It would make the salvation of the individual a joint effort and immediately raises the question of why one man responds and another does not. Does the responding individual thereby demonstrate a superior soul? Is salvation then limited to those of superior nature? Paul says, No! "It is not of him that willeth, nor of him that runneth, but of God that sheweth mercy" (Rom. 9:16). John says that it is not by the will of man but by the will of God that we become his children (John 1:12, 13); and James says, "Of his own will begat he us" (James 1:18).

The same is true of faith. It is not even *our* faith that saves, but the faith of Jesus Christ—not the faith *in* Jesus Christ as some translators would like it to be and interpret it accordingly. Thus we read in Paul's letter to the Galatians (2:16): "A man is not justified by the works of the law, but by the faith of Jesus Christ." And again in Galatians 3:22, "The Scripture hath con-cluded all under sin, that the promise of [the] faith of Jesus Christ might be given to them that believe." So much importance has been attached to the exercise of faith as the basis of salvation that this has become our contribu-tion, as though a dead man could exercise faith in his own resurrection suffi-cient to guarantee it. Man is not saved by his own faith any more than he is saved by his own decision not to resist the Holy Spirit. Because the moment we allow such a thing, we give credit to those who have this ability in distinction to those who do not. And the fortunate ones achieve salvation simply because they are in some way different in themselves. They would have every right to boast in heaven. But boasting is excluded (Rom. 3:27). We are saved by grace through faith—and *that* not of ourselves: it is the gift of God (Eph. 2:8, 9). We do not even contribute our own saving faith. And so boasting is excluded indeed.

Otherwise we have to ask in what way do men differ, for certainly some respond and some believe, while others do neither and are lost. Paul asks accordingly: "Who maketh thee to differ from another? And what hast thou that thou didst not receive? Now if thou didst receive it, why dost thou glory as if thou hadst not received it?" (1 Cor. 4:7). Of course, we don't overtly say, "I was a better man because I was receptive and had faith." But this is tacitly accepted by most of us as the essential difference between the saved and the unsaved, that is, between the *haves* and the *have-nots*. And from the pulpit we appeal to men on this basis. And so we proclaim another Gospel which is not a Gospel at all, for it assumes a capability in man that he simply does not have. Saving faith is not *offered* to man by God: it is *conferred* upon him. This is Paul's Gospel, and the corollary of such a conferring is either an Election that is sovereign but limited in extent to those who are saved, or it is a Gospel that is impotent, the vast majority of those for whom salvation is intended being able to thwart the purposes of God. Then is man stronger than God? No, for Paul quotes the Lord's words to Moses regarding God's own fixed intention: "I will have mercy on whom I will have mercy, and I will have compassion on whom I will have compassion" (Rom. 9:15).

Of course the great difficulty that many have with such a doctrine, presented as it is by Paul with unrelenting logic and without apology, is that it seems to make man a puppet as far as his salvation is concerned so that superficially it seems as though he cannot possibly be blamed for being lost. How could he be blamed if it is not God's intention to grant him the initial responsiveness of soul and the final requisite faith? Indeed! Even this problem Paul does not seek to escape. "Thou wilt say then unto me, why doth He yet find fault? For who hath resisted his will?" (Rom. 9:19). It seemed to many thoughtful people, schooled in the exercise of logic from the Greek masters, that Paul was undermining human responsibility and thus weakening the effectiveness of the threat of punishment in the world to come as an incentive to good behaviour in this world. The sanction of the law was being removed, if man was not responsible for having refused the offer of God's mercy. It seemed essential to restore human responsibility in order to ensure godliness of life.

It was partly because no answer seemed at first to be forthcoming to this question, and partly because man likes to feel he is a free agent, and partly because the influence of Greek philosophy persuaded men that human reason could discover the truth without revelation, that the early Christian apologists looked to their own minds for the answer and concluded that Paul was being misunderstood. Little by little man's inner resources were wrongly estimated and a more humanly reasonable view of the way of salvation was substituted for the Pauline theology. Man still needed salvation, but it was now seen as something possible with God's help—man cooperating by a certain willingness to acknowledge his need and express his faith. This much of human goodness had remained to him in spite of his fallen nature.

The extent to which the adulteration of the Gospel had proceeded by Augustine's time will be seen in quotations from two of his contemporaries who were among the great leaders (or "Fathers" as they are called) of the Church. The first is Chrysostom (c. 350-407), Bishop of Constantinople, who wrote: "Since God has placed good and evil in our power, He has granted free decision of choice and does not restrain the unwilling but embraces the willing." And "Just as we can never do anything rightly unless we are aided by God's grace, so we cannot acquire heavenly favour unless we bring our portion." And "In order that not everything may depend on divine help, we must at the same time bring something ourselves." "Let us bring what is ours: God will furnish the rest."[1] The whole sentiment here is clear: man is required to make a contribution towards his own salvation.

We meet with the same sentiment in the work of Jerome (c. 345-419), perhaps the greatest linguistic scholar of his time and translator of the Vulgate or Latin Version of the Bible, which for centuries was the "Authorized Version" of the Church of Rome. Jerome wrote: "Ours is to begin, God's to fulfill; ours to offer what we can, his to supply what we cannot."[2]

The writers who came after Chrysostom and Jerome went from bad to worse until it came to the point that man was commonly thought to be corrupted only in his sensual nature while retaining a perfectly unblemished reason and a will largely unimpaired.

And it was into such a theological climate that Augustine, later Bishop of Hippo in North Africa, was introduced when, under the influence of Ambrose, he was wonderfully converted. The story of his conversion is beautifully set forth by himself in his *Confessions*. Let us see how it came about, as far as possible in his own words, for he was a truly eloquent man.

---

1. Quoted in John Calvin, *Institutes of the Christian Religion*, II.ii.4.
2. Ibid.

2

AUGUSTINE

Aurelius Augustinus (354-430), Bishop of Hippo Regius in Roman North Africa, was undoubtedly the greatest of the Latin Fathers. He is called a Latin Father partly because he spoke and wrote in Latin, and partly to distinguish him from the Greek Fathers who wrote in Greek. Many of the latter were influential chiefly in the Eastern half of the Christian world which later became the Greek Orthodox Church, whose religious capital was Constantinople. Augustine's influence was chiefly in the Western world.

Augustine was born of middle-class parents at Tagaste in North Africa, but he seems to have been financially assisted as a young man when he had perhaps proved himself to be what today would be called "scholarship material." His father, Patricius, remained for most of his life a pagan, but was converted shortly before his death in 372 when Augustine was just eighteen years of age.

In so far as the specific subject matter of this volume is concerned, Augustine's enormous literary output is of less immediate interest than his autobiography in which he detailed the circumstances that finally led to his conversion. It is in this autobiography, his *Confessions*, that we see the background of the long struggle he had with his own unruly nature, and how he became increasingly aware of both the fundamental depravity of the human heart and the futility of appealing to the unsaved to turn themselves towards the Saviour.

Augustine begins his *Confessions* with the famous and often quoted (or misquoted) words, "Thou hast formed us for Thyself and our hearts are restless till they find their rest in Thee" (I.i.1). He then proceeds to give the reader some idea of his life before he became a Christian. He began very early to be a troublemaker, perhaps when he was only eight or nine years old, and his experience thereafter was what Hogarth would have painted under the title *The Progress of a Rake*. He was not converted until 386 A.D. at the age of thirty-two.

So he continues:

> I will now call to mind my past foulness and the carnal corruptions of my soul, not because I love them but that I may love Thee, O my God. For love of thy love I do it, recalling in the very bitterness of my remembrance my most vicious ways that Thou mayest grow sweet to me—Thou sweetness without deception! And recollecting myself out of that my dissipation in which I was torn to pieces, while, being turned away from Thee, I lost myself among many vanities. For I even longed in my youth formerly to be satisfied with worldly things, and I dared to grow wild again with various and shadowy loves; my form consumed away and I became corrupt in thine eyes, pleasing myself and eager to be pleasing in the eyes of men. (II.i.l)

So even as a child he sought the thrills of crime on a petty scale of theft for the fun of it, making mischief for people simply for the pleasure of seeing their distress. He describes it thus:

> I had a desire to commit robbery and did so, compelled neither by hunger nor poverty but through a dislike of doing the right things, and a certain lustiness of iniquity. For I pilfered that of which I had already sufficient, and much better. Nor did I desire to enjoy what I pilfered but only the theft and the misdeed itself. (II.iv.9)

Inevitably he tired of these adolescent delinquencies, having now reached the age at which the opposite sex became an object of interest. And so he went to Carthage, perhaps the most wanton city of the time "where a cauldron of unholy loves bubbled up all around me" (III.i.1). Into this cauldron he plunged with energetic abandon, and he recounts the steady degeneration of his soul which took place: "Woe, woe, by what steps was I dragged down to the depths of hell!" (III.vii.11).

Meanwhile his mother, Monica, a most devout and godly Christian woman, watched his slow degradation with agonizing concern. Augustine was now in his early twenties and was quite aware of his mother's distress. "My mother, thy faithful one, wept to Thee on my behalf more than mothers are wont to bewail the physical deaths of their children" (III.xi.19).

Augustine's "progress" is remarkably typical of many modern young people who have a similar measure of economic independence. It seems clear that as a young adolescent he became involved with a gang of potential troublemakers who sought escape from the boredom of life by being destructive just for the fun of it. But in due time this palled, and as he grew into manhood he sought more sophisticated forms of escape. And so he went to Carthage, "the big city." But this, too, in time began to sicken him so that like many in similar circumstances today he turned hopefully to philosophy and in a sense "attached" himself to the founder of Manichaeism, the equivalent of the modern guru. He describes this change in lifestyle. "During the space of nine years, then, from my nineteenth to my twenty-eighth year we went on seduced and seducing, deceived and deceiving, in

divers lusts; outwardly practicing a lifestyle which they call 'liberal' "
(IV.i.1). In disgust at the emptiness of this life, therefore, he turned to a
pagan philosophy which saw the universe as being divided into two eternal
kingdoms, the kingdom of good and the kingdom of evil, neither of which
could ever wholly conquer the other. Man might seek by the proper exercise
of will to live increasingly in the one or the other but the strife was unending
and there was no guarantee of complete victory either here or hereafter.

And so Augustine struggled on, gradually establishing a reputation as a
teacher of rhetoric, while at the same time becoming increasingly disillusioned with Manichaeism. He found no peace, no meaning, no sense of purpose: only a growing sense of dis-ease of spirit and dissatisfaction of mind.
He was disturbed also by his own inability to temper his unruly will. To be
good attracted him, but he could not find within himself the resources to
achieve goodness. And so he went to Rome because he learned that students
there lived under more restrictive influences bringing some measure of control to their disordered lives. He recounts the circumstances of this decision
as evidence, when seen in retrospect, of the overruling providence of God in
his life.

> It was not my desire to go to Rome because greater advantages and
> honours were guaranteed me by the friends who persuaded me to do this,
> but my principal and almost my sole motive was that I had been informed
> that youths there studied more quietly and were kept under the control of
> more rigid discipline (V.viii.14).

This remark is a reflection of a struggle which seems to have gone on in
his life for many years. The unruliness of his will, indeed the unruliness of
every man's unredeemed will, was to be a key point of emphasis in his subsequent theology and profoundly influenced Luther's thinking a thousand
years later. In spite of the fact that his personal problem appeared to him at
the time to be the basic reason for his deciding to cross the Mediterranean to
Rome, he later saw this as just one more instance of divine supervision in his
life (V.viii.15).

Evidently his stay in Rome did not fulfill his expectations for he was soon
attracted to Milan, accepting an invitation from that city to teach rhetoric.
He notes that his traveling expenses were paid by the city fathers (V.xiii.23)!
Here he discovered the saintly Ambrose, Bishop of Milan; and to his
mother's enormous relief, this godly minister came to have a tremendous influence on his life. With refreshing frankness he tells why he was first attracted to Ambrose. It was the Bishop's eloquence! And here we have a
beautiful example of how the talents of a godly man, for surely eloquence is
a talent, can be used in God's service in ways that are unexpected. In words
which are equally as eloquent as the Bishop's, Augustine describes what
gradually happened.

For although I took no trouble to learn *what* he spake but only to hear *how* he spake (for that vain concern alone remained to me, despairing of finding any way for man to approach Thee), yet along with the words which I prized there came into my mind also the things about which I was careless; for I could not separate them. And whilst I opened my heart to admit "how skilfully he spake," there also entered with it, but gradually, "how truly he spake"! (V.xiv.24).

I resolved therefore to become a catechumen in the catholic church, which my parents had commended to me, until something more positive should manifest itself to me whither I might steer my course. . . . After that, O Lord, little by little Thou didst persuade me, drawing and calming my heart with a most gentle and merciful hand (VI.v.7).

The process was slow at first. As Augustine wrote:

And I, puzzling over and reviewing these things, marvelled most at the length of time that had lapsed from my nineteenth year when I began to be inflamed with the desire for wisdom, resolving when I found her to forsake all the empty hopes and deceiving insanities of vain desire. Behold I was now getting on to my thirtieth year, still stuck in the same mire and eager for the enjoyment of things present which fly away and destroy me (VI.xi.18).

But Augustine was aware of the continuing pursuit of Him whom Francis Thompson so aptly named the "Hound of Heaven." This conviction strangely strengthened as the misery in his own soul deepened. In his growing despair he found himself nevertheless unexpectedly filled with praise for God!

Unto Thee be praise, unto Thee be glory, O Thou fountain of mercy! While I became more wretched, Thou became more near. Thy right hand was ever ready to pluck me out of the mire and to cleanse me: yet I was ignorant of it (VI.xvi.26).

By inward stings didst Thou disturb me that I should be dissatisfied, until Thou wert made sure to my inward sight. And by the secret hand of thy remedy was my swelling lessened, and the disordered and darkened eyesight of my mind was made whole from day to day by the sharp anointing of healthful sorrows (VII.viii.12).

And I enquired what iniquity really was. And I discovered it not to be a substance [as Manichaean philosophy had viewed it] but a *perversion of the will* bent aside from Thee, O God. . . . And I marvelled that I now loved Thee and not just a fantasy instead of Thee. (emphasis mine: VII.xv.22, 23).

Here then we find a clear recognition of where the real problem of human wickedness lies. Pelagius (c. 390 A.D.) had taken the view that the wickedness of man was really something foreign to his nature, taught him through example and precept by his own corrupt society. The right appeal to his best nature would bring improvement and under the proper circumstances man had the power to correct his faults and achieve his own salvation.

In due course, Augustine, out of the depths of his own experience, was to become such an opponent of this hopeful humanism that Pelagius' teaching would subsequently be condemned by the Church of Rome. Salvation by self-effort was declared to be an impossibility for fallen man. Because of his own experience in Italy, Augustine very early came to the conclusion that the Church of Rome was the sole instrument or vehicle of the grace of God in bringing salvation to the individual. There was no salvation outside of its orthodoxy. Augustine, in fact, by the cogency of his arguments, the eloquence of his writing and speaking, and the profundity of his own personal experience while searching for the truth, had a tremendous influence upon the Church of Rome's theology in this respect; and by many Protestant scholars he is considered to have been the founder of Roman Catholicism in its basic expression.

In the end, Augustine's main emphasis came to be not on the exclusive character of the Church of Rome as a vehicle of God's grace but on the total incapacity of man to turn himself about and contribute in any way to the effecting of his own salvation. As he wrote later:

> And I sought a way of acquiring strength sufficient to enjoy Thee; but I found it not until I embraced that "mediator between God and man, the man Christ Jesus," "who is over all, God blessed forever," calling unto me and saying, "I am the way, the truth and the life" (VII.xviii.24).

And so Augustine came home at last to his God. And his heart was overwhelmed by love.

> O my God, let me with gratitude remember and confess unto Thee thy mercies bestowed upon me. Let my bones be steeped in thy love and let them say, Who is like unto Thee, O Lord? "Thou hast loosed my bonds; I will offer unto Thee the sacrifice of thanksgiving." And how Thou hast loosed them will I declare; and all who worship Thee when they hear these things shall say: "Blessed be the Lord in heaven and in earth, great and wonderful is his name" (VIII.1.1).

Yet the struggle with his unruly will continued, as it did for Paul (Rom. 7), and as it does in all of us. Witness how he cried out in some surprise:

> Whence is this monstrous thing? And why is it? The mind commands the body and it obeys forthwith; the mind commands itself and is resisted. The mind commands the hand to be moved, and such readiness is there that the command is scarce to be distinguished from the obedience. . . . The mind commands the mind to command the will, and yet though it be itself, it obeyeth not. Whence this monstrous thing? It commands itself to will and would not give the command unless it willed, yet is not done that which it commandeth. But it willeth not entirely; therefore it commandeth not entirely (VIII.ix.21).

Augustine's protest is eloquent, and his analogy is striking. He was perhaps the first after Paul to realize the Total Depravity of man.

Man unredeemed is spiritually incapable of truly willing the smallest step towards God unless he is enabled to do so through the offices of the Holy Spirit. We may suppose that men do seek the Lord on their own initiative because we see them apparently doing it. We may suppose we ourselves did it because we were aware of a desire within ourselves. The very act of willing leads us to believe that we are willing of our own accord. We do not stop to ask, Why did I will to seek the Lord? Why did I, but not my neighbour, will to seek the Lord? Was it something in myself which distinguished me from my neighbour, and indeed from the multitude around me? And here is the crux of the matter, for if it was I who initiated this movement in my soul, then could I not be said to be a better man than my neighbour? Would I not be indeed in a position to boast, both here and hereafter?

But there is no reason to suppose that there are levels of spiritual deadness. We are all dead in trespasses and sins, and death is the great leveller. In this unregenerate state we have no power of ourselves to help ourselves. A corpse does not cry out for help. "The dead know not anything" (Eccles. 9:5). The sad truth is that even after we have been born again, we carry part of this death with us until we slough it off in the grave. Thus even after being born again, we still have two wills to contend with. This was Augustine's experience and it generated and coloured his whole understanding of the truth of the Gospel of grace. Indeed, it was out of this experience that he really recovered for the Christian Church the doctrine of the sovereignty of God in the salvation of man. For man being spiritually dead could not possibly initiate out of his own inner being the seeds of spiritual life nor, having been redeemed, generate out of the old life that which is pleasing to God. Augustine's past continued to press heavily on his soul and agonizingly thwarted his aspirations after holiness, until he reached a crisis.

> I flung myself down, how I do not know, under a certain fig tree, giving free course to my tears. I was saying these things and weeping in the most bitter contrition of my heart when, behold, I heard a voice as of a boy or a girl, I know not which, coming from a neighbouring house, chanting and oft repeating, "Take up and read: take up and read." I grasped [the New Testament manuscript in his hands], opened, and in silence read that paragraph on which my eyes first fell: "Not in rioting and drunkenness, not in chambering and wantonness, not in strife and envying; but put ye on the Lord Jesus Christ and make no provision for the flesh to fulfill the lusts thereof" (Rom. 13:13, 14). No further would I read, nor did I need; for instantly, as the sentence ended—by a light, as it were, of security infused into my heart, all the gloom of doubt vanished away (VIII.xii.28, 29).

And so he went in at once to his mother to tell her what happened: "We make it known to her—she rejoiceth! We relate how it came to pass: she leapeth for joy [she was then nearly sixty years old] and triumpheth and blesseth Thee who art 'able to do exceedingly abundantly above all that we ask or think' " (VIII.xii.30).

So was this great warrior consecrated to the Lord's service.

Francis Thompson's beautiful poem "The Hound of Heaven" seems almost as though it were written to describe Augustine's experience. It opens with these words:

> I fled Him, down the nights and down the days;
>   I fled Him, down the arches of the years;
> I fled Him, down the labyrinthine ways
>   Of my own mind; and in the mist of tears
> I hid from Him, and under running laughter.
>   Up vistaed hopes, I sped;
>   And shot, precipitated,
> Adown Titanic glooms of chasmed fears,
>   From those strong Feet that followed, followed after.
>   But with unhurrying chase,
>   And unperturbed pace,
> Deliberate speed, majestic instancy,
>   They beat—and a Voice beat
>   More instant than the Feet—
> "All things betray thee, who betrayest Me."

An edition of this poem was published in 1926 with perceptive comments on the text by Michael A. Kelly. I found his remarks on line 114 of the poem particularly interesting. The line is a short one. It reads, "I am defenceless utterly." At this moment in the poem Francis Thompson, after a long chase through the years, was now in the position of being nearly overtaken by God. Upon this Kelly comments as follows:

> This is a terrible revelation to some souls (for we are all Pelagians at heart and would wish to be able to work out our salvation without God's grace)—the fact that with all their striving they get no closer to God, for they hit wide of the mark all the time by not preparing for and awaiting God's coming to them. What we *can* and must do is to co-operate with God's grace.

This is a noteworthy comment, for while Kelly is suggesting that Pelagianism is an error, he simply substitutes Arminianism instead. Pelagius said, "If a man sets his mind to it he can save his own soul without God's help." Arminius said, "Not so. He must have God's help. He must co-operate with God since he alone cannot save himself." Augustine, in complete contrast to both these positions, held that man is so totally corrupted in his being that he cannot contribute anything whatever. He is spiritually dead and entirely incapable of co-operating with God in any way. Augustine's own experience had taught him that he could not *assist* God in any way, and his own experience had also taught him that he could not *refuse* God in any way either. In his comment, Michael Kelly reflects the view so widely held today, that while man is not able to save himself, he can at least prepare himself to receive the salvation God offers by opening his own heart or at the very least by not resisting the overtures of the Holy Spirit. Modern man's experience, as he licks the wounds of the last two great wars, probably does not encourage too many Pelagians. But the great majority of men still prefer to believe that they have enough autonomy left to be in a position to refuse or to accept the offer of God's salvation just as they have a mind to do.

Augustine died in 430 A.D. at the age of seventy-six. He never left his beloved North Africa for any substantial length of time. His life must have been exceedingly busy, for in addition to his duties as a bishop, his pen was constantly at work. Through his writings, his influence on the development of theology for centuries to come has been enormous. It is sometimes said that in the period of forty-four years between his conversion and his death he produced over a thousand treatises on every aspect of Christian doctrine. As a reflection of the influence of these writings, it may be noted that a bibliography listing works on Augustine published between 1950 and 1960 numbered in excess of five thousand titles.

We have already noted that Augustine's initial emphasis upon the unique role played by the Church of Rome in his conversion strongly influenced him to think of it as the only vehicle of God's mercy. This was seized upon by that institution as the basis for an exclusiveness which, there is little doubt, Augustine in his later years would have abhorred. Augustine's subsequent emphasis upon the Total Depravity of man and the corruption of his will was to play a very significant role in the formulation of the teachings of the Reformers. It thus came about that out of the voluminous works of a single individual there emerged finally two strongly opposed schools of theology, the Roman Catholic and the Protestant. Perhaps in a manner of speaking the second would not have emerged with clarity without the first, and we may therefore praise God for the whole of Augustine's ministry of writing, despite its sometimes contradictory nature. At any rate, Augustine stands as a major link between Paul and Calvin.

From Paul to Augustine the major emphasis theologically had been on the nature and Person of Christ as God-made-man, and experientially, on repentance and faith as the basis of salvation, and on good works (such as almsgiving, prayers, and submission to certain sacraments of the Church such as baptism) as proof of the reality of conversion. Increasingly there had developed a kind of tacit agreement that conversion resulted from a co-operation of wills, the human and the divine. By threat or argument or appeal men were persuaded to respond. Long before Arminius left his personal impress upon the Church of God, Arminianism had swept the early Christian world. Men are *by nature* Arminian. It is easy to believe that man has a say in his salvation, a contribution to make, a frame of mind for which he is personally responsible and without which God is powerless. Pelagius drops easily into a ministry to the elite in society who seem likely to be most amenable, since good breeding is easily mistaken for an improved nature. In such a theological environment it is obvious that Paul's insistence upon Predestination and Election will be toned down until it means no more than that God can foresee who will by nature be responsive and who will not. There are clearly some who don't respond and some who do. The difference is not in the sovereignty of Election but in the responsiveness of the individual. Some men seem to have a form of natural goodness which makes them more susceptible to persuasion, more amenable to reason, more sensitive to the overtures of God, more aware of personal need. Predestination in this view is simply based on foreknowledge. The decision to believe rests ultimately with the individual. Man elects for God, not God for man.

There is no doubt that in spite of this erroneous view of how God's grace is made effectual, the grace of God in saving some guaranteed the continuance of the Body of Christ as a vital living reality through these early centuries, even as it continues today. It is therefore no hindrance to the work of God that those whose lives are effectively renewed do not at all understand the circumstances of this renewal or the theology which underlies it. It is not necessary to a vital Christian experience to comprehend, or even be aware of, the mysteries of divine Election and Predestination. Christian piety is possible without theology provided there is a true conversion; and alternatively, a sound theology is no guarantee of Christian piety. Wesley almost certainly saved England from a "French Revolution," though he embraced the Arminian heresy and left to his followers a legacy of piety without theology.

There is a warfare going on, an unending struggle between falsehood and truth regarding the nature of man and his destiny. This falsehood, which encourages man to believe he has powers of self-redemption (powers which experience nevertheless demonstrates he does not have), is prosecuted forcefully by means of propaganda in printed form that is cogent and reasonable and effectively produced. It is everywhere, in our romantic novels, in our idealistic film themes, in our reconstructions of history, in our philosophy of education, and even, alas, in many of our churches. What is needed to combat this steady stream of propaganda is not merely piety and the ambiguous testimony of individual experience, but an equally reasoned and powerfully convincing presentation of the truth. In short, we need a recovery of sound doctrine rather than emphasis on emotional experience.

History has largely decided the fate of Methodism already. Thousands of church buildings which once housed active and devout Methodist congregations all over North America now stand entirely deserted or have been taken over by congregations whose mission is almost wholly social betterment on a worldly level and whose "theology" is nothing more than a humanism parading as Christian endeavour. A substantial part of the so-called Christian community is either Pelagian or Arminian. That which gives to the individual equal power with God is either humanism, or it is a distortion of the Gospel. And such a distortion, being untrue, is really no Gospel at all. It is no Gospel to an utterly defeated human being to tell him that if he will co-operate with God in the right way God will save him.

What Augustine did was to preserve the Church of Christ in the West from losing sight of the truth of man's hopelessness and helplessness before God. He awakened God's people to the creeping disease of Christian humanism which was evident even then from the successes of Pelagius in Rome and from the growing "Arminianism" which was reflected in the writings of Chrysostom and Jerome and many other Christian theologians by the end of the fourth century A.D. If man did not have it within his power to save himself as Pelagius claimed he did, neither did he have it within his power to embrace the salvation of God made possible through faith in the finished work of Jesus Christ. Both erroneous views credited man with a kind of freedom of will that he does not have.

Man, Augustine argued, has freedom only in one direction. He is free when he sins. As a sinner, man can achieve a curious integrity when he makes no attempt to hide his sin. An Anglican Bishop said recently, "Modern young people are so delightfully wicked!" And Augustine spoke of the unabashed wickedness of pagan man as exhibited in his "splendid vices." Years before this, the Roman writer Scaevola is reputed to have said, "A totally evil man has an irresistible charm and excites the envy and admiration of those who dare not display their own true selves so completely. Total evil has a kind of virtue of its own, an honesty." This kind of freedom is like that of the free fall of the man who jumps from his plane and delays opening his parachute. There are virtually no experienced restraints. The anticipated enjoyment of such an activity is like those who "promise themselves liberty" (2 Peter 2:19), yet are really wholly in bondage to gravity. They become momentarily "free among the dead," as the Psalmist put it poetically (Ps. 88:5).

What Augustine had learned by experience was that the human will is corrupted at the source. When unregenerate man struggles against the evil propensities of his nature, he does so by exercising his will—the dynamic force which lies at the root of those evil propensities. The very exercise of his will in this struggle has the effect only of making it stronger! Augustine found such a struggle spiritually self-defeating because it served in the end only to reinforce at the core of his being the source of the sinfulness he so much hated. The man who of his own will determines to overcome evil is defeating his own purposes by strengthening the very will that is the seat of his evil desires. The power for evil is self-reinforced, and thus self-reformation becomes a wholly self-defeating exercise. It is a vicious circle.

Quoting 2 Peter 2:19, Augustine expressed this idea by saying, "Of whom a man is overcome, of the same he is brought into bondage." The man who overcomes himself becomes in bondage to himself. And this self is sinful. It was one of the defects of Puritanism that by laying emphasis upon outward acts and concentrating energies on suppressing this or that particular fault, the man who overcomes is credited with having overcome sin itself. What he may suppress are only the symptoms, not the disease. But like the man who uses aspirins freely, there comes such ready and long-lasting relief that he is in danger of forgetting the disease itself and ignoring it until it is his undoing.

Or alternatively, a man can surrender to the disease and learn to accept it willingly; he can even learn to enjoy it. So sin also has its pleasures. As Augustine puts it:

> What kind of liberty, I ask, can the bondslave possess except when it *delights* him to serve sin? For he only is free in his bondage who does with pleasure the will of his master. Accordingly, he who is the servant of sin is free to sin. Hence he will not be free to do right until, being freed from sin, he shall begin to be the servant of righteousness. . . . "If the Son shall make you free, ye shall be free indeed" (John 8:36). And before this freedom is wrought in a man, when he is not yet free to what is right, how can he talk of the freedom of his will?[1]

Well, he can of course, but he can speak of freedom only in one direction. He acts freely when he does evil because that is natural to his will. It is a unidirectional freedom, the kind of freedom that the man enjoys in "free fall." Not until a man tries to reverse his course does he suddenly become aware of his bondage. Augustine became intensely aware of his bondage as soon as he tried to break out of it and govern his own unruly spirit.

Augustine argued rightly that man as created was truly free, free to sin or not to sin. Man in Adam lost this kind of freedom of will by an act of disobedience which was a demonstration of how free he had originally been. Augustine was a striking analogy: "A man who kills himself must, of course, be alive when he kills himself, but after he has killed himself he ceases to live and cannot restore himself to life."[2] But by the same token he will not even *want* to restore himself to life! So, again, he is "free among the

---

1. *Enchiridion, XXX.*
2. Ibid.

dead." It *is* a kind of freedom. What is true of physical life is paralleled by what happens in man's spiritual life. Sometimes it is objected that a man can always refuse a gift. He has this much freedom at least. But there is one gift which he cannot refuse: and that is the gift of life. He will not be *offered* it because he is dead. It can only be *conferred* upon him and it is not within his power to refuse it.

The intensity of Augustine's nature, and the seriousness of his search for holiness and for fellowship with God, set him pondering why that which he so earnestly desired was not at all within his grasp as a pagan, and still often eluded him even when he had been so wonderfully converted. Daily he wrote down his thoughts and it became the consuming passion of his life to understand why the human will is so corrupted by nature and so powerless for good.

Augustine saw man as not merely misguided in his search, or defective in his understanding, or blurred in his vision of the truth, or sick in the moral fibre of his being. He saw man as hopelessly lost, blind and dead. Man cannot respond to God's love merely by being told about it, any more than a corpse of a loved one can respond to the appeals of the bereaved. Man needs resurrecting first: to be made alive in order that he may love God, not to love God in order that he may be made alive. The initiative must always be with God. Nor can he hinder the grace of God. The dead cannot refuse resurrection any more than the dead can ask for it. Divine Election and sovereign grace, not human inclination, are what account for man's salvation. Yet it *is* human inclination that accounts for man's lost condition. The intending suicide acts according to his *own* will; but should he succeed he is certainly totally unable to undo what he has done, and even unable to wish it undone.

The question of the bondage of the human will as it sets itself against the will of God was the crucial issue in Augustine's thinking, and his works upon the subject constitute the basis of Luther's *Bondage of the Will* and of Calvin's absolute assurance that salvation is entirely the work of God. Augustine's thinking along these lines was undoubtedly largely stimulated by his conversations with Ambrose. Ambrose had said, in fact, "If you are an unbeliever (when you die), Christ did not die for you."[3] Nothing could be clearer than this. The Election of God is sovereign. No man elected to salvation could possibly die or be killed unsaved. If he died unsaved, he was not one of the elect. There was no thwarting of the purposes of God in this.

Towards the end of his life, Augustine went back over his works and sought to remove some of the potential contradictions that arose as a consequence of his developing understanding. He published his thoughts under

---

3. Quoted in Jerome Zanchius, *Absolute Predestination*, p. 20.

the title *Retractations*, by which he meant not "withdrawals" but "re-drawals" or "re-views". But he did correct a few earlier statements. Thus he wrote in one place: "I could never have asserted that God in choosing men to life had any respect to their faith had I duly considered that faith itself is His own gift."[4] This agreed entirely with an observation he had made regarding John 15:16: "Since Christ says, 'Ye have not chosen Me,' I would fain ask whether it be scriptural to say we must have faith before we are elected, and not rather than we are elected in order to our having faith." He returned to this theme again and again. Common faith is the possession of all men: faith in the word of a friend, in the laws of nature, in the witness of one's own senses (what one hears and sees as being real). But *saving* faith is entirely a work of God and beyond man's natural ability. "God hath from the beginning elected you to salvation, through sanctification of the Spirit and *belief of the truth*" (2 Thess. 2:13). Election is first: faith with respect to the truth of God comes as a consequence. So "as many as were ordained to eternal life, believed" (Acts 13:48) and no others. This was the theme about which Augustine structured his thinking during the last half of his writing ministry. As he put it:

> Whatsoever persons are through the riches of divine grace exempted from the original sentence of condemnation are undoubtedly brought to hear the Gospel, and when hearing they are caused to believe it, and are made likewise to endure to the end in the faith which works by love, and should they at any time go astray, they are recovered and set right again.[5]

Here are Election and eternal security. Later he adds: "All these things are wrought in them by that God who made them vessels of mercy and who, by the election of his grace, chose them in his Son before the world began." And here then is Predestination. As Augustine put it elsewhere: "The grace of God does not *find* men fit to be elected, but *makes* them so . . . . The nature of the divine goodness is not only to open to those who knock but also to *cause them* to knock and ask."[6] Thus John wrote, "We love Him, because He first loved us" (1 John 4:19).

The crucial issue is this. Some men respond and some do not. Why do some and not all men respond to so manifest a good as the eternal salvation of their own souls? Because they are different! In what way? In some way that makes them better judges of what is good? Or just a kind of natural disposition less hostile to the things of God? Are not all such distinguishing marks, if they really exist, but evidences that all men are *not* equal before God, that it is *not* out of the same lump that some are made vessels of

---

4. Ibid., p. 62.
5. *On Rebuke and Grace*, XIII.
6. Quoted in Loraine Boettner, *The Reformed Doctrine of Predestination*, p. 102.

honour while others are made vessels of dishonour? But we know these things are not true. It is "of the same lump" that both kinds of vessels are made (Rom. 9:21). There are not any differences between men (1 Cor. 4:7) as there are no differences in the responsiveness of the bodies of the dead. Their response is wholly predictable: it is nil. The spiritually dead are all alike: dead and unresponsive unless first quickened by the Spirit of God. The Psalmist cried: "Quicken us and we will call upon thy name. Turn us again, O Lord God of hosts . . . and we shall be saved" (Ps. 80:18, 19). It has to be God's initiative, not man's; for "the dead know not anything" (Eccles. 9:5).

Augustine did not believe that man could or did will to be saved. But rather he believed that God graciously converted his will. He was "made willing" by God's grace. Man is an entirely passive participant in this work of God. Just as we may change a man's mind by demonstration of a truth without destroying the mind's power of independent thought, so God can change a man's will by gracious intervention without destroying the will's power of independent expression. Demonstration is to the mind what persuasion is to the will. Neither is destroyed by the change which may be brought about in each case. Augustine gladly admitted that man is capable of exercising saving faith, for clearly the converted man is doing just this. The capacity for exercising this kind of faith is present in man but is dormant until it is awakened by the Holy Spirit and given a direction and a content and a character which were formerly entirely foreign to it. To the unregenerate soul, the things which we as the Lord's children believe are simply "unbelievable." There is no way unaided man can change the character of his faith for himself. Saving faith is a gift. Man has "power" to exercise saving faith but there is no power but comes from God (Rom. 13:1).[7]

This empowering of God is not, however, applied to a creature who has not the requisite capacity for receiving and exercising it. In the elect, saving faith acts upon what Luther refers to as a "passive aptitude" in man. It is a *passive* aptitude but it *is* an aptitude implanted in human nature by the Creator which distinguishes all men from all other creatures, angelic or animal. It makes man unique in that he is a potentially redeemable creature. Man does have the power to exercise will. It is only that his will is corrupted in such a way that it is by nature in opposition to the will of God. Because we are conscious of volition, we suppose our volition is free. What we discover by experience is that our freedom of will is unidirectional. We are truly free only when we sin, for we are then acting according to our nature, a fact which accounts for the pleasures of sin (Heb. 11:25). It comes as a surprise to many people, when they make this discovery.

Originally Augustine had allowed that man has some freedom of choice

---

7. Augustine, *On the Spirit and the Letter*, LIV, LX.

in the matter of his salvation. In his work *On the Predestination of the Saints* (III.7) he had written: "The grace of God consists merely in this, that God in the preaching of the truth reveals his will; but to assent to this Gospel when it is preached is *our own work* [my emphasis] and lies within our own power." But in his *Apology* (XVIII.vii.8) he says: "I have erred when I said it lies within our power to believe and to will." Pelagius had held the maxim, "It is mine to be willing to believe; it is the part of God's grace to assist." In this manner the Gospel of Jesus Christ had been corrupted almost unrecognizably. But such was the enormous influence of Augustine's pen that the Church of Rome was convinced of the propriety of his rejection of Pelagianism and they officially condemned it by the Synod of Orange in 529 A.D. By contrast, the same Church slowly rejected his doctrine of the Total Depravity of man. With this rejection went also the eclipse of the truth of Predestination and Election. Growing emphasis was placed upon formal membership in the Church of Rome, assent to its dogmas, and participation in its sacraments and its ritual. The works of Augustine were seldom studied or even read by Luther's time, except among a few persecuted fragments of the Body of Christ such as the Waldensians.

The cardinal truth of the sovereignty of grace and the total incapacity of man had been recovered by Augustine and explored in a way entirely new. It was he who had crystallized the theology of Predestination and Election which are the corollary of man's total incapacity and helplessness and God's sovereign grace. The Reformation was essentially a revival of Augustinianism, as Augustinianism was a recovery of Pauline theology; and Paul's theology was a clear enunciation of the Gospel as applied to man's need.

I cannot do better to set this in historical perspective than to quote from a great theologian of the recent past, Benjamin B. Warfield. In his book *Calvin and Augustine* (pp. 320 f.), he wrote:

> The great contribution which Augustine has made to the world's life and thought is embodied in the theology of grace, which he has presented with remarkable clearness and force, vitally in his *Confessions* and as a thesis in his anti-Pelagian treatises. . . .

> A new Christian piety dates from him in which, in place of the alternations of hope and fear which vex the lives of those who, in whatever degree, hang their hopes on their own merits, a mood of assured trust in the mercy of a gracious God is substituted as the spring of Christian life. And a new theology corresponding to this new type of piety dates from him; a theology which, recalling man from all dependence on his own powers or merits, casts him decisively on the grace of God alone for his salvation. Of course, this doctrine was not new in the sense that it was Augustine's invention; it was the doctrine of Paul, for example, before it was the doctrine of Augustine, and was only recovered for the Church by Augustine, though in that age, dominated in all its thinking by the dregs of Stoic rationalism, it came with all the force of a new discovery. . . .

It required ten years before the revived Paulinism attained even a fully consistent positive enunciation (first in the work *De diversis quaestionibus ad Simplicianum*, A.D. 396); and, though the leaven worked steadily thereafter more and more deeply and quietly into his thought, death intervened before all the elements of his thinking were completely leavened. . . .

His doctrine of the Church he had received whole from his predecessor, and he gave it merely the precision and vitality which insured its persistence. His doctrine of grace was all his own: it represented the very core of his being; and his whole progress in Christian thinking consists in the growing completeness with which its fundamental principles applied themselves in his mind to every department of life and thought. . . .

It is Augustine who gave us the Reformation. For the Reformation, inwardly considered, was just the ultimate triumph of Augustine's doctrine of grace over Augustine's doctrine of the Church. This doctrine of grace came from Augustine's hands in its positive outline completely formulated: sinful man depends for his recovery to good and to God entirely on the free grace of God; this grace is therefore indispensable, prevenient, irresistible, indefectible; and being thus the free grace of God, must have lain in all the details of its conference and working, in the intention of God from all eternity. . . .

If the necessity of prevenient grace was thereafter [after the second Council of Orange, 529] the established doctrine of the Church, the irresistibility of this prevenient grace was put under the ban and there remained no place for a complete "Augustinianism" within the Church, as Gottschalk and Jansen were fully to discover. Therefore, when the great revival of religion which we call the Reformation came, seeing that it was on its theological side a revival of "Augustinianism," as all great revivals of religion must be (for Augustinianism is but the thetical expression of religion in its purity), there was nothing for it but the rending of the Church.

3

FROM AUGUSTINE TO THE REFORMATION

It would be a rare thing indeed for a man as prolific with his pen as Augustine was to live a long and eventful life without ever modifying his theology. Inasmuch as he had written down his thoughts in both the earlier and later stages of development, it was inevitable that there should be some divergence of opinion in what he wrote. The intensity of his experience was reflected in the depth of his conviction at each stage of his spiritual progression, so that he seemed at one time to recognize nothing but the crucial importance of the Church as an institution for the mediation of God's grace to man and for the preservation of truth. Later, the same intensity underlies all that he writes about the appalling depravity of human nature. Augustine was a man of deep feeling.

It thus came about that two diametrically opposed streams of theology stemmed from one man's thoughts, the Roman Catholic and the Reformed theologians both drawing the inspiration for their particular theologies very largely from the writings of this one profound Christian scholar and philosopher: the Roman Catholics from his earlier writings, the Reformers from his later ones. In the confrontation which finally occurred between Luther and the Roman Catholic Church and which came to a head in the Council of Trent (1545-1563), both parties appealed for their authority to the same great "Father" of the Church, Augustine.

Augustine had owed his conversion to the church *in* Rome and as a consequence, not unnaturally, came very early to believe that the Church *of* Rome was the sole vehicle of God's grace. But as his Christian understanding matured, his interest was turned from the vehicle of God's grace to the object of it and he became increasingly convinced that spiritually man was utterly impotent. In his own struggle to rise above the rebellious nature that was part and parcel of his greatness as an original thinker, Augustine discovered the Total Depravity of his own heart, and his writing was occupied increasingly with the exploration of this fact. Thus his earlier writings placed more emphasis upon the Church as God's vehicle of blessing and his later ones upon sinful man as the object of God's grace. These two emphases were later to lead on the one hand to the claim of the Church of Rome that it is the sole vehicle of man's salvation on earth, and on the other hand to the commitment by the Reformers to the position that man is totally depraved. The first led to the arrogant claims of exclusiveness as God's agent of salvation which were to characterize the Roman Catholic Church, and the second led to the tremendous emphasis upon the sovereignty of God which was to characterize the great *Confessions* of the Reformers.

But it was to be centuries before this confrontation would come to such a head as to split Christendom into two opposing camps on a scale which was to become worldwide. Meanwhile from Augustine to the Reformation one has the impression that true faith was virtually eclipsed, and that centuries of almost complete spiritual darkness intervened. Here and there a few kept the faith in almost total isolation but no substantial body of believers existed in Europe with sufficient status to seriously challenge the Church of Rome. At least this is the impression one is apt to gain. Of course, it was not entirely so. It was rather that giants stood at each end of this bleak corridor of time who shone so brightly that they seemed by their very brilliance to darken the road between, even as a searchlight casts deeper shadows by its power to concentrate its beam. William Cunningham in his *Historical Theology* remarked in this connection:

> The substance of the matter is this: the apostolic fathers (prior to Augustine) generally use the language of Scripture upon these subjects, but they scarcely make any statements which afford us materials for deciding in what precise sense they understood them. They leave the matter very much where Scripture leaves it, and where, but for the rise of errors needing to be contradicted and opposed, it might still have been left. He who sees Augustinian or Calvinistic doctrines clearly and explicitly taught in the Bible, will have no difficulty in seeing also plain traces of them at least in the works of the apostolic fathers; and he who can pervert the statements of Scripture into an anti-Calvinistic sense, may, by the same process, and with equal ease, distort the apostolic fathers.[1]

And Cunningham said with keen insight, apropos of the conflict which was to come at the time of the Reformation:

> Calvinists and anti-Calvinists have both appealed to the early Church in support of their respective opinions, although we believe it cannot be made out that the fathers of the first three centuries gave any very distinct deliverance concerning them. These important topics did not become subjects of controversial discussion during that period; and it holds almost universally in the history of the Church, that until a doctrine has been fully discussed in a controversial way by men of talent and learning taking opposite sides, men's opinions regarding it are generally obscure and indefinite, and their language vague and confused, if not contradictory.[2]

---

1. Vol. I, p. 180.
2. Ibid., p. 179.

These long years of apparent barrenness were not without their flashes of light and many great figures emerged to keep alive a testimony to the truth. What was lacking was not persecution but open controversy between contestants who had power enough to force their opponent to meet them on a more or less equal footing. The persecuted "minorities" of these intervening centuries were not silent or ineffective, but they were never in a position to force the issues into the open as Luther did, and Calvin, and the Reformers generally.

It was this open confrontation along a wide front with the backing of powerful men with strong convictions, and wealth and independence, that seems to have made the difference. For it allowed the contestants to hone their terminology and crystallize the issues in an entirely new way, and it gave men "handles" with which to wield the weapons of truth they had now seized so firmly and begun to use with such effectiveness. As a consequence, the Council of Trent was virtually forced upon the Roman Catholic Church and it marked the *end* of the *reformation* of that Church for several centuries, even as it marked the *beginning* of the *revolution* among Protestants.

And so the lines of divergence between Roman Catholicism and Protestantism really have their roots in this one man, Augustine,* though the process of divergence was not to be made manifest fully until the convergence of two circumstances which were largely responsible for the Reformation. The first was an almost total breakdown of Christian morality in the Roman Catholic Church, and the second was the appearance of a new spirit of free enquiry and independence in every area of human endeavour, including the exploration of the true meaning of the Gospel.

Pelagius had come to Rome at a crucial moment, for there stood to oppose him one man, Augustine, who could best profit by the challenge to the true Gospel which was presented by his humanism. There thus were opposed what are really the only two wholly consistent positions with respect to man's salvation. Either man is his own saviour, or God is his saviour. There is really no middle ground that is logically defensible. If man plays any crucial part whatever, he must in the end have the final say. If this is the case, every man in heaven will have reason to boast, since it will have been by his own will that he has gained admission. But it was pride that caused Satan's fall (Isa. 14:12, 13) and Satan who caused man's; so pride is probably at the root of all man's sin. And a heavenly community assembled on

*It was Pope Gregory (I) the Great (540-604) who took certain aspects of Augustine's theology and made them explicit as a foundation for the exclusiveness of the Church of Rome. Augustine's theology thus became the religion of the Middle Ages and underwent but little further development. (See "Gregory I" in *The New Schaff-Herzog Encyclopedia of Religious Knowledge*, ed. S. M. Jackson [Grand Rapids: Baker, 1969].)

such a basis as to justify pride could scarcely be a heaven. The issue is clear. The salvation of man must be all of God, or heaven is worthless and we have hope only in this world—a bleak prospect indeed!

It might be thought that there could be many alternatives, each tending more or less to one or the other extreme and all of them offering equally reasonable paths to salvation. But logical analysis shows that these alternatives do not form a succession of options approaching more and more nearly to the truth until they effectively merge in a continuous series from salvation achieved by man alone to salvation achieved by God alone. They do not have this character at all. Every alternative which attributes to man any part whatever in securing his own salvation ultimately falls within a single category which must be titled under the general heading, "Man is his own saviour." And the other alternative, that which makes God the sole and absolute saviour of man's soul, stands entirely by itself as the only representative of the other category. There are but two categories.

Inevitably, when man plays any role whatever he plays the crucial role, for fulfillment ultimately hinges entirely upon himself. There can never be an equal partnership, for in such a co-operative process man, and not God, must always have the last say. Man either does or does not perform his part: if he does, he is saved; if he does not, he is lost. That is the end of the matter. The part which God plays is secondary in this scheme of things.

The truth is that every theological system that allots to man some responsibility in the saving of his own soul inevitably ends up by making man his own saviour. And hereby we see an illustration of the principle that error can assume a thousand forms but the truth has only one, even as a line can be crooked in a million ways but straight in only one. So salvation as a co-operative exercise can be presented in many different forms, but there is only one way that is the true way and it is not co-operative at all.

Now, it would be natural, were there various degrees of self-help genuinely open to man, to conclude that some men stand a better chance of helping themselves than do others. And were this true, there would be every reason to suppose that God, whose foresight is perfect, would take note of such differences in potential and would elect to salvation those whom He knows would be most likely to respond to his offer of help—if that kind of help is really the true nature of saving grace. But saving grace is not an offer of help. Saving grace is unmerited favour—favour (not rewarded), and unmerited because it is not contingent in any way on forseen human response.

While it is clear, accordingly, from many intimations in Scripture that Election to salvation is not based on foreseen worthiness or any kind of merit resident in the individual but is based solely on God's good pleasure, it is also clear that there is another kind of election which is not to salvation but to the performance of specific tasks which require special gifts, special endowments. And such endowments are themselves the result of God's providential oversight of the distribution of genetic materials, and the ordering of circumstance. And both of these factors, being of his arranging, are assuredly foreknown to Him who thus ordains them. Such a form of election to service clearly applies to the saved and unsaved alike. Thus we have Judas among the elect (John 6:70, 71), but clearly not to salvation; and certain angels (1 Tim. 5:21) who also were not elected to salvation for we know that they never fell. In both instances election must be to a role to be played in the working out of God's purposes. Moreover, the Lord Jesus Himself was elect (1 Peter 2:6), but certainly not to salvation.

But the Election which is unto salvation and is related to the destiny of fallen man is a biblical principle which has been admitted by the great theologians of the Roman Catholics and Protestants alike. In the latter case it is admitted equally by the Calvinist and Arminian branches of the Protestant community. But the problem is, On what is this Election based? On divine foreknowledge of the response of the individual?

It does not seem that the Bible as a whole supports any such view. Only one passage of Scripture can be appealed to in this regard—Romans 8:29: "For whom He did foreknow, He also did predestinate to be conformed to the image of his Son." But a closer examination of this passage indicates that the word rendered "foreknow" in this instance does not have the simple meaning of *foreknowing* that we commonly ascribe to it in English (see pp. 134 ff.).

The problem is that an Election to salvation based on nothing that can be to the credit of the individual seems wholly arbitrary and the non-elect appear to be appointed to reprobation by a process that is equally arbitrary— and therefore inherently unjust. For if God has predestinated some to be saved for no apparent reason, has He not automatically condemned the rest to be lost for no apparent reason? But the proposition is a *non sequitur*. If all men are sinners to begin with (an assumption few will dispute), then all men are *already* under judgment. Men are not placed under judgment simply because they are not elected to salvation. Predestination to judgment is conditioned by the fact that the wages of sin is death (Rom. 6:23) and all have sinned (Rom. 3:23). We live in a universe that is governed not only by natural law but by spiritual law also. These spiritual laws are as absolute in their operation, barring miracle, as the material laws are—barring miracle. The stone is destined to fall to the earth if it is not held up; the soul that sins is destined to judgment if it is not redeemed.

Election to salvation is a reflection of the will of the Creator who determined to perform a miracle in order to reverse the spiritual law which operates everywhere in the universe. But the performance of the miracle of redemption is not the *cause* of the fate of the unredeemed. It is a sovereign act which God has every right to perform when and where He will. He does not need to act to bring the rest to judgment—they are *already* under condemnation by their own choice.

But it has never appealed to the natural man to be warned that he is under judgment and cannot redeem himself, nor improve his standing in the sight of God by his own good behaviour. Pelagius was realistic enough to admit that the improvement of human nature was not likely, but he did see it as possible, as a goal to strive for by education, cultural conditioning, and good breeding. The virtue of Jesus Christ, as he saw it, was not in some penal aspect of his sacrifice but in the example He set by it and in the principles of living which were part and parcel of his teaching. To teach men that no amount of effort on their part would avail to improve their standing was, he felt, a counsel of despair. Unlike Luther he did not view such despair as being "near to grace." Besides, such a proposition clearly undermined any incentive to holiness even in the Christian. Man cannot be blamed for failure if his constitution is such that failure is inevitable. Why then should he strive to be good? And Pelagius had many followers. As we have seen, not a few of the Church Fathers were already teaching that man must do his best to merit the grace of God.

Pelagius regarded it as a fatal mistake to suppose that the nature of man could be so corrupt that his will is powerless to obey God's commands. For it seemed to him essential to the very notion of morality that in all sin there is a personal assent, and that without this assent there could be no guilt. He was therefore driven to conclude that in a newborn child there could not possibly be either guilt or sin, since there is no power of assent. What makes the innocent child to become guilty is actual sin, inspired by example.[3] If such a child could be brought up to follow the supreme moral example of Christ, he could inherit eternal life. And Pelagius was convinced that such a thing would happen if the circumstances were favourable enough. We should therefore seek to create those favourable circumstances.

Granted that there is no root of corruption inherited from Adam, the newborn child could be viewed indeed as a clean sheet, with all the potential of maintaining that purity provided that the circumstances are such as to eliminate bad example. If, on the other hand, the newborn begins life already corrupted by sinful nature, the situation is very different. The heart of the problem was then, as it is now, to know precisely what it is that has been inherited. Is it some sort of disease that inevitably and fatally corrupts the spirit in due course, or is it a spiritual corruption to which is added imputed guilt? And can infant baptism wash away either the corruption, or the guilt?

Pelagius was convinced that the spirit of the child is uncorrupted to begin

---

3. Henry Chadwick, *The Early Church*, p. 228.

with, and even after committing actual sins and thereby becoming guilty the individual still retains some of the goodness with which God had endowed man in Eden. When Pelagius spoke of *grace* this is what he meant, this remanent capacity for goodness.[4] His use of this term, to which he applied his own personal meaning, at first confused his contemporaries who assumed his orthodoxy. They apparently supposed he meant by grace what they meant, but gradually it became clear that he was far from orthodox.

In time, due to Augustine's relentless pursuit, Pelagius was declared a heretic and his Christianized humanism was temporarily nipped in the bud. Though his followers in England (whence he had originally come) carried on his teaching, Pelagius himself seems to have withdrawn from the fray and disappeared from history, probably dying in Egypt.

Almost immediately after Augustine's death in 430 A.D., a reaction set in against his teaching regarding the spiritual depravity of man. If grace alone makes man acceptable in the sight of God, the call to a life of holiness by way of preparation to receive this grace has little practical importance. If Augustine was correct and man has no power to prepare himself, he therefore has no responsibility for doing so either. This seemed a clear invitation to spiritual indifference if not outright lawlessness.

One of Augustine's contemporaries was a man named John Cassian, an introvert with a great love for the contemplative life of the monastery and a yearning for holiness and purity. He was probably of Scythian stock, coming from somewhere near the Black Sea and uprooted by the turmoil of the period that witnessed the sack of Rome by Alaric in 410 A.D.

Settling in southern France near Marseilles, he established a monastery. Many people in those turbulent days were attracted to the life of retreat. Here, convinced in his own soul of the fundamental truth of Augustine's assessment of human nature, and having supported him in his attacks against Pelagius, Cassian now devoted himself to the working out of Augustine's theology as a way of life. But as he observed the effects of the doctrine of free grace upon those who joined his community, he came to the conclusion that Augustine had gone too far.

Men (and women) came to him, desiring to live a life of holiness that they might make themselves worthy recipients of the grace of God and receive the free gift of his salvation. Cassian found it necessary to encourage them to persevere when the flesh and the world proved too much for them. But he soon faced a dilemma—if such a striving after holiness contributed nothing towards ensuring the grace of God unto salvation, then on what basis could he persuade them to continue the struggle? If Augustine was right, the incentive towards godliness was undermined. If such preparation of the soul

---

4. Ibid., p. 230.

was not at all necessary, then would not God extend his salvation equally to those who took advantage of their freedom and lived immoral lives and to those who struggled earnestly to prepare themselves?

Cassian did not at first suppose that good behaviour formed the basis of man's salvation, but reason suggested to him that it must surely predispose God to look with favour upon the earnest endeavour of the suppliant and, though it was still an act of pure grace, to be more ready in granting salvation to the prepared soul. But Augustine had insisted that the grace of God preceded any such personal fitness. Man was not called upon to seek to be holy in order that he might be the recipient of grace; he became the recipient of grace in order that he might be holy.

Cassian's theology was, of course, not the theology of revelation but of common sense. The kind of preparatory holiness which he was promoting came to be known as *precedent grace*, and in a very real sense it was a reflection of the natural grace which Pelagius believed remained to man even in his fallen state. In Cassian's view it did not contribute directly to the salvation of the suppliant but it predisposed God to look upon him with more favour. Cassian did not suppose that man could ever achieve that measure of holiness which would merit eternal life but he did believe that man contributed something by proving himself worthy of God's favour and grace. And he was convinced that unless this was true, the whole concept of monastic life and man's endeavour to seek after holiness would be without purpose. He was not Pelagian in his theology, but in a sense he became the founder of *semi-Pelagianism*. He was by nature strongly drawn to cloistered life at a time when cloistered life had a tremendous appeal to those who saw the impending collapse of Western civilization. And he saw this kind of life in jeopardy. As a result he made his fears widely known, even though he still considered himself a true disciple of Augustine in every respect.

One individual who learned of these new doubts about Augustinianism was a man named Prosper Tyro of Aquitaine (c. 390-463), about whom comparatively little is known save that he had been an ardent disciple of Augustine though he had never actually met him face to face. Prosper attempted to answer Cassian's criticisms but without apparent success. Accordingly, he wrote to Augustine and asked him to intervene. As a consequence Augustine wrote two treatises: the first was entitled *On the Predestination of the Saints*, and the second *On the Gift of Perseverance*. In the first, Augustine reaffirmed that Predestination is in no way based upon foreseen merit in the elect. All a man's strivings in his own strength to achieve holiness of life apart from the indwelling presence of the Holy Spirit are in vain, and Augustine explained why this is so. In the second treatise Augustine showed that the Perseverance of the Saints, by which he meant (in modern terminology) the eternal security of the believer, is not dependent upon the good works of the individual believer which would result from his conversion, but entirely upon the constancy and unchangeableness of God's elective choice. Both these replies clearly downgraded the importance of good works or holiness of life in so far as these were regarded as contributing to a man's salvation. Good works were not relevant to salvation. They were, however, relevant to man's fellowship with God and his enjoyment of his Christian life. The reason for "being good" was not to the end of being saved but to the end of living a holy life pleasing to the heavenly Father. These two treatises were sent to Prosper and a co-worker named Hilary, and although neither appears to have made any great contribution of their own, Prosper himself did become a leading representative of Augustinian theology after Augustine's death. Yet he departed from one facet of his master's teaching, which others have also found difficult: namely, that Christ died only for the elect. This doctrine was to be termed Limited Atonement by the Reformers who, like Augustine and Calvin, saw it not merely as a view logically consistent in the light of the sovereignty of grace but as the plain teaching of the New Testament.

Gradually Augustinian theology was emasculated by Roman Catholic theologians as a whole, who retained only his emphasis upon the Church of Rome as the sole vehicle of God's dealings with man and the sole channel of salvation. Through the succeeding centuries, semi-Pelagianism became the basic theology of Catholicism; less and less attention was paid to the spiritual impotence of fallen man while more and more was paid to the remanent grace and inherent goodness of man's religious impulses. Man could not be saved apart from the sacrifice of Jesus Christ but that sacrifice alone was not sufficient in itself. It was necessary that man not only accept the Lord's sacrifice but that he strive sincerely after holiness in order to balance the debit account of his own sinful ways. Neither man alone nor Christ alone could save him. Human grace and divine grace must be wedded. Penitence and penance made up for what was lacking in human grace, and God for Christ's sake would then forgive what remained of offence after man had done his best. Baptism, as a rite with magic that worked whether performed by believer or unbeliever, restored the capacity of a person for salvation; good works and faith in Christ's redemption did the rest.

Here and there individuals appeared on the scene who recaptured something of the theology of Augustine in its wholeness, but some of these overemphasized one aspect of this theology and some another, and the wholeness was distorted into a new error. One of these was Gottschalk of Orbais (c. 805-869), who argued that if God had predestinated some men to salvation, He must necessarily have predestinated the remainder to reprobation. "There is a twofold predestination," he said, "of the elect to blessedness, and of the reprobate to death." Augustine had come to this conclusion also, as Calvin was later to do.

But like Calvin, Gottschalk was not altogether convinced that this was a logical corollary. It is not essential that the non-elect be driven to reprobation. They may merely be allowed to have their own way, being passed by and permitted to remain in the way they had freely chosen for themselves. But Gottschalk was so insistent that he came very near to making God the author of sin.

This unhappy man whose life was so plagued by misfortune and injustice that he was attracted by the works of Augustine, who had also experienced much misery in life, had been placed as a child in a Franciscan monastery at Orbais against his will. Subsequently in 829 at the age of twenty-four he was officially released from his vows on the ground that he had been coerced as a minor. Unfortunately his abbot Rabanus Maurus refused to let him go, arguing that all such vows were irrevocable. As a means of escape from his wretched predicament, Gottschalk immersed himself in the study of the works of Augustine.

Looking deeply into his own soul he saw in himself what Augustine had seen. And he came to realize that both he and the Church were carrying semi-Pelagian hearts under a cloak of pretended Augustinian orthodoxy. But the issue which really captured his imagination above all was the fact of Election, and in due time he became trapped in the logic of Double Predestination. Whether he wholly believed it or was merely writing in the hope of resolving the problem for himself, is uncertain. At any rate his superiors assumed that this was his opinion and that he was in fact guilty of making God the author of sin. Neither he nor his superiors considered the alternative possibility that God did not *need* to predestinate men to be lost in the sense that He predestinated the elect to be saved. He had only to leave the non-elect to suffer the consequences of their own free choice.

What was very clear to Gottschalk was that little or no importance could be attached to the natural goodness of man or to any supposed works of merit performed before conversion. God's elective choice was in no way influenced by precedent grace, whether witnessed at the time or foreseen. As he wrote and preached about his convictions, especially during a lecture tour of northern Italy, he aroused much consternation in many quarters, and the authorities decided it was time to act.

Gottschalk was accused of heresy, tried, and condemned. He was allowed no opportunity to defend himself or present his own case in a reasoned form. He was flogged mercilessly and imprisoned under cruel conditions until his death. Even some of his foes protested at the unchristian character of his treatment. Yet he died without recanting and apparently with great peace of mind, holding firmly to his Augustinian theology. He is one in a long line of martyrs for the Gospel, and in a manner of speaking his was the last personal protest against the corrupted *theology* of the Roman Catholic Church until Luther awakened to the truth some six hundred years later. Some of the great figures in church history who came later protested against the *morality* of the Roman Catholic Church but they did not, like Gottschalk, have a clear vision of the Church's theological error. As J. L. Neve observed, semi-Pelagianism retained its great hold upon the Church's theology throughout the entire Middle Ages. But one of the ironies of this circumstance is that because of the breadth of Augustine's theological sweep, even this fundamental departure from his position was justified as orthodox by appeal to certain of his earlier writings (which he had later retracted) and came to be known as "the preaching of Augustine" *(Sermo Augustini)!*[5]

The result was inevitable. Precisely because man's will is utterly corrupt, his strongest exertions to build a credit balance in the sight of God only carried him further and further in the corruption of all that was holy, until the religious communities which had started out to make themselves the guardians of truth and purity of life became the most appalling dens of iniquity. The corruption of the good always produces the greatest potential for evil.

The kind of holiness that self-effort thus produces is not sanctity but sanctimoniousness, and there is something pitifully powerless about it. It is a "form of godliness but denying the power thereof" (2 Tim. 3:5). It is powerless because it springs out of the activity of the corrupted will of natural man. Just because it *is* an expression of man's sinful will, it only confirms that will, making it stronger even while appearing to suppress it. If circumstances later encourage the enjoyment of sensual things, it is all too easy to slip from one kind of exercise that seems to have the appearance of purity, into the opposite kind which has all the earmarks of debasement. The man who has so strengthened his will that he can resist great temptations may later reach a position where he can exercise the same will power to get what he wants even when it is evil. And this happened all too frequently when "holiness" achieved by self-control was afterwards rewarded with authority and power over others. What transpired in monastic life may well have inspired the Reformers to declare that good works done out of Christ, precisely because they are expressions of human wilfulness, no doubt "partake of the nature of sin," as the Church of England in Article XIII has aptly expressed it.

Approximately two hundred years after Gottschalk, Anselm was born in Aosta in Piedmont in 1033 of a pious mother, Ermenberga, and an indifferent though well-to-do father. From a very early childhood his mother's influence played a strong part in his development and he occupied himself in meditation on the things of God as he grew. His relations with his father were much less happy, and when he was a young man he left home to travel

5. J. L. Neve, *A History of Christian Thought*, Vol. I, p. 178.

in France. In due time under Lanfranc he became a monk in the monastery of Bec. In 1063 he became its prior, and finally in 1078 its abbot. In 1093 he was called to be Archbishop of Canterbury.[6]

In a remarkable number of ways Anselm was like Augustine: in his gentleness, in his love for man and for God, in his contemplative nature, in his desire for holiness of life, and in his zeal to suppress his baser nature. Augustus Neander in his *General History of the Christian Religion and Church* says, "He was the Augustine of his age." What gave him his great importance was the unity of spirit in which he thought and did everything, a harmony between life and knowledge which in his case nothing disturbed. And love seems to have been the inspiring soul of his thought.

He was constantly occupied with public duties appropriate to each station of his life as he rose to become Archbishop. Rather like Augustine he felt himself throughout to be a wretched sinner unworthy of his office and privately longing to be free to return to a life of contemplation. When he died in 1109, in spite of the many conflicts in which he unwillingly became involved, he seems to have had no enemies but was completely at peace with God and everywhere revered by man.

There was one important difference, however, between the two men, Augustine and Anselm, namely, in the turmoil of the former's life as he grew up as contrasted with the comparative tranquility of the latter's.

Both men agreed absolutely upon this fact, that faith precedes understanding. Interestingly, both seemed to have based their conviction in this not upon Hebrews 11:3 ("through faith we understand. . . .") but upon the Septuagint version of Isaiah 7:9 which reads: "If ye believe not, neither will ye at all understand." Anselm's principle of handling Scripture was to sit down as a little child before the Word of God and accept its statements. Then, believing, to seek for understanding. Augustine's guiding principle had been that obedience to the Word in faith was the key to understanding it: "If any man will do his will, he shall know of the doctrine whether it be of God" (John 7:17). Similarly Anselm wrote: "Self-confident human wisdom will sooner break its own horn than succeed in overturning this rock." Faith, he held, precedes intellect.[7] In Anselm we find heart and mind beautifully balanced. Yet he made singularly little use of Scripture itself.[8]

In his *De Libero Arbitrio* ("Of Freedom of Will") Anselm controverts any idea of free will in man as being the power to choose between good and evil.[9] Man has only the power to choose between evils and since he sometimes chooses the lesser evil, he appears to be choosing the good. Pelagius

---

6. Augustus Neander, *Church History*, Vol. VIII, pp. 93 f.

7. Ibid., p. 104.

8. A. C. McGiffert, *A History of Christian Thought*, p. 187.

9. Neander, *Church History*, Vol. VIII, p. 261.

had argued that the effect of Adam's Fall was not inherited by his descendants, that every man is born as Adam was created, with complete freedom to choose between good and evil. This freedom is partially but not wholly lost as the individual matures, and this loss can be corrected by following the example of Jesus Christ. Anselm, with Augustine and Paul, denied this possibility. Since salvation was an absolute good, man could not choose it. The realization of this truth seems to have sprung out of Anselm's own experience with himself, as it had with Augustine. Augustine appears to have tried always to bring his thought captive to Scripture, combining the Word of God with every means at his disposal in order to base his theology on something more secure than experience. This policy transformed Augustine's thinking and theology and gave it a more secure foundation, besides vastly illuminating it. Anselm agreed with this principle entirely but did not exploit the Word of God as Augustine had done. Consequently their agreement is more implicit than explicit.

Increasingly as time went by, the emphasis in so-called Christian life had been shifted towards making man responsible for the preparation of his own heart to merit the infusion of the grace of God. This had not improved the spiritual life as a whole; it had tended only to increase the severity of the penalties imposed upon those who were manifestly failing. But this, too, had little effect in correcting the steady decline in Christian morality. Men remained selfish and inhumane and carnal as they had always been. And the question began to be asked, Why do Christian principles generate so little genuine goodness? Why if some men so earnestly desire to be holy, and if the reward for holiness of life is so great and the penalty for failure so terrible, do not men of good intent achieve their goal? Was there, after all, something really wrong with man's *will* to good?

Such was the lasting influence of Augustine's thought upon the centuries following that a number of Church councils still paid lip service by denying man's free will in the matter of salvation. Anselm in this spirit wrote not only his *Dialogue on Free Will* but also a treatise on the harmony between foreknowledge, Predestination, grace and free will. But while the theologians in their councils admitted that the will of fallen man was in bondage, the authorities in their religious houses in whose hands were the lives of the Church's flock continued to operate on the principle that man's will is free and therefore responsible to do something about achieving holiness.[10]

Anselm struggled to reconcile the apparent contradiction. He used an analogy: the will of man has a capacity for good as the eye has a capacity for light. But so long as the eye is in the dark its capacity is ineffective and undiscovered. The capacity of man's will for good is like this, latent only

---

10. Ibid., p. 301.

until the sunlight of God's grace shines upon it.[11] By Luther's time this "capacity" had become a "passive aptitude." It was an aptitude because it was already present waiting to respond, but it was passive because the light that effects this response must be supplied from outside. It was a light *receptor*, not a lamp. The eye of the soul is blind until God shines into it. It is God, not the eye, who gives the light of the knowledge of his glory (2 Cor. 4:6). Until God moves in the will, according to Anselm, the will is impotent towards spiritual good. Yet God does not bend the will by force. The will is drawn in such a way that it follows without resistance as if impelled by an inner necessity.

There is a deeply rooted feeling in the heart of man that he ought to contribute something of his own to his salvation. This contribution has taken a number of different forms. The most obvious contribution he can make is good works, but good works can operate in several different ways. They may secure his salvation directly by some kind of overbalance against his faults, or they may predispose God to favour him and grant him salvation as a gift otherwise unattainable, or they may be added to the weight of merit in the sacrifice of Jesus Christ which by itself is not sufficient. In most cases, the salvation is viewed as a co-operative effort. Yet it has always been felt by theologians that the idea of co-operation is not a worthy one. And so the effort is made to introduce co-operation without letting it *appear* as such.

Many Roman Catholic theologians took the position that man must prepare himself to merit the grace of God without which he cannot be saved. Arminian theologians have modified this somewhat and now take the position that while man cannot by good works merit the grace of God, he can prepare himself to receive it by declaring his willingness to do so. The end result is much the same; the one is as much a co-operative process as the other, and Roman Catholics have as easily adopted the non-resistance alternative as they adopt the preparatory works alternative. In either case, man plays a vital role is his own salvation. Thus while Lutherans today teach that man's vital role is non-resistance of the Holy Spirit, the older Roman Catholic theologians like Cardinal Robert Pullein held virtually the same position. Pullein, who died in 1146, wrote:

> As often as grace offers itself to anyone, the individual either acts in co-operation with that grace or, rejecting it, still goes on in sin. The first cause of all goodness is grace. But the free will also has a part to perform, though a subordinate one. Free will also has some merit; namely this, that *it ceases to resist the divine will* (emphasis mine).[12]

---

11. Ibid., pp. 301 f.
12. Quoted in Neander, *Church History*, Vol. VIII, p. 302.

The contrary will that resists the grace of God is not constrained to yield against its own inclination but is inclined to a willingness by the same grace. This was the logical maneuver by which some token acknowledgment was made to the autonomy of man's will. It was in effect the same device by which Lutheranism (though not Luther himself, I think) was to skate around the problem of the sovereignty of grace.

Luther was to struggle with this same problem and arrived at much the same conclusion, speaking of how the Spirit of God "sweetly breathes" upon the will to cause it to act "not from *compulsion but responsively*" (his emphasis).

Like Luther, Thomas Aquinas (1224-1274) had also postulated a "certain susceptibility" in man which was required for the operation of grace. But Aquinas traces even this susceptibility to the "preparation of God." He was nearer to Augustine in this than Anselm had been.

In his *Summa Theologica* written between 1265 and 1273, Aquinas adopted a technique for the expounding of his theology which others before him had employed, including Anselm in his famous little work *Cur Deus Homo*. This involved a kind of question-and-answer approach which in Aquinas took the following form: first, the stating of the question; second, the presentation of opinions contrary to his own; third, his own view of the matter; and fourth, his reply to each of the contrary opinions treated seriatim. In dealing with the matter of free will he begins by posing the question: "Can man merit eternal life without grace?" (Q. 109, art. 5). This is one of ten questions appearing in the section of his work under the general subject of the "Grace of God."

The first contrary opinion, which Aquinas terms *Objection 1*, is stated as follows: "It would seem that man can merit eternal life without grace. For our Lord says (Matt. 19:17), *'If thou wilt enter into eternal life, keep the commandments,'* from which it would seem that to enter into eternal life rests with man's will. Hence it seems that man can inherit eternal life of himself."

A second contrary opinion, *Objection 2*, is given as follows: "Further, eternal life is the wage or reward bestowed by God on men according to Matthew 5:12, *'your reward is very great in heaven.'* But wage or reward is meted by God to everyone according to his works, according to Psalm 62:12: *'Thou wilt render to every man according to his works.'* Hence, since man is master of his works it seems that it is within his power to reach eternal life."

It is interesting to note how subtly error can creep in through the back door and colour all that follows. The very form of Aquinas' question ("Can man merit eternal life without grace?") starts the process of reasoning on the wrong foundation. Grace by definition is *unmerited* favour and eternal life is a gift. If we ask whether man can merit eternal life, we start with an impossibility, and it is no wonder that we end up with a falsehood. And as the error in the question is subtle, so the error in the final answer is subtle.

Aquinas then presents his own view as follows:

> Man, by his own natural powers, cannot produce meritorious works proportional to eternal life, but for this a higher power is needed, namely, the power of grace. And thus, without grace man cannot merit eternal life; yet he can perform works leading to a good which is connatural to man such as *to toil in the fields, to drink* [convivially?], *to eat, or to have friends,* and the like, as Augustine says in his third *Reply to Pelagians.*

Aquinas' reply to *Objection 1* takes the following form: "Man, by his will, does works meritorious of eternal life, but as Augustine says in the same book, for this it is necessary that the will of man be prepared with the grace of God."

In reply to *Objection 2:*

> As the Gloss [i.e., comment] upon Romans 6:23 ("the grace of God is life everlasting") says: *it is certain that everlasting life is meted to good works, but the works to which it is meted belong to God's grace.* What is more, it has been said that to fulfill the commandments of the law, whereby their fulfillment may be meritorious, requires grace.

So here we have Aquinas on the old question of the relation between good works, grace, and eternal life. Grace is necessary to enable man to perform meritorious works of which the reward is eternal life. So has the Gospel been eroded. These good works are within man's reach if he is assisted by the grace of God. Man is saved *with* grace, not *by* grace. Man and God thus co-operate, God enabling man to merit life.

Aquinas' next question is, "Can a man by himself and without the external aid of grace prepare himself for grace?" His hypothetical opponent suggests that "man prepares himself to grace by doing what he has ability to do. And if he does God will not deny him grace." In support of this proposition, his opponent quotes Matthew 7:11: *"God giveth the spirit to them that ask Him."* His own view is that "man cannot prepare himself to receive the light of grace except by the gratuitous help of God moving him inwardly." And in support of this, Aquinas quotes John 15:5: *"Without Me ye can do nothing."*

So we conclude that even though man must work to merit eternal life, he will not even initiate such work without the enabling of God's grace. And thus in the final analysis we seem to be back with Augustine. However, a complication has been introduced. For even though the grace of God lies at the very heart of man's salvation, it is nevertheless a salvation *merited by good works.* It might seem that Aquinas was not in essential disagreement with Reformed theology as to the receiving of grace, but in truth this grace serves a different purpose in each. For the Reformers, it was the beginning and the end of man's eternal life, and the good works which he performed were an expression of something he already possessed. In Aquinas, grace was to enable man to achieve eternal life by his own efforts.

In his exposition of the *Thirty-Nine Articles* of the Church of England, E. Harold Browne said succinctly, "In philosophy Aquinas was a realist; in theology, a disciple of Augustine; and therefore opposed to the belief too prevalent among the Schoolmen, that the gift of grace was dependent on the manner in which men exercised their purely natural endowment."[13] The Church of Rome produced many great minds that harboured strange combinations of profound truth and profound error. One often wonders how it could come about that the conflict between the two did not become more apparent to the individual.

Thomas Aquinas, who thus presumed a grace that conditioned the will, also presumed a predestination which involved such a conditioning. But he held that it is possible to distinguish what proceeds from a genuine free will so conditioned and what from predestination. He wrote, "All leads back to the goodness of God. To this must be traced the reason why some are predestinated and others reprobated."[14] He might have noted Romans 2:4 in which Paul asserts that it is the goodness *of God*, not the goodness of man himself, that leads men to repentance.

Again Aquinas wrote: "It was God's will to manifest his goodness to a part of mankind—those whom He had foreordained to this end, in the form of mercy sparing them; to others, the reprobate, in the form of punitive justice. And this is the reason why He elected some and rejected others; and the ground of this difference lies only in the divine will."[15] Here we have a clear enunciation of the principle of Unconditional Election, and yet Aquinas still struggled to find some way of so presenting the case as to allow man freedom of will. While his doctrine seemed to annihilate the concept of man's free will, he still argued that this is not really what he meant but rather that by divine intervention God constrains the will of man in another direction.[16] But if this is an imposed change, a change that God effects in man willy-nilly, is this not an overriding of man's will? Aquinas answered: "God brings it about that man should freely will the change he experiences and thus all constraint is removed. For to suppose otherwise, namely, that the man did not will the change which is a change in his will, would involve a contradiction." Such was the subtlety of reasoning of the Schoolmen.

---

13. E. Harold Browne, *An Exposition of the Thirty-Nine Articles*, p. 258.
14. Quoted in Neander, *Church History*, Vol. VIII, p. 251.
15. Ibid., p. 252.
16. Ibid., p. 255.

These endless chains of "therefores," without constant reference to Scripture, inevitably left men no wiser and no clearer than they were before.

If the individual can by his disobedience lose his salvation, then it follows that he can in this "lost" position gain back his salvation by appropriate acts of obedience. And so there is once more restored to man a crucial role in his own salvation. The pull towards Arminianism is to man what gravity is to the material world. It is a subtle ever-acting downward pull that is never absent and that once yielded to causes an increasingly rapid debasement of the truth of the Gospel. The believer's intelligence has constantly to be brought into subjection to the revealed Word of God as a monitor of his thoughts. Like Abelard we try first to understand in order that we might believe. But understanding is not the basis of faith. Understanding is only the basis of knowledge. Faith requires a positive exercise of will, and demonstration of any theorem removes the necessity for exercising will. We merely assent. Unfortunately many people assent to the Gospel, supposing that they are thereby believing it.

The determination to restore the place of free will in the exercise of saving faith, on the ground that by this means alone could the incentive to holiness be maintained, was logical enough if there was any merit in such holiness as exhibited in the unredeemed life. But there is no such merit. Indeed, the notion that there is such merit in man is in fact offensive to God for it reflects unfavorably upon the sufficiency of the sacrifice of Christ for man's salvation if man himself must also make his little contribution. As for holiness *afterwards*, this is a different matter entirely, for then such holiness is meritorious because it is now an outgrowth of the life of God in the individual.

But Aquinas, not recognizing the significance of the new birth and its attendant inward revitalizing moral power, championed the benefits of uncertainty, of insecurity, of lack of assurance, and of the practical necessity of *not* believing in the eternal security of the believer, in order to provide the incentive otherwise lacking. Better, then, to retreat from the world with its temptation whereby one might easily lose one's salvation and to take refuge from its conflicts in the monastic life of sheltered contemplation.

But here men gradually surrendered the witness of the Holy Spirit in the inner life and increasingly substituted the man-made and humanly enforced disciplines of the monastery. These disciplines were interpreted and exercised by strong men who often became ambitious and unscrupulous when they found themselves invested with absolute authority over their fellow men. Power corrupts, and absolute power corrupts absolutely.[17] Religious corruption is extremely dangerous because it tends by its nature not to be tempered by conscience. Here and there a few notable souls served God

---

17. Lord John Acton in a letter to Bishop Creighton (1887).

with great zeal and effectiveness, but the great majority became "princes" in the community or in the world. Theological error has many unforeseen consequences.

It has sometimes been asked, Where was Protestantism before Luther? This question in effect supposes that what we now see as a recovery of the true Gospel, which for fifteen hundred years had been almost lost sight of, was in reality a novel invention. Opponents of true evangelicalism could not believe that God would really permit the total eclipse of the truth and leave men in darkness for so many centuries. Had not the Church of Rome during those previous years leavened the whole of European society and created a Christian civilization, as well as evangelized the heathen world in Africa and America? Admittedly, the Catholic Church had its faults and needed cleansing and restoring in its faith from time to time, but surely the truth was never so completely lost that a total revolution of theology was needed! The Western world had been kept Christian, or so men like Chesterton assured us, more Christian in fact than it had been since Luther and Calvin and the Reformers shattered that monumental unity which was Catholic Christendom.

But is this really so? Was this monumental unity an organic unity of the Spirit or merely a religio-political unity preserved essentially by a civil and hierarchical aristocracy working hand in hand for each other's mutual worldly benefit?

The need for reform was increasingly evident as the fourteenth and fifteenth centuries rolled by. In England John Wycliffe (1320-1384) thundered against the Church of Rome and the abuses of religious orders even in his own country where they were less powerfully entrenched than in continental Europe. It is true that in some ways he had comparatively small influence upon England herself until considerably later, but by means of his teaching and preaching in Oxford (where many Bohemian students from Prague were studying) he had a more profound theological influence on the continent through the followers of John Huss.

His theology was clearly Augustinian, though like Gottschalk he went beyond Augustine in the matter of Predestination and virtually made God responsible for man's Fall and therefore for all his subsequent sin. He categorically rejected the idea that man before his conversion can contribute anything by his moral behaviour towards influencing God's sovereign decision to grant him the grace of the Holy Spirit needful to conversion. Dyson Hague considered that five of the *Thirty-Nine Articles* of the Church of England (Articles X-XIV) could almost be taken word for word from Wycliffe's writing.[18]

---

18. Dyson Hague, *The Life and Work of John Wycliffe*, p. 149.

Article X is most explicit:

> The condition of man after the fall of Adam is such that he cannot turn and
> prepare himself by his own natural strength and good works to faith and
> calling upon God. Wherefore we have no power to do good works pleas-
> ant and acceptable to God without the grace of God by Christ preventing
> us that we may have a good will. . . .

Article XIII is equally explicit in this regard:

> Works done before the grace of Christ and the inspiration of the Spirit, are
> not pleasant to God for as much as they spring not of faith in Jesus Christ,
> neither do they make men meet to receive grace or [as the School authors
> say] deserve grace of congruity [i.e., as a consequence]: yea rather, be-
> cause they are not done as God hath willed and commanded them to be
> done, we doubt not that they partake of the nature of sin.

These ideas are directly contrary to the teaching of Thomas Aquinas but
fully in harmony with that of Augustine, who summed up his position on
the matter of works done out of Christ by using the words of Scripture:
"What is not of faith is of sin" (Rom. 14:23).

Julianus of Eclanum (380-c. 455), a Pelagian theologian, postulated the
case of a heathen who covered the naked and did works of mercy, and
asked, "Is this act of his therefore sinful because it is not of faith?"
Augustine replied unequivocally, "It is sinful." And with this Wycliffe con-
curred because, while the act itself was good towards man, it was not pleasing to God since it was prompted by a corrupt will as an expression of a sinful self.[19] We only need to reflect upon the reaction of a man who has done a
good deed (let us say, he has sent an anonymous gift to a person in need)
when someone else is given the credit for it! The true motive is quickly made
apparent. And a good deed may thus prove to be a work of iniquity even
when done in the name of the Lord (Matt. 7:22, 23).

God often turns such works to truly good ends, yet in themselves they
may be works of iniquity when performed out of Christ because they are
expressions of a fallen nature. Indeed it was argued in Wycliffe's day that "a
man sinneth the more by how much the more he laboureth to dispose himself to grace." Or to put it in plainer language, a man's good works are all
the more sinful when they are undertaken with the express hope and purpose of predisposing God to favour the doer by granting him salvation
upon the strength of them.

When performed by the unbelieving in aid of the Lord's children, works
are rewarded in this world, the reward being a form of kudos. But when
they are judged in the moral light of eternity, they can be seen only as works
of iniquity. Wycliffe saw clearly the unreality of man's supposed natural

---

19. Browne, *Thirty-Nine Articles*, p. 324.

goodness, and he recognized piety in the unredeemed for what it was. He spoke against it fearlessly as a snare and a deception, for unredeemed men were being easily persuaded to emulate the saints of the past in the belief that they would thereby make themselves more worthy of receiving God's grace and a passage into heaven. The Gospel had become superfluous except as an assist to men's natural goodness. The grace of God served only to crown the grace of man. There was a need to return to the biblical position which states in no uncertain terms that "all our righteousnesses are as filthy rags" (Isa. 64:6).

It is an extraordinary thing that while Wycliffe continued to thunder away against the heresy of salvation by good works he remained essentially at liberty and unharmed by the religious authorities of his day, and he died peacefully in his bed at the good age (in those days) of sixty-four years. He has rightly been called the "Morning Star of the Reformation," not merely because he cried out against unrighteousness in high places but because he called for a return to the Gospel.

Various reformation movements within the Church of Rome had been witnessed before Wycliffe and were to be witnessed after him, as for example in Florence under Savonarola from 1490 until his death eight years later. These were genuine outcries against the gross wickedness and immorality of the Church. But they were doomed to failure because, while the righteousness of God was exalted and the sinfulness of man was exposed, there was no attendant proclamation of the Gospel of personal salvation by regeneration which is the only basis for any true reformation of the Church or of society. Reformation must always start with regeneration, and regeneration is a personal matter. It is such individuals who then become the salt not for the building of a perfect society but for the preservation of a society from total corruption. A return to the teaching of Paul and of Augustine was what was required, and it was not very far in the future.

Meanwhile the Church's denunciation of the evils of the world were nothing compared with the world's denunciation of the evils of the Church. The famous troubadours or popular singers of the day took as a major theme of their songs the avarice and heartless greed, the cruelty and arrogant use of power, and the craftiness and treachery of all kinds which compacted together blatantly and without shame in the courts of the Church of Rome.[20] Something had to change or be changed.

The change was to come not by a more persuasive call to holiness but by a rediscovery of the fundamental fact that man is spiritually so completely dead that he is without the power to win the approval of God by good works unless God has first of all granted him new life and a saving faith to believe in the total sufficiency of the sacrifice of the Lord Jesus Christ to

---

20. Neander, *Church History*, Vol. VIII, p. 422.

make him once more acceptable in the sight of God. Man is lost and cannot by any means save himself by his works or even prepare himself to be saved. Salvation is entirely an act of grace dependent upon the sovereign will of God and made effective in the life of the individual only in God's time. Luther rediscovered this truth and proclaimed it; Calvin worked it out and made explicit its implications.

Augustine's influence and teachings had never been entirely lost, but neither had they been preserved entire by any one individual, after the passing of Prosper. Gottschalk was clear on the fact of Predestination and Limited Atonement, and he was probably reasonably clear on the Total Depravity of man and on Irresistible Grace. His position on the Perseverance of the Saints was perhaps sound, but it was implicit rather than explicit. The wholeness of Augustine's soteriology was gradually being eroded and the logical cohesion of his theology was not again to be worked out as a total system for centuries. The implications of the Gospel were not exploited in strictly biblical terms as Augustine had exploited them, until Calvin published his *Institutes*. Thomas Aquinas, the great master of the Medieval Schoolmen, caught some of Augustine's vision of the whole, but Aquinas' view was muddied by erroneous embellishments and fanciful extensions dependent entirely upon human reason that introduced all kinds of error which Augustine would have repudiated. These embellishments were soon made the basis of a whole new set of propositions which were far from the pure Gospel, and the Gospel itself was virtually submerged in a sea of error.

John Wycliffe seems to stand out from the mainstream as a lone figure and yet there is no doubt that he stood firmly in the tradition of Augustine, and as the harbinger of the Reformation formed a further link in a continuous chain which reaches from Paul in the New Testament through Augustine, Prosper, Gottschalk, and Anselm, to Luther, Calvin, and the Reformers.

4

LUTHER

It has been said that Luther can be understood without Calvin but not Calvin without Luther. Neither man can be understood without Augustine. It is difficult to know precisely what Calvin owed to Luther because we still do not know the steps in Calvin's theological development that led to the revolution which occurred in his theology and turned him from an ardent supporter of Mother Church into one of its most scornful critics.

The same is true to some extent of Luther. Of the actual conversion of either man we know surprisingly little. Contrary to popular fancy the precise date of Luther's conversion cannot be determined.[1] It can only be bracketed within a period of some four years and the exact details are still unclear except that, one day, while he was reading Romans 1:16 and 17 a whole new light on the meaning of faith began to dawn on his soul. And the details of Calvin's conversion can be known only by implication from remarks he makes in his commentary on Psalms and on Romans, as T. H. L. Parker has explained in his biography of *John Calvin*.[2] About all that can be said is that it occurred quite suddenly, probably in 1533.

The course of Luther's change of heart and mind is traceable in his growing confrontation with the appalling moral corruption of the Church of Rome, especially in the matter of raising money by the sale of indulgences and the circus-like display of supposed relics which the devout paid to see— or were even encouraged to purchase. It was a public scandal because, as Calvin was to point out later with biting scorn, there were several heads of John the Baptist, two bodies of Saint Anne, three of Lazarus, and at least fourteen nails of the cross, along with far more bones than Peter and Paul ever had![3] And now recently, we have been hearing of the supposed finding of Peter's actual tomb, including his real (?) bones. One official, the Elector

---

1. Carl S. Meyer, "Luther" in *New International Dictionary of the Christian Church*, p. 609.
2. T. H. L. Parker, *John Calvin: A Biography*, pp. 162 f.
3. Ibid., p. 136.

51

Frederick the Wise of Wittenberg (where Luther spent some time first as a Friar and later as a Professor at the University), had amassed a collection of some seventeen thousand relics, which included straw from the Saviour's manger, 204 fragments of the children slaughtered by Herod, and even a vial of the Virgin's milk.[4] The whole amazing charade could, of course, succeed only so long as people were kept in ignorance of what was taking place elsewhere. One could believe in the local relic, a nail for instance, provided that one did not know there were thirteen other nails scattered throughout Christendom! Lack of travel and communication kept alive a system of worship that was utterly fraudulent but highly lucrative. And in the midst of all the deception, simple people sought to purify their lives and succeeded only in impoverishing their bodies. Luther had appeared at just the right moment. Under ordinary circumstances, a man confronting Mother Church as Luther did, and being excommunicated for his pains, would either have been forced to repent (recant) and been received back into the fold a chastened (i.e., silenced) man, or handed over to the civil authorities and removed from society either by imprisonment or death. But the situation had changed radically as a result of a series of signal events over the previous two centuries. These included the perfection of gunpowder as an explosive weapon (c. 1320), the Black Plague (1348-1350), the development in Europe of block printing (c. 1450), and the fall of Constantinople (1453).

The contributing ingredients in the new ferment were introduced within a comparatively short space of time. The perfection of gunpowder, as an explosive weapon of war, brought the old feudal form of society to an end. The feudal lord was no longer safe in his castle. Its walls and towers could be demolished with the newly developed cannons that gunpowder had made possible. As a consequence it became necessary for the great barons to form private armies for personal protection, with the result that common men became mercenary soldiers, and these mercenary soldiers earned wages. Thus wealth began to be distributed in an entirely new way, and the whole economy of Europe began to change.

The Black Plague had a traumatic effect on society, for people witnessed on an enormous scale the carrying away by this awful disease of rich and poor, noble and common, saintly and reprobate alike. No one had been spared for their righteousness, while many who had been considered the dregs of human society and most assuredly under the judgment of God had escaped untouched. The *moral* shock of this indiscriminate devastation had been sobering indeed, and a great many orthodox religious assumptions were severely challenged.

The development of block printing had the effect of enormously expanding the available literature. It has been estimated that about 1450 there were

---

4. Edith Simon, *The Reformation* in *The Great Ages of Man*, p. 16.

perhaps a hundred thousand handwritten manuscripts in the whole of Europe.

Fifty years later as the result of the invention of the printing press there were over nine million books in Europe.[5] The consequence of this was a new demand by ordinary people for education, particularly for the ability to read. And mental horizons were stretched, and many new challenges to traditional beliefs resulted. The Church became less and less the keeper of the world's literature.

Finally, the fall of Constantinople in 1453 to the besieging Moslem Turks had an enormous effect upon European history. It resulted in the flight to the West of the Greek scholars who with their learning and their manuscripts had established themselves in the East after the fall of Rome in 410, leaving Europe impoverished by their departure. For the collapse of the West had broken its link with the classical learning of the Greek world, a break which severed the Western world from its very roots, and robbed it of a vital connection with the cradle of most of its intellectual heritage. When these Eastern scholars came back into the West with their ancient learning and their books, they introduced an intellectual blood transfusion which was both healthful but also upsetting to the Western world.

And now the same Turks, who had captured Constantinople and shattered the equanimity of the Eastern branch of the Christian Church, were headed up into Europe and were threatening Western civilization. Charles V, father of Philip II of Spain of Armada fame, saw the remnant of his Holy Roman Empire threatened unless he could present a united front against the Turks now advancing into Hungary under the able leadership of Suleiman the Magnificent (1520-1566). But here was the problem: Charles' empire was sadly divided. It was no longer Roman (i.e., Roman Catholic) for there had appeared on the scene a man named Luther who had already caused a serious rift in the German provinces and made the united front that was so important (since Germany marked the empire's eastern border) virtually impossible.

Luther's intense search for peace with God is well known in its broad outlines and we do not need to detail it here. The larger historical background sketched above contributed to Luther's success in establishing an independent movement because the monolithic structure of the Church of Rome had been weakened by the events of the previous centuries. And Charles V, who might have preserved its cohesion, was distracted by other divisions within his own empire.

Luther was born in 1483. He was converted dramatically somewhere between the years 1514 and 1518. The precise date is not certain, but the *fact* of his conversion most certainly is. Luther was transformed into a new man,

---

5. Ibid., p. 13.

full of tremendous assurance and hungry to search and feed upon the Word of God and to study the works of those Church Fathers (chiefly Augustine) whose writings illuminated his own experience. He had discovered the truth of Augustine's statement written eleven centuries before: "The saved are singled out not by their own merits but by the grace of the mediator; that is, they are justified . . . as by a free favour."[6]

Like Augustine, Luther saw clearly that the root of man's problem lay in a disobedient and rebellious will. Man is *not* free. His will is in bondage. Every effort man makes to secure salvation by his own efforts only strengthens that will, a will basically at enmity with God. The salvation of man must therefore reside not in man's will but in God's.

The great classical and "Christian" humanist of the day was a man named Erasmus (1466-1536) with whom Luther corresponded at length on the crucial issue of the effects of the Fall of man on the freedom of his will. Erasmus was an ethical Pelagianist to all intents and purposes, saying on many occasions that "to imitate the life of Jesus was far more important than to argue about dogma." But to Luther this was a vast oversimplification of the problem. Many were indeed *trying* to do just this, but how few had any peace in their progress! What was wrong was that man's will was corrupt. The most earnest aspirant after holiness of life found himself saying with Paul, "Oh wretched man that I am!"

Erasmus held that the secret was education. Luther argued that the secret was complete transformation of the will. The will, he maintained, is in bondage to wickedness and such a corrupted source of human energy could not, in the very nature of things, turn itself around and wish its own demise. All man's struggles to correct his evil tendencies only confirmed these tendencies. The sole result of these struggles was the strengthening of the very will which by its corrupted nature was the cause of these tendencies in the first place. It was simply impossible for man to will to be truly holy because he had only a corrupt will to carry forward his good intentions. The principle was self-defeating. The situation, humanly speaking, was quite hopeless—as Luther's own experience had taught him.

But this, Erasmus protested, was to invite a total breakdown of morality. Who would try to correct his ways if he was told that even to attempt it was useless? But Luther had the answer. It was indeed useless to attempt self-reformation, but that did not mean that there was nothing left for man to do! He could turn to God alone for his salvation and abandon all dependence upon human effort.

In his justly famous essay to Erasmus *On the Bondage of the Will*, Luther crystallized the issue in section VII:

---

6. Ibid., p. 38.

It is essential for a Christian to know whether or not the will does anything in those things which pertain unto salvation. Let me tell you, this is the very hinge upon which our discussion turns. It is the very heart of our subject. For our subject is this: to enquire what "free-will" can do, in what it is passive, and how it stands with reference to the grace of God. . . .

Wherefore, friend Erasmus, you certainly at the same time assert also that the mercy of God alone does all things, and that our own will does nothing, but is rather acted upon: and *so it must be, otherwise the whole is not ascribed to God* (my emphasis).

This is indeed the crux of the matter. But Erasmus replied (Section XXIII): "What a floodgate of iniquity would these ideas, publicly proclaimed, open unto men! What bad man would ever amend his life!" Whereupon Luther responded (Section XXIV):

Who (you say) will endeavour to amend his life? I answer, No man! For your self-amenders without the Spirit of God do not regard, since they are hypocrites. But the Elect and those that fear God will be amended by the Holy Spirit; the rest will perish unamended. Nor does Augustine say that the works of *none*, nor that the works of *all* are crowned, but only the works of *some*. Therefore there will be some whose lives will be amended.

You say, who will believe that he is loved of God? I answer, No man will believe it! No man can! But the Elect shall believe it; the rest shall perish without believing it, filled with indignation and blaspheming as you describe them. Therefore, there will be some who shall believe it.

Luther next considers how man's will is turned from enmity against the will of God to a wholehearted embracing of it. "When God works in us," he writes, "the will, being changed and sweetly breathed on by the Spirit, desires and acts not from *compulsion* but *responsively*" (Section XXV, his emphasis). Apart from the grace of God, man's will is free only in the sense that a slave is free who has come to accept his slavery as the normal condition of his life. The will of fallen man is immutably the bondslave of evil. "When it acts in character it commits mortal sin." This was a direct challenge to the official position of the Roman Catholic Church which argued that such a doctrine would relieve man of all responsibility for doing evil on the ground that ability determines duty.

Such heretical views could lead only to excommunication but the Church no longer held the absolute power over the individual that it once had and although Luther was excommunicated, he could not be turned over to the civil authorities as he might have been fifty years before.

Luther's boldness won to his side many disciples who had long been chafing at the restraints placed on their personal freedom by a demanding and powerful hierarchy. Though he himself was in sufficient danger that he needed to be "hidden" in Wartburg Castle, reports of his stand against the Church and of his bold statements and challenges to current religious practices were soon being printed and read widely throughout Germany. For a spirit of independence among the German states had come into being and many of their princes were rejoicing in this new sense of freedom. Groups of followers soon began to form themselves into what amounted to "Lutheran congregations."

It was then that Charles V, seeing this crucial segment of his empire becoming divided when he most needed a unified front against the Turks, decided he must heal the rapidly widening theological rift. And so he called a Congress, hoping thereby to reunite the "separated brethren" with the established Church.

On January 21, 1530, the Emperor commanded the Lutherans in Germany to present a Confession of their Faith before a joint meeting with the theologians of the Church of Rome. At this meeting conciliation was to be attempted. The Congress was held at Augsburg.

In the meantime, it should be borne in mind that Calvin (1509-1564) had not yet publicly formalized his theology. The first edition of his *Institutes*, which was presented in much briefer form than the work now familiar to the world, was not issued till six years later. His initial studies and discussions had taken place while he was in France preparing himself for the legal profession. Circumstances had caused him to flee to Switzerland so that it was in Geneva that his influence came to have its greatest impact. He was well acquainted with Luther, who was twenty-six years older than he, and Calvin respected Luther's work. There is no doubt that those who most influenced Calvin when he came to know the Lord had themselves been influenced greatly by Luther. Luther reciprocated this respect. But there was never any close working relationship between the followers of the two men. They were temperamentally different, and subsequent history in many ways reflected these differences. Thus the call by the Emperor to the Lutherans in Germany did not involve the Calvinists in France or Switzerland.

But this command appearance of Luther's followers provided the occasion for the elaborate formalization of Lutheran theology under conditions of considerable challenge. And it was prepared in a remarkably short time.

In the immediate future, Luther thus stood out as a theologian in a way that Calvin did not until sometime later. By the time Calvin had crystallized his thinking sufficiently to issue a fifth edition of his *Institutes* in very substantially enlarged form (1559), Luther had been dead some thirteen years; and Lutherans themselves had departed in certain respects from their master's original position regarding the part played by man in his own salvation. Calvinists, by contrast, did not shift their position significantly for a long time. The precise *direction* of this departure in Lutheran theology was ultimately to have serious consequences, and it is therefore important to observe how this subtle change came about and upon what it hinged.

The document known as the *Augsburg Confession* was read before the assembled churchmen, Roman Catholic and Lutheran, on June 25, 1530. Only five months had been allowed for its preparation. The details and references which follow are taken from the official Lutheran English translation of the *Book of Concord*. The formulators deliberately made a particular effort to emphasize the points of agreement with Rome rather than their differences.[7] This set policy is reflected in a number of the Articles in the arrangement of the wording.

In such matters as the "veneration of the saints" an effort was made to allow that their example should be an inspiration, and even the Emperor's warlike aims were commended by referring to the blessing of God upon David (p. 46).

In the matter of the Real Presence in the communion symbols of bread and wine a compromise was made which many evangelicals would later find dangerous (p. 34).

Baptism is admitted as a necessity for salvation but there is insufficient stress on the fact that it is not the rite itself but the symbolism which is the key to its significance. The grace of God is said to be "offered through baptism," a blanket statement which invites one to believe the mere sprinkling of water *on* the unbelieving *by* the unbelieving would still guarantee this grace (p. 33).*

Confession and absolution of the sinner by the priest are admitted, though the actual word *priest* is avoided. Such a confession seems to be made a prerequisite for receiving communion, which was an easily misunderstood concession to the Roman Catholic view of the offices of the priest as an essential mediator (p. 61).

Stress was laid on the freedoms which man does possess in certain less important areas of social and cultural life rather than on the bondage which enslaves his will in the more crucial aspects of his spiritual life. "Man possesses some measure of freedom of will which enables him to live an outwardly honourable life and to make choices among the things that reason comprehends. But without the grace, help, and activity of the Holy Spirit man is not capable of making himself acceptable to God."

Not unexpectedly, as first drafted, this Confession was objected to by a number of Lutherans. There had not been sufficient time. Everything had been done in haste and under pressure from the Emperor. As a consequence an alternative *Confession of Augsburg* was formulated by opponents of the first one; and although it was not presented at the first Congress, it was

---

7. *Book of Concord*, p. 24.

---

*Clearly a concession to Rome, which believes just this.

subsequently published side by side with the first Confession. This is how it appears now in the official English edition of the *Book of Concord*. Thus the concessions did not go unchallenged even by the Lutherans themselves.

Meanwhile the Church of Rome presented a *Confutation* which was so positive that Charles V presumed it had completely demolished the Lutheran presentation. But the Lutherans were not even provided with a copy of this *Confutation*. Thus when they came to reply to it they had to depend on memory and notes taken down by those present at its reading. A defence of their own Confession was, however, prepared at once, most of the work being done by Philip Melancthon, whose views on some of these vital issues were rather less positive than Luther's were. This defence statement was ready by September 22, but the Emperor refused to give it a hearing.

Melancthon then further revised the defence and continued working at it, assisted now by a copy of the Roman Catholic *Confutation*, until it had become a far more elaborate defence which was in time to form a kind of official Lutheran Confession. This document, along with certain other documents of a similar nature, was signed by a number of Lutheran representatives in 1537.

Melancthon's reply was thereafter referred to as the *Apology of the Confession* and it disagreed with the original in subtle ways. Particularly was this the case with reference to the subject matter of this present volume. The total inability of man to initiate his own salvation in any way whatsoever was underscored (p. 101). And even more pointedly it is stated: "Men really sin even when they do virtuous things without the Holy Spirit; for they do them with a wicked heart and (Rom. 14:23) 'Whatsoever does not proceed from faith is sin.' " Melancthon reflected the current of thought in his day when he explained this by adding: "Such people despise God when they do these things, as Epicurus did in not believing that God cared for him or regarded or heard him. This contempt for God corrupts works that seem virtuous, for God judges the heart" (p. 112).

One needs to bear in mind that for centuries men had sought, by retreating to the monasteries and endeavouring to fill their lives with good works often having the nature of genuine self-sacrifice, to gain merit in the belief that such a life would predispose God to favour them with saving grace. This pervasive emphasis on the merits of the "religious life" was so entrenched in the medieval mind that the Reformers were forced to counteract it with statements which must strike the ordinary reader as extreme. Entrenched error requires strong measures which to the casual reader may seem equally erroneous.

The issue here is a recurring one. We are too easily convinced that a man's natural goodness will not only predispose him to desire salvation but will also predispose God to respect his desire for salvation more than He will that of an evil man. Yet we know this is not so. Sinners and harlots go into heaven before the worldly righteous (Matt. 21:32). It was certain devout and honourable women who were first stirred up *against* the Christians (Acts 13:50). These were not irreligious people; they were people who had achieved recognition in the community as being devout. And they were not sinners particularly, for they were considered "honourable" people. Being women they were presumably more religiously inclined and less aggressive than many of their contemporaries. Yet they were among the first anti-Christian Gentiles! Wesley was later to make the same discovery. But we still persist in the impression that such-and-such a person, because he or she is such a nice individual, is a good prospect for conversion. Election is clearly not contingent on any such predisposition towards natural human goodness in man himself. All experience proves this and yet we cannot shed the feeling that it ought to be. Melancthon in his Article on *Justification* (IV. 322) quotes with approval Augustine's words: "God leads us to eternal life not by our merits but according to his mercy."[8]

In 1536 the *Smalcald Articles* were issued in an attempt to reach an even more general agreement among the Lutherans. It was at the time anticipated that certain concessions would be required to achieve unity among themselves for it was believed that they would soon be called up by the Pope (Paul III) to a Council to be held in Mantua in 1537. However this Council never actually materialized. Luther himself had been growing increasingly weary of the divisions among his followers and the failure of some of them to adorn the Gospel by their lives. It was therefore Luther personally who drafted the *Smalcald Articles* under orders from the Elector of Saxony. Among those called to sign them was Melancthon who, not unexpectedly, did so only with reservations. For Melancthon and Luther had been growing steadily apart in their theology.

Upon Luther's thinking in the *Smalcald Articles*, Augustine's influence was clearly revealed throughout. One of these Articles holds that it is "an error and not to be believed . . . that man has free will to do good." Nor is it to be believed that "if man does what he can, God is certain to grant him grace" (p. 302). This was the point at issue increasingly between Luther and Melancthon.

The divisions continued among Luther's followers and it was not until 1580, or fifty years to the day after the first attempts had been made to reach concord for the Augsburg Conference, that a measure of agreement was finally achieved permitting the issuance of the *Formula of Concord*, which was to become the official Confession of the Lutheran Church. By

---

8. Augustine, *On Grace and Free Will*, IX.21.

this time Luther had been dead for thirty-four years. Both the Roman Catholics (who seemed by then to have accepted Lutheranism as a permanent part of the German scene) and the Calvinists (who did not view with favour the divisions within the Protestant movement) had been putting pressure on the Lutherans to come to some agreement. The internal peace of the land was felt by the German princes to be threatened until this was achieved. For three years draft after draft was proposed until it reached a form sufficiently acceptable to all shades of opinion within the German Lutheran Church that 8,188 theologians, ministers, and teachers in the participating territories finally signed what came to be called "The Solid Declaration." On June 25, 1580, the complete *Book of Concord* went on sale.

It is a revealing document but it unfortunately holds within it the seeds of betrayal of the basic truth which Luther stood for at the beginning. For he had said that man contributed nothing whatsoever towards his own salvation. In this he was in entire agreement with Calvin's view that man was not merely spiritually *sick:* man was *dead.* Perhaps it was Melancthon's subtle influence that modified this stern but realistic view. Whatever the cause, the end result was a document which ended up by allowing man a small part to play in his own salvation. It *is* a small part, truly. Yet because it is essential, it once more made man the determiner of his own destiny. Man, not God, was sovereign in his salvation. To see how this came about, we must briefly review the *Formula.*

The *Formula* started well. It seems so very explicit that as one reads it one rejoices in its faithfulness to the Word of God and its realistic view of fallen man. Thus in Article II on *Free Will*, under the heading of *Contrary False Doctrines* (Section 4), it is stated:

> We reject, likewise, the teaching that while before his conversion man is indeed too weak by his free will to make a beginning, convert himself to God, and whole-heartedly obey God's law by his own powers, yet after the Holy Spirit has made the beginning through the preaching of the Word and in it has offered his grace, man's will is forthwith able by its own natural powers to add something (though it be little and feeble) to *help,* to *co-operate,* to *prepare itself* for grace, to *dispose itself* to *apprehend* and *accept* it, and to *believe* the Gospel.[9]

I have added the emphasis, but even without the italics what could be more plain and positive in denying to unregenerate man any role whatever in his salvation? So also in Section 9: "Likewise Luther's statement that man's will in conversion behaves 'altogether passively' (that is, that it does nothing at all) must be understood as referring to the action of divine grace in kindling new movements within the will."[10]

---

9. *Book of Concord*, p. 471.
10. Ibid., p. 472.

Regarding the place of foreknowledge in Election, the *Formula of Concord* is equally explicit. Article XI, Sections 2 and 4, reads:

> God's foreknowledge extends alike over good people and evil people. But it is not a cause of evil or of sin which compels anyone to do something wrong: the original source of this is the devil and man's wicked and perverse will. Neither is it the cause of man's perdition; for this, man himself is responsible. God's foreknowledge merely controls the evil and imposes a limit on its duration so that in spite of its intrinsic wickedness it must minister to the salvation of his elect. . . .
>
> Predestination or the eternal election of God, however, is concerned only with the pious children of God in whom He is well pleased. It is a cause of their salvation, for He alone brings it about and ordains everything that belongs to it.

The theme of the Total Depravity of unregenerate man and the powerlessness of his will towards good is reaffirmed so frequently and with such emphasis that it would almost seem monotonous were it not of such crucial importance. It was a crucial issue then, and it is a crucial issue still. In the treatment of *Original Sin* (Article I, Section 7) it is stated:

> Likewise we reject and condemn those that teach that although man's nature has been greatly weakened and corrupted through the Fall, it has nevertheless not entirely lost all the goodness that belongs to spiritual and divine matters, or that the situation is not the way that the hymn we sing in our churches describes it, "through Adam's fall man's nature and being are wholly corrupted," but that human nature has of and from man's natural birth something that is good—even though in only a small, limited, and poor degree—such as the faculty, aptitude, skill, or ability to initiate and effect something in spiritual matters or to co-operate therein.[11]

This complicated Article was apparently directed rather specifically against Melancthon's tendency to take a softer and more humanistic view of the depth of human depravity.

Once again this subject is broached under the heading of *Free Will or Human Powers*. With great firmness is stated the following (Article II):

> In order to settle this controversy in a Christian way according to the Word of God, and by God's grace to bring it to an end we submit the following as our teaching, belief, and confession. We believe that in spiritual and divine things the intellect, heart, and will of unregenerate man cannot by any native or natural powers in any way understand, believe, accept, imagine, will, begin, accomplish, do, effect, or co-operate, but that man is *entirely and completely dead* and corrupted as far as anything good is concerned.
>
> Accordingly, we believe that after the Fall and prior to his conversion not a spark of spiritual powers has remained or exists in man by which he

---

11. Ibid., p. 512.

could make himself ready for the grace of God or to accept the proffered grace, nor that he has any capacity for grace by and for himself or can apply himself to it or prepare himself for it, or help, do, effect, or co-operate towards his conversion by his own powers either altogether or halfway or in the tiniest or smallest degree, "of himself as coming from himself," but is a slave of sin (John 8:34), the captive of the devil who drives him (Eph. 2:2; 2 Tim. 2:26). Hence according to its perverse disposition and nature, the natural free will is mighty and active only in the direction of that which is displeasing and contrary to God.[12]

The formulators of the *Concord* have virtually exhausted the English language to make their point. What else could have been said! Again it is apropos to add that they seem to have been particularly concerned to protect their Confession from any taint of Melancthon's softness in the matter, for they state quite simply before making this lucid and exhaustive declaration that Melancthon ("one part" he is euphemistically called) "held and taught . . . that man nevertheless still has so much of his natural powers prior to his conversion that he can to some extent prepare himself for grace and *give his assent to it*" (my emphasis).

Augustine had struggled with the matter of human assent. The formulators of *Concord* evidently felt it appropriate to underscore their rejection of Melancthon's doctrine of assent and to set forth the circumstances regarding Augustine's similar rejection of the doctrine of assent. Accordingly, they comment on 1 Corinthians 4:7 ("What have ye that ye did not receive? If then ye received it, why do ye boast as if it were not a gift?") by saying:

> It was this passage in particular which by St. Augustine's own statement persuaded him to recant his former erroneous opinion as he had set it forth in his treatise *Concerning Predestination:* "The grace of God consists merely in this, that God in the preaching of the true Gospel reveals his will; but to assent to this Gospel when it is preached is our own work and lies within our own power." And St. Augustine says further on, "I have erred when I said that it lies within our power to believe and to will, but that it is God's work to give the ability to achieve something to those who believe and will."[13]

In summary, the wording could not be more explicit. Having declared that man *cannot* "prepare himself, or help, do, effect, or co-operate towards his conversion by his own powers, either altogether, or halfway, or in the tiniest or smallest degree,"[14] the formulators of *Concord* reinforced this by saying: "In his own conversion or regeneration man can as little begin, effect, or co-operate in anything as could a stone or block or lump of clay."[15]

---

12. Ibid., p. 521.
13. Ibid., p. 526.
14. Ibid., p. 521.
15. Ibid., p. 525.

They continue: "Therefore men teach wrongly when they pretend that un-regenerate man still has enough power to *want* to accept the Gospel."[16]

And yet, having spoken so clearly on the issue, having declared their position so unequivocally, having exhausted the dictionary to find words to reinforce their affirmation of man's Total Depravity of spirit, the formula-tors of *Concord* then gradually shifted the emphasis and ended up with a final pronouncement which undid the whole thrust of their Confession! Man *does* have a say! Man *can* refuse the grace of God! Man *has* the power of assent! It is on page 532 that we see the first concession to semi-Pelagianism:

> When the Word of God is preached, pure and unalloyed according to God's command and will, and *when people diligently and earnestly listen to and meditate on it,* God is continually present with his grace and gives what man is unable by his own powers to take or to give.

Thus begins the leaven of synergism again. The pejorative phrase is underlined. It is a crucial error. The *Formula* has just finished saying, and rightly, that man's heart or will or whatever it is that might respond by lis-tening diligently and earnestly, and meditating upon the Gospel, is a *stone*, a *block*. It is indeed a stone, inanimate, without life. The lump of clay can-not listen earnestly or reflect upon what is said. The dead know not anything at all. As reasonably would one go to the morgue and preach to the corpses laid out there for burial! What could they possibly hear and reflect upon?

But now it is being argued that man's part is of his own will "to attend" to the Gospel: to expose himself to it, to prepare himself for it, not merely to hear a sermon which might be entertaining or intellectually stimulating but to hear the Word of God, to understand it, to receive it with the inner ear. He is therefore no longer a mere object upon whose ears the Word of God impinges like all other sounds. He is to make himself an attentive listener, consciously seeking to know the will of God. And he is to do this, apparent-ly, entirely as the result of the inner promptings of his own heart. This is to be his contribution; this is what he can do and must do as his part towards his own salvation. Thus in spite of what has been said in this respect, we are now told: "In this case it is correct to say that man is *not* a stone or a block."[17] We are therefore to understand that although man *is* a stone or a block he is not to *behave* like one.

Now, in his powers of reasoning man is certainly not a stone or a block. But in his ability to comprehend spiritual truth he is. He does have a heart of stone (Ezek. 36:26). He is spiritually inanimate. We know this by revela-

---

16. Ibid., p. 530.
17. Ibid., p. 532.

tion and it is amply confirmed by experience. We hear the Gospel preached but it does not speak to us at all until the Lord opens our ears or our hearts that we may inwardly "attend" to it (Acts 16:14). We in turn speak to others and set forth the way of salvation to them as clearly as it is possible to do so by using the Word of God, but until they, too, are born again they hear nothing either. A newly converted man will frequently say afterwards, "Why did you not tell me these things before?" He has heard a voice, as the bystanders heard the sound of a voice when the Lord spoke to Paul on the way to Damascus (Acts 9:7). But he, like them, has heard only sounds within meaning. There is something supernatural about this. Any other piece of information communicated in the same language at the same level of sophistication will normally be grasped immediately. But spiritual truth is totally incomprehensible to the natural man. Something actually does not get through, as though the channels of communication were closed. There is no way of accounting for this fact except by saying that sin has closed man's understanding to certain kinds of truth. This is true of every unregenerate man. Apart from the prevenient grace of God no man either will or can consciously and deliberately place himself in the position of listening for the Word of God. It is something entirely outside his experience to listen *in this way*.

And so the formulators, ignoring this fact or simply failing to recognize it, begin to question "whether man in his conversion (i.e., at the time of his conversion) behaves like and really is a block," or whether he may not in fact be sufficiently alive to deliberately close his mind to what is being said, as though he actually knows what is being said. And they conclude "in the light of the previous discussion" that they are to be condemned who argue that God coerces the wills of men and compels man to be converted against his will.

Here, then, is man's contribution. He puts himself deliberately in the way of hearing the Gospel, and when he hears it he does not resist it. As the formulators finally sum up the situation: "Towards this work the will of the person who is to be converted does nothing *but only lets God work in him until he is converted*" (my emphasis).[18] How Luther would have grieved at this fatal concession to the autonomy of man! As Charles Hodge said on this issue, "The Lutherans themselves admitted it as a 'divinely necessitated logical inconsistency' once they had rejected the consequences of their avowed belief that man really was spiritually dead."[19]

How did this change come about? It was the result of the search for a rational explanation of why some are elected and others are not. It is clear

18. Ibid., p. 539.
19. Charles A. Hodge, *Systematic Theology*, Vol. II, p. 724.

from Deuteronomy 29:29 that this is one of the secret things hidden in the mind of God. "The secret things belong unto the Lord our God: but those things that are revealed belong unto us and to our children for ever. . . ." It *is* revealed to us that we are "chosen in Him before the foundation of the world" (Eph. 1:4). It is not revealed to us *why* we are chosen and not others. It is revealed to us that the saved were formerly even as the unsaved (Eph. 2:3) and that it is of the same lump of clay that one vessel is appointed for honour and another for a contrary purpose (Rom. 9:21).

There is no doubt that the raw material of elect and non-elect alike is basically the same. We are made of the same stuff. This is revealed. What is still hidden is "Why me and not my neighbour?" And our minds being what they are, we become locked in with the problem, particularly at certain stages of our development. We cannot let it go. We become certain in our own minds that there is an answer, and that the answer will be humanly satisfying and so comprehensible in its rationality that men will be persuaded to believe it. We ourselves believe the fact of Election and wonder at the goodness of God, and gain unbounded assurance from it. "Ye have not chosen Me, but I have chosen you" (John 15:16) becomes food for the soul and we worship the Saviour and glorify God, but it is still a certainty born of faith and not of reasoned assent. Nevertheless we try to uncover the rationale behind it.

Lutherans at that time, and a host of thoughtful men since, have argued thus among themselves: If God elects some to be saved, He must have allowed others to be lost. The judicial reason they are lost is their own guilt. But the fact that others equally guilty were not left to suffer for their sins (for the elect are saved from them) rests in the sovereign good pleasure of God, which pleasure was manifestly not extended to include the non-elect. If it is not God's good pleasure that *any* should be lost, a fact to which Scripture bears abundant testimony, then for what possible reason would He not exercise his sovereignty and good pleasure over all the lost rather than over only some? Does He not then displease Himself arbitrarily and unnecessarily?

If unnecessarily, is it not also unjustly? His foreknowledge tells Him that men will resist his grace. That is why Election to salvation has to be a divinely initiated and sovereignly effected act. Those who are allowed to resist are clearly being allowed to resist unnecessarily if the initial resistance of the elect can be overridden at God's good pleasure. And so it almost seems that we have to "save the face of God" by supposing that the reason some are saved is that these by nature (and of their own free will) do not resist. The saved in no way contribute positively to their salvation, except in so far as they *negatively* do not offer resistance to the Spirit of God.

We are on the horns of a dilemma if we must rationalize Election. Either God condemns men unnecessarily, though not unjustly—for they are sinners. Or men are different, some being by nature unresisting and others resisting. God foreknows who will not resist, and thus elects them to salvation on the basis of that foreknowledge. Such human reasoning leads us inevitably to contradict what is revealed, for what is revealed tells us that unregenerate man is dead and all dead men are equally dead with neither the will to resist or yield. So that it is *not* of him that willeth but of God that showeth mercy (Rom. 9:16), and Scripture everywhere affirms this fundamental truth. The whole process is initiated and completed by God in Christ who is the author and finisher of our faith.

Did those who tried to rationalize Election in this way not remember that Paul was coerced by the sovereign grace of God? Did they not remember, too, how a certain man made a feast and sent out invitations, only to have every one of the invited guests decline the invitation so that the lord who had thus been rebuffed said to his servants, "Go out and *bring* them in" (Luke 14:21)? And when there was still room, had he not said, "Go out now and *compel them to come in*" (v. 23)? It is significant, moreover, that in Matthew 22:10, which is part of an account of the same event, we are told that those who were thus brought in were "both good and bad."

Some are brought, some compelled. In either case the initiative is God's. Lot, his wife, and his daughters were "taken by the hand" and brought out of Sodom (Gen. 19:16). Paul was turned about with violence because he "kicked against the pricks" of the goad of God's grace (Acts 9:5).

Unregenerate man does not listen attentively to the Gospel—though he will listen to the preaching of what is not the Gospel (2 Tim. 4:3). If men are in church because they seek salvation in God's way, they are there because God has first begun to awaken them to their need. If they are there for any other reason it is for the wrong reason. They seek social recognition, or commercial advantage, or to satisfy intellectual curiosity, or for purely esthetic reasons, or because they need to belong somewhere, or because they are determined to prove their own merit in the sight of God, or for a hundred other subtle reasons. "The heart is deceitful above all things, and desperately wicked: who can know it?" (Jer. 17:9).

No! Dead men do not consent to being given life. They can neither refuse nor consent until after life has been given. Only then can they ratify it. The formulators of *Concord*, after all their care to do otherwise, end up by making men necessary co-operators with God, who evidently requires their consent to have his Election confirmed in the elect. Man, not God, becomes sovereign after all. As Louis Berkhof said: "Notwithstanding the strong assertions that man owes his salvation entirely to God, it is held that man can frustrate the divine operation effectively, so that the decision really lies with him."[20]

---

20. *History of Christian Thought*, p. 219.

5

CALVIN AND CALVINISM

Throughout this whole controversy there runs a single thread, rooted in human pride and demanding the right to be personally responsible in the decision-making process at some critical point in the conversion experience. Many men desire to be saved, or say they do, until they discover that God's way makes them entirely dependent upon his grace, thus discounting completely any supposed merits they may have counted upon to improve their chances of being saved. Such are they who would take the Kingdom by force (Matt. 11:12).*

The Gospel is that we are saved by faith alone without works of any kind, not even the working up of ourselves into a state of readiness or willingness to be saved, nor even the exercise of our own faith. Here is the heart of the matter. This is the "offence of the Gospel" (Gal. 5:11). Salvation is all of God; and since it is clearly a selective process (for only some are saved), it must be a sovereign act of God's Election. Man can neither choose to be saved nor can he initiate the process.

The issue is whether we are called upon to co-operate in helping God (or conversely to ask God to help us), or whether we are simply clay in the hands of the Potter. Clay has no say. Reason tells us that we ought to be able to co-operate if we wish; pride tells us that we do co-operate. We offer our own willingness, or non-resistance, *something* of ourselves at least, *anything* of ourselves will do no matter how small it is. The great thing is

---

*In Luke 13:24 the Lord seems to speak of *many* who "will seek to enter in and shall not be able," as though men did indeed desire salvation but were refused. The answer to this apparent anomaly seems to lie in the fact that these many individuals did indeed wish to enter in—but on their own terms. Like the man who crashed the gates of the wedding and sat down to enjoy the feast—but without the appropriate wedding garment, such improper entry can result only in being rejected as soon as the King discovers their presence (Matt. 22:11-13). It is interesting to see that the individual in this little story knew perfectly well he was in the wrong place and had no excuse. He was speechless. And it is also significant perhaps that it was by this little story that the Lord introduced one of the most famous of all passages to be quoted in connection with Election: "For many are called, but few are chosen" (v. 14).

that it is of ourselves. As autonomous beings we demand the right of making some essential contribution. It need not be much—but it must be essential.

Many, with all the self-assurance in the world, come loaded with good things to be credited to their account. The poorer souls may seem to come more humbly, but they too hug the only possession they have to offer, their own willingness. It is quite possible to be as proud of this as it is of a large account. Surely this is as great a thing, seeing their circumstances, as the goods their affluent neighbours can bring along! Certainly it is as offensive to the soul to have a humble contribution (humble by force of circumstance) set aside as it is for the affluent man to have his set aside. Pride is a mighty assertive force, and rather than cause offence, ministers all too frequently yield to pressure and adulterate the Gospel. It must be embellished, added to, completed by the pitiful works of man.

This adulteration, this challenge to the perfect sufficiency of the Lord's sacrifice, is technically termed by theologians "the evil leaven of *synergism.*" Synergism is a word which means "joint-effortism." If there is one pervasive theme above all in Calvin's system of theology it is this: *Solus Deus.* God alone! God alone is man's Saviour; the act of regeneration is monergistic, a solo work of God without man's help in any way whatsoever.

Many years ago Warfield put it this way:

> Thus it comes about that monergistic regeneration—"irresistible grace," "effectual calling," our older theologians called it—becomes the hinge of Calvin's soteriology [i.e., doctrine of salvation], and lies much more deeply embedded in the system than many a doctrine more closely connected with it in the popular mind.
>
> Indeed, the soteriological significance of predestination itself consists to the Calvinist largely in the safeguard it affords to the immediate supernaturalness of salvation. What lies at the heart of this soteriology is absolute exclusion of creaturely efficiency in the induction of the saving process, in order that the pure grace of God in salvation may be magnified.
>
> Only so could he express his sense of man's complete dependence as a sinner on the free mercy of a saving God; or exclude the evil leaven of synergism by which God is robbed of his glory and man is encouraged to attribute to some power, some act, some initiative of his own, his participation in that salvation which in reality has come to him from pure grace.[1]

The controversy as carried forward by men like Gottschalk was essentially the same, but there was a different emphasis. Predestination to Election was the basic theme, not the grace of God as the sole means whereby that Predestination is realized in the life of the individual. Grace alone: this

---

1. Benjamin B. Warfield, *Calvin as a Theologian and Calvinism Today*, pp. 16 f.

is really Calvin's message. All else in his theology is subservient and derivative. Indeed, to Calvin, as to Owen and Spurgeon and a host of other spiritual giants of subsequent generations, this was the one theme that held all else together. Once admit man's spiritual deadness and total ineptitude in the matter of his salvation and everything else follows. Once abandon this, and the whole Christian system becomes indefensible and fragmented. Spurgeon wrote of Calvinism: "I have my own private opinion that there is no such thing as preaching Christ and Him crucified unless we preach what is called nowadays Calvinism. It is a nickname, to call it Calvinism; Calvinism is the Gospel and nothing else."[2]

Now John Calvin was born on June 10, 1509, at Noyon in Picardy. Like so many other young men who became great warriors in the Lord's service, he had a notably devout mother. His father was quite well off and had sufficient influence with the ecclesiastical authorities that he could secure for his son certain benefices that allowed him a higher education and professional status. John had set himself to become a Man of Letters par excellence.

Unlike Augustine, Calvin was a quiet student and his youth a blameless one seriously devoted to his calling. But he was an individualist and had no tendency to become a mere rubber stamp reiterating the words and phrases of his teachers. He was open-minded and affectionate and, contrary to the stern picture we tend to have of him in later life, he had a genuine and refreshing sense of humour as some of his letters show. By the time he was twenty-two he was an established humanist scholar, settled in Paris, with a well-earned reputation through his publication in 1532 of a commentary on a treatise by Seneca (c. 8 B.C.—A.D. 65) entitled *On Clemency.*

And then due chiefly to the influence of men like Ulrich Zwingli (1484-1531) and Martin Bucer (1491-1551), who had been greatly influenced by Luther, the whole direction of his life and interests changed. In due course he was solidly converted, the exact circumstance not being altogether clear. From that time, Calvin had no doubt that his goal was now henceforth to be a Man of Letters for God. And his pen became busy at once, but his forthrightness soon made it unwise for him to remain in France where there was a growing pressure against Protestants. He fled to Basel.

In the spring of 1536 he published what he variously referred to as "An Apology," "A Manifesto," and a "Confession of Faith." It was a brief document of less than a score of pages. It is not altogether certain but it is generally believed that this was a first draft of what was to become the *Institutes of the Christian Religion.* Although it was brief, the title certainly was not. It read:

The Institutes of the Christian Religion, Containing almost the Whole Sum of Piety and Whatever It is Necessary to Know in the Doctrine of Salva-

---

2. J. I. Packer, Introductory Essay in John Owen, *Death of Death*, pp. 10 f.

tion. A Work Very Well Worth Reading by All Persons Zealous for Piety, and Lately Published. A Preface to the Most Christian King of France, in which this Book is Presented to Him as a Confession of Faith. Author, John Calvin, of Noyon *(Basel, MDXXXVI)*.

Three years later he expanded his "little book" into an ample treatise on theology. The question of the precise relationship of these works and whether the 1539 issue was indeed merely an expansion of the 1536 draft is in some doubt. But this was certainly the beginning of his worldwide influence as a Reformed theologian and a Man of Letters for God. As already indicated, Predestination had only brief treatment in his initial statement. It was not a key issue at this point in the development of Calvin's theology. The key issue was the grace of God.

After some moves back and forth between Geneva, Basel, and Strassburg, he began almost reluctantly an active ministry that kept him from his beloved books more than he wished but resulted in the establishment out of a group of French refugees like himself the first "model Church" under his shepherding.

It was at Strassburg that his literary activity as a truly great Man of Letters really began, and it was from Strassburg that at thirty years of age he published the more elaborate form of his original "little book." Such was the prolific output of his pen subsequently that it was to require fifty-nine volumes to contain all the "Works of John Calvin."

In 1559 he published the definitive edition of his *Institutes*, probably the most influential single work on Dogmatic Theology ever to have been written after the close of the New Testament Canon. The works of Augustine were certainly as influential, but they did not in quite the same way constitute a single thesis. As Benjamin Warfield put it:

> As the first adequate statement of the positive programme of the Reformation movement, the *Institutes* lies at the foundation of the whole development of Protestant theology, and has left an impress on evangelical thought which is ineffaceable. After three centuries and a half, it retains its unquestioned pre-eminence as the greatest and most influential of all dogmatic treatises.[3]

The same writer underscores the debt which Calvin owed to Augustine. Calvin's doctrine of the Church was not his own creation, though he gave it a precision and vitality that was truly a reformation. It was his doctrine of grace that was so peculiarly his own as to be called thereafter *Calvinism* rather than *Augustinianism*. Yet as Warfield says:

> It was Augustine who gave us the Reformation. For the Reformation, inwardly considered, was just the ultimate triumph of Augustine's doctrine

---

3. *Calvin and Augustine,* p. 8.

of grace over Augustine's doctrine of the Church. This doctrine of grace came from Augustine's hands in its positive outline completely formulated: sinful man depends, for his recovery to good and to God, entirely on the free grace of God; this grace is therefore indispensable, prevenient, irresistible, indefectible; and being thus the free grace of God, must have lain in all the details of its conference and working in the intention of God from all eternity.[4]

Now the so-called Five Points of Calvinism, which were not really Calvin's to begin with though truly representative of his theology, were formulated implicitly by Augustine, who drew his inspiration for them from Paul. All through the centuries thereafter down to Luther's time these same five points have been argued over, denied, believed, explored, written about, and misunderstood. Whether man is totally depraved and spiritually dead or only very sick,* whether Election is based entirely on God's pleasure or on foreseen merit, whether the sacrifice of Christ is intended for all men or only for the elect, whether men can or cannot resist the grace of God, and whether the saints are eternally secure in their salvation or can fall away and be lost again: these are the basic issues of debate in the theology of salvation. Calvin did not put an end to the debate but he so crystallized the issues, and showed so compellingly the logic of their relatedness, that it has ever since been understood by the truly informed that they all stand or fall together. And Calvin showed *why* they all stand or fall together. He set forth in lucid terms the logical consistency and coherence of the doctrine of sovereign grace and showed that, granted any one of these Five Points, the rest must follow inevitably: deny any one of them and the whole structure is endangered. One cannot satisfactorily defend some points but not others.

Charles Hodge has a beautiful summary of the heritage that belongs to Reformed theology.

> Such is the great scheme of doctrine known in history as the Pauline, Augustinian, or Calvinistic, taught, as we believe, in the Scriptures, developed by Augustine, formally sanctioned by the Latin Church, adhered to by the witnesses of the truth during the Middle Ages, repudiated by the Church of Rome in the Council of Trent, revived in that Church by the Jansenists, adopted by all the Reformers, incorporated in the creeds of the Protestant Churches of Switzerland, of the Palatinate, of France, Holland, England, and Scotland, and unfolded in the Standards framed by the Westminster Assembly, the common representative of Presbyterians in Europe and America.[5]

---

4. Ibid., p. 322.

---

*Pelagius said man is *well*; Augustine said man is *dead*; Arminius said man is *sick*.

---

5. Charles A. Hodge, *Systematic Theology*, Vol. II, p. 333.

When people today think of Predestination they associate it with Calvinism. This is unfortunate for it far antedated Calvinism and is one of the few doctrines about which there has been almost universal agreement in all the Churches. There is not the same agreement, of course, as to its precise meaning; nor is there the same agreement as to its basis. But as a fact of Christian theology it has not been challenged. It is also unfortunate that it should be so closely associated with Calvinism because it is only one facet of Calvinism and not the central one. It is a logical element in the doctrine of sovereign grace but it is a consequence rather than a cause. The cause of our Election lies in the good pleasure of God and the ground for it is not Predestination but the full, perfect, and sufficient sacrifice of the Lord Jesus Christ. Election is a necessity because man is so spiritually dead that the Lord's sacrifice would never have become effectual but for the sovereign grace of God. Had his sacrifice merely been offered to man it would never have been accepted. And foreknowledge has nothing to do with Election because there is nothing good in man to be the grounds of that foreknowledge except negatively.* The only thing that God could foresee was that man would never be able to turn to Him for salvation unless He Himself first turned man. As the Psalmist said: "Quicken us and we will call upon thy name. Turn us again, O LORD God of hosts . . . and we shall be saved" (Ps. 80:18, 19). If man is to be saved at all, God must not only provide the means but undertake the entire initiative in making those means effectual. If *any thing* is left to man there is no hope. Man is totally dependent because he is totally depraved, and unless God predestines some and elects them to be saved, man is entirely without hope. Salvation is all of grace and that grace is sovereign. Such was the burden of Calvin's message.

John T. McNeill, who has provided an Introduction to the English edition of Calvin's works published in Philadelphia by Westminster Press in 1960, seeks to correct a commonly held view that Calvin's mind was a kind of factory turning out and mechanically assembling the parts of a neatly jointed structure of dogmatic logic.[6] Throughout his work it is manifest that, like Augustine, Calvin's heart and mind were in beautiful balance. The spiritual, emotional, and intellectual aspects of his being were joined in the effort. He was not a professional theologian but a deeply religious man who made warm friends and who also happened to possess a genius for orderly thought. "The secret of his mental energy," McNeill wrote, "lies in his piety." The first great object of his pen was to make the way of salvation

---

*In the matter of Double Predestination, some theologians have seen Predestination to reprobation as based entirely on foreknowledge of guilt.

---

6. John T. McNeill, Introduction in John Calvin, *Institutes of the Christian Religion*, p. li.

plain; the second was to persuade men to believe it; the third was to encourage the elect to adorn their faith by their lives.

In order to deal in depth with Calvin's doctrine of salvation, it is appropriate first of all to examine the circumstances which led to the formulation
of the so-called Five Points to which reference has already been made. As
will be seen these Five Points did not originate with Calvin's pen but with
those who opposed his doctrine. Nevertheless they provide a very good
starting point for a consideration of the structure of Calvin's theology of
salvation.

Throughout the whole controversy between grace and works, between
synergism and monergism, between the Total Depravity of man and a resi-
due of natural human goodness, between divine sovereignty and human responsibility, there was always a concurrent issue the solution to which is
probably one of God's secrets, but it is an issue which has refused to go
away. This was the question of Double Predestination, a question which
has kept cropping up throughout the history of Christian thought. It will be
remembered that the term originally meant that men were divinely predestined either to be saved or to be lost. The assumption was made that if some
were predestined to be saved then the rest of mankind was automatically
predestined to be lost and God was accordingly accused of injustice.
Augustine held it in the sense that the sinner is, by reason of the very moral
fabric of the universe, destined (and so predestined) to suffer the consequences of his guilt, *or* predestined to be saved from those consequences by
the sacrifice of Christ. One or the other is necessarily man's destiny. But
while God clearly knows beforehand what is to happen in every individual
instance, it is not necessary to assume that this foreknowledge means that it
was also his intention that many should be lost. It can just as easily mean
that man is allowed to suffer the consequences of his guilt as a sinner and is
therefore predestined to reprobation, a reprobation which God clearly foresees and foreknows.[7] It is a case of divine permission of a certain course of
events predetermined by the very structure of the moral order. God gave
man free will and in Adam man made his choice freely. Thereafter human
nature prefers the course of action which leads to destruction. Man chooses
destruction as a free expression of his fallen nature and God allows him this
choice. The end result is that man by nature is predestined to reprobation
but the foreknowledge of God relative to this fact is not the cause of it.

On the other hand, Election to salvation is causative because man's will,
freely expressed, would not otherwise allow Election to salvation to be effectual. Thus Predestination to reprobation is caused by man; Predestination to salvation is caused by God. The first is a natural consequence of the

---

7. Louis Berkhof, *History of Christian Thought*, p. 136.

will of man; the last is a supernatural consequence of the will of God. Yet both may fairly be described as predestined events.

Thus the situations are essentially different. The Predestination which is the natural consequence of man's corrupted will is self-fulfilling, inevitable, in one sense uncaused except by the spiritual laws which God has built into his universe. But there was always a tendency to confuse these two very different kinds of Predestination. The concept of Predestination was taken to mean the same thing in both cases, thus making God responsible for man's unhappy destiny. God became in fact the author of sin. And those who thus understood Calvin's view on the matter could justify this position (as Zanchius did) by an appeal to certain passages in Scripture which can be interpreted to support it. Calvin himself never seems to have been quite able to make up his mind on the matter. He *seems* in certain places to be teaching Double Predestination (he called it *Decretum Horribile*, an awful decree), by arguing that God really planned that man should fall in order to work out his divine purposes to his own glory by the saving of a certain number of the fallen. The important point here is that God so planned *before* He created man. He did not first create man, permit him freedom of choice, and therefore leave the way open for the Fall to occur. God made his plan before creating man and then, being sovereign, determined that this plan should be followed. Calvin said, "It is an awful decree, I confess. . . . God not only foresaw the Fall of the first man and the ruin of posterity in him, but arranged all by the determination of his own will" *(Inst.* III.xxiii.7). It may well have been pointed out to Calvin that his reasoning here was of doubtful validity for it would surely be just as true to say, "God foreknew what end man was to have (if and when he fell) before creating him, because He had so ordained reprobation to be the inevitable consequence of disobedience." What God did was to allow man to fall; but man having fallen, God then predetermined what would be the consequences.

In his study of Calvin's doctrine of Predestination, F. H. Klooster notes Calvin's asseveration that there could be no Election to salvation without its opposite, Election to reprobation *(Inst.* III.xxiii.1), and adds with propriety, "This assertion is not a logical deduction."[8] I believe he is right.

If a group of guilty men are in prison for their crimes and one is reprieved by the decree of a State Governor, it is not the State Governor's decree in freeing the one man that caused the other men to remain in prison. They remain in prison because they have not yet completed their sentence. They *remain* in prison because they are in prison to begin with, and under judgment not yet fully satisfied. Men who do not believe in the Lord are not condemned because they do not believe; they are condemned *already* (John 3:18) and simply remain so.

---

8. *Calvin's Doctrine of Predestination*, p. 36.

If I hold a golf ball in my hand it does not fall. Because I am holding it, I am in the strictest sense the cause of its *not* falling. If I let it go, nature takes its appointed (predestined) course and it falls. It is only in a manner of speaking that it falls because I let it go. The real reason that it falls is gravity. In a spaceship, away from the gravitational forces of the earth, I could let it go and it would not fall. If I throw it down I am contributing directly to its fall, but if I let go of it I am not a direct *cause* of its falling. The principle is a very wide one, and it is very easy to use language loosely and therefore to confuse the issue.

These two alternative effects of Predestination both appear to be grounded in the same phenomenon, the intention of God. But they are not really so at all. Predestination to salvation is causative, the will of God being the cause of salvation; Predestination to reprobation is consequential, reprobation being the consequence of the disobedience of man. The first is therefore the result of God's intention, the second of God's permission. It should be pointed out perhaps that by this circumstance those who find themselves in heaven have only God to thank, whereas those who find themselves under judgment have only themselves to blame. To make the analogy of the men in prison complete, one might therefore say with equal propriety that the one who was reprieved has only the Governor to thank, whereas the ones who were left in jail have only themselves to blame.

Calvin quotes Matthew 15:13, "Every plant which my heavenly Father hath not planted shall be rooted up," and comments on this by saying that the hearers are being "plainly told that all whom the heavenly Father has not been pleased to plant as sacred trees in his garden are doomed and devoted to destruction" *(Inst.* III.xxiii.1). The implication here is quite specific. Those who do not reside in Paradise are not of God's planting. God is not the author of such trees. For this reason they do not belong in the garden. Thus the analogies we have used above are reflected in Scripture by implication if nothing else. For the divine Gardener did not plant these foreign trees in the first place. It is as though, like weeds, they had planted themselves.

It seems clear that Calvin's own logical mind sensed the illogic of Double Predestination and yet never quite succeeded in resolving the issue to his own satisfaction. J. L. Neve in his *History of Christian Thought* says: "Calvin did not express himself clearly or consistently on this matter."[9] Certain passages in Calvin's writings can be quoted in favour of Double Predestination and others against it. This caused some dissension and disagreement among his followers. A scholarly layman, D. V. Koornheert of Holland, wrote against this teaching, and demanded that the *Belgic Confession*, which incorporated it, be revised. Jacob Arminius (1560-1609), known for

---

9. Vol. II, p. 16.

his dialectic skill and for his loyalty to Calvin, was invited to reply to him. But the effect of the studies which Arminius made in preparation, carried out specifically to formulate his rebuttal, converted him to a non-Calvinistic position!* He turned against the whole system of Calvinistic theology, perhaps because he realized for the first time that there was no room for any kind of sentimental humanist acknowledgment of man's innate goodness, a discovery which he did not like. He became so actively hostile that a serious schism arose affecting the whole Reformed Church in Holland.

Though Arminius died in 1609, his followers produced a number of able spokesmen. These met together in 1610 and drew up the Statement of Faith setting forth the grounds of their opposition to Calvinism and their alternative interpretation of the whole question of Predestination, foreknowledge, and Election. Their Articles were called *Remonstrances*, and they themselves were accordingly called Remonstrants. The Calvinists issued a counterstatement, but to no good purpose. So the matter was introduced before the famous Synod of Dort in 1618 at which representatives were present from England, Scotland, the Palatinate, Hesse, Nassau, East Friesland, and Bremen.

The representatives of Arminianism were treated with great discourtesy, and the Five Articles of their *Remonstrance* were condemned. Five Calvinistic canons were drafted and the *Belgic Confession* and the *Heidelberg Catechism* were formally adopted. In spite of the rather unlovely procedure, the end result was a magnificent Statement of Faith that eloquently reflected Calvin's theology.

The Five Articles of the *Remonstrance* have ever since served as one of the most effective backdrops against which to set the Reformers' position. They may be summarized in the following way. They are here arranged not in the original order in which they were presented but to reflect the order in which they were answered.

(1) *The Fall left man spiritually very sick but not in a state of total incapacity.* He still has some freedom to good. His will is not entirely enslaved to a sinful nature. He needs only God's assistance in his coming to conversion. In this he brings his *own* faith and his *own* willingness.

(2) Accordingly, *Election* is *based upon foreknowledge.* God foresees who will be willingly disposed and who will refuse, and elects those whom He knows will assent. If some oversimplification is permitted it might be said that Arminians held that God's foreknowledge related to those who would seek salvation. In the Lutheran system this foreknowledge related to those who would not resist God's call. In the Methodist system God's foreknowledge related to those who He knew would persevere.

---

*An excellent and sympathetic biography of Arminius has been written by Carl Bangs, and published by Abington Press, 1971.

(3) *Christ died for all men*, for the salvation of all men was God's original plan. It is not God's will that any should perish but, having been given freedom, man is able to accept or reject salvation and only a few are saved. (The fourth point was joined to this third point, though these two points are generally set forth as two separate articles.)

(4) *Man is entirely free to resist the grace of God.*

(5) *Even after yielding to God and accepting the Lord as Saviour, a man may so resist the influence of the Holy Spirit thereafter* in his life *that he becomes a castaway*, a reprobate, disapproved, "turning again to his former wallowing," and so in the end losing his salvation.

It will be obvious that these Five Points of the Arminian *Remonstrance* have the same kind of logical coherence as the system of Calvin does. One point follows from the other and all hold together in a kind of organic unity, granted the premise. The premise of the *Remonstrance* is that man is able to contribute to his own salvation because he is not totally depraved, and that God requires this contribution to make salvation effectual. From this it follows that man can subsequently cease to support his part of the bargain so that the work of God then fails in its objective and man is finally lost. Since the sovereignty of God in salvation is thereby surrendered and his predeterminate elective purposes can no longer be considered the cause of man's salvation and perseverance, Election is the result simply of foresight relative to the individual's anticipated response.

The crux of the matter in these two logical (or theological) systems is the sovereignty (or otherwise) of the grace of God, and its co-ordinate—the freedom (or otherwise) of the will of man, determining his own destiny. It has been rightly said that evangelism based on Calvinism lays the emphasis on the sovereign grace of God; evangelism based on any form of Arminianism is dependent upon man's powers to persuade. The world has developed highly successful techniques of high-pressure advertising in the hands of the so-called Persuaders, and Arminian evangelism has tended to adopt many of the same tactics. Power lies with man and must be applied with maximum effect, As in all advertising the emphasis is often laid more on the method than the message.

Although the great Confessions of the Reformed Churches (*Thirty-Nine Articles, Westminster, Heidelberg*, and so forth) are Calvinist, and although ministers in the denominations that once drew their inspiration from these Confessions are therefore Calvinist by profession, the great majority of them have long since adopted an Arminian approach to evangelism and depend far more upon techniques of persuasion than upon the truth of their professed Reformation theology. There is today a great need for a return to the Gospel of sovereign grace as the sole remedy for man's Total Depravity.

These two streams of theology, the Calvinist on the one hand, and the

Semi-Pelagian-Arminian-Lutheran-Methodist on the other, seem always to have existed side by side within the household of faith almost from the day the Church was born. Undoubtedly God uses both streams to create saints and to forge their characters. But in many important ways there can never really be complete fellowship between the Lord's people in the two camps. The basic premise of each is so totally opposed to the other and its effect so pervasive on each system of thought that conversation quickly deteriorates into argument as soon as it becomes seriously involved with fundamental issues. As long as we remain at a superficial level we can praise the Lord together. But one is aware always of skating together on thin ice. Since such arguments can never be wholly resolved unless both parties adopt the same basic premise there can never be real reconciliation. If the logical constructs in each system were simply abandoned there might be hope of reconciliation, because equally illogical adjustments would either pass unnoticed or would not disturb those who employed them. But such is man's constitution that irrational thinking never really proves an adequate base for peace of mind *or heart*. Fellowship on such grounds is always a fragile thing on the edge of collapse if some unexpected thought should intrude itself. Guarded conversation is not conducive to openness of heart which is essential to true fellowship.

And so we seek desperately to "sink our differences" and this serves merely to produce a unity among us which is theologically emasculated and powerless to challenge a sinful world.

Having set the historical background in some perspective, we now turn to an in-depth study of these two *Five-Point* alternatives to see what Scripture has to say on the matter.

The chronological table on page 79 will help the reader to see the historical relatedness of the events we have outlined.

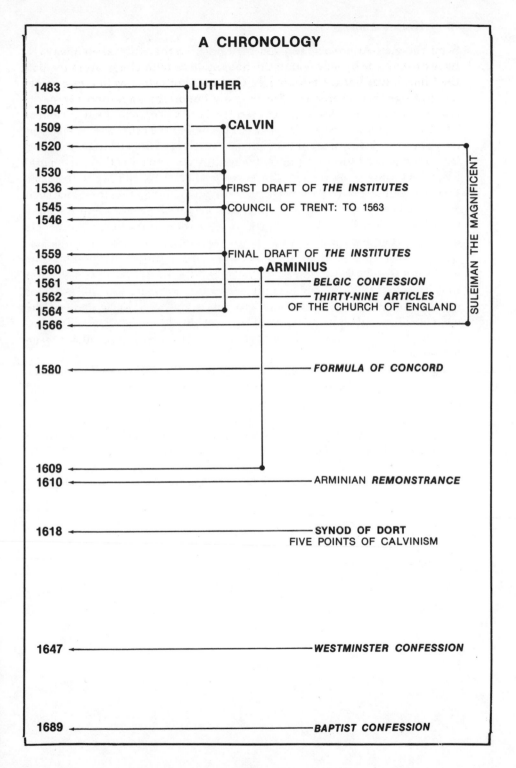

A CHRONOLOGY

1483 ← ● LUTHER

1504 ←

1509 ← ● CALVIN

1520 ←

1530 ←

1536 ← ● FIRST DRAFT OF *THE INSTITUTES*

1545 ← ● COUNCIL OF TRENT: TO 1563

1546 ←

1559 ← ● FINAL DRAFT OF *THE INSTITUTES*

1560 ← ● ARMINIUS

1561 ← *BELGIC CONFESSION*

1562 ← *THIRTY-NINE ARTICLES*
OF THE CHURCH OF ENGLAND

1564 ←

1566 ←

1580 ← *FORMULA OF CONCORD*

1609 ←

1610 ← ARMINIAN *REMONSTRANCE*

1618 ← SYNOD OF DORT
FIVE POINTS OF CALVINISM

1647 ← *WESTMINSTER CONFESSION*

1689 ← *BAPTIST CONFESSION*

SULEIMAN THE MAGNIFICENT

PART TWO

The Crystallization
of the Theology of Grace

INTRODUCTION

The *Canons of Dort* (1618-1619) were the response of the Synod of Dort to the Five Points of the Remonstrants. They formed an extended Statement of Faith under the following headings: Divine Election and reprobation; the Death of Christ and the redemption of man thereby; the Corruption of man, his conversion to God, and the manner thereof; and the Perseverance of the saints. Each of these headings was treated by a series of Articles numbering fifty-nine in all with additional comments on errors which were to be rejected. This statement of faith has since been greatly simplified for ordinary teaching purposes into five points which correspond in substance but not in the order of presentation to the Five Points of the Remonstrants. These are now widely known under the acronym T U L I P, each letter standing for a simple descriptive phrase. These five descriptive phrases together summarize the Calvinist position. They are spelled out as follows:

T . . . . . Total Depravity
U . . . . . Unconditional Election
L . . . . . . Limited Atonement
I . . . . . . Irresistible Grace
P . . . . . Perseverance of the Saints

Each of these requires a word of explanation and clarification.

Total Depravity is not intended to signify that unregenerate man is wholly evil in everything he does, but rather that nothing he does is ever wholly good. In so far as motive determines the moral character and spiritual significance of an act, every deed has something of sinfulness about it because man's will is fatally corrupted by his fallen nature. Not all motives are equally sinful, but no motive is wholly pure. Hence, from a moral and spiritual point of view, human activity is always poisoned as to its motive, to a greater or lesser extent. This fundamental impurity of motive is the reason for saying that man is totally depraved. This depravity is reflected in man's entire impotence towards any spiritual good; in this respect unregenerate man is not merely sick but *dead*. Consequently the salvation of man is altogether a work of God, initiated and carried through by Him without the help of man, man being able neither effectively to resist nor to assist the elective purposes of God directed towards his salvation.

Unconditional Election means that the Election of an individual to salvation in no way hinges upon foreseen merit in that individual. The Election of one as opposed to the by-passing of another rests entirely with God, and is according to his own good pleasure. Moreover, this choice was made before the foundation of the world (Eph. 1:4). It is a sovereign act, predetermined without respect to the merit or demerit of the individual either before or after regeneration.

Limited Atonement signifies that the death of the Lord Jesus Christ, though *sufficient* for all men, is *efficacious* only for the elect. In the purposes of God, a full, perfect, and sufficient penal satisfaction for sin was provided and will be effectively applied only against the sins of those elected to a saving faith. The sufferings of Christ were not needlessly expended on behalf of those who the Father foresaw would not avail themselves of their benefits.

Irresistible Grace indicates that because the grace of God in electing some to salvation is sovereign, it is not possible that the elect will effectively resist his grace. Nevertheless, for reasons known only to Himself, God may sometimes allow this work of grace seemingly to be delayed.

Perseverance of the Saints denotes what today is commonly referred to as the eternal security of the believer. A more suitable expression might be the "Preservation of the Saints" since this is more precisely what is involved. The security of the believer is bound in with the sovereignty of God, the unchangeableness of his purpose, and the constancy of his good pleasure. It is the faithfulness of the Lord Jesus Christ and not the faithfulness of the believer that guarantees this security.

Now these Five Points form an organic unity, a single body of truth. They are based on two presuppositions which Scripture abundantly supports. The first presupposition is the complete impotence of man, and the second is the absolute sovereignty of the grace of God. Everything else follows. The meeting place of these two foundation truths is the heart of the Gospel, for it follows that if man is totally depraved, the grace of God in saving him must of necessity be sovereign. Otherwise, man will inevitably refuse it in his depravity, and will remain unredeemed.

That man is wholly impotent to save himself does not signify, however, that he cannot be redeemed. He is redeemable: he has a capacity for salvation. Man is a redeemable creature such as no other creature appears to be, whether animal or angel. He was designed for this. He was fashioned of the dust of the ground in human form as an appropriate vessel for the housing of a redeemable human spirit.

It is clear that as man's body lay on the ground, awaiting the infusion of a spirit when God would breathe into his nostrils the breath of life, his body was wholly unconscious of any need of any such infusion and quite incapable of either preparing itself to receive it or refuse it. His inanimate body had an aptitude for spiritual animation but it was a passive not an active aptitude. This also is the position of the spiritually dead who thus await the infusion of new life by a process of re-creation. The spiritually dead are recipients of a process of reanimation which must be as wholly a work of God as the infusion of spirit into Adam's body was. Adam's body could no more prepare itself to become the receptacle of an animating spirit than the man who is dead in trespasses and sins can prepare himself as a receptacle for the grace of God in salvation.

Thus in man's fallen state he is truly without strength (Rom. 5:6), and in no position to prepare himself for the grace of God. The *Westminster Confession* (XI.2-5) describes man's situation thus:

> Man, in his state of innocency, has freedom of power to will and to do that which is well pleasing to God. . . .
>
> Man, by his fall into a state of sin, wholly lost all ability of will to any spiritual good accompanying salvation; so that a natural man is dead in sin and is not able by his own strength to convert himself, *or to prepare himself thereunto* [my emphasis].
>
> When God converteth a sinner and translateth him into the state of grace, he freeth him from his natural bondage under sin, and by his grace alone enableth him freely to will . . . that which is spiritually good; yet so as that, by reason of his remaining corruption, he doth not perfectly, nor only, will that which is good, but doth also will that which is evil.
>
> The will of man is made perfectly and immutably free to good alone, in the state of glory only.

Here we see four stages. Unfallen man was free to choose either good or evil. Fallen man's will has become free in one direction only, unidirectionally towards evil. By his grace, God undoes this unidirectionality of the will and sets it free again to choose either good or evil. This is the third stage. But it is not the final stage, for in heaven we shall have a will constitutionally with the capacity only of willing good. The human will therefore is capable of operating under four different conditions: bidirectionally to good or evil as unfallen, unidirectionally to evil as fallen but unredeemed, bidirectionally to good or evil as redeemed, and unidirectionally to good only as glorified.

None of us can recover Adam's innocence even in our redeemed state for the bidirectionality of our will is not the same as the bidirectionality of Adam's fallen nature, for we, the redeemed, still have a bent towards evil in spite of the liberating effect of our redemption, a bent which Adam did not have to begin with. So profoundly has Adam's Fall affected human nature that even regeneration does not entirely undo it. Not until these mortal bodies are laid aside, and we are rehoused in a new and glorious body like the Lord's resurrection body (Phil. 3:21), shall we be finally free. As Paul said in Romans 8:23: "Ourselves also which have the first fruits of the Spirit, even we ourselves groan within ourselves, waiting for the adoption, to wit, the redemption of our bodies." And Paul has already in chapter 7 of Romans made it clear how much of our spiritual defeat originates through this defective housing.

We may suppose therefore that the transmission of the effects of the Fall in Eden has resulted primarily through the acquisition by natural generation of a defective, corrupted, mortal body which early in life infects the spirit which it was designed to house.

Now one's view of the nature of Original Sin determines one's view of the nature and extent of man's depravity. For if sin is an inherited disease which is inescapable and which inevitably bears fruit in the form of sins, then man is lost indeed so long as he is naturally born. There is no natural way in which the course of events can be circumvented. By his disobedience one man, Adam, made human nature sinful; thereafter human nature has made every man a sinner. We do not inherit an active sinfulness but we inherit a fatal disease, the morbid symptoms of which inevitably find expression if we survive childhood. On the other hand, if, as Pelagius held, sin is *not* an inheritable disease but an alien condition acquired sometime later in life in the process of growing up and as a result of yielding to temptation, then some men will not be sinful as soon as others are, because they have been hedged in during the growing-up process and protected against some of the temptations which have brought about the downfall of other men. Pelagius believed that man could be educated into a highly cultured being, and thus so preserved against failure that, with God's help, human nature could be humanly perfected. He admitted that God's help was needed, but he did not mean that this help came by divine intervention. It came by the illumination of the mind by which a man would be enabled to emulate the example of Christ and obey his instructions for living. For this purpose, God had sent his Son into the world as an example and not as a sacrifice for sin. Pelagius' thesis was in effect a Christianized humanism. Sin was thus to be kept *out*, not merely kept down.

Pelagius viewed each child that was born as being like unfallen Adam, and that child's subsequent growth in experience as being like Adam's subsequent temptation and fall. As Adam might have turned innocence into virtue but failed to do so by yielding to temptation, so every newborn child faces the same possibility. Education and culture are the means whereby innocence might become righteousness. In this sense the child that sins and

fails to achieve this desirable goal has sinned "after the similitude of Adam."
It is to combat this vain hope implicit in Pelagianism that Calvinists are
careful to include a statement to the effect that each man becomes a sinner
but *not* after the similitude of Adam. We become sinners because we inherit
a fatal disease which inevitably exhibits its characteristic symptoms. We are
born with the disease, or, to put it slightly differently, we are *born* in SIN
(singular). But we are not born in SINS—an accusation which the Pharisees
wrongly made against a certain man (John 9:34). On the other hand, the
Lord spoke with precision when He told these same Pharisees that they
would *die* in their SINS (John 8:21). The difference between these two
terms, though they look so similar, is really profound, and it is a difference
which is consistently recognized throughout the New Testament and emphasized in Paul's epistles. Calvin put the matter this way:

> We are not corrupted by an acquired wickedness but do bring an inborn
> corruption from the very womb. . . . All of us, therefore, descending from
> an impure seed come into the world tainted with the contagion of sin.
> (*Inst.* II.i.5).

It is noteworthy that Augustine in his *Anti-Pelagian Writings* said,
"Original Sin is derived from the faulty condition of the human seed" (*On
Marriage and Concupiscence*, chap. 20). It is even more remarkable that
Luther himself attached this inheritable factor to the *male* seed, when he
wrote: "Through the fall of Adam SIN entered into the world and all men
have as a result sinned. For the paternal sperm conveys the corruption from
generation to generation" (*Luther's Writing*, Erlangen ed., 10, 304; 11, 246;
19, 15). It is interesting also to find that Karl Barth in his *Credo* claimed that
the "sin-inheritance is transmitted through the male parent only."[1]

My object in this introduction has been to show that human nature has
been corrupted at its source in such a way that it is incapable of any kind of
self-help. Man is not merely lost and searching consciously for a way out of
his predicament: he is lost so completely that he can no longer recognize the
nature of his lost condition for what it is.

There are only two basic positions that one can take in this matter. The
first is that man's lost condition, though severe, is nevertheless only partial,
leaving him with some hope of self-redemption. This self-help may take the
form of active good works, or it may take the form merely of an earnest desire to be helped, or it may take the form only of a spirit of non-resistance
towards the help that is provided. But always there is some supposed faint
glow in the embers of man's heart which God uses to fan into a new flame.
In the other view the fire has simply gone out. There is *nothing* which can
be fanned alight. Which of these two positions one takes determines vir-

---

1. Quoted in R. G. Gromacki, *The Virgin Birth: Doctrine of Deity*, p. 119.

tually all else in one's theology. Do we start with man and some imagined potential for goodness or do we start with God who must be the author of salvation in its entirety? Do we start with the effectiveness of evangelism in generating a responsiveness in man's heart which then becomes the entree for the grace of God, or do we start with the sovereign grace of God as the only basis for man's hope? The Arminian view, and also the view of much modern evangelism, takes as its starting point the ability of man to respond, making the assumption that he has at least this much goodness upon which God can then act. The Calvinist position is that man is completely dead spiritually and all the initiative must be of God. This position, I believe, is the biblical one.

It is in this light that we must consider how and why the Five Points of the *Remonstrance* were ordered and arranged as they were, and how the order of the Calvinist reply differed in its emphasis. The difference reflects the contrasting importance attached to the starting point, which in turn reveals much about the attitude of the two parties in their view of the potential of human nature. The Arminian *Remonstrance* attaches prime importance to man's freedom of will, and insists that he is only partially debased in his nature. There is a contribution which man must make and *can* make before God will act. The Calvinists saw this as a basic fallacy: man is not free to make such a contribution, being spiritually dead. Hence while Election was freely admitted by both parties, it was given first place in the *Remonstrance* and was presumed to be based upon God's foreknowledge of man's ability to respond out of the residual goodness of his heart. For the Calvinist the starting point for man must always be recognition of his own total spiritual impotence. The rest of the Points in each statement are ordered accordingly. In the tabulation which follows the arrows indicate which Points on each side are actually in counterbalance.

REMONSTRANTS	CALVINISTS
1 PREDESTINATION BASED ON FOREKNOWLEDGE	1 **T**OTAL DEPRAVITY
2 CHRIST DIES FOR ALL MEN	2 **U**NCONDITIONAL ELECTION
3 MAN IS ABLE TO RESPOND AND THIS IS HIS CONTRIBUTION	3 **L**IMITED ATONEMENT
4 MAN CAN REFUSE THE GRACE OF GOD IF HE WILLS TO DO SO	4 **I**RRESISTIBLE GRACE
5 THE CONVERTED CAN FALL AWAY AND BE LOST	5 **P**ERSEVERANCE OF THE SAINTS

THE ACRONYM T-U-L-I-P IS A MNEMONIC AID.

6

TOTAL DEPRAVITY

The tremendous optimism which characterized the period immediately prior to World War I, reflected in the writings of H. G. Wells and many others, and which originated in the Age of Enlightenment when Rousseau wrote imaginatively about the noble savages of North America living without the encumbrance of debasing civilization, has disappeared almost entirely. Man is no longer seen as perfectible. Despair has overtaken the humanist idealism of those days, and sin has come to be recognized as a depressing fact of life. The depravity of man is no longer questioned except by a few blithe spirits whose feet are in the clouds and whose dreams for society are about as unrealistic as it is possible to imagine. Nevertheless we still have among us a few ministers of the "Gospel" who have high expectations for the supposed innate goodness of man, but the children of this world are wiser in their own generation.

On the other hand, psychiatrists like Karl Menninger tell us that man is sick and that the root of his sickness is a basic depravity of human nature that has to be reckoned with. T. H. Huxley, Darwin's great defender, was wiser than those who followed him when he said:

> It is the secret of the superiority of the best theological teachers to the majority of their opponents that they substantially recognize these realities. . . . The doctrines of original sin, of the innate depravity of man . . . appear to me to be vastly nearer the truth than the liberal, popular illusions that babies are all born good, and that the example of a corrupt society is responsible for their failure to remain so; that it is given to everybody to reach the ethic ideal if he will only try . . . and other optimistic figments.

Would that we heard this today from the pulpit! Louis Berkhof in his *Systematic Theology* (p. 227) speaks eloquently on this issue:

> Sin is one of the saddest but also one of the most common phenomena of human life. It is a part of the common experience of mankind, and therefore forces itself upon the attention of all those who do not deliberately close their eyes to the realities of human life. Some may for a time dream

of the essential goodness of man and speak indulgently of those separate words and actions that do not measure up to the ethical standards of good society as mere foibles and weaknesses, for which man is not responsible, and which readily yield to corrective measures; but as time goes on, and all measures of external reform fail, and the suppression of one evil merely serves to release another, such persons are inevitably disillusioned.

They become conscious of the fact that they have merely been fighting the symptoms of some deep-seated malady, and that they are confronted not merely with the problem of sins, that is, of separate sinful deeds, but with the much greater and deeper problem of sin, of an evil that is inherent in human nature. This is exactly what we are beginning to witness at the present time.

It needs only one kind of circumstance to bring this deeply rooted malady in human nature to the surface. That circumstance is the acquisition of power over others. Most men have very little power over others which is absolute. We all have some power, but it is so circumscribed and hedged about by social restraints of one kind or another that very few have the opportunity to learn what would happen to themselves if these restraints were removed. But recent history has amply demonstrated what people are capable of in their treatment of fellow men when they are given absolute power to do with them what they will. People who seemed cultured, restrained, law-abiding, and considerate of others have been converted into beasts to the surprise of the civilized world—and perhaps to their own surprise, if the truth were known. The Nazi concentration camps were often administered by people who spent their spare time listening to classical music or surrounding themselves with great works of art. But any disappointment they may have felt in themselves seems to have been short-lived as they took increasing delight in the infliction of pain and injury upon others. Dostoyevsky, in his *Brothers Karamazov*, tells how at one period in Russian history, girls whose social behaviour was considered immoral in the extreme were punished by severe flogging. He points out a curious fact the authorities had discovered, that when young unmarried men were given the responsibility for inflicting the punishment upon these outcasts of society, they almost always ended up by marrying their victims. It is as though some deep-seated satisfaction came to them in the fulfillment of their "duty," so deep-seated that it led to permanent attachment to their victim. More recent history under Stalin in particular has shown that if man's power over his fellows extends far enough to allow him the privilege not merely of punishing severely but of utterly destroying, then he will utterly destroy both them and himself in the process. It is because we are externally restrained in our self-expression that the power to do some good remains with us, even as it did with Dostoyevsky's young men. Since then, we have seen ample evidence that when there are no restraints, human behaviour becomes altogether evil and degraded. Solzhenitsyn observed this and wrote about it eloquently in his description of the Russian detention camps under Stalin. The cruelty of men seems to have been directly proportional to their power.

Recent Russian history, and Nazi history before that, abundantly justifies the statement made by Lord John Acton in a letter to Bishop Mandell Creighton in 1887: "Power tends to corrupt; absolute power corrupts absolutely." And D. R. Davies in his masterful study of raw human nature under the title *Down Peacock's Feathers* points out that in America before the introduction of slavery, there were many high-minded people who protested against it. But once it had become a *fait accompli* these same people not infrequently became the most inhumane among slave owners. Given power over their fellow men, they discovered within themselves evil impulses of which they had been previously unaware.

Perhaps one of the profoundest evidences of the sinlessness and incorruptibility of the Lord Jesus Christ lies in the fact that although his power was absolute, He remained absolutely uncorrupted by it. He had power over life (He cursed the fig tree and it died—Matt. 21:19), and He had power over death (He called Lazarus forth from the grave—John 11:43, 44). He had power to heal every conceivable kind of sickness, and He had power over men who would have taken Him and murdered Him because of their hatred. He merely walked untouched through their midst (John 8:59). He had authority, that "something" which seems to be essentially rooted in the morality of man, which enabled Him to challenge the evil institutions of his day (as when He cleansed the temple—Mark 11:15-18); and no man lifted a hand against Him. He had power to forgive sins and He had power to condemn. He had moral, physical, social, and intellectual authority over men, such as has never been observed in any single individual before or since that time. He towered above mankind, and still does. This is not literary fiction: such a figure cannot be invented. Yet He remained totally uncorrupted. The absolute power which elevated *Him* to the very heights of heaven degrades *fallen* man to the very depths of hell.

Herbert Butterfield, the Oxford historian, adds his warning to those who attempt to understand human history while ignoring the effects of the Fall. He says, "What history does is to uncover man's universal sin." And subsequently, "We create tragedy after tragedy for ourselves by a lazy unexamined doctrine of man which is current amongst us and which the study of history does not support."[1] He points out that it is the restraints of culture that prevent human nature from showing itself as it really is, or at least prevent some men from appearing as bad as they really are. Other men are not so prevented, and increasingly more and more people are showing their true colours as the restraints of society break down. "In some cases," Butterfield writes, "human nature looks better than in others because it can go through

---

1. Butterfield, Herbert, *Christianity and History*, p. 45 f.

life without being subjected to the same test." And he remarks by way of illustration that if we had no rules of the road, a nasty side of human nature would make its appearance among motorists more often than it does at the moment. Human nature needs only opportunity to declare itself for what it is.

So it is widely agreed that man is depraved. But *how* depraved? Totally, or only very seriously? Was human nature merely *injured* by the Fall, as Roman Catholic theologians would say, or completely ruined, as the Reformers would say? Has this fatal injury been communicated to every individual by inheritance, or does each individual start with a clean sheet, as Pelagius argued, becoming sinful only by example? Has human nature been severely corrupted but not so severely that the grace of God cannot cooperate with the spark of human goodness which has not quite died, as Arminians believe? Or is man hopelessly, totally depraved, his nature so corrupted through the Fall that the whole motivation of his life is evil, being self-centred and rebellious against God? Is man truly a total moral catastrophe?

Is man then only sick but in a humanly curable way; is he injured by the sad example of society but capable of being good if given the opportunity; or is he spiritually dead—his nature utterly ruined, his will free only to sin, his understanding darkened, and his heart a heart of stone?

Then what of all the evidence in history of human kindness, restraint, mercy, self-sacrifice and nobility? And what of human creativeness, of beauty in handiwork, of truth in thought, of success in the harnessing of Nature? Are all these illusory? What does "Total" Depravity mean in this context? Isaiah 1:5 and 6 tells us, "The whole head is sick, and the whole heart faint; from the sole of the foot even unto the head there is no soundness in it." And Jeremiah 17:9 warns us: "The heart is deceitful above all things, and desperately wicked: who can know it?" How sick is man: how desperate is his situation? When Paul said, "There is none that doeth good, no, not one" (Rom. 3:12), was he inspired to write the plain truth or was he merely reflecting upon the appalling corruption of Roman society at its lowest ebb under the frightful tyranny of Nero? In short, what precisely did the Fall do to human nature: how deeply has man been wounded, and how is the effect transmitted?

DEFINITION OF *TOTAL*

First, then, what did Calvin himself mean when he spoke of man's *Total* Depravity? To begin with, he was dealing essentially with motivation rather then with action. He never denied that men *do* good deeds, and

Scripture supports him in this. For example, the Lord Himself spoke of those who "being evil, know how to give good gifts" (Matt. 7:11). There is nothing incompatible between Calvin's conception of the Total Depravity of man and man's performance of deeds which, by the most rigid standards of judgment, would have to be characterized as good. The ability of man to *do* good deeds in no way challenges his basic depravity. For what is corrupt in human nature is motivation, the inability of man to *be* good. But what do we mean when we speak of man being able to do good but not being able to be good?

Henri Fabre once spoke of animal instinct as *inspired wisdom*. This is a beautiful thought and worthy of reflection. In Nature one observes this inspired wisdom in animals at every level in the scale of complexity. Man alone seems to be without instinct.

Yet unregenerate man is not without *inspired wisdom;* we simply have not recognized it for what it is. In spite of the Fall he has tremendous creative capacities, and these capacities are usually most successfully demonstrated when his work springs from something akin to inspiration. A great deal of creative activity is simply a form of ingenuity, but there is a creative activity observed most clearly in artistic effort of all kinds which appears to arise as the result of inspiration. No one knows where this inspiration comes from. Those who are inspired in the creation of music, or art, or literature, or architecture, or in any other field of human endeavour whether it is strictly practical in objective or purely ornamental, have acknowledged the part played by the strange and little understood phenomenon of inspiration. Such inspiration is often described and experienced as a form of tyranny. It seems to spring from some source other than the will itself, for the will becomes captive.

When we add to these circumstances the confusing fact that some of the most creative individuals have also been some of the most wicked, immoral, selfish, cruel, and egocentric individuals known to history, we are not only baffled by the nature of this inspiration but by its choice of victims. It could even be said as a general rule, to which there are nevertheless many exceptions, that the more inspired a man's work is the less inspiring that man is apt to be.

We have to ask, then, Whence comes this inspiration? We know from Scripture that it may come directly from God, though this does not guarantee that it always does. For example, in Exodus 31:2-11 and 35:30-35 we are told that a certain man named Bezaleel was an inspired craftsman appointed by God to oversee the beautification of the Tabernacle whose furnishings were to reflect the perfection of God's handiwork. Naturally, we assume he was a godly man. But history shows that many ungodly men have created things which in their way contributed to the glory of God, like the architects and stonemasons of many of the cathedrals whose wages were paid out of money received in exchange for indulgences to sin with impunity. Furthermore, some of the most beautiful artifacts in the world (such as ancient Egyptian jewelry) and some of the most beautiful buildings in the world (such as the Taj Mahal) owed nothing to Christian inspiration. I think it would be true to say that the poetry of people like Robert Browning, Elizabeth Barrett, Percy Shelley, William Shakespeare, and hundreds of others who, while not anti-Christian, seem personally to have been largely indifferent to the Lord's claim upon their lives, was nevertheless inspired in this sense.

It may well be that the inspiration which produces such masterpieces of man's creative ability is part and parcel of the Common Grace of God by which the special aptitudes of men are appointed to ameliorate human life and to give pleasure and satisfaction in a world cursed by sin. And within the orbit of this Common Grace would surely also have to be counted the inspired hunches and guesses and ventures in faith which have led men throughout the ages to dedicate their lives to fruitful research towards alleviating human suffering. Thus have been produced new preventatives that have slowly eliminated, or show great promise of doing so, some of man's most terrible scourges in the form of communicable diseases like smallpox. And we would have to add the inspiration which has produced many great humanitarian reform movements. All of these, I suggest, invite us to equate this kind of inspiration with Common Grace, for many of the moving spirits in these ventures *felt* inspired.

That this capacity for inspired activity in man should all too frequently be turned to frightful ends is not surprising. If this is a capacity divinely ordered for man at his creation and surviving the Fall, it can obviously be used by Satan, whose design is to counteract the Common Grace of God. The stimulation in both cases is supernatural. And there is this that can also be said of both kinds of inspiration: Satan does not always find his most effective servants among wicked men as we might suppose, nor God his most effective servants among the saints. It is sad, but true. There seems to be no apparent connection between the character of the individual and the degree and objection of his inspiration. As with Election to salvation, God's choice is solely according to his good pleasure.

God has often displayed his Common Grace without regard to the stature of the chosen vessel. Some of the most notably successful and sought-after evangelists, conference speakers, and Christian leaders, have been personally the most proud, unforgiving, self-centred individuals imaginable. It is sometimes better not to know too well those from whom one receives the greatest help and inspiration along the way. What a man can *do* under God's inspiration and what he can *be* under his own, are very different things.

Now the fact that animals are so beautifully equipped for the ordering of

their lives by the inspired wisdom of which Fabre wrote so eloquently suggests that Common Grace may apply in our world on a far larger scale than
we have recognized. In their "interpersonal" relationships animals show a
wonderful constraint which is only now being sufficiently acknowledged.
The authenticated stories of animal co-operation in the wild are legion, and
they include insects, fishes, birds, and of course the higher animals. One
possible exception, curiously enough, may be the whole order of snakes
which seem to lack even a semblance of maternal spirit, a fact which makes
the snake a peculiarly appropriate symbol of Satan. The apparent cruelty of
animals, of which Darwin made so much, is increasingly being viewed in a
rather different light as we discover more about the pain reflexes of the
preyed upon and the killing instincts of the predators. Where we do find
wanton destruction by predators, it can almost always be shown to be the
result of man's interference upsetting the behaviour of either the prey or the
predator. As Professor Ronald Good of England has been saying for some
years, Nature is not a battlefield with all the combatants red in tooth and
claw but in ordered and beautifully harmonious co-operative society whose
behaviour ultimately tends towards the benefit of every member.

Man by contrast seems alien to this whole co-operative scheme of things.
His instincts, if he has any at all beyond swallowing, are fundamentally
suicidal in nature. No other creature is persistently so destructive of his own
well-being. The Roman author Cicero said, "Man is a disaster." He is not so
much diseased, as himself the disease. But for the Common Grace of God
man's life would be unbearable and his suicidal tendencies would probably
lead to the total destruction of the human race. Operating through the
merits of the sacrifice of the Lord Jesus Christ, this Common Grace truly
constitutes Him the Saviour of the "world."

Apart from man, the rest of the natural order operates as an expression of
the Kingdom of God. The laws of Nature are his laws, "written in" as they
are written once again into the heart of every man who newly becomes a
member of that Kingdom (Heb. 8:10). Animals are obedient to the law of
God as appointed for them and *by their obedience* live out their lives under
divine protection. It must be for this reason that Satan and his emissaries
have to ask permission of the Lord to invade this Kingdom where animals
are concerned, as the demons did before entering the swine on that
Gadarean mountainside in Matthew 8:31.

God rules these creatures from within, but He also overrules them when
necessary, and so they are always obedient to his will. Thus He *stops* the
mouths of lions (Heb. 11:33), and exceptionally orders the behaviour of
other animals wherever necessary as in the case of the tribute money needed
by the disciples on one occasion (Matt. 17:27). It is just such a belief in this
obedience of the animal world to the divine will that prompted a medieval
traveller who had taken refuge in a cave during a storm only to find himself

face-to-face with a deadly snake, to address this creature with the words, "If thou hast leave to strike me, I do not say thee nay."

And we have one extraordinary record of just such an occasion in 1 Kings 13:24-28 where both a lion and an ass unite in serving the Lord's purposes in a very special circumstance. The story is worth recording. A certain prophet who had obediently fulfilled the Lord's mission was later tempted, on the strength of his success, to disobey the Lord's further express command that he must go straight home without tarrying. Unfortunately he allowed himself to be detained on the way with the result that when he resumed his journey again to go home, riding his ass, he was attacked by a lion and killed. As the text says cryptically:

> A lion met him by the way, and slew him: and his carcase was cast in the way, and the ass stood by it, the lion also stood by the carcase.
>
> And, behold, men passed by, and saw the carcase cast in the way, and the lion standing by the carcase: and they came and told it in the city where the old prophet dwelt.
>
> And when the prophet that brought him back from the way heard thereof, he said; It is the man of God, who was disobedient unto the word of the Lord: therefore the Lord hath delivered him unto the lion, which hath torn him, and slain him, according to the word of the Lord, which he spake unto him.
>
> And he spake to his sons, saying, Saddle me the ass. And they saddled him.
>
> And he went and found his carcase cast in the way, and the ass and the lion standing by the carcase: the lion had not eaten the carcase, nor torn the ass.

Note particularly in the last verse how carefully the Word of God explains the circumstance that the lion did not attack the ass nor did the ass flee from the lion, both creatures being divinely inspired to behave contrary to their inborn nature. These two witnesses stood obediently by, as a rebuke to the disobedience on the part of the now dead prophet: "In the mouth of two . . . witnesses it shall be established" (Matt. 18:16).

When God is about to bring judgment upon a city, He has respect to such lower creatures just as He has respect to those of humankind who have not yet reached the age of moral accountability. Thereby He acknowledges that both animals and children alike are still part of his Kingdom (Jonah 4:11 and Mark 10:14). Satan's emissaries are permitted to possess only those who are not members of God's Kingdom (Luke 22:3), but not those who like Peter are his children (Luke 22:31, 32).

To re-enter the Kingdom of God a man must be reborn (John 3:3) and adopted back into it (Gal. 4:5, 6). Then, and only then, is something akin to the God-given instincts which guide animals implanted in the soul of the believer as a like form of inspired wisdom. And thus is exhibited the *Special*

Grace of God. But meanwhile his *Common Grace* generates in the world that which is beautiful and which contributes to man's well-being both in animal and human behaviour. This Common Grace is perhaps little more than the expression of God's great goodness towards all his creatures, a great goodness which would quickly turn this blessed vale of tears back into the Paradise it was intended to be if (and when) his dominion is wholly restored as it one day will be.

And is it any more anomalous that God should Himself inspire even the wickedest of men to create things of great beauty according to his own plan and as an expression of his Common Grace, than that He should reach down to even the chiefest of sinners and redeem them and turn them into saints as an expression of his Special Grace?

Thus the statement that the Common Grace of God results in some measure of goodness in human society is not intended to demonstrate that man *is* basically good, but only that by divine restraint of evil the way is left open for men to *do* better than they otherwise would. Common Grace is a reflection of the benevolent sovereignty of God whereby He maintains in fallen man his ability to *do* good, while Special Grace is a reflection of the same sovereignty whereby He creates in man the ability to *be* good. Common Grace acts generally in the world; Special Grace is at work only in the elect. The acts of men and the motives of men must be considered separately, for they are clearly separable. As Kuyper said: in view of man's Total Depravity, "the world goes better than expected," and in view of the fact of its redemption, "the Church goes worse than expected." This is certainly true, for if man is totally depraved, the world is a remarkably good place to live in. But why does the Church fail so badly?

Why does the community of the redeemed fail so badly? This is an important question for a proper understanding of what God does with his people. We are accustomed to thinking that the first thing He undertakes to do with us is to eliminate, or at least to restrain, the evil that is in our nature, what is sometimes referred to as the *bad* "old man." We suppose that He will leave the *good* "old man" and perhaps make use of it. But if this good is basically evil in its motivation, it is no more worthy to be encouraged than the bad. If the *whole* of human motivation in the natural man is evil whether it finds expression in good deeds or bad, it cannot find any favour in the sight of God, who is of purer eyes than to countenance evil in any form, even under the guise of good works. Consequently when God begins a new creation in the redeemed individual He also begins to remove all the evil *and* the good that is rooted in the old nature. The natural goodness of man is not the promise of a new life but the remnant of a dying Adam. By the providence of God, man's natural capacities can be used for the general welfare of society but only on a horizontal and temporal plane—in their vertical and moral context the same actions must be viewed as sinful. Thus they can be allowed in the unredeemed but they cannot be allowed in the redeemed. Consequently the world may seem to do better on a horizontal plane than does the Church of God, which must operate on a different principle.

It should be recognized that a distinction must be made, in speaking about the natural goodness of man, between those endowments which enable a man to contribute to society by the work of his hands or the creativeness of his mind, and what he can contribute to the moral fabric of society; that is to say, what he can contribute on a social level as opposed to what he can contribute on a spiritual level. It is in the latter that the child of God must normally expect to make a unique contribution, and it is towards this contribution that the specific work of redemption is by the Special Grace of God uniquely directed. This is why God's chief concern with his people has to do with motivation. And in order to correct this in our fallen state, it is often necessary to sacrifice, at least for a time, some of our natural endowments which might otherwise seem to have such promise. Thus it is not merely the bad old nature which must be changed but the good old nature as well, for the whole natural man is depraved in his being though still remarkably capable in his creative endowment. This is what Total Depravity really means: not total inability but total *spiritual* inability.

It often happens that a man who has a certain natural ability and is filled with high ideals and is known for his good works, will, when he is converted, become for a season a far less admirable and effective individual. The good old man is slowly undermined because it is good only in an accidental way. This form of natural goodness has to be replaced by a supernatural goodness. It is the work of Special Grace to convert natural goodness, which is counterfeit in the sight of God, into supernatural goodness that is genuine because the motivation has been freed from the bondage of sin, and brought into conformity to the will of God (Rom. 6:18). In a real sense, all goodness in the natural man is simple self-indulgence.

Common Grace deals with man's doings; Special Grace concerns his being. It is quite possible in the Judgment for a man to claim truthfully, "Lord, Lord, in thy name have I done many wonderful works" (Matt. 7:22). The claim is not unjustified because it has reference only to deeds themselves and nothing more. The Judge can say with equal truth, "Depart from Me, ye that work iniquity" (v. 23), for a deed, no matter how good it is in itself, is really a work of iniquity when the motivation behind it is wrong. Article XIII of the *Thirty-Nine Articles* states this very carefully:

> Works done before the grace of Christ, and the inspiration of his Spirit, are not pleasant to God for as much as they spring not of faith in Jesus Christ, neither do they make men meet to receive grace . . . yea rather, in that they are not done as God hath willed and commanded them to be done, we doubt not but that they have the nature of sin.

It sounds extraordinary that good deeds which accrue to the benefit of society as a whole should nevertheless partake of the nature of sin, yet in the light of what has been said above, there is no doubt that they do. It is not the deeds but motives that count, and herein is man *altogether* sinful. A man may therefore be full of good works and outwardly have the appearance of a beautiful marble building, spotlessly clean. Yet the building itself may be only a sepulchre painted white on the outside (Matt. 23:27), while inside is a rotting spiritual corpse. This is a saddening truth. The spiritual depravity of man is total. The totality has reference to his motive, not to his works.

How has this disparity between the good that man can *do* and the evil that man can *be* come about? Judging by the good that man can do, we must assume that he was formed with enormous potential for creativity in art, literature, music, technology, and so forth; but he has been fatally corrupted in his nature. His mind can serve him well enough (in mathematics, for example) for the discernment of truth as perfectly as God can know such truth; but his heart is self-deceived and self-deceiving and utterly incapable of genuine purity of *motive*.

This brings us to the problem of the constitution of man, and the question of whether he is a composite of all kinds of elements—physical, spiritual, intellectual, and so on—or of only two, a physical and a spiritual. We know whence comes his physical body. It is derived ultimately from the body of Adam and Eve who had poisoned themselves into a state of mortality by eating the forbidden fruit. But what is the origin of man's soul, or his spirit, of that part of his being which is non-material? And is this spiritual component itself *single* or composite?

It has traditionally been the view of believers throughout the Christian era that man is a dichotomy, a creature composed of body and spirit. This was a view held by the early Church Fathers for the most part, and the view held by Augustine and consequently by the Reformers and by Roman Catholic theologians, both of whom drew much of their inspiration from Augustine in this. The view that man is a trichotomy composed of body, soul, and spirit is comparatively recent, and is largely inspired by Greek philosophy. Only two passages of Scripture seem in any way to demand the trichotomy view. The balance of Scripture, particularly in the New Testament, forms in general a harmonious picture of man as being constituted of body and spirit, each of which he *has*, uniting to form a soul which he *is*. In the following discussion, the view of man as a dichotomy is assumed to be the correct one.

The origin of man's soul has presented far greater problems than has the origin of his body. It is clear enough that if man derives his body by natural generation there is no problem in understanding how it has come about that his body is defective in so many ways. This kind of inheritance is familiar. The question is, How does his spirit or his soul come to be corrupted also?

There are essentially two views on this matter. (The concept of pre-existence, which was favoured by Origen and a few other early Church Fathers, never gained wide acceptance and is today rejected by Protestant and Roman Catholic theologians alike.) One view holds that we derive our soul from our parents by some kind of process of division and recombination even as we derive our body from them. This view is referred to as Traducianism. It is favoured by Arminians generally, and officially by the Lutherans as a body. It is believed that it accounts most effectively for the inheritance of a fallen nature. One of the most common arguments in favour of it is the fact that in the account of the formation of Eve out of Adam there is no mention made of the creation of her soul. However it is of interest to note that when Adam was presented with Eve, he exclaimed, "This is now bone of my bones and flesh of my flesh" (Gen. 2:23), omitting any reference to the derivation of her spirit from himself. A further objection which is raised against Traducianism is that it makes the soul divisible. The souls of the mother and the father are in some way fragmented and the fragments combined to form the soul of their child. It is also difficult to account for the fact that Jesus Christ did not share the corruption of our nature even though He was born of a human mother.

The other view is that God creates a new spirit or soul for each individual. This view of direct creation assumes that the soul is perfect as it comes from the hand of God but is in some way corrupted by its introduction into the body which carries the defect of fallen Adam. This view is termed Creationism. The only serious challenge to it seems to be the argument that God supposedly ceased creating after the six days' work (Gen. 2:2, 3). But in the light of 2 Corinthians 5:17 this cannot be true, since every regenerate child of God is here said to be "a new creation."

Now whether the soul is thus acquired by inheritance or by direct creation, the problem of its present corruptedness remains an issue of debate. Precisely how man becomes a sinner as he matures is not clear. The light of Scripture on this matter is capable of more than one interpretation. That all men do become sinners is unquestionable, both Scripture and personal experience bearing abundant testimony to the fact. But how this universal process of deterioration is initiated in the individual soul is still an open question, and *when* this process begins remains equally uncertain.

It seems likely that we cannot do much more than reach an approximation as to how and when this physical corruption which we inherit is transmuted into a spiritual one also. For Scripture is not entirely clear. The transmission of inheritable corruption from generation to generation through some genetic mechanism no longer presents the kind of problems that it did to the Reformers. The difficulty which remains to be elucidated is how a physical corruption can damage the spirit of man, which is a direct creation of God. It is the old problem of the interaction between body and spirit, or as Descartes spoke of it, between matter and mind.

We have certain facts regarding the Fall of man which are reasonably assured if we assume that the story of Eden is truly historical. By eating a forbidden fruit Adam and Eve introduced into their bodies some mortogenic factor, perhaps in the nature of a poison, which destroyed their original created perfection and the physical immortality which characterized it. And this was brought about in such a way that physical death became the lot of mankind so universally as now to be termed "natural." But it was not *natural* at first. By their disobedience, Adam and Eve did not merely *shorten* their lives, but introduced death as an entirely new experience. As Romans 5:12 says, "By one man sin entered into the world and by sin death"—and death passed upon all men.

We know that all men have inherited this disease, not only because all men die but also because all men become sinners. As F. W. Farrar noted, volumes have been written upon the precise meaning of Paul's statement, "for all have sinned." A substantial number of modern authorities would interpret the Greek at this point to mean "in view of the fact that all men have sinned." Another group of scholars would interpret these same words to mean "upon which account all men have sinned." Whichever is the correct rendering of the crucial words *eph' hō*(ἐφ' ᾧ), the universality of sinfulness is a clear demonstration of the universality of the disease.

It is therefore apparent that there is some causal connection between this inherited mortogenic factor resident in the body and man's corrupted spirit. The factor itself is passed from generation to generation. It was not identified by the early Church Fathers as something in the nature of a poison, but it was recognized as having real physical existence. Terming it Original Sin, Augustine said it is derived from faulty condition of human seed.[2] Five hundred years later Peter Lombard, as we have seen, concluded that the male seed is the chief offender, it being stained in the act of procreation by concupiscence—which he assumed to be something evil. Calvin *(Inst.* II.i.5) indicated his belief that the corrupting factor is essentially physical by saying, "We are not corrupted by acquired *wickedness* but do bring an innate corruptness from the very womb. . . . All of us, descending from an impure seed, come into the world tainted with the contagion of sin." Luther, as we have also noted, was even more specific, stating his belief that the "paternal sperm" conveys the corruption from generation to generation. Franz V. Reinhard (1753-1812) in his *System of Christian Morals* explained the Fall as a kind of poisoning and hereditary sin as the inheritance of a poisoned constitution. The Roman Catholic Church at the Council of Trent (1545-1563)

---

2. *Anti-Pelagian Writings: On Marriage,* II.20.

sought to state its position on this issue by declaring that the corruption which passes from generation to generation is not in itself a moral defect but rather something which inclines to moral defect, a "fuel of sin" which was technically termed *fomes peccati*.[3]

Whatever the nature of this contagion, it was foreign to man as originally created, it was introduced in Eden, and it is inherited by every natural born child of Adam. Its effect is to mortalize man's body and corrupt man's spirit. It is capable of transmission from body to body by the mere fact of procreation, and from body to spirit as the individual matures. Man inevitably returns to the dust and he unfailingly becomes a sinner if he lives to maturity. In Original Sin we therefore have a case of an acquired character which has been inherited. Physiologically this no longer presents the serious problem that it might have presented a few years ago. For we now know that certain types of acquired characters can indeed be transmitted by inheritance, not via the nuclear genes, however, but by what are called plasmogenes, certain bodies resident in the cytoplasm rather than in the nucleoplasm, which, by a process of dauermodifications, can be permanently modified by factors outside the cell wall in such a way that the daughter cells which arise with each division are changed even in the absence of the factor which caused the modification in the parent cells. Today we not only have much evidence that such a mechanism exists but we have a fairly clear idea of how it operates.

Man's first act of disobedience introduced not only physical death to himself and his descendants but also spiritual death so that all men naturally born of Adam's seed have since that time turned the innocence of infancy into the sinfulness of adolescence and manhood as they matured. Somehow the defect of the body becomes the ruination of the spirit, even though that spirit is perfect when first created and implanted by God in the body.

The question is, How does the body corrupt the spirit? Does Scripture actually encourage belief that such an interaction, such a transmission of contagion from body to spirit, really occurs? It all depends upon how we interpret the use of the term *flesh* in the New Testament. Does the word normally mean actual flesh and only occasionally mean carnal desire, or does the word normally mean carnal desire in the physiological sense and only occasionally mean the actual body tissue, tangible, physical in the corporeal sense?

We do not need to ask the *how* of such a mechanism unless we are first satisfied that this is what Scripture says actually does happen. If we once establish this, then we can perhaps usefully ask what the nature of the mechanism is; and although at the moment there is no clear picture here, we

---

3. "Concupiscence" in *A Catholic Dictionary*, p. 214.

do begin to discern some of the somato-psychic (body-psyche) mechanisms behind the interactions that we experience in daily life. This new area of enquiry may shed light for us on a very ancient problem that puzzled Augustine, as it has puzzled all who have sought to elucidate the matter since his time. It was *this* aspect of the problem—the interaction between body and spirit—that led inevitably to the debate between the Traducianists and the Creationists, a debate to which Augustine contributed only his own uncertainty. If Traducianism is true, the spirit derives its impurity by a kind of spiritual procreation process in which the fallen nature of Adam and Eve is directly transmitted to every descendant. If Creationism is true, then the spirit begins its personal existence pure, and is corrupted by the body. We have already considered some of the difficulties of Traducianism: the divisibility of the soul and the problem of the perfection of the soul of Jesus Christ. But Creationism presents us with a difficulty of its own, the fatal interaction between body and spirit, between "flesh" and "soul."

That such an interaction does occur is intimated in Romans 8:3, where Paul speaks of what the law could not do, in that it was "weak" (*asthenei:* ineffective, without sufficient force) on account of the flesh. This, he says, is why the law is so impotent in regulating conduct. It is not that the spirit is unwilling but rather that the flesh is "weak" (*asthenēs:* Matt. 26:41). The law sets the standard which every individual is called upon to meet. But why does a child with a pure created spirit not meet it? Because the law of itself is impotent in the face of the contrary urgings of the body. Because the eager desire of the flesh must have its own way. In the innocence of childhood, how else could we suppose temptation to come at first except through some appetite of the body?

How early, then, does the fatal contagion perform its deadly spiritual contagion? It is difficult to establish this from Scripture. Some of the Reformers clearly viewed even prenatal life as sinful and morally corrupt, even if only by imputation. In Isaiah 48:8, for example, they read the words "from the womb" as meaning from *within* the womb. But it is not required of the Hebrew that *from* should be read as *within*. "From the womb" is a common enough expression meaning only "from the very beginning"; and it need not signify more than it would if we were to say of someone, "He was *always* a happy child."

We have seen how some of the Confessions viewed the matter and we observed that in regard to human sinfulness they considered the neonate not merely as corrupted in nature and as already guilty, but even as actually sinful. Perhaps the earliest possible time marker in the Old Testament is to be found in the regulations regarding circumcision, which was to be performed on the eighth day. It is possible that this indicates the arrival of some kind of moral accountability—though that seems rather unlikely. It is more likely that the timing is important for physiological reasons since it happens to be an almost ideal time for such an operation. It avoids potential excess loss of blood due to insufficient development of the anticoagulating mechanism on the one hand, and on the other hand it avoids too gross an assault on the infant nervous system because the operation is performed before that system has matured and become too highly sensitive. We do know that when David's first son by Bathsheba died on the seventh day it had not yet been circumcised, yet David by implication was quite certain that he would meet his child again in heaven. In 2 Samuel 12:23 he said, "I shall go to him, but he shall not return to me." At the age of seven days a child therefore, though uncircumcised ("unbaptized"?), may be assumed to be fit for heaven.

In Deuteronomy 1:39 there is an indication that those children who had not yet learned the difference between good and evil were in a state of innocence and would inherit the Promised Land, though their parents who had halted at the entrance through unbelief would not do so. Presumably this would include children at least up to a year old.

In Matthew 19:14 children are said by the Lord to be "the stuff of heaven". We do not know how old these children were, but while Matthew says only that He laid his hands upon them, Mark (10:16) tells us that He actually took them up in his arms. This may indicate something about their size and age. If these children were two or three years old, they were evidently still "of such" as is the Kingdom of heaven.

Jonah 4:11 tells us that God respected the repentance of the people of Nineveh and spared their city for a season. But He also took into account the many children in it who, we are told, had not yet learned to discern the right hand from the left. These children were, of course, strangers to the covenant of Israel and in no sense children of believers. Yet apparently they were accounted worthy of sparing.

Genesis 8:21, with some precision, tells that "the imagination of the heart of man is evil from his youth." But how old is a youth? Beyond childhood surely! Yet we do not know where the line of demarcation between childhood and youth is to be drawn, though if we are guided by the time at which a Jewish boy traditionally becomes a man we have reason to believe that the line of demarcation from youth to manhood is somewhere in the early teens.

There is a transitional period in here, and about all we can say on the basis of what is written in Scripture is that the time at which a child first discovers there is a difference between right and wrong seems to mark the age of accountability. When the time comes to make an actual choice between the two, a previous age of innocence becomes an age of virtue if the choice is made correctly, but an age of culpability if the choice is wrongly made. This may not, of course, actually occur at the same time of life for each individual. Samuel was an obedient and godly child—yet just how obedient we cannot be sure, for when the Lord called him by name he did not respond as Eli had instructed him to do. In 1 Samuel 3:9 the aging High Priest advised him to answer, "Speak, Lord, for thy servant heareth." But in verse 10 we observe that Samuel said only, "Speak, for thy servant heareth." And in verse 7 we are told why: "Samuel did not yet know the Lord nor had his word yet been revealed to him." This observation seems about the clearest possible indication that he had not been converted up till then. Admittedly the Old Testament does not give us a clear picture of the steps that led to conversion in those days, nor precisely what such a conversion meant in the life of the individual. For while Saul was given a new heart and turned into another man, and anointed with the Holy Spirit (1 Sam. 10:6, 9), he seems clearly to have departed from the faith shortly afterwards (1 Sam. 16:14).

We are therefore somewhat in the dark except in so far as we have two brackets, the first being David's uncircumcised seven-day-old son who was clearly innocent, and secondly, the statement in Genesis 8:21 which tells us that man is corrupted by sin from his youth. Somewhere between the two, the process of corruption is initiated and the spirit becomes dead towards God. Yet I do not think we need to assume that the stage of innocence passes in one stroke into a stage of guilt. There may well be an interim during which the child resists temptation for a while, passing from innocence into virtue of a sort. But it is probably a brief interlude and for many children may not exist as an interlude at all. So many grow up in an environment of selfishness and violence. Samuel was perhaps especially sheltered —and there must still be "Samuels" among us, though sadly their destiny is to mature as we all do. It is only a matter of time before all flesh corrupts its way and every man falls short of the perfect righteousness which God requires. The corruption of the spirit by the body, the "spotting" of the garment by the flesh (Jude 23), comes about inexorably with the passage of time as we mature.

But does the word *flesh* really mean the physical tissue of the body or only some kind of psychological impulse that, though it operates through the body, originates in the soul? A study of this word *flesh* (σάϱξ, *sarx*) is revealing because it does not bear out the meaning which is often attached to it by those who habitually conceive of man as a spirit who happens incidentally to inhabit a body, rather than (as Scripture sees him) as a body/spirit entity.

To begin with, there are many passages in which only the physical sense of the word can be intended. "The Word was made flesh and dwelt among us" (John 1:14) is unequivocal—and because of the nature of its context is a very powerful witness. Another such reference is John 6:51, 52, 53, 54, 55,

56, and 63, where the Lord hammers home to the Pharisees that He really means his *body*, for his sacrifice was to be a physical as well as a spiritual one. It was in his body that He bore our sins on the cross (1 Peter 2:24). In Acts 2:26 it is clearly the physical body that rests in hope of the resurrection, and in verse 31 it is his physical body that did not see corruption.

In Romans 9:3 Paul speaks of physical relationship to his Jewish brethren as a thing of the flesh, and in verse 8 those born of the flesh are natural kin, as also in Romans 11:14. In 1 Corinthians 5:5, where the reference is to a grossly disobedient brother in the Lord whose presence is an offence to the Body of Christ, "the destruction of the flesh" clearly means the putting to death of the body, as many similar passages indicate. In 1 Corinthians 15:39 all flesh is rightly said not to be the same kind of flesh. The meaning is only that fish, fowl, and other animal foods differ in texture, taste, and value. In short, flesh is equivalent to meat. Paul suffered from some as yet unidentified bodily ailment which left him physically depleted, his real trial being an actual disease of some sort (Gal. 4:14). He spoke of this as being "a thorn in the flesh" (2 Cor. 12:7).

In such recurrent phrases as "flesh and blood" (Matt. 16:17; 1 Cor. 15:50; Eph. 6:12) and "flesh and bones" (Luke 24:39) the reference is clearly to the body, which demonstrates that when Scripture means physical tissue it is not limited to the use of the word *body* (soma). Such a compound phrase as "the body of his flesh" (Col. 1:22) is a Hebraism translated into Greek and means simply "his fleshly body." This is a common circumlocution in Hebrew, as when David speaks of "the mountain of his holiness" (so the original Hebrew of Ps. 48:1), meaning simply "his holy mountain." Similarly Paul speaks of the "body of this death" (Rom. 7:24), meaning "this mortal body" whence arose so many of his trials, for, physically speaking, he was a frail man (2 Cor. 10:10).

To "live in the flesh" (Phil. 1:22) meant, for Paul, to remain in the body, though he desired rather to leave it and go to be with the Lord. To see his friends face to face was to meet them "in the flesh," personally, physiologically (Col. 2:1); while to be absent in the flesh meant only to be physically absent.

In 1 Timothy 3:16 God is described as manifest in the flesh, that is to say, He was physically incarnate, to be seen and heard—indeed, to be *handled* (1 John 1:1). These were "the days of his flesh" (Heb. 5:7), of his embodiment. When John wrote that a test of true spiritual understanding is frank acknowledgment of the fact that Messiah has indeed appeared in the flesh, he is talking about the incarnation and he sees no reason not to use the term *flesh* where the word *body* might have been more appropriate (1 John 4:2).

When Peter says, "All flesh is grass" (1 Peter 1:24), he is speaking of living tissue, not of some psychological impulse; and his simple observation expresses a profound physiological truth, for in the final analysis, if the word *grass* is allowed to stand for any type of plant life, all flesh *is* grass.

Now depending exactly on how the count is made, the word *flesh* is to be found approximately 120 times in the New Testament. Of these, only eleven cases seem to be clearly used metaphorically, while another five may also be so used though they are equivocal. But at the most, sixteen cases can be pointed to which do not seem to be synonymous for "the body." The balance, 104 out of 120, are almost certainly to be taken literally. Even allowing for some differences of opinion in matters of this sort where personal bias may affect the outcome, it is clear the view held in some circles that the word *flesh* has primarily a psychological connotation rather than a physical one is not supported by the evidence of the majority of cases in the text.

Charles Hodge, in presenting the case for Creationism, refers to a classic "proof text" which is found in Hebrews 12:9, where it is said that we have derived our flesh by descent from our fathers and have received our spirit directly from the Father in heaven. He notes the obvious antithesis here between body and spirit, and between the source of each, and he adds: "This is in accordance with the familiar use of the word *flesh*, where it is contrasted, either expressly or by implication, with the soul."[4] He then lists some of the passages to which reference has been already made above, where the word *flesh* is used in a literal sense, and observes: "In all these, and in a multitude of similar passages, flesh means body and 'fathers of our flesh' means fathers of our bodies."

When Paul therefore speaks of "the works of the flesh" (Gal. 5:19), he is really only saying that the symptoms of the disease which afflicts our bodies are these unhappy expressions of our fallen nature. So also when he speaks of "the sins of the flesh" (Col. 2:11), and "the lusts of the flesh" (Gal. 5:16). He is not really using the word *flesh* in some symbolic sense. These symptoms of a fallen nature are rooted in this body of death from which we, like Paul, desire so earnestly to be delivered (Rom. 7:24).* For he discovered, as we all do, that in us, that is, in our *bodies*, dwelleth no good thing (Rom. 7:18).

It may seem that we are viewing the body as inherently evil, as something we might far better be without. It is inherently diseased, corrupt, defective; but we could not do without it, for God has constituted man as a composite

---

4. Charles A. Hodge, *Systematic Theology*, Vol. II, p. 71.

---

*When Paul speaks of the conflict within, he speaks of it as a conflict between the intentions of his mind and the demands of his body, the "members of his body" being the source of his defeats. For this reason he cries out, "O wretched man that I am! Who shall deliver me from this body of death?" The phrase "this body of death" is a familiar Hebraism, such as is to be observed in a different context but in the same form in Psalm 47:8 and 48:1.

of body and spirit, more like a centaur of classical antiquity than simply a rider on a horse. Paul says rightly that we do not want to be disembodied, but re-embodied with a perfect body as was originally planned for our spirit to animate. "For in this [body] we groan, earnestly desiring to be clothed upon with our new house [new body] which is from heaven. . . . For we that are in this tabernacle do groan, being burdened [by its defectiveness]: not that we would be unclothed [disembodied] but clothed upon in order that mortality might be swallowed up of life" (2 Cor. 5:2-4). And in verse 5 he adds significantly: "He that hath wrought us for the self-same thing is God."

So we have perhaps a clue here to the etiology of our problem, how the body interacts with the spirit to communicate its own defectiveness to something which comes perfect from the hand of God. Our body *inherits* a disease. In due course this disease, acting from within, infects the created spirit by imposing upon it temptations to disobedience to which it ultimately yields. Some yield very early in life; some a little later. But all yield in the end, save He who did not have this disease within his flesh; for though He also was tempted, his temptations always came to Him from outside. If we are right in applying the word *sin* to the disease itself, then it would clearly be more correct to translate Hebrews 4:15: "[He] was in all points tempted like as we are, yet *apart from* sin." The Greek word *chōris* (χωρὶς) translated "without" in most versions is elsewhere frequently rendered "apart from." There is no doubt that this is the more correct rendering as most lexicons bear out. And indeed some modern translations have observed this fact (Young's *Literal Translation*, Rotherham and Williams), though a great many have not done so.

Smith and Goodspeed have rendered the phrase "without committing any sin," but it is almost certain that if this had been the intention of the author he would not have employed this construction at all. This kind of sinlessness is unequivocally intended in John 8:7, where we find the words "Let him that is without sin," etc., represented in the original by the single Greek word *anamartētos* (ἀναμάρτητος). That is not what Hebrews 4:15 is telling us. What we are being told here is that when the Lord Jesus was tempted there was nothing in Him which would provide a foothold for Satan to weaken his defences. He said, "The prince of this world cometh and hath nothing in Me" (John 14:30). Both the first and the last Adam were alike in this that the first temptation came to them entirely from outside. Unlike ourselves, their bodies were not corrupted in such a way as to pressure the spirit towards evil, in the sense that our bodies do. The Lord's hunger in the desert was not in any way a corrupted appetite. "In Him is no sin" (1 John 3:5), no disease.

We know now that there are strange and formerly unrecognized interactions between the chemistry of the body and the behaviour of the spirit. If the chemistry of the body has been deranged, it is obvious that the spirit must suffer some damage also. We know that this chemistry is deranged in some types of people whose spirit is disturbed. There is growing evidence in certain forms of depression that the lithium level is responsible. We also know from personal experience that spiritual depression is characteristic of physical fatigue, a fact which should have been apparent enough in the light of the disciples' sleepiness at the time of the Lord's special need (Mark 14:37). But we also recognize today that coronary insufficiency (a purely physical defect) can cause a similar depression that may be quite profound and seems to be unmanageable unless the physical root cause is corrected somewhat.

Aberrant forms of behaviour are known to arise from certain environmental contaminations such as lead in the air, and from dietary deficiencies (lack of salt for example), and from unwanted chemicals ingested or inhaled, or even admitted percutaneously from salves or lotions or dressings of one kind or another. This is a whole new area of modern research and even the present findings should give us cause to rethink the theological problems involved in the relationship between Original Sin and our individual response to it.

The reverse reaction is also true. An outflow of spiritual energy can leave the body physically depressed. Ministers often face Monday morning with physical energies severely depleted. Elijah won a tremendous spiritual victory on Mount Carmel, only to find himself so exhausted that the proper divinely appointed therapy was purely physical in nature: sleep and food, sleep and food (1 Kings 19:4-8). Searching within his own soul Elijah mistakenly saw himself as spiritually depleted, and despaired for the spiritual welfare not only of himself but of his people (verse 4). But God knew better where the trouble really lay. Some of us have not yet learned to apply this truth in our own lives. It is obvious that there is a continuous interaction between body and spirit and between spirit and body, and all too frequently it is to the detriment of the spirit. It is not too difficult to see how a diseased body could infect a spirit which, though perfect at first, is so closely engaged in its processes and so intimately dependent upon its operation.

Augustine held that we each inherit from Adam by natural generation the *corruption* of his body, and by imputation the *guilt* of his sin by which that corruption was introduced. Pelagius, his contemporary, entirely rejected this view. Each individual starts, he held, as a perfect being free from defect of spirit or body, as Adam was when first created. It is by active sin, imitating as it were Adam's history, that each man becomes a sinner and subject to death. It ought therefore to be possible by the right environment and correct training, education, and example, for a man to grow up sinless.

Calvin and the Reformers followed Augustine and held that man inherits a defective body and assumes by imputation the guilt of Adam's sin. Between the two, man's nature is wholly corrupted from the very beginning of his individual existence and is under just condemnation. Arminians have held a view midway between the Augustinian and the Pelagian views. We indeed inherit Adam's corrupted nature, but not his guilt. Infants are therefore innocent by nature, whether baptized or not, until they become guilty when they commit actual sins. That they inherit their souls from their parents does not make them guilty, though it does inevitably lead to guilt when voluntary expression is given to the inherent fallen nature by yielding to temptation. Thus Original Sin is transmitted and in due time erupts into sinful action which results in actual guilt. No child needs to be taught to sin.

Midway in time between Augustine and the Reformers (and Arminius, of course) we have Peter Lombard and his contemporaries at the school of St. Victor (Hugo and Abelard among them) attempting to formulate a more precise doctrine. Peter himself was not so sure about the inheritance of *guilt*, but he concluded that we certainly inherit the injury itself, and with this injury we inherit the inevitable penalty of becoming a sinner.

Infant baptism was predicated by Augustine on the presumption of inherited guilt. By baptism in the name of Jesus Christ this inherent guilt is removed and a kind of righteousness (perhaps *innocence* would be a more appropriate word) replaces the imputed guilt of Original Sin until the time of accountability is reached. Baptism does not remove the corruption itself, but does cover the inherited guilt. Although Lutherans believe that the soul is derived from the parents by a process akin to spiritual generation, they believe that the corruption that is inherited is strictly physical. According to Luther the propagation of sin is exclusively physical. Augustine held a somewhat similar view, though he inclined towards Creationism in the matter of the origin of the soul. Nevertheless he believed that the corruption of human nature was propagated by "bad seed." But he does not seem to have been able to crystallize his own thinking completely. Perhaps the problem he had as a creationist was to account for the corruption of a pure spirit created by God merely by its introduction into an impure body procreated by the parents. How did the flesh corrupt the spirit?

Peter Lombard struggled with this problem and concluded that the male seed is somehow "stained: in the act of procreation by concupiscence ("eager desire") which he, like Augustine, assumed to be something evil. Yet in Scripture concupiscence is not necessarily evil. In Luke 22:15 it is applied to the Lord's eager desire to share a certain Passover with the disciples. In 1 Peter 1:12 it is used of the angels' eager desire to understand the purposes of God in the matter of man's salvation. In Hebrews 6:11 it refers to the genuine concern that the Lord's people may have for one another's spiritual welfare. Peter Lombard presumably shared a rather widespread feeling that the act of procreation had something inherently sinful about it.

In whatever way the factor is inherited, the factor itself is by Calvin and in Scripture frequently designated by the word *SIN* (in the singular). This *sin* is the root of all physical evil (sickness and death) and all spiritual evil. It is a disease, transmissible from body to body by procreation, and in the individual from body to spirit—where the symptoms appear as SINS. These sins are not merely like boils that erupt at the surface as a deeper infection runs its course. They are willed expressions of a corrupt nature for which the individual is not merely pitied as a sick man but held responsible as a guilty one. The disease itself cannot be treated or cured by being forgiven or punished, but must be healed. The symptoms which are expressions of it must be either punished, or forgiven on the grounds of penalty borne by someone else. To ignore these symptoms is not only to encourage their expression but to conceal the disease, and this has been habitually man's unfruitful method of dealing with the ills of human society. But in order to prevent the total corruption of the individual from becoming the total corruption of society itself, God has exercised the Common Grace of restraint. And part of this restraint has been the creation of the true Church, that body of the redeemed who are placed in the world not to redeem it by saving all men but to preserve it from total corruption by acting as a light to dispel the darkness and as salt to preserve against its total self-destruction.

This, then, is the background of the concept of the Total Depravity of man, how it may have come about, how the roots of it are transmitted from generation to generation in every natural born individual, and what it has meant in human history. It is a depravity of the most profound kind because it has made human behaviour fundamentally suicidal, and it is Total Depravity because in every individual naturally born the motivation of all behaviour has been poisoned at the source. While the individual may, by the restraining Common Grace of God, be kept from actions as evil as they might otherwise be, only the transforming experience of spiritual rebirth, amounting to a re-creation of the image of God in the heart of the individual, can fundamentally change this motivation and consciously bring it into conformity with the will of God.

DEFINITION OF *DEPRAVITY*

Now, the *Belgic Confession* (XV. 1) holds that "sin is a corruption of the whole nature and a hereditary disease wherein even infants in their mother's womb are infected, and which produces in man all sorts of sin, being in him as a root thereof." Calvin saw *sin* as the definitive term for the root, and *sins* as the fruits of this root (*Inst.* II.i.8). Calvin recognized that while we have an inherited defect we do not actually inherit the wickedness which results from it. The defect and what results from the defect are causally related (*Inst.* II.i.5), but we cannot blame upon our parents the fruits of the defect which we ourselves exhibit by allowing or encouraging them. Every man is to bear the guilt of his own sin.

Calvin wrote on this matter thus:

> Pelagius [rose up] with the profane fiction that Adam sinned only to his own loss without harming his posterity. Through this subtlety Satan attempted to cover up the disease and thus to render it incurable. But when it was shown by the clear testimony of Scripture that sin was transmitted from the first man to all his posterity (Rom. 5:12), Pelagius quibbled that it was transmitted through imitation, not propagation. Therefore, good men (and Augustine above the rest) laboured to show us that we are corrupted not by derived wickedness, but that we bear *inborn defect* from our mother's womb. (my emphasis)

And Augustine had expounded the same view when he wrote *(City of God,* XVI.xxvii): "Infants are . . . born in sin *not actual* but original" (my emphasis). The Lutherans likewise interpreted the relationship between SIN and SINS *(Formula of Concord,* I.5):

> It is an established truth that Christians must regard and recognize as sin not only the actual transgression of God's commandments but also, and primarily, the abominable and dreadful *inherited disease* which has corrupted our entire nature. . . .
>
> Dr. Luther calls this sin "natural-sin" or "person-sin" in order to indicate that even though a (natural) man were to think no evil, speak no evil, or do no evil—which after the Fall of our first parents is of course impossible for human nature in this life—nevertheless man's nature and person would still be sinful. This means that in the sight of God *original sin, like a spiritual leprosy,* has thoroughly and entirely poisoned and corrupted human nature. (emphasis mine)

And so we have this basic pattern of relationships:

SIN	SINS
The Root	Fruits
The Disease	Symptoms
The Defect	Manifestations
Not accountable	Accountable
Merely "repugnant"	Under moral judgment, or morally reprehensible

Although this defect or disease called SIN is the direct cause of SINS, we nevertheless are not held morally accountable for the root itself. God has taken upon Himself the responsibility of dealing with it and therefore of dealing with the physical mortality which it causes.* SIN, being a disease, is accordingly not *forgiven*, but in the Old Testament is "covered" (Ps. 32:1), and in the New Testament it is to be "cleansed" (1 John 1:7) until it will be "taken away" (John 1:29) or "put away" (Heb. 9:26). Hence the Lamb of God became in respect to this aspect of the Fall "a ransom [from death] for all men to be proven in due time" (1 Tim. 2:6), when as "in Adam all die, so in Christ will all men be made alive" (1 Cor. 15:22)—not merely resurrected like Lazarus who later must have returned to the grave, but placed beyond the power of physical death. It is in this sense that by the grace of God the Lord Jesus Christ "tasted death for every man" (Heb. 2:9).

Thus Original Sin is not itself to be identified with Total Depravity. Yet it is the root cause of it. The newborn babe bears the defect of Original Sin but is not yet totally depraved. We are conceived and born in SIN (Ps. 51:5) but not born in SINS, though we die in them (John 8:21). The Pharisees entirely misquoted the passage from Psalm 51 because they did not understand its significance (John 9:34). Adult Total Depravity results from the fact that the spirit is pervasively influenced by the flesh and so weakened by it that the law becomes powerless to convert our initial innocence into demonstrated righteousness (Rom. 8:3). The Lord Jesus became a Saviour by escaping this poisonous stream through the circumstances of the virgin conception. Whereas Paul, speaking for all of us, could say categorically, *"In me*, that is, in my flesh, dwelleth no good thing" (Rom. 7:18); of the Lord Jesus Christ, John could say with equal justification, *"In Him* is no sin" (1 John 3:5).

Original Sin is the cause of man's Total Depravity, and this Total Depravity manifests itself spiritually in man's natural refusal of God's salvation. He is not forced to this position by anything external to himself. When he refuses, he is merely exercising his freedom; but it is clear that this freedom, real as it is in the consciousness of the individual who exercises it, is actually a bondage. Luther said that man's freedom was in his slavery to sin. Augustine explained what happens when a man does will to salvation by saying, "Man is not converted because he wills: he wills because he is converted." The turning of the will necessarily precedes the willing acceptance, and this turning is a work of God, not of man.

Man is free to choose salvation *if he wills it*. Whosoever will may come (Rev. 22:17). But by nature he does not so will. It is not that any man is denied salvation *though he wills it*; it is simply that no man wills it unless God turns his will around. Furthermore, the elect are not saved whether

---

*This view was shared by Semi-Pelagians and the earlier Arminians. Wesleyan Arminians hold that this inborn corruption also involves guilt. See Louis Berkhof, *Systematic Theology*, p. 241.

they will or not. They are saved by the grace of God, because they will it by the grace of God. As Luther put it, "When God works in us, the will, being changed and sweetly breathed upon by the Spirit of God, desires and acts, not from *compulsion*, but *responsively*" (his emphasis).

The *Westminster Confession* deals with this matter (XII.1, 2) under the heading *Of Effectual Calling* as follows:

> All those whom God has predestined unto life, and those only He is pleased, in his appointed and accepted time, effectually to call by his word and Spirit out of that state of sin and death in which they are by nature, to grace and salvation by Jesus Christ: enlightening their minds, spiritually and savingly, to understand the things of God, taking away their heart of stone, and giving unto them an heart of flesh; renewing their wills, and by his almighty power determining them to that which is good; and *effectually* drawing them to Jesus Christ; yet so as [i.e., in such a way that] they come most freely, *being made willing by his grace.*
>
> This effectual call is of God's free and special grace alone, not from anything at all foreseen in man, who is altogether passive therein, until, being quickened, and renewed by the Holy Spirit, *he is thereby enabled to answer* this call, and to embrace the grace offered and conveyed in it. (emphasis mine)

A. H. Strong in his *Systematic Theology* (p. 640) has this statement regarding the nature of man's impotence resulting from Original Sin:

> In opposition to the plenary [i.e., complete] ability taught by the Pelagians, the gracious ability taught by the Arminians, and the natural ability of the [Liberal] theologians, the Scriptures declare the total inability of the sinner to turn himself to God, or to do that which is truly good in God's sight.

Strong goes on to point out that this is not to deny man has a range of freedom in acting out his nature, even as there is a range of freedom in slavery though that slavery is inescapable. The freedom which man lacks towards God is supplied by God. He is "made willing in the day of God's power" (Ps. 110:3). John Owen in Volume X of his *Works* (p. 127) underscores the fact that there is not only impotency towards God which might be considered negative but enmity towards God which can be highly active. Berkouwer spoke of this as the "dynamism of sin."

Such enmity towards God is like enmity towards life itself. And enmity towards life is by definition *suicidal.* James Gall *(Primeval Man Unveiled,* p. 91) considered that one of the most profound differences between animal nature and human nature lies in this, that human nature is suicidal in its tendency. And SIN is the suicidal powerhouse of the human will.

One of the most profound questions to occupy the mind of man is the extent of his freedom. The right to make free choices has been battled for throughout history. It has been fought for even by those whose outright materialism forces them to admit that they themselves are merely bundles of electrochemical activity, the course of whose doings are absolutely predetermined by all that has gone before. Pure materialism reduces all willed activity to mere mechanism and locks all behaviour into a chain reaction from which there is no escape. Mind is reduced to brain, soul to central nervous system. Freedom becomes an illusion. Yet the most ardent of materialists, like Bertrand Russell, spoke eloquently in defence of man's right to self-determination as an individual!

Moralists are likewise on the horns of a dilemma. We recognize in ourselves and in others, as a universal part of experience, that we have a sense of making decisions where alternative choices are open to us. We are aware of exercising volition. And the whole concept of moral responsibility deeply embedded in the culture patterns of every human society is predicated on the freedom of choice, on the ability, and therefore the responsibility, to choose what is right and reject what is wrong. Even if cultures define right and wrong differently, they still recognize these two categories of human behaviour which tend in opposite directions.

Some theologians, convinced of the Total Depravity of man, perceive as a corollary of this depravity total absolvement from all moral accountability. If a man cannot do good, is he then culpable for failing to do it? Can God judge man for not obeying his commands if man is constitutionally unable to obey them even if he wants to? Is not ability to perform the test of duty?

This was Pelagius' argument: "Ability is always the measure of responsibility."[5] It was also the argument of Arminius. Their followers have therefore said: If God commands man to repent and believe, it must be assumed that he is capable of repenting and believing, otherwise God is unjust in his demands. But it was observed by the Reformers that both Pelagians and Arminians were mistaken in their assumptions because a logical extension of this argument leads to an absurd and manifestly erroneous conclusion. If a man's responsibility to obey is to be gauged by his ability to perform, then as his behaviour degenerates and his ability is progressively reduced, he has less and less duty. The wholly evil man thus ends up by having no responsibility whatever, and must be accounted blameless! In point of fact, the measure of our duty is not our capability to perform but God's requirement of us whether we can perform it or not. That we cannot perform it is our fault, not his; and there is no injustice in his refusal to lower his standard of requirement on account of our failure.

So it is apparent that man's total incapacity does not absolve him from

---

5. Quoted in A. W. Pink, *Gleanings from Scripture: Man's Total Depravity*, p. 227.

full responsibility. The reason that he is culpable is that he has willingly allowed himself to degenerate to the point of total incapacity. Man now takes pleasure in unrighteousness (2 Thess. 2:12). He is not incapacitated against his will. His bondage to sin is embraced willingly. Man finds his freedom in this way. Being a bondslave of corruption man promises himself liberty by accepting this corruption as normal (2 Peter 2:19). Thus when man sins he is acting as a truly free agent, though he is in bondage. As Dostoyevsky says in his *Letters from the Underworld,* "Man commits sin simply to remind himself that he is free." The most abject slave who willingly embraces his slavery is no longer a slave perforce: he has found freedom in bondage.

Now the Reformers never denied that man is morally free, in spite of his total moral depravity. He is not a puppet, for a puppet cannot *choose* to be a puppet. Man not only chooses to be a sinner, but by nature prefers to remain one. As originally created, Adam was free in the absolute sense that he could choose either way, to obey or to disobey the command of God. The important thing is that he had freedom of choice in *either* direction, upwards or downwards. As Augustine put it: "It was possible for him not to sin but not impossible for him to sin." But when man made his fatal decision he destroyed this absolute freedom and left himself thereafter with freedom in only one direction. This is still freedom but it is unidirectional. When man finally reaches heaven he will still have freedom only in one direction, but this time it will be in the opposite direction. He will be constitutionally unable to sin, even as now he is constitutionally unable not to sin. That one should be free and yet not free is a difficult concept until we realize what it means. We know from Scripture that God cannot lie (Heb. 6:18), but this does not mean that God is not free; it means that God is free from the possibility of sin. At the present moment in our fallen state we ourselves are, as Paul said, "free from righteousness" (Rom. 6:20). Thus whereas in his innocence Adam need not have sinned, now in his fallen state, *so long as he is acting freely*—so long as he is acting according to his nature—man can do nothing else.

This tendency towards sin and unrighteousness is like gravity. We fall freely. No doubt if stones had consciousness, they would claim to be falling without compulsion. It is only when the free-falling man attempts to go in the opposite direction that he realizes his freedom is unidirectional and downward only. As such, it is in fact an absolute bondage within which, so long as he does not attempt to resist it, he lives with a sense of complete freedom. Total bondage therefore is a kind of total freedom, and it is only when the bondage is not total that a man may discover he is not wholly free. Every time a man says, "I will be free and do as I please," he accelerates his degeneration. In this natural state we are conscious of making choices, but most of the time we do not ask why we make the choices we do. As

Strong says, we never know the force of any evil passion or principle within us until we begin to resist it.[6]

Then why does God command of us what we cannot possibly do? He does so because his requirement, not our capacity or our preference, is the true measure of our duty. His command is not his expectation but his judgment of our fallen nature, the condemnation of our unrighteousness.

Now God undertakes to convert this unidirectionality of will into a bidirectionality, thus setting it free. He does this by a gracious severing of the bondage which we have allowed our inherent corruption to impose upon us. Man redeemed has once again freedom to choose in either direction, to disobey or obey the will of God. But something more than this is accomplished in us by the Holy Spirit. We are not merely given alternatives where we formerly had no alternative, but preference for righteousness. We are not merely transformed from a negative to a neutral position, but from a negative to a positive one. If we walk in his light and allow his grace to work in our hearts, we may increasingly tend upwards *by choice*, for it is God who thereafter works in us not merely to do but also to will his will (Phil. 2:13). We are turned around, converted, as to the direction of our will. The law of God instead of the bondage of self is written in both our minds and hearts (Heb. 8:10). That is, it is written in both our understanding of his will (mind) and our willingness to do it (heart). This is the new covenant which God makes with us. Yet the downward will remains, though it is no longer representative of our true selves (Rom. 7:18-20). Not until we reach heaven shall we be truly free, in such total bondage to righteousness that to will downwardly will be constitutionally impossible. We could perhaps set forth this sequence of events diagrammatically as shown in the chart on page 120.

Thus man unredeemed is able only to sin, though various restraints which are both internal and external and which may or may not be part of the Common Grace of God have placed limitations even on this form of freedom which remains to him. But whatever freedom he is permitted, its direction is always downwards whether he goes only a little way along the road of sin, or plumbs the depths of sin.

Luther was very clear on this matter and one of his most famous and earliest works dealt with the subject. In his essay *On the Bondage of the Will* (Section XXV) he wrote:

> If it be proved that our salvation is apart from our own strength and counsel, and depends on the working of God alone (which I hope I shall clearly prove hereafter, in the course of this discussion), does it not evidently follow, that when God is not present with us to work in us, every-

---

6. Augustus Strong, *Systematic Theology*, p. 577.

MAN IN EDEN	FALLEN MAN	MAN REDEEMED	MAN IN HEAVEN
NEED NOT SIN	CANNOT BUT SIN	CAN SIN BUT NEED NOT	CANNOT SIN
FREEDOM TO DO GOOD OR — — — — — EVIL	FREEDOM TO DO ONLY EVIL	FREEDOM AND PREFERENCE TO DO GOOD BUT — — — — — TO DO EVIL— STILL SOME FREEDOM	FREEDOM ONLY TO DO GOOD

thing that we do is evil, and that we of necessity do those things which are of no avail unto salvation? For if it is not we ourselves, but God only, that works salvation in us, it must follow, whether or not, that we do nothing unto salvation *before* the working of God in us.

But by *necessity*, I do not mean *compulsion*; but (as they term it) the *necessity of immutability*, not of *compulsion*: that is, a man void of the Spirit of God, does not evil against this will as by violence, or as if he were taken by the neck and forced to it, in the same way as a thief or a cut-throat is dragged to punishment against his will; but he does it spontaneously, and with a desirous willingness. And this willingness and desire of doing evil he cannot, by his own power, leave off, restrain, or change. . . .

When God works in us, the *will*, being changed and sweetly breathed on by the Spirit of God, desires and acts, not from *compulsion*, but *responsively*. . . .

Salvation means not merely the payment of penalty as the basis for forgiveness, but also the breaking of the bondage of the will towards sin. In the Fall, man ruined his spiritual life absolutely. But the ruin was not quite as complete with respect to other elements of his nature. Because of the interaction of his spiritual life and his relationship to other men, he severely crippled his social life. Because of the poisoning of his body and therefore of his brain also, he made his intellectual life defective in certain areas, but not in all. And because of this same poison ingested from the forbidden fruit he robbed himself of an original physical immortality and has become a dying creature from the moment of his birth. Physically we are but rubbish compared to Adam as created. We thus suffer fom spiritual death, social malaise, the darkening of our understanding, and physical mortality. When we are born again, the new birth restores our spiritual life (John 10:10); revitalizes our ability to relate to our fellow men (Rom. 15:5); renews our mind (2 Tim. 1:7); and gives us promise of physical resurrection in a new and glorious body (I Cor. 15:52, 53 and Phil. 3:21). This regenerative process which touches every aspect of our being is entirely the work of God; without it man's condition is hopeless.

The hopelessness of man's unredeemed condition is, however, not always apparent because the Common Grace of God acts to mask the fatal consequences of the Fall. Remove these restraints and the appalling evil which lies barely suppressed in man's heart is revealed in all its terrible reality. Potentially we are all capable of being a Nero or a Hitler. It is largely a question of lack of opportunity for self-expression. The simple act of coveting (which we have euphemistically renamed *ambition)* is stealing but for lack of opportunity. Lust is adultery but for lack of opportunity. Hatred is murder but for lack of opportunity. There is no difference between men in their potential for wickedness: only the accidents of life place different kinds of restraint upon each of us. In spite of man's tremendous creative energy, human nature is totally depraved at the source and any other view of man is dangerous in the extreme. This sad fact is recognized very clearly by the formulators of the *Westminster Confession* (XVIII.7):

> Works done by unregenerate men, although for the matter of them they be things which God commands, and of good use both to themselves and to others; yet because they proceed not from a heart purified by faith; nor are done in a right manner, according to the word; nor to a right end, the glory of God; they are therefore sinful, and cannot please God, or make a man meet to receive grace from God. And yet their neglect of them is more sinful and displeasing to God.

There is perhaps no better way to state the matter truthfully—man is essentially reduced only to the choice of evils. Of course, man may do some good by choosing the lesser of possible evils. Those who consistently manage to do this benefit mankind. But this is a deception. For a lesser evil is not in fact a positive good.

In the New Testament Jesus Christ expressly states that men do good to one another. On a horizontal plane and in man-to-man relationships there is this kind of goodness. Luke 6:33 records the Lord's words as follows: "If you do good to them that do good to you, what reward do you have? For even sinners do the same." That there should be no reward for this kind of goodness implies that it is not meritorious, but expedient only. Seen in the light of hidden motivation, man's goodness is destitute of true virtue because it springs from a poisoned source and is indeed fundamentally self-serving. We have only to observe in ourselves our reaction when some supposedly genuine deed of kindness is credited to someone other than ourselves. We are at once offended, hurt, aggressive or withdrawing. We resent being robbed of that ministry.

In the process of conversion there are several discernible steps, each of which is divinely initiated. Man is purely the recipient, making no more contribution towards his spiritual birth than he did towards his natural birth, or than inanimate Adam did towards his own animation when God turned him into a living soul. Whatever the circumstances surrounding any particular conversion, we normally view the process as being one of repentance followed by saving faith.

Repentance may or may not mean "sorrow for sins." It often does, but not always. Sometimes there is no very great sense of guilt at the time of conversion, as I know from personal experience. Some tremble with an overwhelming apprehension of the terrors of the judgment to come, and casting themselves before God they cry aloud for mercy. Others experience a kind of emptiness and meaninglessness and say, "Oh, that I might find Him!" And then there are those who are suddenly stopped in their tracks as Paul was, and immediately exclaim, "Lord, what wilt Thou have me to do?" People who experience little sense of personal wickedness at the time often become increasingly conscious of unworthiness as they mature in their Christian life. It is a growing experience. Paul began as the "least of the apostles," though an important individual because an apostle (1 Cor. 15:9). Later he described himself as the "least of all the saints" (Eph. 3:8), yet, as a saint, enormously privileged. But finally he had to confess himself the "chiefest of sinners" (1 Tim. 1:15).

Unbelievable as it may seem, this was progress! It was progress in truth, progress in integrity, progress towards the Lord. The closer we come to his glory the more clearly must we see our own unworthiness and shame, and our own darkness of soul. I am persuaded that when we are truly ready to go home to be with the Lord we shall hate sin with a perfect hatred, and be able to identify it in ourselves where we had been previously quite unaware of it.

Repentance really means "change of mind." This is the root meaning of the Greek word *metanoia:* a turn-around in attitude and point of view. We begin to look towards eternity with a new longing—and hence sometimes also with new apprehension lest we prove unworthy of it. This change is brought about by the renewing of the mind by the Holy Spirit, who in some mysterious way unlocks a deep-rooted mental barrier, making a new kind of thinking possible. Things that were unreasonable previously suddenly begin to appear as reasonable, and the unbelievable begins to become believable.

Repentance is thus a multidimensional word that signifies change in a number of directions. It is filled with the seeds of a new liberty of understanding. It is filled with promise of a new kind of spiritual vitality divinely engendered. It is above all the first step towards light and life and salvation. It is in no way self-generated, nor is it argued into being by the use of reason. It is supernatural. It is a gift of God. Scripture is very explicit on this subject, and rightly so because it is the first step towards eternal life.

Consider Romans 2:4: "Despiseth thou the riches of his goodness and forbearance and longsuffering; not knowing that the goodness of God *leadeth thee* to repentance?" It is the goodness of God and not the goodness of man that effects this fundamental reorientation. For this reason we are to be patient with those who seem unable or unwilling to understand. They are only acting according to their nature as we too acted according to ours until the Lord intervened. "In meekness instructing them that place themselves in opposition; lest God peradventure will *give them* repentance to the acknowledging of the truth" (2 Tim. 2:25).

So in Acts 5:31: "Him hath God exalted with his right hand to be a Prince and a Saviour for to *give* repentance to Israel and forgiveness of sins." Not only to Israel is this gift given but to Gentiles also. Thus Peter rejoiced greatly when he witnessed the rebirth of Gentiles so that he and his co-workers glorified God, saying, "Then hath God also to the Gentiles *granted* repentance unto life" (Acts 11:18).

The Old Testament reflects the same gracious truth. Psalm 65:4 reads: "Blessed is the man whom Thou choosest and causest to approach unto Thee that he may dwell in thy courts." And so likewise Lamentations 5:21: "Turn Thou us unto Thee, O Lord, and we shall be turned." It is the Lord Himself who gives a new heart (Jer. 24:7; Ezek. 11:19) and the Lord who opens the closed doors of the heart, making our response possible (Acts 16:14).

That such repentance unto life comes *before* saving faith is clear from many Scriptures. We do not live because we believe: we believe because we are made alive. The dead know not anything. "Whosoever liveth and believeth . . ." (John 11:26)—in that order. When Jesus said, "Ye do not believe because ye are not my sheep" (John 10:26), He was not saying, "Ye are not my sheep because ye do not believe." Similarly He said, "Ye therefore hear not [God's Word] because ye are not of God" (John 8:47); He did not say, "Ye are not God's children because ye will not hear his Word." Until the Spirit of God awakens the soul we *cannot* hear, for "the natural man receiveth not the things of the Spirit of God, for they are foolishness unto him: neither *can* he know them, because they are spiritually discerned"

(1 Cor. 2:14). Acts 13:48 illustrates the hedge that is set around the outcome of all preaching when it tells us that only as many as are "ordained to eternal life" actually respond believingly. Like the case of Lazarus, who must first have been animated before he could respond to the command to come forth from the tomb, so life precedes faith. "Whosoever believeth [present active participle, i.e., is believing] that Jesus is the Christ is born [perfect indicative passive, i.e., has been born] of God" (1 John 5:1).

It would be foolish to preach in a cemetery, trusting that some of the interred dead would hear the Gospel and come to life; and yet this is what many ministers are doing. Their congregations are cemeteries of spiritually dead people. Unless God makes some of them alive, they cannot possibly respond with saving faith and be redeemed. This is why Paul in writing to the Ephesians says that when we were dead in sins, we were quickened first and then raised up (Eph. 2:5, 6).

Moreover, it is not even our own faith but a faith given to us from the Father, channelled through the Son, and made effective through the power of the Holy Spirit. It is "by Him" (Jesus Christ) that we believe in God (1 Peter 1:21), a truth perceived by Peter from the very beginning of his ministry: "The faith which is by Him" (Acts 3:16). In both these instances the Greek is *dia autou*, through Him. Saving faith is not the human contribution of a sinner seeking salvation but the divine contribution of the gracious God seeking a sinner (Acts 18:27). We are saved by grace through faith (Eph. 2:8) and that not of ourselves. It is through faith as a channel that we are saved and not because of a faith of our own which is taken as a kind of guarantee of our earnestness. So also in 1 Corinthians 3:5, where Paul speaks of himself and Apollos as those *by* whom the Corinthians had believed. He does not speak of either of them as the originators of their faith but as the channels of it (*dia* with the genitive). To indicate the actual originator of this faith in the sense that a painter is the originator of his painting, the Greek word *dia* would have to be followed by the accusative, not by the genitive as it is in these instances. As Paul said to the Philippians (1:29), it had been *given* them to exercise saving faith. It was a gift.

The *Canons of Dort* rightly say: "That some receive the gift of faith from God, and others do not receive it, precedes from God's eternal decree. . . . According to which decree He graciously softens the heart of the elect, however obstinate, and inclines them to believe" (Chap. I, Art. 6). Calvin was even more specific when he wrote:

> But here we must beware of two errors: for some make man God's co-worker, to ratify election by his consent. Thus according to them, man's will is superior to God's plan. As if Scripture taught that we are merely given the ability to believe, and not, rather, faith itself! Others . . . make election depend upon faith as if [that election] were both in doubt and ineffectual until confirmed by faith. (*Inst.* III.xiv.3)

As Warfield put it, justification is through faith not on account of faith.[7] Augustine said, "We are not numbered among the elect because of foreseen faith but because of foreseen unbelief." It is man's natural inability to exercise saving faith while he is yet unsaved that makes Election so necessary. It is not an Election because of faith but an Election *to* faith. The Lord Jesus Christ is truly the "author of faith" (Heb. 12:2), the word *our* (preceding "faith") in the King James Version not being part of the original text. Thus it is really his salvation (Ps. 85:9; Luke 2:30; 3:6); it becomes our own only after we have received it as a gift (Phil. 2:12).

Although repentence and faith are both gifts, it is perfectly proper that God should command men everywhere to repent and believe (Acts 17:30). Such commands exhibit only what God requires of us, not what are his actual expectations. It is most important to realize this fact. God commands men to repent and believe though He knows perfectly that man has no power in himself to initiate such repentance or saving faith. They must be given to man from above. God commands men to love Him and to love their neighbour as themselves, though He knows that this is impossible for fallen man. Then why does He command impossibilities?

There are two answers. The first is in order to show man what are his requirements if man should demand the right to earn his own passage into heaven. God sets these standards of perfection as a man sets a plumb line against a wall (Amos 7:8) in order that the judgment may be just when the time comes. Man can never say, "I did not know what was required of me."

But there is also another reason. The law of God was given with the promise that if any man should fulfill it perfectly he would be declared not guilty of any offence, not worthy of any punishment, and under no sentence of death. As Moses said (Lev. 18:5): "Ye shall therefore do my statutes, and my judgments: which if a man do, he shall live." This was a serious promise, and not as hypothetical as it sounds. It is repeated in the New Testament with emphasis, for example in Romans 10:5 and Galatians 3:12. It is a valid promise, not a mockery. If a man never broke the commandment of God in any point, God would declare him righteous and worthy of heaven. He would enter heaven by right, needing no Saviour for sins. His name would never have been blotted out from the Book of Life.

One day a young man came to the Lord, seeking to *inherit* eternal life (Mark 10:17). In classical Greek this word was used with the meaning of "acquiring as a right." "How can I achieve this?" he asked. The Lord said, "Keep the commandments." Deceived by the simplicity of this, the young man asked, "Which?" And Jesus began to enumerate those commandments which He knew the young man had kept, and which the young man assured

---

7. Benjamin B. Warfield, *Calvin and Augustine*, p. 292.

Him he had kept. But then the Lord said, "If thou wilt be perfect . . ." (Matt. 19:21), and here is the problem. Heaven is for those made perfect.

To a certain lawyer who asked how he might earn eternal life (Luke 10:25-28) the Lord said, "What does the law say?" When the lawyer repeated the Great Commandment about loving God with all one's being, Jesus said, "This do, and thou shalt live!" This was a promise—the covenant of law that God had made with man. As it had been God's promise through Moses in Leviticus 18:5, so it had been the promise of God renewed through Ezekiel 20:11: "I gave them my statutes, and showed them my judgments, which if a man do, he shall even live in them." It was in effect when the Lord was present with us on earth, and so it is today. *If* a man fulfills the whole law, in its great summation of Luke 10:27 which combines Leviticus 19:18 with Deuteronomy 6:5, he has kept unbroken the old covenant of God with man.

Is perfection possible by this route? The answer must be Yes for unfallen man, but No for fallen man. It is no longer possible for us, but it was possible and was realized by the Lord Jesus Christ who fulfilled *all* righteousness (Matt. 3:15). The requirement is to fulfill all or nothing. As James 2:10 tells us: "Whosoever shall keep the whole law and yet offend in one point is guilty of all." While it is true that "he that doeth the law shall live," it is also true that one offence kills. If spiritual death is the consequence of sin in any form, whether great or small, there can be no half successes. "The soul that sinneth shall die" (Ezek. 18:4) is the corollary of "he that doeth the law shall live." Death is terribly once-for-all. As Ezekiel 33:13 states it so clearly: "When I say to the righteous that he shall surely live; if he trust in his own righteousness, and commit iniquity, all his righteousness shall not be remembered; but for his iniquity that he hath committed, he shall die for it." What could be plainer: many righteousnesses (plural) cannot compensate for one iniquity (singular). If the penalty of one offence is death it makes little difference whether a man commits one offence or hundreds of them. When hanging was the penalty for stealing, it was perfectly logical for a man to say, "One might as well be hanged for a sheep as a lamb, so why not steal a sheep?"

But is this principle really worth setting forth in Scripture if it is so hypothetical? Yes, indeed. God is assuring us that righteousness is possible for *man* and that any man who has never departed from the law will be truly without spot or blemish and therefore not worthy of death on his own account. And one Man did indeed perfectly fulfill it! The Lord Jesus Christ, having satisfied all the demands of the law (even the ritual ones) was without spot or blemish or sin of any kind, and was not therefore on his own account worthy of death. That is why He could be a Saviour of sinners by substituting for them. "God made Him who knew no sin to be a sin offering for us that we might be made the righteousness of God in Him" (2 Cor.

5:21). Thus He proved that the law was just and proper and capable of serving to demonstrate the sinlessness of the One who was to become a Saviour of men.

As for the rest of men, conceived in sin and born defective, there is no hope by this route. "There is none righteous, no, not one" (Rom. 3:10). "For all have sinned and come short of the glory of God" (Rom. 3:23). And what is this "glory of God"? It is none other than the Lord Himself (John 1:14), who is to be the plumb line, the standard by which we shall be judged (Amos 7:8), "because He hath appointed a day in which He will judge the world in righteousness by that man whom He hath ordained, whereof He hath given assurance unto all men in that He hath raised Him from the dead" (Acts 17:31).

Were human behaviour to be judged by our own defective standards, there could be no infallible standard of justice, for righteousness is absolute and relates equally to both action and motive. And the human heart is desperately wicked (Jer. 17:9). Man is potentially an appallingly evil creature and only by accident do some men appear less evil than others. But we are all spiritually dead, and there is not in any of us an impulse towards good in spiritual matters. When his mercy overwhelms us and clothes our nakedness, only then can we stand before Him without shame or fear. Otherwise, like Adam, we flee from Him and hide unless He intervenes.

So the initiative must rest with God and the first step has to be his, not ours. This first step is the infusion of life. It is truly a spiritual resurrection. The source of action is God's. This is an essential part of the meaning of Total Depravity.

There is nothing new about all this. It has been said in many different ways with equal force in every one of the great Confessions of churches with a Reformation faith. Thus in 1561 the *Belgic Confession* (Article XV: "Original Sin") made the following statement:

> We believe that through the disobedience of Adam original sin is extended to all mankind; which is a corruption of the whole nature and a hereditary disease, wherewith even infants in their mother's womb are infected, and which in man produces all sorts of sin, being in him as a root thereof, and therefore is so vile and abominable in the sight of God that it is sufficient to condemn all mankind. Nor is it altogether abolished or wholly eradicated even by baptism; since sin always issues forth from this woeful source, as water from a fountain; notwithstanding it is not imputed to the children of God unto condemnation, but by His grace and mercy is forgiven them. Not that they should rest securely in sin, but that a sense of this corruption should make believers often to sigh, desiring to be delivered from this body of death.

So also in the *Thirty-Nine Articles* of the Church of England in 1562 (Article IX: "Of Original or Birth-Sin"):

Original sin standeth not in the following of Adam (as the Pelagians do vainly talk); but it is the fault and corruption of the nature of every man, that naturally is engendered of the offspring of Adam: whereby man is very far gone from original righteousness, and is of his own nature inclined to evil, so that the flesh lusteth always contrary to the spirit; and therefore in every person born into this world, it deserveth God's wrath and damnation. And this infection of the nature doth remain, yea in them that are regenerated. . . .

Likewise the *Westminster Confession* of 1647 (Chap. VI: "Of the Fall of Man, of Sin, and of Punishment"):

By this sin they fell from their original righteousness and communion with God, and so became dead in sin, and wholly defiled in all the faculties and parts of soul and body.

From this original corruption, whereby we are utterly indisposed, disabled, and made opposite to all good, and wholly inclined to all evil, do proceed all actual transgressions.

This corruption of nature, during this life, doth remain in those that are regenerated. . . .

And the *Baptist Confession* of 1689 (Chap. 2: "Of the Fall of Man, of Sin, and of Punishment Thereof"):

Our first parents, by this sin, fell from their original righteousness and communion with God, and we in them, whereby death came upon all: all becoming dead in sin, and wholly defiled in all the faculties and parts of soul and body.

The Reformers recognized that while man is able to reason about temporal matters correctly (mathematics, for example), in all spiritual matters his understanding is darkened and his will is impotent towards righteousness and towards God. The Fall wholly corrupted his will, but only partially damaged his intellect.

Thus when an act is sinful and not merely a mistake, it is an expression of our will, of our fallen nature, just as when Satan lies "he speaketh of his own" (John 8:44), for he was and is a liar by nature. The *New American Standard Version* renders this: "He speaketh from his own nature." So likewise the *Revised Standard Version:* "He speaks according to his own nature." Man, too, is wilfully sinful in heart and mind. "The heart of the sons of men is fully set in them to do evil" (Eccles. 8:11). "Every imagination of the thoughts of his heart is only evil" (Gen. 6:5).

We see men performing good deeds towards their neighbours, as I have often experienced at the hands of my neighbours; and one cannot but be grateful both to them and to the Lord for their kindnesses. Nevertheless long experience teaches that it is the secret motive, the motive often never even consciously recognized by the doer himself, that God judges. For He judges the thoughts and intents of the heart and looks not on the outward man (1 Sam. 16:7). We would recognize that even such kindnesses as these are poisoned at the source if we could only see them as God sees them. In a real sense man's inhumanity to man, to use Shakespeare's famous phrase, is no worse than his *humanity* to man. Both are fundamentally self-serving, though the one has all the appearance of evil and the other all the appearance of good.

The *Augsburg Confession* (XVIII.I) says:

> It is also taught among us that man possesses some measure of freedom of the will which enables him to live an outwardly honourable life and to make choices among things that reason comprehends. But without the grace, help, and activity of the Holy Spirit, man is not capable of making himself acceptable to God.

To act acceptably before men is not beyond most of us for much of our lives, because outward conformity to the cultural standards of our society is usually advantageous and does not require that we be inwardly what we seem to be outwardly. But to act acceptably before God is quite a different thing for He demands *inward* conformity. Concealment is proper in social relationships and is largely covered by the word *courtesy*. In many aspects of social intercourse, human behaviour is acceptable and the exchange of service, ideas, and materials proceeds smoothly and without the effects of the Fall creating any serious disruptions. Thus subsequently there were added to this statement from the *Augsburg Confession* the following words: "We are not denying freedom to the human will. The human will has freedom to choose among the works and things which *reason by itself* can grasp." Yet so many human relations depend upon the integrity of the contracting parties that in the *Formula of Concord* (I.3) the true inner situation is spelled out more darkly: "Original Sin is not a slight corruption of human nature, but is so deep a corruption that nothing sound or uncorrupted has survived in man's body or soul, in the inward or the outward powers." Indeed, "this damage is so unspeakable that it may not (even) be recognized by a rational process, but only from God's Word."

This is a grim picture indeed. Oddly it is a picture that is being increasingly admitted by the more perceptive psychiatrists of our time—as it was by Freud.

When an unregenerate man by the grace of God begins to truly despair of his own nature, he is often, as Luther put it, "near akin to divine grace." To preach that man need not despair of himself is to challenge God's design to bring men near to grace by this means. It is also a demonstration of the damage done to the powers of reason by the very defect which is being denied.

What then does man have in his unredeemed, totally depraved state upon which God can act? He has eyes, but is blind. God can restore his vision. He has ears that are deaf. God can open his ears. He *has* a heart, but it is of stone. God can convert it to a heart of flesh. He has a spirit, but it is dead. God can make it live. So God has made man with the capacity to see, hear, and act responsively to his inspiring, but he cannot act until he is made alive. He cannot come forth from the tomb until he has been given a new life. Only *then* does he hear the voice of God saying, "Come forth."

When the Lord knocks at the door of a man's heart he cannot hear *for he is deaf.* Only when God opens his ears does he hear. And even then *when he hears* he is likely at first to say, "I am in no convenient position to open. My children are in bed, the door is locked, we are 'closed for the night,' please don't bother me now!" (Luke 11:5-8). Only the caller's persistence, not the householder's desire to entertain the caller, drives him in the end to open the door; the Spirit of God acting upon his heart makes him a willing host. It is God's persistent knocking at the door of man's heart and not man's persistent knocking at the gates of heaven that brings the elect finally to salvation.

Such, then, is the nature of the Total Depravity of man.

7

UNCONDITIONAL ELECTION

The Scriptures make it very clear that Election to salvation is in no way conditioned by or dependent upon anything that distinguishes the saved from the unsaved prior to the day of their effectual calling to become members of the blameless family of God. It is "of the same lump" that both saved and unsaved are constituted (Rom. 9:21). "There is no difference, for *all* have sinned and come short of the glory of God" (Rom. 3:22, 23). As persons before God the elect have nothing inherent in their character to make them to differ from the non-elect that was not received either by genetic endowment or the conditioning of circumstances. Wherever we imagine we can detect differences we have to ask the question, "Who maketh thee to differ from another? And what hast thou that thou didst not receive? Now if thou didst receive it, why dost thou glory as if thou hadst not received it?" (1 Cor. 4:7). "We *all* had our conversation in times past in the lusts of our flesh, fulfilling the desires of the flesh, and of the mind, and were by nature the children of wrath, *even as others*" (Eph. 2:3).

Sometimes it is argued that there are differences between us, even though these differences are due to divinely overruled providential circumstances, so that there is really no room for boasting about them. But could not God choose us, then, on the grounds of these foreseen differences which we owe to Him in the first place and which He has been pleased to ordain as useful to his purposes in particular ways? Election might then be based on foreknowledge of special aptitudes which are not to our credit but are advantageous to God.

Undoubtedly there is an election which is not to salvation but to the fulfillment of a specific duty or to the playing of a role. We see this in the case of Judas Iscariot. The Lord said, "Have I not chosen [elected] you twelve, and one of you is a devil?" (John 6:70). Judas Iscariot was chosen. But his being chosen was not to salvation. He had an awesome part to play in the plan of redemption. Since he thus fulfilled a role for which he was appointed as one of the elected apostles, was God just in punishing him? "Thou wilt say then unto me, Why doth He yet find fault, for who hath resisted his will?" (Rom. 9:19). And the answer must be that no man is ever condemned simply for fulfilling the Lord's will. Actions in themselves are not so judged. It is the intent of the heart behind the action that is judged, not the action itself. The same act performed by two agents, one with evil intent and the other with sorrow, believing that God is calling him to such action, may fulfill the same end in carrying forward the purposes of God, but the two agents will certainly be judged differently—the one for his evil intention, and the other for his good. Cyrus was chosen of God (Isa. 45:1-4) to provide for the return of God's people to the Promised Land, because their society was required there to form the receptacle for the Lord Jesus' ministry and witness on earth; yet Cyrus was evidently not elected unto salvation.

To be elected to an evil task or to fulfill an evil role is not necessarily to be elected to an unusual condemnation. Condemnation is destined, and therefore pre-destined, for all who have failed to achieve the moral perfection that God requires of man. Those elected specifically to salvation do not face this condemnation. But it is not because of the mere fact of Election: it is because they are elected *to salvation*. There are many kinds of election. The Lord Jesus Christ was "elect," but certainly not elect unto salvation (1 Peter 2:6). And the elect angels were not elected to salvation, but apparently elected never to fall (1 Tim. 5:21). The non-elect angels who fell, fell by being disobedient—not because they were elected to disobey.

Thus it comes about that among those who raucously added their voices to the murderous crowd shouting, "Crucify Him! Crucify Him!" were some who later were saved by reason of the very death of the One whom they in their wickedness condemned to be crucified. These men were not more wicked than others. They were men caught up in circumstances which gave their fallen nature exceptional opportunity to reveal itself. Circumstances favoured their wicked propensities which were therefore expressed in ways that the wicked propensities of other men have not had opportunity to find expression. But there is no difference fundamentally between us; it is all a matter of opportunity. Natural man, whether yet to be the object of God's favour by Election to salvation or not to be the object of that favour, is everywhere of the same stuff. We are all potentially capable of the worst crimes, until we are re-created in Christ Jesus.

David, Israel's most noble king, and Ahab, Israel's most wicked one, both alike coveted and ended up as murderers. Uriah the Hittite was as surely murdered by David, who coveted his wife, as Naboth was murdered by Ahab, who coveted his vineyard. And both men, curiously enough, lacked the moral courage to carry out the murder personally. David had his general do it for him, and Ahab his wicked wife. It is no wonder that the Reformers spoke of us all as "miserable sinners," for so we are.

Then what advantage is it to a man to be a child of God as David was, as opposed to being a child of the devil like Ahab? The answer is clear enough in Scripture. Ahab was totally indifferent to his wickedness; David in the deep penitence of his soul wrote Psalm 51. The difference is not in the action itself but in what the doing did to the doer. David was not mistakenly chosen by God because God thought he was essentially a good and noble man incapable of any great wrongdoing. He was not chosen of God because he was great, but he became a great saint because he was chosen of God. It was the Spirit of God who brought David to the writing of Psalm 51 and thus distinguished him so radically from Ahab in spite of the similarity of their behaviour in their selfish exercise of power.

As we have already seen, the grace of God does not search for men who are willing to accept it, although the Lutherans finally adopted essentially this position even as the Arminians did. The grace of God *makes* men willing, not *finds* men willing. It is as Romans 9:15 and 16 says: "I will have mercy on whom I will have mercy, and I will have compassion on whom I will have compassion. So then, it is not of him that willeth nor of him that runneth, but of God that showeth mercy." It should be borne in mind that the first part of this sentence is a quotation from the Old Testament (Exod. 33:19), demonstrating that God has always acted on this principle.

Nor are some men elected to salvation because God *foresees* that they will believe, but because He *foreknows that none will.* But for the Election of God the Lord would have died in vain. All alike are "concluded in unbelief" (Rom. 11:32) so that God's mercy is unconditional. As Calvin put it *(Inst.* III.xxii.8): "The grace of God does not find men fit to be chosen but makes them fit." And Augustine said: "Man is converted not because he wills to be, but he wills to be because he is ordained to election." Or again, as J. I. Packer has observed, "Where the Arminian says 'I owe my election to my faith,' the Calvinist says 'I owe my faith to my election.' "[1]

Now the battle lines are drawn more critically within the ranks of those who do not question the fact of Election. Shakespeare said, "The nearer in blood, the nearer bloody," and there are no quarrels so bitter as between those who stand together upon some great doctrine which is rejected by the vast majority of other men. Calvinists and Arminians alike accepted the fact of Election unequivocally. It is not the fact of Election which is in question between them, but the basis upon which that Election is established. Even among themselves not all Calvinists are entirely agreed upon all points, for many who call themselves Calvinistic have rejected one of the Five Points, the Point which is to be discussed in the next chapter, namely, Limited Atonement. But these differences do not cause the same bitter divi-

---

1. Introductory Essay in John Owen, *Death of Death*, p. 7.

sions as do differences of opinion respecting the basis of Election. The Arminians, including in this respect both Lutherans and Methodists, accept the fact of Election since they accept the Word of God which speaks of Election so frequently. But they hold that it is based upon foreknowledge, God's foreknowledge of man's response. The Calvinists hold that such foreknowledge is not the basis of Election since there is no merit in any individual which could be the subject of that foreknowledge. Calvinists hold that the basis of Election is entirely concealed, one of those matters hidden from us in the secret counsels of God (Deut. 29:29). It is not based, we believe, upon any foreseen merit or anticipated worthiness of the individual. It can only be said to be "according to his good pleasure" (Eph. 1:5). Why it should please God to elect one man and pass another by is never revealed.

Arminians, broadly speaking, hold that Election is based upon God's foreknowledge of *who will actively co-operate with God* in the saving of his own soul. Lutherans hold that it is based upon God's foreknowledge of *who will not resist* his invitation to accept salvation as an outright gift. Wesleyans believe that it is based upon God's foreknowledge of *who will persevere* to the end. All have certain key texts to which they appeal and to which they give the weight of emphasis necessary to counterbalance the testimony of the rest of Scripture as a whole.

That Election is based on foreknowledge seems to be clearly stated in Romans 8:29, a key verse in this controversy and indeed the only verse which seems clearly to support the thesis: "For whom He did foreknow, He also did predestinate to be conformed to the image of his Son, that He might be the first-born among many brethren." Let us therefore consider this key passage carefully and examine some of the implications which follow if the word *foreknowledge* as used in this instance means what we customarily assume it to mean.

First of all, it should be observed that almost all modern versions of a scholarly nature have rendered this passage in such a way as to suggest that they do not view the word *foreknowledge* in its commonly accepted sense. They have evidently understood it to mean something rather different from ordinary foresight. The truth is not found merely by an appeal to majority opinion, yet if the majority can be shown to be not unduly biased but to have been guided by principles of sound scholarship even where they disagree with the evangelical position respecting the nature of the Gospel of Grace, then majority opinion carries extra weight. In many versions, the rendering adopted is not based on a prejudice towards Calvinism for the translators are often not Calvinistic in their private theology. Their testimony sometimes carries even greater weight when it is borne in mind that many of these translators do not view with any sympathy the idea of verbal inspiration. By ordinary standards of assessment with respect to personal bias, the broad testimony of the translations which follow is impressive because there is a measure of agreement as to the meaning of the passage in question even among those who would not agree on many other crucial issues which hinge upon it.

Here are some excerpts from eleven of the best-known modern versions. As will be observed by those who know the backgrounds of these translations, they were by no means all produced by evangelicals, much less by men of Calvinistic persuasion. To avoid any appearance of an attempt to build a case by special ordering, I have simply set them down in alphabetical order. I have also carefully respected the use of capitals by the original authors, a use which can have significance since it sometimes reflects the author's reverence and respect for his subject.

ALTERNATIVE RENDERINGS OF ROMANS 8:29

1. *An American Translation* (Smith and Goodspeed; Chicago: University of Chicago Press, 1923): "For those whom he had marked out from the first he predestinated to be made like his Son."

2. *The Emphasized Bible* (Joseph B. Rotherham; Grand Rapids: Kregel, 1959): "For whom He fore-approved He also fore-appointed to be conformed unto the image of his Son."

3. *Good News for Modern Man* (London: British and Foreign Bible Society, 1966): "For those whom God had already chosen he had also set apart to become like his Son."

4. *The Holy Bible in Modern English* (Ferrar Fenton; London: Black, 1903): "For He previously knew them, and appointed them to conformity with the image of his Son."

5. *The Jerusalem Bible* (ed. Alexander Jones; New York: Doubleday & Co., 1966): "They are the ones he chose specially long ago and intended to become true images of his Son."

6. *The New English Bible* (Oxford University Press and Cambridge, 1970): "For God knew his own before ever they were, and also ordained that they should be shaped to the likeness of his Son."

7. *The New Testament: A New Translation*, Vol. 2 (William Barclay; London: Collins, 1969): "For long ago, before they ever came into being, God both knew them and marked them out to become like the pattern of his Son."

8. *The New Testament: A New Translation* (James Moffatt; New York: Hodder & Stoughton, no date): "For he decreed of old that those whom he predestined should share the likeness of his Son."

9. *The New Testament: An Expanded Translation* (Kenneth S. Wuest; Grand Rapids: Eerdmans, 1961): "Because those whom He foreordained He also marked out beforehand as those who were to be conformed to the derived image of His Son."

10. *The New Testament: A Translation in the Language of the People* (Charles B. Williams; Chicago: Moody Press, 1937): "For those on whom *He set His heart beforehand* He marked off as His own to make like His Son." (A footnote says: Literally, *foreknew*, but in the LXX used as translated.)

11. *The Twentieth Century New Testament* (Chicago: Moody Bible Institute, 1967): "For those whom God chose from the first he also did predestinate to be conformed to the image of his Son."

One further rendering is worthy of note, though it is not strictly a translation but an interpretation. *The Amplified New Testament* (Grand Rapids: Zondervan, 1958) reads: "For those whom He foreknew—of whom He was aware and loved beforehand—He also did predestinate from the beginning (foreordaining them) to be molded in the image of His Son (and share inwardly His likeness)." The interesting point here is the introduction of the idea of loving *beforehand* as an essential part of the meaning of the word *foreknow* in this passage. It is fully justified as will be seen.

By contrast many valuable modern translations have made no attempt to clarify the sense of the text beyond giving a more or less conventional rendering. This is true of *The New International Version* and of *The New American Standard Version*, which is beloved by many who still appreciate the "old English" aura of the King James Version.

On the other hand one may read a paraphrase such as *The Living Bible* and suddenly become aware of the extent to which Arminianism underlies the theology of some of the great evangelists of our time, whose ministry is so wonderfully blessed of God and yet whose presentation of the Gospel seems to leave the final decision with man himself. The strong recommendation which such men give to *The Living Bible* cannot but contribute in the end to a faith that is indeed saving yet basically betrays the true Gospel by its emphasis on the part man plays in his own salvation. By such men, Predestination is assumed to be based upon a foreknowledge by God of a deserving earnestness and humility of spirit in those who will, because of a meritorious assessment of their own need, accept the Lord Jesus as their personal Saviour. Their salvation is seen to depend upon their willingness to accept, and the fact that God foresees their willingness to accept is thus made the basis of their Predestination. That these have willingness where others do not implies a difference between men in their unregenerate state, a difference which Scripture does not recognize. To shift the crux of the matter one step further back and say that this willingness arises from the gracious softening influences of God the Holy Spirit does not ease the problem, because we still have to ask, Why does the Holy Spirit succeed in softening only these hearts and not the hearts of others? We are hemmed in on both sides until we have to confess either that the Election of God is based on something that is secret and unrelated to the recipient of grace, *or that the individual determines his own destiny by his response.* Then we must ask further, Why do some respond and not others? And the only answer we can give is that those who respond are in some fundamental way better people. Either God is sovereign and Election is an expression of God's will, or man is sovereign and Election is an expression of God's foreknowledge. *The Living Bible* reveals the author's choice of alternatives by rendering Romans 8:29 as follows: "For from the very beginning God decided that those who came to him—and all along he knew who would—should become like his Son."

This breathes Arminianism and the sovereignty of man, and a certain inherent goodness and merit in all those who become the elect of God. God knows who will come to Him, and on the basis of this foreknowledge makes his plans for them. He decides what *He* will do with them after *they* have decided what they will do with his grace. The ultimate decision rests with the individual, not with God.

As we have already noted, it is not necessary for the individual to be able to formulate or even to recognize the sovereignty of God's grace, in order to be a genuine believer. And thus there are many earnest believers among us who are indeed God's elect and yet live by the supposition that God is really *their* choice. God did not choose them; "they made their decision for God." But the Lord Jesus said, "Ye have *not* chosen Me, but I have chosen *you*" (John 15:16). That this emphasis upon human decision is indeed the emphasis of the great evangelistic campaigns of today is sadly true. And because the decision is accredited to the individual himself, evangelism is largely committed to exploiting techniques of persuasion. And because these techniques as developed by the world have proved so effective in the market place they tend to be uncritically adopted in the evangelistic campaign.

To the Calvinist, the tactic of persuasion is less important: not unimportant, but less so. Much more important is the assurance that God's Word will bear fruit as He sees fit (Isa. 55:11) because God is sovereign and the responsibility for the fruitfulness of the Gospel is not ours but God's. The whole emphasis is thus placed upon the sovereign grace of God and not upon the persuasive powers of the evangelist. It is equally important that the newborn child of God should realize it has not been his own faith, his own decision, his own repentance, his own yielding, his own commitment, his own earnestness, his own sincerity, his own *anything*—that brought about his new birth. His new birth is entirely the result of, and is timed by, the sovereign grace of God from whom he received his faith, his repentance, his yielding, his *everything*. Salvation is a gift of God whether we strive for "results" by pressure or merely present the truth, trusting that God knows what He is about. Such evangelistic pressuring has resulted in the birth of untold numbers of premature babies in Christ who, unless they receive the same kind of personal and constant (often even *heroic*) care that hospitals

provide for premature babies, spend the rest of their Christian lives trying
to catch up, forever demanding milk when they should be receiving meat.
Strong men in the Lord are men brought up on strong meat in the Word.
Spiritual babies kept on the bottle when they should have been weaned
from milk and given meat are slow to mature and many never do so.

In these various excerpts from versions of the last hundred years, it is
clear that the use of the word *also (kai* in the original Greek) separates the
foreknowing from the Predestination. The text does not say that "He knew
that they would be saved" but (a) He foreknew them and (b) also predestined them to be perfected as saints. The majority of the versions quoted
follow the King James Version by introducing the word *also.* The omission
of *also* changes the whole meaning of the passage. It makes the two clauses
dependent and causally related. To say "whom He did foreknow, He predestinated" is to make Predestination dependent upon foreknowledge. To
say "whom He did foreknow, He *also* predestinated" is clearly to separate
the two divine activities. Each of the two clauses stands in its own right as a
separate statement of fact.

The difference is important, for in point of fact the word *foreknew* in this
context is probably not being used in the common English sense of mere
foresight. As noted in Williams' rendering the word has more than one
meaning, and judging by the above eleven translations, this fact was
recognized implicitly. The most explicit version is that of Williams, who attaches to the word the specific sense of "loving concern," a meaning which
the Greek word can actually carry.

The Septuagint (LXX) Greek rendering of the Hebrew Scriptures produced by a group of Jewish scholars sometime in the third century B.C. provides us with a valuable insight as to how the Jews of our Lord's day used
many important words which reappear in the Greek of the New Testament.
The word rendered *foreknow* in Romans 8:29 is *proegnō* (προέγνω), the
third person singular aorist indicative of *proginōskō* (προγινώσκω) which
commonly means "to know beforehand," "to be previously acquainted
with." But this basic meaning can be understood in two rather different
ways in Greek. It can mean to have known *someone* previously or it can
mean to know *something* in advance. In Acts 26:5 Paul wrote, "who *knew
me from the beginning* if they would but testify . . . ," using this word *proginōskō.* The context favours the idea of previous acquaintance with
somebody rather than a foreseeing of future history.

The Septuagint translated the Old Testament Hebrew word *yāda*, which
means "to know," "to regard," "to care for," by the Greek word *ginōskō*
(γινώσκω). In his treatment of *ginōskō* in Kittel's *Theological Dictionary of
the New Testament,* Bultmann comments that the compound form *proginōskō* has the more basic meaning of foreordaining or electing rather than
merely foreknowing, even as *yāda* can also mean "to elect." In Romans 11:2

the implication, he believes, is that in this previous acquaintance God had been caring for his children. A parallel to this kind of usage may be observed in 2 Timothy 2:19: "The Lord knoweth *[ginōskō]* them that are his," by which we are surely to understand that He recognizes them that are his by caring for them in a special way. By contrast, there are those who are turned away from being favoured, to whom the Lord addressed the fatal words in Matthew 7:23—"Depart from Me. . . . I never knew you"— where the word *ginōskō* again appears.

The Old Testament equivalent, as we have noted, is the Hebrew word *yāda*. It is found in Psalm 1:6: "The Lord knoweth [i.e., cares for] the way of the righteous; but the ways of the ungodly shall perish." In Psalm 31:7 David wrote: "I will be glad and rejoice in thy mercy; for Thou hast considered my trouble; Thou hast known [i.e., cared for] my soul in adversities." And so also in Nahum 1:7: "The Lord is good, a strong hold in the day of trouble; and He knoweth [i.e., cares for] them that trust in Him."

One of the most striking Old Testament examples of this use is found in Genesis 18:19: "For I have known [Abraham] that he will command his children and his household after him, and they shall keep the way of the Lord, to do justice and judgment; that the Lord may bring upon Abraham that which He hath spoken of him." In the original, the Hebrew is rather explicit in conveying a slightly more complex meaning. Understood as the King James Version has rendered it, this looks simply like foresight: "I know he will do this and that, and so I shall bring upon him this and that. . . ." The Hebrew actually says: "For I have known him *in order that* he may command," etc. The text is most explicit here: there is no ambiguity. The words *in order that* appear in the original. A number of modern versions have taken cognizance of this fact and so rendered it. These include Rotherham's *The Emphasized Bible*, Smith and Goodspeed's *The Complete Bible: An American Translation*, *The New American Standard Version*, *The Revised Standard Version*, Ferrar Fenton's *The Holy Bible in Modern English*, the *French Crampon Bible*, *The Jerusalem Bible*, a new translation of the Jewish Publication Society which is simply called *The Torah*, and *Today's English Version (The Good News Bible)* just issued.

Here, then, we have a clear case of personal acquaintance which becomes the reason for something predestinated with respect to the subject's future. It is not a case of foresight but of foreordination. "I have cared for Abraham *in order that* certain things may happen to him in the future." The foreknowing (used in this sense) did not signify *foresight of* future events but deliberate *ordination of* those events. What God is assuring his children in Romans 8:29 is not that He has foreseen our favourable response to his call when the time comes and has therefore decided that we shall duly be conformed to the image of his Son. It is rather that He loved us in anticipation and determined, for reasons entirely hidden from us, that we should be conformed to the image of his Son by an act of his sovereign grace. And though we often despair of this conforming ever being fulfilled, yet we have this assurance that He who hath begun a good work in us will carry it on (*epiteleo*, ἐπιτελέω) until the day of Jesus Christ (Phil. 1:6).

If such an interpretation should appear strained, it does so only because we have habitually depended upon the King James Version for so many years and therefore assume the more familiar sense to be the true one. Those who are persuaded that our Election is based on foreknowledge will be reluctant indeed to surrender the only text in Scripture which they can point to that seems clearly to support such a view. That the rest of Scripture either by implication or by plain statement does not support such a view will tend to be neglected. The fact that so many modern translations, written by men individually or in committees, translate Romans 8:29 in a way which shows that the sense is not really that which the Arminians have favoured is a very powerful argument against the Arminian claim. Certainly many of these translations, if they do have a bias, would tend to be towards Arminianism. Yet the translators have refrained from allowing their bias to guide their translation.

The rest of Scripture, Old and New Testaments alike, clearly puts the basis of God's elective choice entirely outside the subject's own worthiness. In the Old Testament this is quite explicit:

> I, even I, am He that blotteth out thy transgressions *for mine own sake*, and will not remember thy sins (Isa. 43:25).

It is purely a matter of his good pleasure and the only other certain thing about it is that the choice was made before the foundation of the world.

> [God] hath chosen us in Him before the foundation of the world . . . having predestinated us into the adoption of children by Jesus Christ to Himself, according to the good pleasure of his will (Eph. 1:4, 5).

> God hath from the beginning chosen you unto salvation (2 Thess. 2:13).

> Who hath saved us and called us with a holy calling . . . according to his own purpose and grace which was given us in Christ Jesus before the world began (2 Tim. 1:9).

> [The names of the elect are] . . . written in the book of life from the foundation of the world (Rev. 17:8).

Now there are two questions which demand serious consideration since they challenge the justice of God if they are answered amiss. In the first place: Is God by electing some on an apparently arbitrary basis in no way dependent upon their worthiness or unworthiness to be chosen, thereby automatically condemning the rest to punishment whether they are worthy to be punished or not?

Formulated in this way, the question inevitably invites reasonable objection. But should the question be so formulated? Is man condemned to reprobation simply because he is not elected to salvation? The answer must be a most emphatic No! He is condemned to punishment for his sins, not for his non-election.

It may be helpful to use an analogy we have previously considered. Suppose ten men are in prison, justly incarcerated for crimes of which they are proven guilty, and let us also suppose for the sake of simplicity that each man has committed a similar crime. Then let us further suppose that the Governor of the State or the Premier of the Province in which they are prisoners has the right to grant a reprieve for one of the men. Since all the men are in prison with equal justification, the choice of the one to be set free is, from the point of justice, an indifferent one. All are equally guilty and *any one* of them might therefore be granted the reprieve with equal justification. None are less guilty or more guilty.

For reasons not in any way related to the individual's worthiness or unworthiness, but in some way reflecting the Governor's or the Premier's good pleasure, reprieve is granted to one man and he is set free. Now it must be asked, Why are the remaining nine prisoners still in jail? Is it really because they were not released? It might at first appear to be so, but in actual fact these other nine men would all be set free if they had fulfilled their prison term. The reason they are not all set free is that they have not yet paid the full penalty of their misconduct. The nine who are left in prison are therefore in prison still, not because they were not reprieved, but because they were put in prison for their crimes and have not yet satisfied the demands of justice. The release of the one reprieved man has no bearing on the retention of the other nine. The reprieved man owes his freedom entirely to the graciousness of the one who has authorized it; the retention of the remainder is owing entirely to their own guilt. To argue that the election of one is the cause of the condemnation of the others is clearly irrational. Those who are granted saving faith and are accordingly redeemed are not the cause of the lost condition of those who remain under condemnation. As John 3:17 and 18 says specifically, "God sent not his Son into the world to condemn the world. . . . He that believeth not is condemned *already.*" The unbeliever is not condemned for his refusal of God's salvation. He merely *remains* under condemnation because he has not believed. The critical term in this case is the word *already.*

Consider another analogy. If I hold a ball in my hand it will not fall. If I let go, it does. But my letting it go does not *cause* its fall; letting it go merely allows it to respond freely to gravitation, which is the cause of its falling. This is easily recognized by the fact that in the absence of gravity I could release it and it would not fall. In a spacecraft, opening my hand would have no such effect. From this we see clearly that *allowing* something to happen is not at all the same as *causing* it to happen. God did not condemn the rest of men to perdition simply because He elected some to be saved. Those not chosen were already condemned by their own guilt and God has simply left them in that position. But it needs to be emphasized that those who are elected to be saved are originally in precisely the same situation. They are not elect because they are less guilty. "All have sinned and come short of the glory of God" (Rom. 3:23). All come from the "same lump" (Rom. 9:21).

If there should be ten apples lying in the grass under a tree and you stoop down, choose one, and pick it up, it would be irrational indeed to accuse you of placing the other nine on the ground. They fell there because they are subject to gravity. This is how they came to be there. You, by your selection, have merely raised one of them which was sharing the same debasement with the others.

For some years Calvin himself seems to have drawn the erroneous and (probably even to himself) unwelcome conclusion that Election to salvation has a necessary corollary "Election to reprobation." He never seems to have quite resolved this conclusion of false reasoning, because he did not see that it really is false. He wrote (*Inst.* III.xxiii.1): "Indeed, many, as if they wished to avert a reproach from God, accept election in such terms as to deny that anyone is condemned. But this they do very ignorantly and childishly since election itself could not stand except as set over against reprobation." Elsewhere, Calvin reaffirms this *non sequitur* by arguing: "Jesus said that 'every plant which my heavenly Father has not planted shall be rooted up' (Matt. 15:13), which plainly means that all whom the heavenly Father has not deigned to plant as sacred trees in his field are marked and intended to destruction." But Matthew 15:13 is quite specific in saying that these bad seeds were not planted by the Father at all. They were planted by an enemy, as Jesus Himself had already made clear in a parable (Matt. 13:28).

Furthermore, it cannot be argued safely that the plants which He had *not* planted were actually intended for destruction unless we assume that God intended their planting. That the sinner reaps the harvest of his own sins is inevitable. This is part of the absolute moral law of the universe, as absolute as its physical laws though not always so immediately fulfilled as to consequences. Because of the existence of this moral fabric, the evil plantings were doomed, destined to be gathered and cast into the fire (Matt. 13:30). Since God sees the future as though it were the present, it was and is not inappropriate to speak of what is destined as being pre-destined. God did not need to do anything save only to allow the moral laws of his universe to work themselves out. Sinners are appointed to judgment as hailstones are appointed to fall to the earth. No divine intervention is required.

It is evident that God's foreknowledge would allow Him to predestine *the non-elect* to reprobation without making Him responsible for their sin. He foresees that because they are not elect to salvation, they will not believe and their destiny will be reprobation. God's foreknowledge of the elect stands in a different relationship, for in this case it is foreknowledge based on his own predetermination to elect them to salvation. The two cases are not parallel. Predestination to Election is not based upon foreseen faith but is *the cause* of that faith. Predestination to reprobation is based on foreseen unbelief. Such foreknowledge is reactive, not causative. Predestination to salvation is the ground (Lat. *materia)* of foreordained faith; Predestination to reprobation is the result of (Lat. *propter)* foreseen unbelief. In the first, Predestination is cause; in the second, Predestination is effect, for here Predestination is not the *cause* of unbelief but the consequence of unbelief.

Divine intervention is required to halt this destined course of events, and so the sovereign grace of God acts upon the same stuff of fallen man to change the destiny of some. As the prisoners who were in jail could blame no one but themselves, so the man who is reprieved can thank no one but his liberator. Those who suffer for their sins have themselves to thank; those who are elect have only God to thank. I think it virtually certain that there will be no recriminations in hell even as there will be no boasting in heaven, for the whole truth will then be known and acknowledged. God will not be blamed by the unsaved for their condemnation, for God's justice will be admitted by all (Rom. 3:19); while the saved will claim no merit, for God's grace will be admitted by all (Rev. 5:9, 10, 12). The elect will acknowledge that they were by nature the children of wrath "even as others" (Eph. 2:3).

Yet one more question still remains. If man's only hope of salvation lies in his Election, why does not God save all men? To this question we have only a partial answer and it is based on logic. Though human reason may be at fault in such matters, we cannot altogether escape the compulsion of this logic. There appear to be only four possible alternatives governing the Lord's actions in this matter. He can either save all by electing all, save none by electing none, save some but not others, or not create man with freedom of choice in the first place. Of course, without such freedom of choice man would have been a mere puppet, his worship would have been meaningless, his obedience as mechanical as that of the toy baby doll which can be wound up, and his devotion would have been a sham. He would have been less than an animal, a mere thing, a mockery of a creation with capacities that were entirely without purpose or reason.

Let us consider, then, the first three alternatives, assuming that man was created in the beginning with freedom to choose either to obey or disobey God's injunctions.

If God were to save all by electing all, what would be the implications? We know that man initially was given freedom to choose to obey or disobey. By his wrong choice, man forfeited his power to will God's will. As a consequence, in order to convert man back to the truth, God must override his will to enable him once more to be free to obey. It is true that He accomplishes this turning around by a gentle process of which the individual is normally scarcely aware. But it is a sovereign act, nevertheless, initiated by God not man. Unless this is done, man remains entirely impotent. All resurrections from death whether physical or spiritual are of this nature. The dead neither resist nor co-operate in the process. The process of giving life to the dead is one in which the dead are entirely passive. It cannot be otherwise. Life is not offered to them but conferred upon them. To this extent it is true to say that man's will is overruled, although there is a sense in which, if the analogy of death is preserved (and Scripture most assuredly preserves it), the dead are raised without either dissent or consent. To this extent they have no will at all in the matter. Continuance in a state of lifelessness being their natural course, that course is turned about contrary to what is natural to their being by an act of resurrection or revitalization that amounts to a second birth. And in this they certainly are overruled.

To save all by electing all therefore means to override what is natural to all, acting upon all despite themselves to reverse the consequences of the choice they were free to make, and invited to make, in Adam at the very beginning. Why, then, allow them to make an initial choice which was later to be wholly overridden? We conclude that if God elected all men to salvation He would be acting inconsistently with his original plan to create a race of free moral agents. We cannot reasonably believe that God would create one situation and then undo it by a second creative act which entirely negates the purpose of the first one. Why create such a race in the first place?

The second alternative fares no better. If in creating man God's purpose was to produce an order of beings with freedom to worship and serve their Creator with a full consciousness of what they are doing, only to find that they all reject the purpose for which they were created, and if there is no intention to take countermeasures of any kind to salvage the experiment in any way, then we must ask, Why create man to begin with?

And so we seem logically to be driven to the position of saying that since God as completely defeats his original purpose if He saves *all* men as He defeats his own original purpose if He saves *none*, He has but two courses open to Him: not to create man at all, or having done so to save at least *some* of them.

Yet one question still arises out of this dilemma which we will attempt to answer at the end of this work. The question is, Can the saving of a few out of so many justify the creation of so many whose fate (even though they determine it for themselves) seems so very terrible? Does the numerical imbalance have the same meaning in the light of eternity as it certainly seems to have to us who live in time? We will return to this when we come to consider the destiny of those who are not among the elect of God.

Meanwhile, as John Owen put it *(Works,* Vol. X, pp. 54 f.): "Before the foundation of the world, out of his own good pleasure, God chose certain men, determining to free them from sin and misery, to bestow upon them grace and faith, to give them to Christ, to bring them to everlasting blessedness, to the praise of his glorious grace." This seems to sum up all that we really know about God's purposes in the saving of the "some."

The elect are the Father's gift to the Son. For these He died, and these will come as gifts to Him at the appropriate time. They do not offer themselves, they are offered by the Father to the Son as a gift. "All that the Father giveth Me shall come to Me; and him that cometh to Me I will in no wise cast out. . . . This is the Father's will who hath sent Me, that of all which He hath given Me I should lose nothing. . . . And this is the will of Him that sent Me, that every one [of them] may have everlasting life" (John 6:37, 39, 40).

"No man *can* come unto Me, except the Father who hath sent Me draw him. . . . Therefore said I unto you, that no man can come unto Me except it were given unto him of my Father" (John 6:44, 65). "Ye have not chosen Me but I have chosen you" (John 15:16). "Of his own will begat He us with the word of truth" (James 1:18). What could be clearer?

Our salvation is entirely in the hands of God, the basis of his choice of any one individual over against another being unrelated to the worthiness or unworthiness of that individual. All whom He has chosen as gifts to his Son will be called, will hear the call, and will respond to the call. And only those will do so.

Whosoever wills to do so, may come because none wills to do so who is not already marked out as part of the Father's gift to the Son. And accordingly whosoever *may,* will come, that is, whosoever is *able* to come because enabled by the Father, *will* come because the Father has already prepared the way. Thus in the simplest possible terms it may be said, *Whosoever will, may come; and whosoever may, will come. And whosoever will not, cannot come.* It is inwardly that the change is wrought, to free the will from its bondage to sin and death, enabling the refugee from God to turn about and seek his face instead of fleeing from Him. Election is unconditional, and in the end we surrender to his will unconditionally. As many as are ordained to eternal life do believe (Acts 13:48).

The rest of men are not condemned to unbelief but merely permitted to continue in their own way, being left where by nature they wish to be. Like the ratchet wheel that is unidirectional in its turning, they freely turn only in the direction that corresponds to the now fallen nature of man. Calvin summed up the matter in this way:

The efficient cause of our election is the good pleasure of the will of God:
The material cause is Jesus Christ:
The final cause is the praise of the glory of his grace: and
The formal cause is the preaching of the Gospel by which the goodness of
God overflows upon us.[2]

The Lutherans argued that a man has at least this much that he can do towards his conversion, namely, that he can place himself in the position that he can hear the Gospel. To quote the words from the *Formula of Concord* (II.53):

The person who is not yet converted to God and regenerated, can hear and read the Word of God externally because even after the Fall man still has something of a free will in these external matters, so that he can go to Church, listen to the sermon, or not listen to it.

But this is surely to ignore the difference between listening to the words, and being alive to their meaning. It was only because God opened Lydia's heart that she actually heard inwardly Paul's words (Acts 16:14). We can see and *not* see, we can hear and *not* hear, even as Isaiah said (6:9, 10). We hear only the words, not their meaning; we see only the evidences, not their significances. As Moses said to the children of Israel (Deut. 29:2), they had seen all that the Lord had done before their eyes in the land of Egypt, and "yet the Lord hath not given you a heart to perceive, and eyes to see, and ears to hear unto this day" (v. 4). There are two kinds of seeing, two kinds of hearing. Merely to be in the Lord's house is not any guarantee that the Word of the Lord proclaimed there will be heard inwardly or the truth seen and grasped by faith. A man may go to church for many reasons which have nothing to do with a conscious obedience to the Lord's command to hear his Word. Whether such a man goes or not has no necessary connection with his conversion. For God can speak to him just as fruitfully in other ways. He may recall to his mind some life-giving portion of his own Word long forgotten since it was first learned as a child. Or as a man walks, He may cause him to glance at a street sign with a Gospel message printed on it, or casually to pick up a tract blown by the wind into his path. The circumstances surrounding a man's conversion really have no necessary connection with his presenting himself in church and sitting there hearing the words with his outward ears. He need not by any means contribute even his presence within the *sound* of the Gospel to become suddenly and wonderfully born again into the blameless family of God. The Church with its conventional pulpit sermon is by no means always the vehicle of God's saving grace, and whether a man decides to subject himself to this vehicle has

---

2. Quoted in Fred H. Klooster, *Calvin's Doctrine of Predestination*, p. 19.

nothing to do with his Election except that it may be a means by which that Election is made effective.

In every sense, Unconditional Election is a direct corollary of Total Depravity. It must be. If we are wholly impotent to effect or assist in our salvation in any way, as totally impotent as a corpse is to assist in its own resurrection or as the newly formed body of Adam was to assist in its own animation, then our personal salvation must of necessity be unconditionally God's doing.

In any other view of the matter, the implication is that Christ saves us only *with our help;* and what this inevitably soon comes to mean is that we really save *ourselves,* though with God's help. To suppose that if we only preach the love of God persuasively enough men's hearts will be softened and they will acknowledge their need of the Lord and of his salvation is to wholly misrepresent the true nature of man's predicament as a sinner.

8

LIMITED ATONEMENT

The concept of Limited Atonement is perhaps the one point of the Five Points of Calvinism about which controversy among those who otherwise hold firmly to the Calvinist position has had the most serious consequences. It is argued that there are far too many passages in Scripture that speak clearly of the universality of the love of God to justify the view that the Atonement was limited in its intention to a chosen few. And we cannot honestly and sincerely present the Gospel to the world at large unless we are convinced that God really desires the salvation of all men equally.

Such a verse as John 3:16, "God so loved the world that He gave his only begotten Son that *whosoever* believeth in Him should not perish," is surely without limitation in its implication. And such passages as those which speak of Christ as the "Saviour of the world" (John 4:42; 1 John 4:14), or "the Saviour of all men" (1 Tim. 4:10), or as the one who gave Himself to be "a propitiation for the sins of the whole world" (1 John 2:2), or which affirm that He is "the bread of God which cometh down from heaven and giveth life unto the world" (John 6:33, 51), are so all-embracing as to defy the concept of a sacrifice confined in its efficacy only to the elect of God while the vast majority of men are passed by. Statements like these, and there are many others, appear to prohibit placing limitations upon the intrinsic worth of that sacrifice or upon its intention in application.

Yet there are reasons to believe that another interpretation is possible, if not indeed more likely, both for these passages and others of a similar nature. That the Lord Jesus Christ should die for all, while only some avail themselves of his sacrifice, is surely to make a provision far greater than is required. It constitutes a kind of divine extravagance which seems inappropriate in view of the appalling nature of the penalty paid in his own Person by the Lord Jesus. In the nature of the case the Father must have foreseen that the sacrifice of his Son would effectively have only limited application. It would seem only appropriate to make the payment limited accordingly: limited punishment to balance limited crime. The Lord Jesus enunciated this principle Himself when He said that the man whose offences were few was to receive few stripes, whereas the man whose offences were great was to receive many (Luke 12:47, 48). It is customary to say that the Lord's sacrifice was *sufficient* for all, but *efficient* only for those who avail themselves of it. But to many people even this appears to be an evasion of the problem, a mere play upon words.

However, a careful reading of what Scripture does say about those for whom Christ died reinforces the impression that He did actually bear only the sins of his people, "Thou shalt call his name Jesus for He shall save *his people* from their sins" (Matt. 1:21). "The good shepherd giveth his life for *his sheep*" (John 10:11). Apparently, He did not give his life for the goats who constitute the other class of mankind in the Day of Judgment (Matt. 25:32, 33). "Christ loved the Church and gave Himself for *it*" (Eph. 5:25). Certainly the implications here are clear enough; yet the argument is still essentially a negative one. It might yet be true that He gave Himself for us, while still dying for other men also.

But it has to be admitted that the extent to which Scripture seems to go out of its way to avoid inclusive statements when speaking specifically of those for whom Christ died is certainly remarkable. Writing to the Galatians, Paul is very specific when he says: "He gave Himself for *our* sins that He might deliver *us*" (1:4). And again in Galatians 3:13: "Being made a curse for *us,*" to the end that *"we* might receive the adoption of sons" (4:5).

Similarly, Peter wrote: "Who his own self bare *our* sins in his own body on the tree" (1 Peter 2:24), a picture reflecting Isaiah 53:5: "He was wounded for *our* transgressions, bruised for *our* iniquities; the chastisement of *our* peace was upon Him, and by his stripes *we* are healed." To the Roman Christians Paul wrote: "He was delivered for *our* offences, and raised again for *our* justification" (Rom. 4:25).

In writing to Titus, Paul said: "He gave Himself for *us* that He might redeem *us* from all iniquity and purify unto Himself a special people" (Titus 2:14). The writer of the Epistle to the Hebrews said, "By Himself He purged *our* sins" (Heb. 1:3), "having obtained eternal redemption for *us*" (Heb. 9:12). And in 1 John 4:9: "In this was manifest the love of God towards *us* because God sent his only begotten Son into the world that *we* might live through Him." Notice here that John does not say that God sent his Son into the world that the world might live through Him. And as John records the Lord's prayer in Gethsemane we read the significant words, "I pray *not* for the world but for them Thou gavest Me" (John 17:9). Note also in Titus 2:14, quoted above, that the selective process had a well-defined objective, not to redeem the world but to create a special people (1 Peter 2:9 also) for a special purpose, who were to be kept from the world, though not taken out of it (John 17:15). The people of God are left in the world not in the hope of converting it to Christ but (like salt) to preserve the world from total corruption (Matt. 5:13), or like a small lamp to keep the world from being enveloped in total darkness (Matt. 5:14).

Now while the Lord said that the world as a whole "lieth in the wicked one" (1 John 5:19), He also revealed that the elect of God, even before they came to Himself to be his sheep, did not lie in the wicked one but already belonged to the Father. Of these who were to be his true disciples, Jesus said to the Father: "*Thine they were*, and Thou gavest them to Me . . ." (John 17:6). Such indeed is the implication also of John 8:47 addressed to those who the Lord well knew were not destined to become his sheep: "Ye therefore hear not [God's words] because ye are *not* God's." By contrast in Acts 18:10 God said to Paul when he went to Corinth, that most wanton of ancient cities: "I am with thee and no man shall set on thee to hurt thee for *I have much people in this city.*" These elect individuals though yet unsaved were nevertheless already in the Father's possession, purchased in anticipation. Those who were not in the Father's possession would not hear the Lord's voice because they were not his sheep, and therefore they did not come to Him for salvation. Conversion does not appear to turn goats into sheep. It is only sheep of other folds that are yet to be brought in as his possession (John 10:16). Ambrose was surely right when he exclaimed, "If you die in unbelief, Christ did not die for you." Christ died for no one in vain.

Would it be proper to speak of the Lord's victory as a triumph if 80 percent of the people for whom He supposedly died repudiated that sacrifice? Yet if Arminianism is true and the intent of the Atonement was unlimited, it would follow that millions for whom Christ died are lost and the salvation of God was enormously overpaid. Since far more appear to be lost than are saved (Matt. 22:14), the greater part of the Lord's suffering for man's sins was to no purpose. This is surely a poor semblance of triumph.

On the other hand, if Christ died for all, then God is either *unwilling* to apply that sufficiency, or He is *unable* to do so. If He is unwilling, then what are we to do with many contrary statements in Scripture which assure us that He takes no pleasure in the death of the wicked? "Have I any pleasure that the wicked should die? saith the Lord God. . . . I have no pleasure in the death of him that dieth, saith the Lord God" (Ezek. 18:23, 32 and 33:11). If on the other hand He is unable, He is clearly not sovereign in the midst of his own creation. If He has some other plan, hidden from us at the present, which if we did but know it would explain why his intention was limited, then we may safely wait upon Him in the certainty that in due course we shall see that the Judge of all the earth has after all done what is right.

Now the passages usually brought to the defence of the universalistic view are all, as we shall see, capable of a different interpretation. Meanwhile it may be asked, Is there any passage of Scripture which can be taken unequivocally to mean that God has deliberately undertaken *not* to extend his saving grace to certain people who, if that grace had been extended to them, would have responded affirmatively? It appears that there is such a passage. Augustine *(Enchiridion,* Chap. 103) has this observation: "The Lord was unwilling to work miracles in the presence of some who, He said frankly, would have repented if He *had* worked them." The passage to which Augustine made reference is Matthew 11:20, 21, where it is written: "Then began He to upbraid the cities wherein most of his mighty works were done because they repented not: Woe unto thee, Chorazin! Woe unto thee, Bethsaida! For if the mighty works which were done in you had been done in Tyre and Sidon they would have repented long ago in sackcloth and ashes." It is difficult to evaluate such a pregnant statement as this without concluding that an immeasurable benefit was at one period deliberately withheld from a group of people who would apparently have gladly accepted it had it been offered to them. Yet we may possibly have some light even on such a mystery as this from other parts of Scripture.

We know that Nineveh repented (Jonah 3:5 ff.), as the result of Jonah's preaching, and yet its people were Gentiles and can hardly be supposed to have partaken of the covenant which God had made with Israel. We are not told that Nineveh was actually saved, only that it was spared (Jonah 4:11). Its doom was merely postponed, though its fate was sealed and in due course it was virtually wiped from the face of the earth.

It seems that Tyre and Sidon might have been spared also had they witnessed the miracles which the Jews witnessed, and such a genuine repentance by a community with its attendant postponement of impending judgment has probably been more common throughout history than we have recognized. Such sparing does not seem to mean salvation: it signifies only a temporary reprieve as an expression of what has been called the Common Grace of God.

Thus such passages as 2 Peter 3:9—"The Lord is not slack concerning his promises as some men count slackness; but is long suffering towards us, not willing that any should perish but that all should come to repentance"— may signify that God is indeed prepared to give man every possible chance of reprieve in this life by delaying judgment whenever man shows concern even though such concern is not divinely inspired and does not produce saving faith. Such delays are as though God Himself shares something of our concern for men who are lost even when He knows they are not to be among the elect. Perhaps it is the children involved who are his special concern, even as Jonah 4:11 seems to imply: "And shall I not spare Nineveh, that great city wherein are more than sixscore thousand persons that cannot discern between their right and their left hand, and much cattle?"

Such sparing acts of God are expressions of a mercy which He commonly bestows upon all men alike. As Matthew 5:45 tells us: "He maketh his sun to rise on the evil and on the good, and sendeth rain on the just and on the unjust." In Acts 14:15-17 we find Paul and Barnabas saying: "Sirs, why do ye these things? We also are men of like passions with you, and preach unto you that ye should turn from these vanities unto the living God who made heaven and earth, and the sea, and all things that are therein: who in times past suffered all nations to walk in their own ways. Nevertheless He left not Himself without witness, in that He did good, and gave us rain from heaven, and fruitful seasons, filling our hearts with food and gladness." So also in Psalm 145:9: "The Lord is good to all: and his tender mercies are over all his works."

Now Augustine held that God, having from all eternity elected some to everlasting life, had special reference to their salvation only when He covenanted with the Son to make atonement. Subsequently Lutherans and Calvinists agreed as to the worth of the Atonement but came to differ as to its design. While Augustine and Calvin maintained that it was designed only for the elect, Luther maintained that it had equal reference to all mankind individually. Charles Hodge observed that what Christ suffered would have been just as necessary if only one human soul had been the object of redemption, yet nothing more would have been required had every child of Adam been redeemed.[1] It was Augustine who, with his characteristic genius for abbreviated statement of truth, gave us the couplet "sufficient for all, efficient for the elect only." Following his insight many others have sought to give expression to the same thought in different ways. It is possible to tabulate these different modes of expression somewhat as follows by saying that the Lord's sacrifice was:

potentially infinite	but	actually limited
unlimited in value	but	limited in intention
infinite in worth	but	finite in application
limitless as to its capacity	but	limited in its effect
unlimited atonement	but	limited redemption

Not all these alternative expressions are precisely the same in implication. There is virtually universal agreement as to the value of the Lord's Atonement being infinite, but it makes a difference whether we oppose to this the doctrine that it was limited in intention or limited in effect. The difference lies in this, that while God's intention may or may not have been limited, since this is really the point at issue, the actual effect was indeed limited by man's wide rejection of it—about which there cannot be any disagreement. The crux of the matter then is summed up in the question: "What *was* God's intention?"

---

1. *Systematic Theology,* Vol. II, p. 545.

The Calvinist position is that in the beginning the Father and the Son entered into a covenant in which the Son undertook to pay the price of ensuring that man's creation as a free moral agent would not fail in its purpose of bringing glory to God, while the Father would guarantee the effectiveness of the Son's atoning sacrifice by exercising his sovereign grace to apply the Atonement effectively to an appropriate number of individuals, the elect. Thus his sacrifice would not be in vain. These elect given by the Father to the Son would in due time without fail be brought to a saving faith. The Lord would thus see the travail of his soul and be satisfied (Isa. 53:11), and his table would be completely furnished with guests, in the words of Matthew 22:10. The elect were therefore chosen in Him from the very beginning.

The *Westminster Confession* (III.6) makes this declaration:

> They who are elected, being fallen in Adam, are redeemed by Christ, are effectually called into faith in Christ by his Spirit working in due season; are justified, adopted, sanctified, and kept by his power through faith unto salvation. Neither are any others redeemed by Christ, effectually called, justified, adopted, sanctified, and saved, but the elect only.

It will be apparent that the Reformers in the Calvinist tradition were very positive in their assertion of Limited Atonement. Yet they also recognized that because the Lord Jesus Christ was not only man but God also, the worth of his sacrifice is accordingly infinite and fully sufficient for the sins of all men. The formulators of the Anglican *Prayer Book* demonstrated that they recognized this by introducing into the communion service a prayer which speaks of the Lord's sacrifice as "a full perfect and sufficient sacrifice, oblation, and satisfaction for the sins of the whole world." The real question at issue here is not, then, Was his sacrifice sufficient for all? but rather, Was his sacrifice *actually intended* for all? On this question, as we have seen, there came to be a critical division of opinion, both sides appealing to Scripture and believing themselves to be clearly guided by it. Yet the issue probably cannot be settled simply by an appeal to the Word of God: it must be settled rather by implications from the Word of God, implications which are drawn from its statements by the exercise of sanctified reason and which, although it may not be possible to find precise proof texts, are nevertheless in no way contradicted by other statements of Scripture, the meaning of which is unequivocal.

Now it must be admitted that there are a number of passages in the New Testament, and a few in the Old, which appear to substantiate the view that the Atonement was unlimited both in extent and intent. It is on the basis of these passages that an increasing number of evangelicals, beginning with Arminius, began to teach that God must have covenanted with his Son to make an Atonement not merely for the sins of the elect but also for all men indiscriminately. Such passages do not mean that all men will be saved but that all men could be saved if they would, that it was God's initial intention that their salvation should be genuinely possible. The Atonement made by the Lord Jesus Christ was sufficient for all men (with which the Calvinists would agree wholeheartedly) and was intended for all men if they should desire it (with which Calvinists could not agree). Calvinists disagreed with this for two reasons.

First of all, the view that Christ's sacrifice was intended for all would make much of that sacrifice pointless since so many do not in fact avail themselves of it; the triumph of the cross is fatally diminished if only a fragment of its original intention is actually to be realized. If, on the contrary, Christ died only for the sins of the elect of God and not for those that are lost, the victory of the cross is total in terms of its intentions. It is hard to believe Satan has been allowed largely to defeat God's intentions. Christ did not die to make the salvation of all men possible; He died to make the salvation of the elect certain, and this will be demonstrated in due time. None of them will be lost (John 6:39, 40 and 10:27-29). Such is the basis of our assurance of eternal security. There was no limit to the worth of his Atonement, but in God's intention there was to be no waste either. The Lord did all that was necessary for the salvation of an elect number whose response was guaranteed by the Father. The original design was and will be entirely fulfilled. The Lord's victory is complete. The completeness of this victory is not dependent upon man's natural inclination to respond to the offer of salvation but upon God's sovereign grace in conferring upon the elect the necessary saving faith.

Secondly, the view that Christ's sacrifice was intended for all could be interpreted to mean that all men will automatically be saved whether they believe or not, since all men indiscriminately would already have had the penalty for their sins atoned for and would not therefore be called upon to suffer any penalty themselves. It is a principle of law in the civilized world that a man cannot be held accountable for a debt which has already been paid by someone else on his behalf and to the full satisfaction of the offended party. But this is precisely what un-limited atonement would involve. For if the Lord Jesus Christ paid the penalty for the sins of every man in particular to the satisfaction of the Father, then every man in particular, regardless of his attitude towards that payment and whether he believes or does not believe, is *ipso facto* rid of his debt. In the eyes of the law he is absolved. It cannot be demanded of him that he also by punishment hereafter pay the debt a second time. He cannot be accused of owing anything. The only reason for such an accusation by a court would be ignorance of the fact that the debt has already been paid—or deliberate deception by the accuser. In the final Judgment no such contingencies could ever arise because the Judge is the Lord Himself, the same who has already paid our debt (Rom.

8:34). Although it has not hitherto been used as a theological term, one might say that there can be no *double jeopardy*. A penalty cannot legally be demanded twice.

Let us state this principle once again. *No man can be held accountable for a debt that has already been paid for on his behalf to the satisfaction of the offended party.* But a double jeopardy, a duplication of indebtedness, is indeed involved if the non-elect are to be punished for sins for which the Lord Jesus Christ has already endured punishment. And this is what *un*-limited atonement means if interpreted in the universalistic sense that Christ died for the sins of all men. It follows therefore that if the unsaved are to be punished, the Lord cannot *also* have been punished substitutionally on their account.

Now it is not logically possible that the Lord might have died for the non-elect or might not have died for the non-elect as though it were a "potential" dying only, the issue to be settled by subsequent events. He either did die for the non-elect or He did not. If He did, the deed is done whether it is applied or not applied. If it is not applied and men are to be punished, we have a double liability involved. If it is to be applied, then all men are saved automatically. If, on the other hand, the Lord Jesus Christ did not die for all men individually, then it cannot be done now. It is too late. The body of Jesus Christ was offered only *once* (Heb. 10:10).

It is thus consistent for us to define our faith simply by use of the term *Limited Atonement.* We should not at the same time attempt to emphasize it by saying what it is not. We should rather stay close to Scripture, which makes it so very clear that the Lord died for the sins of his people, of the sheep. We are not told more than this. There are passages of Scripture which seem to say more than this, but as we shall see they may not really be doing so. Most of the expressions which have been set forth on page 285 should probably be used with great care on this account, since they could be an invitation to a serious error. Logically they may be convincing enough, but scripturally they may go beyond the truth. We can safely say only that the Lord's sacrifice had limited efficacy in so far as it has had limited application.

Whether it is intended or not by those who adopt the thesis in their preaching that "Christ died for the sins of all men," the *logical* consequence is a simple Universalism—"all men will be saved." And Universalism makes preaching the Gospel almost pointless, for the most that can be hoped is that a few individuals will respond in thankfulness as the one leper who was healed did (Luke 17:15-17). Such a sense of thankfulness will certainly be beneficial, but in terms of destiny it will make no difference. The other nine lepers are assured that they are free to do precisely what they like without fear of judgment to come or personal consequence from their action. It would be better not to preach such a Gospel as this. It is only because we are *not* logical so much of the time that we are saved from such ill effects.

It is thus clear that the Lord can have died only for those who have been predestined *not* to have to suffer the penalty of their own sins. Since this does not apply to any but the elect and since we cannot know beforehand who is elect and who is not, we cannot tell, when we are face-to-face with an individual, whether that individual is chosen to respond or will be permitted to refuse, and it is clearly improper to say, "Christ died for you." Indeed this form of statement is nowhere to be found in any of the sermons recorded in Scripture (Acts 2:14 ff.; 3:12-26; 4:8-12; 5:29-32; 7:2-53; 10:34-43; 13:16-41; 17:22-32; 22:1-21), and does not correctly represent the Gospel. We can safely say to a man only something like, "This is a faithful saying and worthy of all acceptation, that Christ Jesus came into the world to save sinners" (1 Tim. 1:15); or "God hath made Him who knew no sin to be a sin-offering for us that we might be made the righteousness of God in Him" (2 Cor. 5:21). It would not even be correct to paraphrase this last passage by replacing the words "for us" with the words "for you," and the words "that we might be" with the words "that you might be." Yet I have heard it done. This cannot be said by one man to another truthfully because we do not have God's knowledge of which men are elect. We can only quote Scripture faithfully and leave the results to God.

In the *Canons of Dort* (III-IV.9) we are told that, in the Gospel, Christ is offered. But in III-IV.14 we are told that salvation is *not* offered, it is conferred. The Gospel is offered but salvation is not. It seems appropriate to quote this Article in full.

> Faith is therefore to be considered as the gift of God, not on account of its being offered by God to man, to be accepted or rejected at his pleasure, but because it is in reality conferred upon him, breathed and infused into him; not even because God bestows the power or ability to believe and then expects that man should by the exercise of his own free will consent to the terms of salvation and actually believe in Christ, but because He who works in man both to will and to work, and indeed all things in all, produces *both the will to believe and the act of believing also.*

Now this apparent conflict that in preaching the Gospel we offer Christ, while salvation is not offered but conferred, seems to be resolved (as Hoeksema observes) by noting that the Latin of Article 9 indicates that "offering" Christ means *presenting* or *showing* Him.[2] In short, there is no question of saying Christ died for *you*, but only of *declaring* that Christ died as a sacrifice for sin. Preaching the Gospel is not to be equated with giving an invitation but with making a declaration. The elect will hear this declaration

---

2. See G. C. Berkouwer, *Studies in Dogmatics: Divine Election*, p. 222.

as an invitation; to the non-elect it will come as a judgment which leaves them without excuse.

Meanwhile, true preaching of the Gospel is something done under divine compulsion. When Paul says, "Necessity is laid upon me; yea, woe is unto me, if I preach not the Gospel (1 Cor. 9:16), he uses a very forceful word in the original Greek (ἀνάγκη) when he speaks of necessity. One might properly have translated it "absolute compulsion." When God thus determines that the Gospel shall be preached, it is only because He has also predetermined that it shall bear fruit (for life or death) as He foreordains. The "tool" is his Word, the agent is his servant, the results are in his own hands.

That the Atonement itself is limited in its effect is not disputed by either Calvinists or Arminians. What is in dispute is the *intent*, not the *extent*, of the Atonement. And on this dispute hinges an important consideration. For if God's intention was limited, we do not know why He was pleased to limit it and are apt to suppose on the basis of human reason alone that the love of God is also limited, and this we find disturbing.

This issue regarding the extent of God's love was a truly basic point of disagreement between Arminius and the strict Calvinists of his day. It is not desirable to enter here into the clash of personalities at the time which undoubtedly contributed to the hardening of battle lines between the two parties, Calvinists and Arminians. Suffice it to say that Limited Atonement became an issue because it led to the belief in certain quarters that if the sacrifice of Christ was intended only for a select minority of the human race, the majority of men were being predestinated to eternal punishment unfairly; and God emerged as a despotic sovereign whose indifference to the fate of the non-elect seemed to stand in clear violation of a number of passages of Scripture which speak of his love for mankind as a whole. How could God so love the world that He would allow his only begotten Son to sacrifice Himself for it and then limit that sacrifice to a few while He predestinated the many to reprobation?*

---

*We are here in the presence of a very difficult question. The two sides to this question have customarily been treated under the terms *Supralapsarianism* and *Infralapsarianism*. Supralapsarianism means that before the Fall, and indeed before the creation of man, God predestined man to SIN. Infralapsarianism means that after man fell, God predestined him to reprobation. It seems to be largely a matter of timing, but the problem is more serious.

Did God decide that man should fall and, thereby, Himself become the author of sin, or did He merely on the basis of foreknowledge determine that, having fallen, man was destined to reprobation? Did He, in short, ordain sin *before* man fell or ordain only reprobation *after* man fell? The first is evidence of absolute sovereignty, the latter of complete foreknowledge. The first is more an act of sovereignty than justice, the latter of justice than sovereignty. Sovereignty is challenged in the latter because it means that man was *not* predetermined by God to fall of his own free will. Since the fact that man was not predetermined to fall but indeed did fall appears to defeat the purposes of God, it seems that man rather than God is sovereign in this matter. For if God were sovereign in this matter, the reasoning goes, He would not have allowed it. Is God more just than sovereign in this case?

Jesus Christ, it was argued, is revealed in Scripture as having died for all men, the saved and the unsaved alike. The difference between the saved and the unsaved as to their destiny was not the result of a narrow atonement which passed the unsaved by but a broad atonement which they themselves neglected to make use of. It was intended for them but it was never appropriated. The fault lay with them, and not with the Saviour. Those who reasoned in this way held that to view the situation in any other light was really to make God the author of unbelief and reprobation.

Arminius at first seems to have held the Calvinist position of Beza, whom he greatly admired but whose theology he finally found unacceptable. Beza's position was that if God elected some men to salvation, He must automatically have elected others to reprobation. This is not a logical deduction, however, for it can be argued with equal force that man elects himself to reprobation by freely choosing to neglect the salvation which is offered to him. For the majority of men, the many who are not chosen (Matt. 20:16), it is not necessary for God to act determinatively. He needs only to permit them to have their own way. He respects their freedom of choice and passes them by. The choice is made freely in that it truly represents fallen man's natural inclination.

For all his acuity of reasoning, Beza never seems to have been able to recognize that Election to salvation for a few whose wills have been set free from within is perfectly compatible with granting to the rest of mankind freedom to go their own way. Double Predestination is not necessary. Calvin in his younger days committed himself to Double Predestination by

---

In Supralapsarianism, the Fall and sin are *ordained means* to the fulfillment of God's purposes; in Infralapsariansim, the Fall and sin are merely *permitted factors* in the fulfillment of his purposes.

The issue seems to boil down to this. Did God create a situation in which his sovereignty had to be surrendered in *allowing* man to decide for himself, or is God the *author* of sin? There cannot be two sovereign wills. If in this matter, man is truly free to decide whether to obey or not, then all else hinges on man's decision, not God's. If God is determined to have his will obeyed, did He not then authorize Adam to disobey—in which case did Adam really *disobey* at all?

When the Lord was speaking to the disciples, He said, "I go to *prepare* a place for you" (John 14:2). By contrast when men are condemned in the Judgment they are sent to a place that was *not* prepared for them. In Matthew 25:41 the Lord said to these men, "Depart from Me, ye cursed, into everlasting fire, *prepared for the devil and his angels.*" These two antithetical statements, antithetical in so far as the destiny of the blessed was prepared for them, but the destiny of the cursed was not prepared for them, may afford some grounds for arguing against Supralapsarianism. If men are predestined to be saved, one might expect a corresponding place of destiny to be prepared. That the place of destiny of the non-elect was not prepared for *them*, but for the devil and his angels, implies that at least for man such a destiny was not foreordained. Whatever may be the order of events relative to the devil and his angels, and whether they were predestined to fall before they were created, we have no clear intimation from Scripture and the idea seems repugnant. But the place of punishment for the non-elect is statedly a kind of emergency, make-do arrangement, serving a purpose which it was not originally designed to serve.

saying: "Many professing a desire to defend the Deity from an invidious charge admit the doctrine of election but deny that anyone is reprobated. This they do ignorantly and childishly since there can be no election without its opposite, reprobation" (Inst. III.xxiii.1). Curiously he sought to reinforce this dismal doctrine by a reference to Matthew 15:13: "Every plant which my heavenly Father hath not planted shall be rooted up." Calvin then comments that the Lord's hearers are here "plainly told that all whom the heavenly Father has not been pleased to plant in his garden are doomed and devoted to destruction."

Far from demonstrating Double Predestination, which would require, by analogy, that the Father would not only root up these reprobate weeds, *but had also been responsible for planting them in the first place*, this passage of Scripture says precisely the opposite: they were *not* planted by the Father at all. But as already noted, Calvin seems to have softened his views on this issue in his later years.

Beza succeeded to Calvin's mantle of authority when the latter died and seems to have hardened his position on this issue, becoming himself perhaps the most ultra-Calvinist of the time. He insisted that the reprobate were as predestinated to be lost as the elect were to be saved; that they were not merely permitted to go their own way, but were willed of God in this direction. To Beza it seemed inevitable that if God predestined them to be lost, He clearly did not covenant with his Son to die for them. This latter deduction seemed to be common sense and it appears that Arminius accepted it at first, and embraced the corollary of a Limited Atonement. But in due course for reasons which we do not need to consider here, Arminius came to feel uncomfortable about certain implications of Limited Atonement, namely, that God's love is not universal unless the intention of the Atonement was universal. God's love would appear to be limited by the intention of the Atonement since the Atonement was in the final analysis the real demonstration of the scope of God's love (1 John 3:16). If we know that He loved us because He gave Himself for us, must we not assume that He did not love the rest of mankind if He did not give Himself for them?

When we say that reactions against Beza's persistence in holding to Double Predestination had the effect of *hardening* his position, we are in effect saying that Beza's mind and powers of logical analysis became separated from all feeling. Unlike Calvin, who softened his position later, recognizing that our finite minds can drive us to extremes, Beza did not pause in his pursuit of logic. Both Calvin and Luther did, recognizing that human logic may break down and that mind needs to be monitored by heart. Arminius went to the other extreme and allowed his heart to warp his powers of logic, so that in the end he found himself convinced by his own heart to adopt a position regarding man's capacity of response to the love of God which was logically inconsistent and yet which he attempted to defend by logical means. He agreed wholeheartedly that man's salvation is wholly of God and that man contributes nothing by way of good works towards it. When asked, "Why does one man respond to the love of God but not another?" he replied, "Because that man has grace enough to do so, while the other man has not."

"Whence comes this grace?"

Arminius replied, "From God."

"Then why does not God give that grace to the other man?"

Arminius replied, "He does, but the other man refuses it."

And here is the crux of the matter. For it is necessary to assume either that the one man has an element of goodness which the other does not (which Arminius denied), or that God's love does not extend to both men equally (which Arminius also denied). His theology gradually became inconsistent and logically indefensible.

Once the set of his mind began to be freed from the compulsion of Beza's logic, Arminius appears to have become increasingly aware that there are a number of passages of Scripture favouring the broader view of God's love to all men. But Romans 9:13 ("Jacob have I loved, but Esau have I hated") faced him with the fact that God did not love all men equally. In the end he resolved this problem to his own satisfaction in a way that is rather interesting. He recognized that the majority of men do not accept the salvation of God, but this did not seem to him to require the assumption that prior to their rejection God did not love them. He resolved the question of Jacob and Esau by suggesting that Jacob represented all who believe and accept God's salvation and Esau all who reject God's salvation. The love of God is extended towards all those therefore who have not actually rejected his salvation. Once an individual has irrevocably rejected the love of God, the love of God is no longer extended towards him and, by contrast with Jacob, that man stands in the position of Esau. But if God loves all men prior to their rejection of his salvation, then must He not have prospectively provided a sufficient Atonement for all men in order that the offer of salvation may be made to them sincerely? And thus there arose within the Reformation movement a growing body of evangelical believers (for Arminius had many secret supporters) who rejected the concept of Limited Atonement and favoured its antithesis, the concept of the universality of God's love for the world and the provisional universality of the Atonement.

The fact that man is saved purely by the grace of God and apart from any works of his own was not really being questioned. For these dissenting minds, the part which man plays involves only a willingness to accept, a spirit of non-resistance. But neither Arminius nor any of those who have followed in the Arminian tradition have ever really been able to resolve the problem of how it is that some men resist the love of God and some do not. Yet Arminius held firmly to the view that until the resistance is final, the love of God reaches out to them still. Scriptural support for the universality of God's love and, as a corollary the unlimited intent of the Atonement, is based upon a number of passages of Scripture which must now be examined carefully.

It is appropriate to start with 1 Timothy 2:1-6 because the statement is both sweeping and apparently unequivocal. In order to establish a context it is desirable to quote the whole six verses, which in the King James Version read as follows:

> I exhort therefore, that, first of all, supplications, prayers, intercessions, and giving of thanks, be made for all men; for kings and for all that are in authority; that we may lead a quiet and peaceable life in all godliness and honesty. For this is good and acceptable in the sight of God our Saviour; who will have all men to be saved, and to come unto the knowledge of the truth. For there is one God, and one mediator between God and men, the man Christ Jesus, who gave Himself a ransom for all to be testified in due time.

We are, therefore, exhorted to pray for *all men*. And yet we know from John 17:9 that the Lord Jesus Christ Himself deliberately refrained from praying for all men, "I pray for them [the chosen few]: I pray not for the world but for them Thou hast given Me." It is of course perfectly true that the Lord Jesus knew who were to be the sheep of his flock even before they became part of his inner circle of disciples, and He also knew the spiritual battle which lay ahead for them all. It might therefore be argued that He prayed for them specifically, and not for the world, for this very reason. But are *we* being called upon to engage our prayer life on behalf of all men indiscriminately? Would this not so dilute our prayers as to be meaningless and ineffective? To pray for everyone is really to pray for nobody.

It seems more likely that the phrase "for all men" should be translated more selectively to read "for *all sorts of* men." Such a translation is perfectly consonant with the original Greek, for the word *all* frequently has the less inclusive meaning of "all kinds of," or "all manner of." The simple form *pas* (πᾶς) is translated "all manner of" in the following places, all of which provide a more precise definition of its meaning:

Matthew 4:23—"all manner of disease"

Matthew 5:11—"all manner of evil"

Matthew 10:1—"all manner of sickness"

Luke 11:42—"all manner of herbs"

Acts 10:12—"all manner of four-footed beasts"

Romans 7:8—"all manner of concupiscence"

1 Peter 1:15—"all manner of conversation"

Revelation 21:19—"all manner of precious stone"

If Mark 3:28 is compared with Matthew 12:31, which has reference to the same occasion, it will be observed that the *all* of Mark appears in Matthew as *all manner of*, though in both the same Greek word is used. Either translation is therefore perfectly legitimate.

The point scarcely needs labouring. Every lexicon of New Testament Greek and of Classical Greek agrees upon the validity of the expanded translation. Thayer, for example, gives a number of references by way of illustration and adds this comment: "So especially with nouns designating virtues or vices, customs, characters, conditions, etc." On numerous occasions it greatly illuminates the text to convert the simple "all" (whether of things or men) into "all kinds of" or some such alternative. No special pleading is involved. For example, Mark 11:32 tells us that "all men counted that John was a prophet" but obviously only people aware of what was going on could have been intended. In John 8:2 we are told that "all people came to Him" but we know the Pharisees did not do so. In both cases it would be more appropriate to say "all kinds of" people.

In Romans 5:18 Paul wrote: "Therefore, as by the offence of one judgment came upon all men to condemnation, even so by the righteousness of one the free gift came upon all men unto justification of life." As it stands we might be forced to conclude that every man is condemned in Adam but every man is justified in Christ: every man, without exception. All are lost, all are saved. Both these *all* need to be understood in the same way to justify the sentence structure. Since only some men come "unto justification of life" we are driven to conclude that what Paul intended by his words was *not* that all men are both condemned and justified but rather that, as all kinds of men have suffered the penalty of Adam's disobedience, so all kinds of men have benefited from the rewards of Christ's obedience.

Romans 14:2 tells us how one man "believeth that he may eat all things" whereas another eats only herbs. The obvious intention of the passage is that some men allow themselves meat as well as herbs whereas others avoid meat. But a subservience to a strictly inclusive interpretation of the word *all* would require us to assume that the first individual would eat absolutely anything, an unreasonable assumption.

In writing to Titus (2:11) Paul declares that "the grace of God that bringeth salvation hath appeared to all men." It is almost certain that this would more appropriately be rendered "to all sorts of men." Calvin wrote on this passage as follows: "The apostle simply means that there is no people and no rank in the world that is excluded from salvation, because God wishes that the Gospel should be proclaimed to all without exception. The present discourse relates to classes of men, and not to individual persons."[3] It is important to remember that in Paul's time slaves had no status whatever.

---

3. *The Pastoral Epistles*, p. 55.

They were not even counted as persons. There may have been new Christians to whom it had scarcely occurred that the Gospel was also to be preached to slaves.

Thus in 1 Timothy 6:10, while it is doubtful if the love of money could be the root of all evil—such as blindness due to accident in childhood—it certainly is the root of all *kinds* of evil. And in John 12:32, unless we assume that the Universalists are right, it is more reasonable to read the text: "I, if I be lifted up from the earth, will draw* *all kinds of men unto Me.*"

When John 1:7 tells us that John the Baptist was sent as a witness to the Light which is Christ, in order that all men might believe, we are surely nearer to an understanding of what this means if we read it as "that *all sorts of* men might believe," the "all sorts and conditions of men" of the Anglican *Prayer Book.* The principle may very well be reflected in the familiar promise made to Abraham in Genesis 12:3 that in him "should all the families of the earth be blessed."

Augustine in his *Enchiridion* (Chap. 103) wrote about such passages as these. He said:

> We are to understand by "all men" the human race in all its varieties of rank and circumstance—kings, subjects; noble, plebeian, high, low, learned and unlearned; the sound in body, the feeble, the clever, the dull, the foolish, the rich, the poor; and those of moderate circumstances; males, females, infants [note!], boys, youth; young, middle-aged and old men; of every tongue, of every fashion, of all arts, of all professions, with all the innumerable differences of will and consciousness, and whatever else there is that makes a distinction among men.

Perhaps we still need to be reminded of this. Some men we think too good or too high; and perhaps if we did but understand sufficiently, we might include imbeciles whom we now tend to neglect in this respect. And precisely what did the Lord act upon when He healed lunatics?

---

*The word *draw* in this passage is a strong one. According to Moulton and Milligan *(Vocabulary of the Greek New Testament)*, the Greek form *helkō* or *helkuō* has almost the sense of dragging by force. It is used of *hauling* bricks, of *towing*, of *dragging along*, and even in connection with *impressing* people as labourers. Thayer *(Greek-English Lexicon of the New Testament)* says it is used of dragging people, as when Paul is dragged into the market place (Acts 16:19) or out of the Temple (Acts 21:30). John uses it in 18:10 of drawing a sword, and in 21:6 and 11 of failure and then success in dragging a net. James 2:6 uses it in the sense of dragging the poor before a judge. In the Septuagint the use follows very much along the same lines. Obviously there is something here much stronger than the mere attractiveness of a sweet personality, and it is significant that even in John 12:32 the same word is employed: "I, if I be lifted up, will draw all men unto Me."

The mere presentation of the drama of Calvary, no matter how effectively or appealingly it is made, will not be enough to attract men. Contrary to popular sentiment, there is a real sense in which sinners are not attracted to the cross but dragged to it. Such is the deadness of the human spirit.

So we may quite safely translate 1 Timothy 2:1 as an exhortation not to pray for all men indiscriminately, but rather that we should remember to pray for all sorts of people, not discriminating against any merely by reason of their station in life or any other distinguishing mark. In verse 2 Paul reinforces this alternative by saying that we should include kings and all in authority over us, a surprising exhortation at the time of writing when Nero was the Emperor and an almost wholly corrupt hierarchy derived their authority from him.

If this much is allowed, then verse 4 becomes less all inclusive and more probable, when it tells us that God our Saviour "will have men of all sorts to be saved and come unto a knowledge of the truth."

It should also be noted that the words *will have* in this passage represent the more determinative verb *thelo* in the original, a verb which in many instances seems to be stronger than the alternative verb *boulomai*, from which it seems to be distinguished as representing intention rather than merely desire. It is as though God our Saviour does not merely *desire* that men from every class of society will come to acknowledge the truth but actually *intends* them to do so. The Body of Christ is to be made up in a truly representative way. Paul did not say "not *any* noble are called" but "not many" (1 Cor. 1:26).

As though to reinforce this, Paul is inspired to write that there is only "one mediator between God and men" (v. 5): not one mediator for the high-born and another for the commoner, or one mediator for the free and another for the slave. Men of all sorts stand equal in the sight of God and a single mediator, the Lord Jesus Christ, can make any one of them acceptable before God. And why? Because (v. 6) the same Lord Jesus gave Himself a ransom on behalf of the elect, no matter what class of society they come from.

We do not seem to be required to read this as an expression of the universality of God's love for all men indiscriminately. The wording can be reasonably understood in much more particular terms. But that such a translation is not found in modern versions tells us no more than that where two alternatives have equal validity the one chosen will almost certainly always be the one which best reflects the current climate of theological opinion. And that theological opinion today is undoubtedly universalistic in this sense, both among liberal humanistically oriented expositors and among evangelicals of Arminian persuasion. That God desires or would have all men to be saved is most assuredly assumed by virtually all modern translators. Yet I do not believe that this really reflects the mind of God as revealed elsewhere in Scripture.

But this does not mean that the opposite is true! As we have already noted, Scripture makes it clear that God takes no delight in the death of the wicked but would rather that men should turn from their wickedness and live. Nevertheless, God is a realist and knows that men will not turn and live unless *He* turns them; and to turn all men indiscriminately is simply to render meaningless Adam's original endowment of freedom of choice to good or to evil. Our problem is that we tend to equate our own sentiment with the strong love of God. As one older writer put it: "The love of God is without mercy." Unlike human love, the love of God is without partiality. Arminius was nearer to the truth than were some of his later followers when he limited the love of God to those who have not yet refused Him. We should remember Jehu, the son of Hanani, who rebuked King Jehoshaphat for "loving" a man who hated God (2 Chron. 19:2).

In 2 Peter 3:9 we read: "The Lord is not slack concerning his promise [i.e., the return] as some men count slackness; but is long-suffering towards us, not willing that any should perish, but that all should come to repentance." Here, behind the words *not willing* we have the less determinate Greek verb *boulomai*, that is "not being *desirous* that any should perish." There is a beautiful consistency here with Ezekiel 18:23: "Have I any pleasure at all that the wicked should die? saith the Lord God: and not that he should return from his ways and live?" And verse 32 of this same passage reads: "For I have no pleasure in the death of him that dieth, saith the Lord God; wherefore repent ye and live." Thus God desires that men would come to repentance, and delays the coming Judgment not because He hopes for what He knows cannot be but because He is reluctant to bring to pass that which must be. The love of God and the pity of God are two different things.

Then we meet with another factor of importance in understanding the meaning of many passages which employ the verb rendered "to save" or some derivative of it. In 1 Timothy 4:10 it is written: "For therefore we both labour and suffer reproach, because we trust in the living God who is the Saviour of all men, especially of those that believe." The sentence structure here seems to require that we attach to the word *Saviour* the same implication for unbelievers as we do for them that believe. We know that He is indeed the Saviour of the latter. Is He then in the same sense also the Saviour of the former, of the "all men" of the text? Or is it that the word *Saviour* does not mean in this instance what it usually does in the context of saving faith?

The root verb here is sōzō (σώζω), the meaning of which is either "to save" in the evangelistic sense or "to preserve" in the physical or physiological sense. Both meanings are found in the King James Version. Thus in 2 Timothy 4:18 Paul speaks of his confidence that the Lord will preserve him unto his heavenly kingdom. In 1 Timothy 2:15 Paul gives assurance that women will be preserved in childbearing, for such seems to be rather clearly his meaning. It is also quite possible that in 1 Timothy 4:16, the same alternative ought to be understood: "Take heed unto thyself, and unto the doctrine; continue in them: for in doing this thou shalt both preserve thyself and them that hear thee." It does not seem likely that Paul would commit to Timothy, who was already the Lord's child, the responsibility of *saving* himself. We meet with a similar situation in all probability in Mark 8:35 and 15:30 where the word *preserve* would possibly be more appropriate, for at that time it was a far more dangerous thing to stand for the Lord than it is in our society at the moment, and many people did not preserve their lives on account of their testimony. And perhaps this was Peter's intent when he said, "Preserve yourselves from this untoward generation" (Acts 2:40). James 5:20 may be another case in point: "Let him know that he who turneth the sinner [a brother in the Lord, be it noted, from verse 19] from the error of his way shall preserve a soul from death. . . ." And so, too, perhaps in James 5:15.

Even the Old Testament makes use of both renderings of this verb in the Septuagint Greek translation, as for example in Psalm 36:6: "O Lord, thou preservest man and beast." It is clear that God does preserve his creatures as long as He can as an expression of his compassion as though like a merciful judge He postpones the passing of judgment. As Psalm 145:8 and 9 tells us: "The Lord is gracious and full of compassion; slow to anger and of great mercy. The Lord is good to all: and his tender mercies are over all his works." This is one aspect of his exercise of Common Grace. Perhaps Common Grace is an expression of God's pity for man, rather than his love. God was merciful to Esau—but did not *love* him (Rom. 9:13).

It is for this reason that we, his children, are called upon to pray for all men and to give thanks *on their behalf* unto God and the Father. Ephesians 5:20 has not received an altogether appropriate translation in either the King James Version or many modern versions, for we can hardly be expected to give thanks always for all things. Are we to give thanks, for example, for our own defeats, for our silence when we ought to speak for the Lord, for our own selfish enjoyments when we might instead have blessed others by our giving? Are we to give thanks for the appalling diseases that afflict innocent children in many parts of the world? Are we to give thanks for the prison camps in Russia of which Solzhenitsyn has written so eloquently? And what of a million and one other evils that result from carelessness, or indifference, or the sheer wickedness of men? The Christian is indeed counselled to give thanks *in* everything (1 Thess. 5:18), but surely not *for* everything.

If we should take this to mean that we are to give thanks *on account of* everything, the Greek of Ephesians 5:20 does not serve to establish this recommendation, for the preposition *huper* followed as it is here by the genitive does not mean "on account of" but *on behalf of*. The thought behind this injunction is beautifully expressed in the Prayer of General Thanksgiving in the Anglican *Prayer Book* which reads: "Almighty and most merciful Father, we thine unworthy servants do give Thee most humble and hearty thanks for all thy goodness and loving kindness to us and *to all men. . . .*" The word *things* in Ephesians 5:20 is an interpolation by the translators—the word *men* would have been more appropriate. Certainly the words "on behalf of all men" is the clear intention of 2 Corinthians 5:14 where precisely the same construction occurs. Yet curiously, almost all modern translators have misunderstood the intent of Ephesians 5:20 and presented it as a call to give thanks *for* everything, improbable as such an injunction would be in a world like ours.

Now there is a large group of passages which employ the word *world* (Greek *Kosmos*, κόσμος). It is widely agreed that this word often has the somewhat abstract meaning of "the human race" or "human species," and that to save the human species required only the saving of a sufficient number of members, not the saving of every member. There are not a few passages where such a key improves our understanding of the meaning.

It has been suggested that there are at least four different meanings to this word. It can mean (1) the natural order, (2) the arena of human history, (3) a segment of society, and (4) the human species. Let us examine these usages.

(1) *The natural order.* In a passage such as John 1:10, "the world was made by Him," it seems clear enough that the creation is intended. It would not seem appropriate to consider this in the more confined sense of either human society (which is after all man-made) or even the human race, for the human race is fallen and not the race that God made. As C. S. Lewis rightly said, when man sinned he brought into being a human species which was not the species which God created. It seems that in this case the word *world* means the natural order as a whole, for He was truly its Creator (Col. 1:16).

But in the same sentence (John 1:10) the words "the world knew Him not" must have a more restricted meaning. In view here is a segment of society at one particular point in time, the people who were the Lord's contemporaries when He walked this earth. Thus a single word in the original can have somewhat different meanings depending upon the context, even in a single sentence. When Acts 17:24 tells us that "[God] made the world and all things therein," we seem clearly to have a reference to the natural order at any period of time; but in 2 Peter 3:4-7 we have a more restricted natural order, the old world, being replaced by an equally restricted natural order, the world that now exists.

(2) *The arena of human history.* In a passage such as Matthew 4:8, "all the kingdoms of the world," the reference is surely to the human scene, and would not include areas where man does not or has not lived (for example, the polar region), which are still nevertheless part of the "natural order." Indeed in the parallel passage in Luke 4:5 the statement is expressed slightly

differently by employing the Greek word *oikoumenē*, meaning "the *inhabited* earth."

(3) *A segment of society*. John 1:10, where we find the words, "He was in the world," seems to have specific reference to the particular society to which Christ came in a special sense by being born as one of them. This was the world which did not recognize Him. It was a world which ought to have recognized Him because it was a segment of society which had received special preparation to this end.

(4) *The human species*. In John 3:16, 4:42, and in many other places, the meaning seems clearly to be the human race as a species, since it was to save this species from total self-destruction and loss that Christ came and offered Himself as a sacrifice. The suicidal nature of the human species has long been recognized as one of its most distinguishing marks *as a species*, setting it apart from all other animal species. Such is the effect of sin that virtually everything natural man plans to do in isolation or co-operatively with other men tends towards the destruction of the species. In the light of eternity the creation of the human species would have been a *total* tragedy but for the saving work of the Lord Jesus Christ. God sent his Son that He might save enough members of this species to preserve the species, and in this sense to become the Saviour of the "world."

Thus in seeking to understand the meaning of 1 Timothy 2:1-6 we have to take into account all these factors: that the word *all* has a number of shades of meaning which modify its universality; that the words *will have*, applied to God or man, may mean either intention or preference; that the word *save* often has the sense of preserving rather than redeeming; that the preposition *for* may mean either "on behalf of" or "on account of"; and that the word *world* has often the connotation of the human race as a whole, rather than every member of it individually. None of these alternatives are in any way exceptional or rare. They are commonly observed in both New Testament and Classical Greek. There is no question of "tampering" with the original. It is a matter of making an intelligent choice among legitimate alternatives, and the guiding factor must be the principle that Scripture is in harmony with itself, and alternatives may not be allowed to create contradictions between single passages and the rest of Scripture as a whole.

There is a further class of passages which seem to belong together and which may indeed be interpreted to signify a certain universalistic aspect of the Lord's death which cannot be denied but which in no way conflicts with the doctrine of Limited Atonement as formulated by the Reformers. We may introduce this aspect of the problem by reference to 2 Corinthians 5:14, 15. Here it is written: "For the love of Christ constraineth us; because we thus judge that if one died for all, then were all dead; and that He died for all, that they which live should not henceforth live unto themselves but unto Him which died for them, and rose again." Now, it seems that there might be two possibilities here whereby this passage may be understood in such a way as to be in harmony with the rest of Scripture, for in harmony with the rest of Scripture it must assuredly be when rightly understood.

The first proposed solution is that one ought to be guided as to the intention of the writer by the fact that the words are addressed to believers (saints at Corinth) who are therefore the referents of the "us" of the text, that is, the love of Christ constraineth *us* believers. Then the words, "we thus judge that if one died for all," should be understood to mean, "If one died for all of us, then we were all dead." That such could very well be the intention seems to be borne out by the words "that they [i.e., the saints] which live should not henceforth live unto themselves." Being the beneficiaries of his death by which we are now among the spiritually alive, we therefore ought to follow his example in this, namely, that we like Him should not live unto ourselves.

There is another possibility. There are a number of passages which speak in universalistic terms of the Lord's death as being for (i.e., on behalf of) all men. Such is the case in 2 Corinthians 5:14. But even more specific is Hebrews 2:9 which reads: "He, by the grace of God, should taste death for every man." There is also 1 Corinthians 15:22: "As in Adam all die, even so in Christ shall all be made alive." Now there is little doubt that Adam experienced death in the sense of terminating his physical life as a penalty for an act of disobedience in eating the fruit of the tree of knowledge of good and evil. That he need not have experienced physical death had he not disobeyed has been the belief of the Christian Church since the days of the Church Fathers, and was believed even before that by Jewish commentators themselves. Roman Catholic theologians have also officially held this view. Adam did not merely shorten his life but actually by disobedience introduced physical death as something new for the human race. Romans 5:12 puts it very precisely: "By man sin entered, and by sin death . . . and so death passed upon all men." Or as 1 Corinthians 15:22 puts it: "In Adam all [men] die."

We are thus mortal creatures, as presently constituted, contrary to what God originally made possible for us when He created Adam and formed Eve. This defective condition of our bodies is the result of our being conceived of corrupted seed. In the sight of God we are defective in this respect, and while the fault is not immediately our own, we come under judgment, the penalty of which is that in the end we are all brought to a condition of both spiritual death and physical death. God is just to pass this judgment of death upon us, but just also in recognizing that we are not personally guilty of the corruption which brings us to physical death. In his justice, God took it upon Himself to pay the price of this mortal defect for all men alike, universally and individually. It is in this sense that the Lamb of God takes away the *sin* of the world (John 1:29), that inheritable defect by which all men are brought to the grave, having tasted death for all men (Heb. 2:9), so that as in Adam all die, in Christ shall all be not merely resurrected but made alive (1 Cor. 15:22), that is, put once for all beyond the power of physical death. Perhaps it is in this sense that 2 Corinthians 5:14, 15 is to be understood.

There would, then, be a truly universalistic aspect to the Lord's sacrifice, not for men's sinful *actions* but for man's sinful *condition*, that condition which renders man a mortal creature. In this aspect of his Atonement there are no limitations placed upon it since all men equally will be raised from the dead, freed forever from this present physical defect, and will therefore face judgment in bodies no longer subject to death. As Jesus assured his hearers: "The hour is coming, and now is, when the dead shall hear the voice of the Son of God . . . and shall come forth: they that have done good, unto the resurrection of life, and they that have done evil unto the resurrection of condemnation" (John 5:25, 29). The ransoming of all men's bodies from the grave is one of the universal effects of the Lord's sacrifice, one real sense in which He died for the world, that is, for all men indiscriminately.

There is one other truly universalistic aspect of the Lord's Atonement which is often overlooked. The Old Testament prescribes sacrifices which are to be offered for all kinds of sins. One special type of sin to be covered by sacrifice was sin done in ignorance. Such sins were called trespasses and the appropriate offering was a trespass-offering. Leviticus 5:15, 17, and 19 provide the following instructions: "If a soul commit a trespass and sin through ignorance . . . then he shall bring for his trespass unto the Lord a ram without blemish . . . for a trespass-offering. . . . And if a soul sin . . . though he wist it not, yet he is guilty and shall bear his iniquity. . . . [The ram] is a trespass-offering: he hath certainly trespassed against the Lord."

Now the Israelite would normally only make such an atonement if he were notified somehow of the offence of which he was otherwise unaware. In the larger context outside the Israelic Covenant with God, no such arrangement existed for men, yet men everywhere and throughout all history have been guilty before God of offences of which they were unaware. This is not to deny the fact, of course, that all men have also been guilty before God of offences of which they were *fully* aware—either accusing themselves or excusing themselves accordingly, their conscience bearing witness (Rom. 2:14, 15). It is not these known offences that we speak of here but the unknown ones: in short, their *trespasses*. What is to be done about these in the Judgment? Would it be just for God to condemn men for sins committed unawares?

Well, God is just indeed. As 2 Corinthians 5:19 assures us: "God was in Christ, reconciling the world unto Himself, not imputing their trespasses unto them." Thus the judgment of God is entirely fair. Among the effects of sin are therefore two consequences for which in fairness man could not appropriately be held responsible: the defect of his body, and the fruits of that defect—sinful actions which are committed without awareness. The first is covered by the sacrifice of Christ when he took upon Himself the sin of the world, and the second when He took upon Himself the world's trespasses. And in these two areas of judgment God was satisfied and man was reconciled. In both of these aspects of man's sinful estate the Atonement appears to have unlimited application. It is possible that not a few passages claimed by those who hold an Arminian position have direct reference to these aspects. Yet in the sense in which Calvin spoke of the Lord's sacrifice as being a Limited Atonement, I do not think these two forms pose any essential challenge to his theological position. Man is still guilty for his deliberate sinful actions.

In short, Limited Atonement is specifically in relation to our SINS, the sinful acts of believers; Unlimited Atonement is in relation to the SIN not only of the believers but of the whole human race (John 1:29). Only if we keep these two words (SINS and SIN) distinct and separate can we reconcile those passages of Scripture which clearly seem to imply Limited Atonement, such as that "the good shepherd giveth his life for the sheep" (John 10:11) and not for the goats, with those which tell us unequivocally that the Lamb gave Himself for the whole world (John 1:29). His sacrifice was indeed *sufficient* for all but *efficient* only for the elect, since otherwise we face the problems of (1) over-compensation (which signifies faulty assessment of the need) and (2) double jeopardy (which introduces a serious legal dilemma).

Only one passage remains to be considered. In 1 John 2:1, 2 it is written: "My little children, these things write I unto you, that ye sin not. And if any man sin, we have an advocate with the Father, Jesus Christ the righteous: and He is the propitiation for our sins: and not for ours only, but also for the sins of the whole world." This passage is admittedly a difficult one for those who hold to a Limited Atonement. Yet it is impossible to believe that there could be in Scripture a very general (though quite specific) theme favouring Limited Atonement only to be countered by a single passage unequivocally presenting precisely the opposite view. I think we have to assume that there is a meaning to this passage which will perfectly satisfy the original Greek while harmonizing with the rest of Scripture. What, then, can be done with these words by way of elucidation?

For centuries, theologians have struggled with this passage and found themselves baffled. It has often been suggested, following Augustine's lead, that we have here an enunciation of the grand principle that the sacrifice of Christ was efficient in intent for the elect of God only, but sufficient in extent for the whole world. Or, to put it slightly differently, his sacrifice was of limited intended application but unlimited in intrinsic value. Its worth was sufficient to cover the sins of all men, but it was not designed to do so; its design was limited to the elect. Augustinians and Calvinists have not denied that Christ died for all men. They have denied only that He died *equally* for all men. In so far as all men will be made alive in Christ and forgiven their sins of ignorance, thus far He died for all men. In so far as He died for the sins of his people (Matt. 1:21) or for this sheep (John 10:15) or for his Church (Eph. 5:25), thus far is his atoning sacrifice limited in its application. In so far as all for whose sins He paid the penalty will come in due time in faith to be redeemed, thus far his victory will be complete. But He did not die for the *culpable* sins of any individual who never avails himself of that sacrifice. Ambrose said that if a man dies unconverted, Christ did not die for him. Such is the usual method of handling this apparently contradictory passage.

There is, however, a remote possibility that John may have had a slightly different thought in mind. John's Epistles in most modern versions are placed among the Epistles directed initially towards Hebrew Christians scattered abroad after the fall of Jerusalem. If it is these Christians, rather than Gentile Christians, that John originally had in mind as he penned these words, then the "ours only" which is contrasted with "the whole world" could conceivably be a reflection of the view held by Jews almost universally at that time that there was a real bifurcation of human society in this respect. The world was composed of two classes of people: the Jews and the Gentiles. To the Jews, the Jews were "we," the Gentiles were "they."

John would then be saying to his Hebrew Christian readers, "Let us remember that our advocate, the Lord Jesus Christ, is the propitiation for our sins—but not for ours only, but also for the sins of Gentile believers throughout the world." In other words, because the reference to "our sins" might be misunderstood as limited to Jewish believers, among whom John included himself, John hastens to add, "And not for ours only, but also the sins of the whole world," thereby including all Gentile believers who enjoyed precisely the same advocacy.*

A rather similar parallel may be observed in 1 Peter 5:9, which reads: "Resist [your adversary the devil] steadfastly in the faith, knowing that the same afflictions are accomplished in your brethren that are in the world." It could be that the Jewish believers to whom Peter addressed his words had a tendency to forget that they belonged to a larger fellowship rooted in the

---

*Caiaphas' prophetic utterance in John 11:52 seems to bear this out. He spoke of Jesus' dying not for "that nation only" but also that He "should gather together in one the children of God that were scattered abroad."

Gentile world. Peter and John may both have desired to remind their brethren of this, in order to strengthen the bonds of Christian unity.

Perhaps the first solution, which is also by far the more commonly employed, is really better. Yet it must be admitted that even this solution has some element of begging the issue about it. But it is true that the Atonement clearly was limited and is limited *in its application* to all who are believers, though there are no such limits to be placed upon its intrinsic worth. Did every man, woman, and child lay claim to it, it would easily support those claims. As 2 Samuel 18:3 indicates, a human king may have such superior worth as to overweigh the deaths of ten thousand ordinary men. How much greater in value must be the death of the very Son of God?

It is always difficult to change the thinking habits of a lifetime. Many of the passages which we have examined in this chapter have for so long been read with a universalistic colouring that it will not be easy to reorient to them, especially when most modern versions continue to reinforce their broader meaning. That this reinforcement may be unwarranted in the light of the rest of Scripture does not make it any easier to reorient oneself. If scholars in their translations of these universalistic passages had from the first been guided by Calvinistic presuppositions, such verses would have struck us very differently, though still faithfully reflecting the original.

In summary, taking into account alternative renderings of the word *all* and of the word *world*, and taking into account an extended meaning of the word *saved*, the three words which play a crucial part in almost every one of the passages of Scripture which seem to challenge the concept of Limited Atonement, it has to be said that these passages may very reasonably be shown to be in harmony. The case against Limited Atonement is not a strong one if these passages are removed from the controversy.

In so treating these apparently contrary passages we may be accused of bending Scripture to support the doctrine we favour. But we may say in reply that our opponents, Arminian-oriented evangelicals, must in like manner face the many passages that we can point to which clearly oppose their position. For example, "Ye have not chosen Me, but I have chosen you" (John 15:16), or "No man can come unto Me, except it were given him of my Father" (John 6:65). Have they ever seriously attempted to retranslate these passages from the original Greek in such a way as to show that there really is nothing exclusive about God's Election? Indeed, do our opponents even try to find an alternative rendering that by its very reasonableness would find wide acceptance? It is difficult to imagine how passages such as these can ever be made to mean anything less than that the Father elects certain ones to be his sheep, and that these sheep are the ones for whom the Shepherd has given his life—while the rest are passed by, being allowed to go their own way.

9

IRRESISTIBLE GRACE

If a man *by nature* always resists the grace of God, then in order for that grace to be effectual it must in some sense be irresistible; for if the grace of God were ineffectual none would be saved, and this we know is not the case.

We know by experience that "the natural man receiveth not the things of the Spirit of God: for they are foolishness to him; neither indeed can he know them because they are spiritually discerned" (1 Cor. 2:14). On the other hand we also know that "to them that received Him gave He the power to become the sons of God, even to them that believe on his name" (John 1:12).

Thus to speak of the grace of God as irresistible is not to say that man cannot resist it, for he does. It is only to say that human resistance is allowed to proceed so far and no further than God pleases. The Jewish authorities were allowed to resist the Holy Spirit to the very last (Acts 7:51), but Paul was allowed to resist only to a point—when his resistance was suddenly brought to an end (Acts 9:5, 6). The grace of God is sovereign; but it cannot be said to be irresistible, for men do resist it. Loraine Boettner suggested that it might indeed be better to employ the term *Efficacious Grace* instead, for this is really what the saving grace of God is. This would spoil a widely accepted mnemonic aid, the acronym T U L I P, beloved of catechists for many generations, but in the interests of greater doctrinal precision it might be well to abandon it.

Now while it is true that man cannot continue to resist the grace of God if the purposes of God require otherwise, there is no doubt that even the elect are sometimes reluctant at first—if not actively hostile, as Paul was. What does this resistance signify? What of the man who seems anxious for the Lord's salvation and yet hesitant about accepting it, perhaps "not far from the Kingdom of God" (Mark 12:34), yet procrastinating on the very threshold as though both longing for and fearing it at one and the same time? If the natural man *cannot* receive these things, how can a man half receive them and half resist them? Is he half-dead? Is such a position possible? Or is it that being born again is a *process* rather than an *event*? The question is an important one to answer.

Was Paul actually already born again that he could recognize the Lord against whose pricks he had been kicking so hard, even though he continued to kick? Was he like Francis Thompson who so eloquently spelled out his flight from God whom he yet was seeking longingly? When did the saving grace of God first reach out to him? When he began to flee Him, or only after he was overtaken? Would the truly dead be aware of the pursuing God of love, "the Hound of Heaven" as Thompson so aptly named Him? Or was there already a spark of spiritual life that made him aware of the divine pursuit long before the moment of capture? Paul must have known of the "prickings" of God—but *how* did he know? The truly dead know not anything (Eccles. 9:5). Was there then a glimmer of life already engendered? In short, when does the *process* of being born again actually begin? Was not Lazarus made alive while he lay in the darkness of the tomb and before he came forth into the light?

Psalm 80:18 and 19 surely sets the sequence of events in their right order. "Quicken us and we will call upon thy name . . . . and we shall be saved." First, quickening; then, calling upon his name; and finally, salvation. Then must we not suppose that the man who kicks against the pricks like Paul, or who comes from the grave still bound hand and foot with the garments of death like Lazarus, or who has progressed along the way so that he is not far from the Kingdom of God like the scribe, even though he has not yet been wholly set free to rejoice in the assurance of salvation, is nevertheless already spiritually alive in some sense? But when, then, was the spark of life actually introduced?

The most apt analogy of all is certainly the analogy of birth. It is the analogy which is associated inevitably with our Lord's conversation with Nicodemus, but it is an analogy adopted in both the Old and the New Testaments alike, as will be seen by the following references.

Of the Rock who begot thee thou art unmindful . . . (Deut. 32:18).

Shall a nation be born at once? (Isa. 66:8).

. . . who were born not of blood, nor of the will of the flesh, nor of the will of man, but of God (John 1:13).

Except a man be born again, he cannot see the kingdom of God (John 3:3).

Of his own will begat He us with the word of truth (James 1:18).

Blessed be the God and Father of our Lord Jesus Christ who, according to his abundant mercy, hath begotten us again unto a lively hope . . . (1 Peter 1:3).

Being born again, not of corruptible seed, but of incorruptible, by the Word of God . . . (1 Peter 1:23).

See also 1 John 2:29; 3:9; 4:7; 5:1, 4, 18.

Consider what this analogy implies. We customarily think of a new birth, the overt and public manifestation of conversion, as the starting point of all Christian experience. Yet is this really so? Is not birth preceded by a period of covert growth and development which follows the act of union of two seeds at the conception of the individual? Life begins with conception, not with birth. And perhaps this is where spiritual life really begins. In natural life a seed is germinated and a period of development is initiated as a consequence, until after a certain number of days or months of prenatal life, depending on the species, gestation is complete and the new living organism comes forth into the world. Thus delivered, the newborn becomes an independent source of life.

If we transfer these sequences of events to spiritual birth we have to conclude that, before actual conversion, there is probably a gestation period. This gestation period is not fixed in duration as it is in the natural world, for some move quickly from their first introduction to the things of God towards actual conversion, while others move very slowly. A few seem to come to birth only after a gestation period occupying years. In either case it is a period of hidden growth, of uneven growth seemingly, of fleeting evidence of life followed by such stillness that we despair of the individual's viability. Many people pass through this gestation period unevenly, at times eager to learn and to talk and to read the Word of God, and at other times showing almost total dormancy or disinterest. And throughout this time the individual invariably lacks assurance. Like the foetus, he or she is dependent entirely upon the protection and encouragement and concern of others. There is no genuine spiritual vitality that is truly self-sustaining.

These things are commonly observed by those who are involved in personal evangelism, who therefore have opportunity to witness a kind of spiritual life which the Lord must have seen in the young scribe who was not far from the Kingdom, and to witness a kind of resistance to the promptings of the Lord which must have characterized Paul's kicking against the pricks before he was finally brought to the place of non-resistance.

It could be, then, that conception and not birth is the *initial* step taken by God in making effectual the Election of one of his children. It must be taken in secret, hidden from both the individual himself and from those who are observing him. The seed which is germinated in the soul is the implanted Word, and the germination is the work of the Holy Spirit of God who makes it alive. In due course after a gestation period the foetal child of God comes to birth, sometimes quietly and sometimes dramatically. And perhaps there are false labours, false alarms, or even births induced before the proper time. But none are stillborn.

Spiritual conception is an act of God. As John 1:13 says, it is "not of the will of the flesh, nor of the will of man, but of God." And as the Lord said to Nicodemus, "That which is born of the flesh is flesh; and that which is born of the Spirit is spirit" (John 3:6). It is of his own will that He *begat* us (James 1:18)—not of any corruptible seed such as is physical but of an incorruptible seed which is the Word of God (1 Peter 1:23), *germinated* by the Holy Spirit in what can be described only as a form of virgin conception. This process is irresistible because there is no one there to resist. This is a work of God clearly, wholly of his initiation and without human consent or refusal. The Lord's people may indeed play a part in it, for it is their privilege to plant the seed, but the recipient of life plays no part in this process whatever.

Do we have any intimations in Scripture that such a period of secret development akin to gestation and initiated by something akin to spiritual conception really does precede the actual coming to birth of a soul? I believe we do. Let us examine four passages of Scripture which when placed in juxtaposition shed a remarkable light on this matter. I propose to set forth these passages first of all without comment, and then to review them by drawing attention to certain remarkable and highly significant parallelisms in the language and symbolism employed by each of these four writers:

> Cast thy bread upon the waters; for thou shalt find it after many days . . . . He that observeth the wind shall not sow; and he that regardeth the clouds shall not reap. As thou knowest not what is the way of the spirit, nor how the bones do grow in the womb of her that is with child: even so thou knowest not the works of God who maketh all [literally, who is doing the whole thing]. In the morning sow thy seed, and in the evening withhold not thine hand: for thou knowest not whether this or that, or whether they both alike, shall be good (Eccles. 11:1, 4-6).

> The kingdom of God is such, as if a man should cast seed into the ground; and should sleep and rise, night and day, and the seed should spring and grow up, he knoweth not how. For the earth bringeth forth fruit of herself; first the blade, then the ear, after that the full corn in the ear (Mark 4:26-28).

> Jesus answered and said unto him, Verily, verily, I say unto thee, Except a man be born again, he cannot see the kingdom of God. Nicodemus saith unto Him, How can a man be born when he is old? Can he enter the second time into his mother's womb, and be born? Jesus answered, Verily, verily, I say unto thee, Except a man be born of water and of the Spirit, he cannot enter into the kingdom of God . . . . Marvel not that I said unto thee, Ye must be born again. The wind bloweth where it listeth, and thou hearest the sound thereof, but canst not tell whence it cometh and whither it goeth: so is everyone that is born of the Spirit (John 3:3-8).

I [Paul] have planted, Apollos watered; but God gave the increase. So then, neither is he that planteth any thing, neither he that watereth; but God that giveth the increase. Now he that planteth and he that watereth are one [in objective and in importance]: and every man shall receive his own reward according to his own labour. For we are labourers together with God (1 Cor. 3:6-9a).

Notice in these quotations the recurrence of such words as *sowing, seed, wind, womb, born, water,* and so on. The passages clearly reflect the same motif: the birth of a soul is like the sowing of a seed which germinates in secret by a mysterious process followed by a time of hidden development that we call gestation. Remember throughout that the seed is the Word of God, for we are born again "not of corruptible seed, but of incorruptible, by the Word of God" (1 Peter 1:23). "Of his own will begat He us with the word of truth" (James 1:18). "Faith cometh by hearing and hearing by the Word of God" (Rom. 10:17). "The seed is the word of God" (Luke 8:11).

In the natural order of things the actual infusion of *individualized* life does not begin at the time of birth but at the time of conception. *Conscious* life begins with birth. What a man may remember with extreme vividness is his spiritual birth. But who can recall or who ever detected when the whole wonderful process was actually initiated? Only God knows which seed of the many portions of the Word of God that may have penetrated and lodged in the womb of the soul will actually germinate, being fertilized by the Holy Spirit. It is our privilege to plant this seed, and it is our privilege to water it, but I doubt if this is anything more than a privilege. I doubt whether we are any longer absolutely essential, for the Word of God in printed form has run to every part of the world for men to read. There are many places where it is not yet known, and here it is our responsibility, and perhaps we are indeed essential for its planting. But by and large the seed can be planted now through a printed portion of Scripture or a tract or a billboard sign without personal human attendance. We know this by experience. Men have been saved by reading a page blown from a worn New Testament. But it is our privilege to plant the seed and it is our privilege to be there also to assist in the prenatal development of the newly conceived yet unborn soul. Most of us have witnessed the entire lack of assurance of those who are still seeking but have not yet come to birth. They are dependent upon our constant stimulation or encouragement. Men do resist this coming to birth, even as Paul kicked against the pricks of God. And who has not exclaimed in eager anticipation, "Thou art not far from the Kingdom!"

How could the dead, those in whom there is no spiritual life whatever, possibly kick against something of which they have not the slightest awareness? And how could the dead so act as to give the impression of having gone a long way towards being alive? Such resistance at the time of conversion could mean only that there is already life present, and at what time in the cycle of coming to birth could such life have been introduced other than at the time of conception? So if we should ask, "What kind of life can the spiritually dead soul have before that soul is born again?" we can only answer, "It can have the kind of life we all have before we are born the first time—prenatal life." For this, only conception is necessary, the germination by the Holy Spirit of the seed which is the Word of God implanted in the soil of the soul. Though the soul is indeed spiritually inert as a seedbed, yet it has a passive aptitude to nourish that implantation if God sees fit to give it life. At this point in time there *can* be no resistance. The implantation and germination are unresisted and irresistible because, while man may sow the seed which the ground cannot refuse, only God can germinate it; and ungerminated it comes to nought. Here, then, we must suppose the birth of a soul begins with an act in which the recipient plays no part; here Election becomes effectual; here the Lord's Atonement is first made applicable; here a new creation is initiated. In this gestation period of prenatal existence the real life of a child of God begins. Here is fashioned in secret, like the stones of the Temple which were later brought to the site, one more member of the Body of Christ, a brother or a sister in the blameless family of God for whom Christ died. There is no resistance to the grace of God in this genesis of the Christian soul, nor indeed in the very nature of the case can there possibly be. It all begins with the seed which is the Word of God, sown through the agency of God's children, germinated and caused to begin its growth in secret through the agency of the Holy Spirit, and watered and nourished by the Lord's people. We become co-workers with God but we never usurp the creative power which rests only in his hands.

Thus as we analyze these four lengthy quotations we see the picture emerging. As the Lord's children and bearers of the seed, we are encouraged to sow wherever there is any hope of a return, "beside all waters," as Isaiah 32:20 puts it. "After many days" the returns will become manifest. Not all the seeds will be germinated. Indeed very few of them probably, for this is God's way. After how many days? We are not told because different soils and different environments produce different harvests. We are encouraged only to have patience because the results will be "after many days" and not immediately. There is no fixed gestation period in spiritual matters. But the possibility of delay ought not to become an excuse for putting off the sowing. He that keeps his eye constantly on the weather will not sow at all! And whoever spends his time studying the sky rather than the soil will find he has no harvest to reap. We do not know "the way of the Spirit" nor precisely how the seed grows in secret before it demonstrates its viability by bursting through the surface of Mother Earth. This is surely the message of Mark 4:26-28. Sow faithfully, and then go about normal business. By all means cultivate the ground and water it regularly, but do not try digging up the seed. Have patience—it takes time. It is God who is working at it, God who is working it all out. Thus we keep sowing in hope (Isa. 55:11).

Here then we have a situation in which it is clear that while others cooperate with God in the birth of a soul, that soul does not himself make any contribution whatever in the initiation of life. The soil is dormant, having only a potential, a capacity for life; but there is no active will either to seek or to refuse the spiritual germination.

Whether the foetus at full term plays any conscious part in coming to birth is a matter about which there is still disagreement. Sometimes it almost looks like it, but the appropriate chemical stimulation can cause extraordinary responses in organisms which have no brain whatever (such as plants), and even more amazingly in decerebrated or effectively brainless animals, and, alas, in anencephalic infants born without the gray cells which constitute the vehicle of mind in normal individuals. Electrochemical reactivity in an unborn body equipped with animal life can cause responses to stimuli that have all the appearance of consciousness which nevertheless can be shown to be absent. That Jacob in the womb should grasp his twin brother's heel (Gen. 25:26) is not an exceptional circumstance, for contact with the palm of the newborn will often induce a grasping reflex even before the cortex (the gray matter of the brain) has developed. Such activity is still entirely reflex. Thus the appearance of an "urge" to be born before actual parturition is sometimes observed, but it is not at all certain whether it is a *conscious* urge involving will or only a reflex action in response to a change in the chemistry of the immediate environment surrounding the foetus.

What can be said with absolute certainty is that in the natural order, until the two seeds unite successfully, there is no coming to be born. And until the seed which is the Word of God takes root in the soil of man's soul wherein lies the seat of his God-given capacity for redemption, and until this seed is germinated by the Holy Spirit in a process somewhat akin to what happened in Luke 1:35, there is no coming in due time to the rebirth of the spirit. Natural birth is not an improper analogy in that it is the climax of a gestation period in which growth has taken place largely in secret. The whole process culminates suddenly in the emergence of a new individual whose independent life is initiated by the inbreathing of the Holy Spirit (John 20:22), in a sudden opening of the eyes to a new understanding (Luke 24:45), in the acquisition of a voice to prove his viability, and in a new form of hunger. It is also the beginning of a different kind of dependence upon others, for nurturing and for fellowship. All these things occur after birth in ways that are different from those vaguely analogous needs which existed during the gestation period.

There can be no resisting by the not-yet-conceived. There can be no desiring for life either. There is, in fact, at this point no one there. And so it is with the divine conception of the new man in Christ Jesus, begotten by the will of God alone. We can examine personal experience for words to describe the *effect* of conversion, but Scripture alone can tell us about the *process* itself. There must surely be much yet that is revealed in Scripture which up to now we have not recognized as relevant. But the great Confessions which formalized the Church's understanding of the process have with one accord sought to preserve and crystallize two aspects of the truth: first, that conversion is a sovereign act in which the recipient plays only a passive role; and secondly, that it results from the combined effect of the Word of God sown and the Spirit of God germinating it. The Confessions have not viewed this sovereign act as being effected by coercion of the will but rather as by a form of persuasion making the will responsive so that the unsaved "come most freely, being made willing by his grace" *(Westminster Confession,* XII. 1), or as Luther put it: "When God works in us, the will, being changed and sweetly breathed on by the Spirit of God, desires and acts not from compulsion but responsively" *(Bondage of the Will,* XXV).

When an individual matures and acts for the first time disobediently and the spirit dies, all that remains to the will is a natural bent towards unrighteousness. With the creation of a new man within, the will towards righteousness is re-created and the original bidirectional freedom of will which Adam first enjoyed is restored. In due time, the elect will reach the place where the old will to unrighteousness has died and there will thenceforth be freedom only to righteousness even as at the present time man by nature has freedom only to unrighteousness.

The creation of this new potential is a sovereign act of God's grace. It is not derived out of the old will, as though the old will were by some process purified in part. But it effectively breaks the bondage of the individual to the old will by creating an antagonist to it. The new life introduces a new kind of motivation, new desires, new goals, new aspirations. The old desires, goals, and aspirations are now challenged. The will to righteousness is not derived by some corrective process within the old will which gives it powers that it did not have before. The will to righteousness is identified with the creation of the new man in Christ Jesus (2 Cor. 5:17).

Conceived as it were "virginally," this new man by the very nature of his being begotten of God partakes of the divine nature (2 Peter 1:4). This is what Paul in Romans 7:22 refers to as "the inward man," a phrase which, in keeping with the original Greek, might quite properly have been rendered "the man inside"! It is only embryonic until it is brought to birth; and it is immature until it is brought to perfection when God's molding and chastening work is completed (Phil. 1:6; Heb. 12: 6-11).

Now life comes before faith. The gradual change which is observable in the elect before they come to birth is spoken of as repentance. Like life, repentance also precedes faith. Faith is exercised by the living, not by the dead. "He that liveth and believeth . . ." (John 11:26). As is clear from John 10:26 we must already be Christ's sheep to be believers. The Lord did not say, "Ye are not my sheep because ye believe not," but "ye believe not because ye are not of my sheep"—which is a very different thing. Faith is not the cause of this life but the proof of it. We are not saved because we believe, but we believe because we are his sheep. Whenever repentance and faith are spoken of in juxtaposition, repentance is placed before faith (Acts 20:21; Heb. 6:1). But if faith is the *result* of life, then whence does repentance originate? One can hardly see repentance, even when commonly interpreted as "sorrow for sins," as occurring before the spirit has been made alive. Yet we normally think of it as a kind of precondition to the new birth. But if man is spiritually dead until he is born again, how can he fulfill such a precondition as that kind of repentance which seems to require that he be already alive? Does a corpse sorrow over its deadness? Can the spiritually dead sorrow over his sins, except perhaps to regret that they did not succeed as he hoped? This is what Judas did when he "repented himself" in vain (Matt. 27:3). Must there not already be some form of spiritual life within the heart to make godly repentance possible? Otherwise, like Judas, a man merely changes his *own* mind.

Repentance in the more basic sense of the word means "change of mind," and it is reflected in experience as a changed attitude in the unbeliever towards the things of God. The idea of a change of attitude on the Lord's part which does not involve sorrow for sins is frequently observed in Scripture as the following verses indicate: Genesis 6:6, 7; Exodus 32:14; 1 Samuel 15:11, 35; 2 Samuel 24:16; 1 Chronicles 21:15; Jeremiah 18:8, 10; 26:3, 13, 19; Amos 7:3, 6; Jonah 3:10; and Hebrews 7:21. And the word also refers to human repentance which has little to do with sorrow for sin, as a comparison of Genesis 27:34 f. with Hebrews 12:17 clearly shows.

What we often witness in those whom we seek to lead to the Lord, before they are born again, is just such a change of attitude. The idea of sorrow for sin is by no means always apparent. Often it is rather a new interest in spiritual matters, a new desire to find meaning, a new openness in discussing the things of God, a new willingness to listen to the message of the Gospel. Such new attitudes do not merely appear after conversion; they are often observed before conversion. They seem to be part and parcel of what is meant in Scripture by repentance. They represent the beginning of a genuine change. Then must we not presume that the seed of spiritual life has already been germinated even though the individual has not yet come to birth? What else can this possibly indicate other than that conception has taken place though the gestation period has not yet run its course? And this period of gestation is by no means an uninterrupted progress forwards. It is often accompanied by periods of dormancy and apparent lack of interest. If in our concern we then try pressure tactics we often run into resistance, the kind of resistance that was clearly manifest in the life of Paul before he was converted. We thus seem to come close to resolving a serious problem in the ordering of events.* There *is* a real kind of spiritual aliveness in embryonic form prior to the new birth. This new life is God-given. It is given unsought and unresisted. It is given secretly so that we, the sowers, can never be sure until later whether our sowing of the seed has been fruitful in the way we hoped. This is a sovereign act, centered in the will of God and not according to the will of man. It is the beginning of the effective realization of God's purposes in Election.

One further point in this connection seems worthy of a moment's reflection. If the course of events associated with the second birth is not altogether unlike that associated with the first, perhaps we can enlarge our understanding by the consideration of one factor in the physical process which may conceivably apply also in the spiritual one.

There are times when, in the natural process, coming to birth seems unduly delayed, and what is known as *induction* is resorted to. Induction is giving artificial assistance (mechanical or chemical) to bring about parturition. May it not be that we are sometimes called upon to give the same kind of assistance to one who is about to be spiritually born? We may properly be reluctant to use any form of pressure to *hasten* the soul into its new life, because we seem thereby to be appropriating the office of the Holy Spirit. But this is not really the case if the crucial work of the Holy Spirit is not in parturition but in conception. We should certainly be prepared in the case of imminent spiritual birth to encourage the soul that is about to be born, though premature interference is to be avoided.

---

*In dealing with the order of repentance and faith, Dabney (Lecture #55 of his *Lectures in Systematic Theology*, p. 655 and 657) remarked: "Let anyone look at the scriptural definition of Repentance, and he will be convinced that none but a regenerate heart is competent to the exercise". And later: "Both these graces are the exercises of a regenerate heart alone; they presuppose a new birth. Now, Calvin, with perhaps the current Calvinistic divines, says that 'Repentance not only immediately follows faith but is produced by it'. And again: 'When we speak of faith as the origin of repentance, we dream not of any space of time which it employs in producing it; but we intend to signify that a man cannot truly devote himself to repentance unless he knows himself to be of God'." But Dabney himself does not feel that this ordering of events is justified. "In our view it is erroneous to represent faith as existing irrespective of faith, in its very first acting, and as begetting repentance through the medium of hope. On the contrary, we believe that the very first acting of faith implies some repentance as the prompter thereof". At the same time he would make "no gap of duration between the birth of the one or the other". This seems to be necessary in order to avoid having repentance (which is a sign of life) precede saving faith (which is also a sign of life). But this problem is obviated very simply if we assume that rebirth *is* preceded by a period of gestation. Repentance is then effectively initiated at the time of conception and active saving faith at the time of birth; the first indicating covert spiritual life, but life nevertheless, and the second overt spiritual life. Dabney's "no gap of duration" would then be replaced by the period of gestation.

If the individual has increasingly shown spiritual concern and hunger for the life that is in Christ Jesus, and is manifestly eager to come to the issue but seems unable to take the final step, ought we not to help him by decisive action? We are not thereby usurping the authority of God; we are merely offering ourselves as active co-workers in his service. Perhaps such induction can be the meeting place between a strict Calvinism that recognizes the sovereignty of grace and a wise and concerned evangelism that actively seeks to remove some of the hindrances to its effectual fulfillment. The householder in Luke 14:16 ff. who prepared his feast sent out his servant into the highways and byways to find guests to fill his table; he did not go himself to fetch them, though he surely might have done so. He sent his servant to bring them in (v. 21) and in some cases even to "compel" them (v. 23). In the latter, the Greek *anagkazo* (ἀναγκάζω) genuinely has the idea of "forceful" constraint.*

But we should not see this as a form of co-operation in the salvation of a soul in the sense that Arminians have used the word *co-operation*, which is now technically termed *Synergism*. The kind of co-operation we are advocating is not between the Lord and the sinner in the initiation of life *at conception*, but between the Lord and his people in bringing a soul to birth after the period of gestation is complete. The older Calvinists sometimes termed irresistible grace *Monergistic Redemption*. And they were certainly putting the emphasis in the right place, for the sinner does not co-operate in any way in his own spiritual conception. This is indeed solely a work of God.

But there is a place for God's people to involve themselves actively when the gestation period seems to have run its course, even as Paul spoke of "persuading men" (2 Cor. 5:11), persuasion which must upon occasion have been tantamount to spiritual *induction*.

The key point of Calvinistic soteriology is the fact of man's complete non-involvement in his own spiritual conception. As Warfield observed, Monergism "has been much more deeply embedded in the system than the doctrine of predestination itself which is popularly looked upon as its hallmark." The contribution which the individual is supposed to make to his own salvation is the exercising of repentance and faith, out of his own inner resources. At the time of the Reformation when Luther was unequivocal about the absolute impotence of man, it was Melancthon who began to interject the idea that man is able to exercise his will by giving free active assent to the Gospel, to "comfort himself" through faith so that the

---

*See on this, Grundman, in Kittel's *Theological Dictionary of the New Testament*, Vol. I, p. 345.

Holy Spirit is then granted, as God comes to his aid.[1] Man's response to the hearing of the Gospel is to believe it; God's response is then to send his Holy Spirit to seal the believer.

According to Warfield: "It was perceived by all the Reformers that the free grace of God must be preserved in its purity in the saving process by insisting upon the elimination from it of all the leaven of synergism." Otherwise God is "robbed of his glory and man is encouraged to attribute to some power, some act, some initiative of his own, his participation in that salvation which in reality has come to him from pure grace."[2] And again, Warfield wrote:

> To God alone . . . belongs salvation and the whole of salvation; He it is, and He alone, who works salvation in its whole reach . . . . Any intrusion of any human merit, or act, or disposition, or power, as ground or cause or occasion, into the process of divine satisfaction—whether in the way of power to resist or of ability to improve grace, or the opening of the soul to the reception of grace, or of the employment of grace already received—is a breach with Calvinism.[3]

And it is a breach with the Gospel!

The crux of the matter is in the initiation of the process, and here I believe we find the safest and truest biblical analogy not in the actual new birth of the new man but in the conceiving, in the germination of the seed, which is the Word of God, by the supernatural life-giving power of the Holy Spirit.

In his *Systematic Theology* under the general heading *The Synergistic Controversy*, Charles Hodge wrote as follows:

> If the soul is not merely morally sick and enfeebled but spiritually dead [as taught in the great Confessions: the *Augsburg, Smalcald Articles*, and finally in the *Formula of Concord*], then it follows: (1) That man since the Fall has no ability to anything spiritually good. (2) That in order to return to God he needs the life-giving power of the Spirit of God. (3) That the sinner can in no way prepare himself to be the subject of this grace, and cannot merit it nor can he co-operate with it. Regeneration is exclusively the work of the Spirit, in which man is the subject and not the agent. (4) That, therefore, it depends on God and not man, who are to be and who are not to be partakers of eternal life. (5) That consequently God acts entirely as a sovereign. . . .[4]

All these inferences are in harmony with the theology of Paul, Augustine, and Calvin, and were freely accepted at first by Luther. But before his death he had begun to lean towards some mild form of Synergism, influenced

---

1. J. L. Neve, *A History of Christian Thought*, Vol. I, p. 258.
2. Benjamin B. Warfield, *Calvin as a Theologian and Calvinism Today*, pp. 5, 16.
3. Ibid., p. 24.
4. Vol. II, p. 720.

perhaps chiefly by Melancthon but also in some measure by the many factions within the Lutheran party which seem to have been concerned to preserve some means of stimulating evangelism, which was in danger of losing its incentive. If man contributed nothing, then why attempt to persuade him? Perhaps, said the Lutherans in the end, man's contribution is not an active one; but it could be a passive one—*non-resistance*. And so as we have seen, for what may have been the best of reasons, namely, concern to keep alive a vital missionary spirit among their members, the Lutherans allowed this small but essential contribution to be made by man. As the *Formula of Concord* (p. 539), after half a century of earnest discussion, finally concluded: "Towards this work the will of the person who is to be converted does nothing *but only lets God work in him until he is converted.*"

But if man must work with God in any essential aspect of his own salvation, then he becomes the ultimate arbiter of his own destiny. He can yield and be saved, or he can resist the grace of God and be lost. Whether his Election is to be made effective or not rests with him and not with God. As we have seen, the Reformers in the Augustinian tradition stood firmly against any such synergistic system of soteriology. They were unbendingly monergistic.

But in recent years, as we shall see in Part IV, even the Christian Reformed Church has witnessed rumblings towards a departure from this firm resolve. Once again the issue is the feeling that pure Monergism is deadening missionary zeal. If man has some real part to play in his own salvation, would this not provide the stimulus required for the Lord's people to go out and exercise their persuasive powers more earnestly, seeking to turn the unsaved back to the Lord? It looks like it. It seems that persuasion would be fruitful and greater eagerness in persuading men would surely turn more men towards God, seeking salvation. But is this *really* true? Would this change the number of the elect?

Or would it bring to the birth prematurely many who as a consequence would recover a normal healthy Christian faith only after years of corrective teaching? Does this not put the whole burden upon man, the persuader, rather than upon God, the Giver of Life; upon the *techniques* of evangelism rather than upon the true message of God's sovereign grace?

Melancthon taught that "some men assent willingly and do not resist the Word of God." If we assume that actual rebirth is the sum and substance of the conversion experience, then there is some evidence that man does have the power to assent willingly, for some men come very easily and quickly to birth, as though they were already fully prepared in their own spirit. Others seem to delay their coming for years. Is this not proof of Melancthon's position? But if we consider that birth must always be preceded by conception and foetal development, and if we admit that man cannot possibly delay or resist his own conceiving, then the situation is different. For what part could

man possibly have in his own conception, when the Word of God is germinated by the Spirit of God and a whole new creation is initiated which had
no existence before its conception?

But once this conception has occurred, others may witness evidences during spiritual foetal development of a new kind of life, of new movements of
the emerging organism long before actual birth. We see a man hitherto
totally indifferent to the things of the Spirit, disinterested in hearing or
reading the Word of God, avoiding Christian company, and shunning all
discussion of spiritual matters, suddenly showing an interest, genuinely,
earnestly, often unashamedly. It is sporadic and evanescent at first. We, the
observers, become excited, wondering if our friend is already born again;
but we learn by many disappointments to be cautious and not prematurely
hopeful. But we ought to be hopeful! It may not be birth but conception
that has taken place and these are the twistings and turnings of a healthy but
yet unborn organism which God has engendered and which in due time He
will bring to birth.

In terms of the soul to be saved, God alone is responsible, monergisti-
cally, for the giving of life, but we meanwhile have the privilege of working
with God synergistically in sowing the seed, and in its cultivation and
watering. "I have planted," Paul writes (1 Cor. 3:6, 7), "Apollos watered;
but God gave the increase. So then, neither is he that planteth any thing,
neither he that watereth; but God who giveth the increase [Greek, *auxanon:*
growth, increase in size]."

Thus we are privileged to co-operate with God in planting the seed but
not in the germination of it. And the soul in whom the seed is thus planted
and germinated plays no part in the germination process.

Jesus said: "All that the Father giveth Me *shall come unto Me* and him
that cometh unto Me I will in no wise cast out . . . . No man *can* come unto
Me, except the Father who hath sent Me draw him . . ." (John 6:37, 44).
This last observation, which proved so offensive when it was first spoken
(even as it proves offensive today) because it challenges man's imagined
freedom, was very deliberately repeated by the Lord (v. 65): "Therefore
said I unto you, that no man can come unto Me, except it were given unto
him of my Father." And we are told that "from that time many of his
disciples went back, and walked no more with Him" (v. 66).

What could possibly be a plainer statement than this of the fact that
salvation is conferred upon a select number who are conceived by the Holy
Spirit and born again by the will of God alone (John 1:13; Rom. 9:15, 16;
James 1:18)? Whoever thus comes to birth does not by this dramatic experience become a child of God, but actually has already become a child of
God (John 17:6) by a prior experience of supernatural conception. When he
comes to birth, he has already been introduced into the family of God, and
for this reason and for no other reason is able to hear God's words (John

8:47). We are thus quickened first and only then do we call upon his name for salvation (Ps. 80:18b; Rom. 10:13). Were the grace of God not irresistible, none would be saved, for none would call upon his name.

In a fallen world, and in the matter of man's salvation, either man *or* God must be free to have the final word. Both cannot. If man is free, God is bound by man's freedom. If God is free, man must be bound by the will of God. In an unfallen world this would not be so, for then all wills would be one. God's grace must be irresistible or man's will would remain eternally opposed to God's, and the creature would override the Creator. Grace has to be irresistible.

10

THE PERSEVERANCE OF THE SAINTS

Eternal security for the believer! The greatest of all assurances—or an invitation to moral laxity? A biblical doctrine plainly rooted in Scripture and part and parcel of the revelation of God along with the promise of forgiveness and cleansing—or simply a logical deduction from the fact of Election? If a promise of God, what of the many passages which seem to warn of the danger of falling away unto perdition and being lost in the end? And if it is up to the believer "to endure," do we not then shift the final responsibility for salvation to the individual himself? Are we then to be *kept* by our own good works after being saved by faith without them?

But if once saved means always saved, should we not then speak rather of the *Preservation* of the Saints than of the *Perseverance*, for must it not be that God preserves rather than that the believer perseveres? Where does our responsibility to maintain good works begin and where does it end? And does this maintenance of good works have a bearing upon our relationship in the family of God as sons of the Father, or only upon our continued fellowship with Him?

Such were the issues that revolved around the central fact of Predestination and Election, issues which divided the Reformers into two factions that found it increasingly difficult to resolve their differences because Scripture seemed to be equivocal, supplying proof texts for the advocates of both positions. In the end not merely two but three streams of theology emerged: the Reformed, the Arminian, and the Roman Catholic. And these three streams have tended only to harden their differences even while all three point to the same Scriptures as their authority. Meanwhile, of all the differences between these three theological systems, the fundamental point at issue might be said to be summed up in the basic question, Does the believer preserve himself or is he kept solely by the power of God?

The issue has been considered of great importance because it seems to be crucial for the maintenance of a godly life. If the believer is kept solely by the power of God—and what other view of the matter could possibly guarantee real security—then it would seem that there is no vital incentive to godly life. What need of learning even the rudiments of the doctrine of the faith, and what need of penitence, and what need of exhortation to obedience? What need of separation from the world and its contamination of spiritual life? What need of good works? Might we not turn around a familiar saying to read, "Eat, drink and be merry, for tomorrow we *live?*" Indeed what need of anything, for are we not free to do exactly as we please without fear of serious consequence in this world or of judgment in the world to come? Does not liberty become licence? Is not this what Paul was inviting when four times he repeated the words, "All things are lawful unto me" (1 Cor. 6:12 twice and 1 Cor. 10:23 twice)? Should we not logically all join hands with the Antinomians who drew just such a conclusion as this and repudiated all controls entirely, claiming the right of each man to do precisely what he chose as he felt inclined, by what he called the inner leading of the Holy Spirit? If such lawlessness was not dangerous, could it possibly be wrong at all?

Thus while the issue might seem to be merely a theological one, its resolution had wide practical consequences for the Lord's people and formed the basis of divisions between believers as well as between branches of the institutional churches, divisions which have confounded all attempts at healing and have so far rendered futile every effort to reunite Christendom into a true organic unity. So unlikely is it that the issue can be resolved that it would almost appear to be a providential device whereby the existence of active controversy keeps the issue vital and the truth constantly under examination, and doctrine in a state of perpetual refinement.

As we have noted already, William Cunningham in his *Historical Theology* stressed the fact that the early Church Fathers often presented contrary views on the same issues.[1] As a result they have often been appealed to for support by opposing parties of later centuries. These contradictory opinions were not matters of grave concern to the Church at that time, but later, when it came time to resolve them, their very existence proved beneficial in some important ways. They had previously received little notice because the issues were not sharply enough defined. But sharper definition was achieved as a direct result of the later controversy to which earlier imprecision had now given rise. These controversies focussed attention, clarifying the issues and refining the answers. Conflict of opinion has thus had the beneficial effect of deepening conviction and enlarging understanding. While the Council of Trent directed Roman Catholic theology along a false trail, Reformed theology honed and refined the truth.

Now the Calvinist position is grounded securely in Scripture, but it is also logically defensible. It may not seem important that it should be logical if it

---

1. Vol. I, p. 179.

is truly biblical. But it is important, because a system of faith that will not bear logical analysis is a faith that becomes indefensible at certain critical points except by emotional reinforcement. When faith is challenged at these points and we find we cannot meet the challenge reasonably we become emotionally defensive, and if the challenge persists long enough we may come to suspect human reason altogether. But if then asked why we reject reason, we inevitably find ourselves searching for reasonable explanations for our rejection, and thus we fall back upon the very thing we are seeking to repudiate. The Lutherans tended to accuse Calvinists of basing the doctrine of eternal security upon reason rather than upon Scripture, making it a logical consequence of their faith in the fact of Election. The Lutherans had to do this because while they accepted Election they rejected eternal security in the Calvinistic sense of being a certainty. They could not allow, therefore, that the doctrine of eternal security was to be found in Scripture, and accordingly they insisted that Calvinists discovered it only by a process of logic.

If God has elected man to be saved and if God is truly sovereign, then man will be saved and cannot end up in any other way. The logic seems unchallengeable. But we have to ask, Upon what *grounds* does God elect? Calvinists say, "Solely upon the grounds of his own good pleasure." But the Lutherans say, "Not so. God elects men on the grounds of foreseen Perseverance." This puts a new complexion on the matter. Because God can foresee who will persevere to the end, He can safely elect those more promising individuals to be conformed to the image of his Son. Thus both parties agree to Election but upon different grounds, and allowing these two different grounds permits a logical extension to two different conclusions regarding the security of the believer. To the Lutherans Election hinges upon foreseen Perseverance; to the Calvinists Perseverance hinges upon Election.

Now the Lutherans were as convinced as the Calvinists that a man is saved by the grace of God, but they differed as to how he is kept. To say that he is also "kept by the power of God" (1 Peter 1:5) was, if taken literally, to invite total indifference on the part of the believer to what he did with his life thereafter. And Lutherans felt that many Scriptures demand that the child of God exercise himself continually towards godliness or he will *not* be kept. Only he that endures to the end will be saved (Matt. 10:22). God's keeping of the believer is contingent upon the believer's endurance. The believer is therefore called upon to mortify the flesh (Col. 3:5), to keep the body under control lest by any means he should himself become a castaway (1 Cor. 9:27). We are to strive to walk worthy of our calling (Eph. 4:1), and to abide in the Lord lest we be cut off and thrown into the fire and burned (John 15:6). The incentive to godly life is the need to preserve the salvation which has been initiated solely by the grace of God. Though this initiation was not a co-operative effort but wholly a work of God, the preservation of it is man's work. Both Lutherans and Calvinists agree that the grace of God in bringing salvation is effectively sovereign. It might be resisted for a season by the elect but it cannot be resisted forever. Once saved, however, a man might indeed resist the grace of God. Calvinists believed that such resistance would be to the hurt of a man's fellowship with God but not his sonship; Lutherans believed that it might be to the hurt both of a man's fellowship and his sonship. Thus the grace of God is both irresistible and resistible, depending on whether we are talking about the experience of regeneration or our walk thereafter with the Lord. Issues which appear sometimes to be very simple and straightforward prove upon closer examination to have nuances which allow for great diversities of opinion.

The compulsiveness of the logic of Calvinism which argues that if man must preserve himself he becomes his own saviour was not lost on the Lutheran Reformers. Consequently, they had to reject the use of logic and insist only upon an appeal to Scripture. And Calvinists replied by underscoring the many passages of Scripture which support the doctrine of eternal security. For example, in John 10:28 the Lord said to his disciples: "I give unto them eternal life; and they shall never perish, neither shall any man pluck them out of my hand." But the Lutherans countered by quoting many passages which seemed to state the reverse, and they sought to take the force out of their opponents' words by reinterpreting such proof texts as this. "True," they said, "no man can pluck us out of his hand. But we by our own disobedience can escape from his hand and be lost." They did not argue that Perseverance was impossible; they argued only that it was up to the believer. It was not guaranteed merely by the fact of Election, for Election itself was based on foreseen Perseverance.

But the Calvinists believed that they need not depend upon logic, though logic is certainly in their favour. They believed that Scripture itself places the security of the believer not in himself but in the Father's good pleasure; and then, having committed themselves to this, they sought a better understanding of those passages which their opponents pointed to as standing against their doctrine. In this they were behaving no differently from the Lutherans and Arminians who supported the contrary view, except in so far as they have concerned themselves more intensively with these apparently contradictory passages with the result that, by sharpening their understanding, a great refinement of doctrine has resulted. By and large Lutherans and Arminians have not been able to refine their position to the same extent, partly because every effort to do so has led to reasoning which is circular. A study of the written works of Arminius shows this very clearly. That it should be impossible, apparently, to break out of this circularity and to reach a final conclusion suggests that the system is basically at fault, not so much in its logical structure but in its premises. By contrast, Calvinism does not suffer in the same way; its logic is linear and it allows the extension of understanding almost indefinitely—one might say, to the limits of human reason, provided that the premises accord with revelation. What Arminius, and what evangelicals of Arminian persuasion, have consistently failed to produce is a logically defensible theology that is not circular in its reasoning; for what they seek to prove is introduced into the argument as part of the proof.

This kind of reasoning was particularly true of Arminius, whose position on this matter closely resembles the Lutheran. In his arguments with his contemporaries he never seems able to escape from circularity of reasoning. What he seeks to prove is first assumed to be true and then forms an essential part of his proof. It should be recognized that Arminius was a most worthy man and undoubtedly a very earnest believer. He often remarks upon the fact that the object of all his theological dissertation was only to lead men to Christ, not to defeat his opponents. He was a man of genuine humility and profound learning. His reputation was admitted equally by friends and foes alike. Beza, one of his most persistent opponents, highly respected his scholarship nevertheless. Arminius admired Calvin and recommended to his students the reading of Calvin's *Institutes* and *Commentaries* as essential to their proper training. He was a gentle man, constantly seeking to avoid raising controversial issues and anxious to find and explore points of agreement rather than disagreement. His early life was marked by tragedy when, in his absence from Amsterdam as a youth, his whole remaining family—mother, brothers, and sisters—was massacred by Spanish forces bent on stamping out the Protestant Reformation Movement in Holland. And the last decade of his comparatively short life was plagued by increasingly incapacitating illness (probably tuberculosis) and constant attacks by strong Calvinist proponents who doubted not only his orthodoxy but also his integrity.

It must be admitted that his persecutors had some grounds for their concern. Arminius occupied a sensitive position as a prominent member of the Dutch Reformed Church and even more as a Professor of Theology at Leiden University where many Reformed students received their basic training. The situation was acerbated by the fact that Arminius hedged regarding his own position in the crucial matters of the capabilities of the natural man, the extent of free will, and the question of the eternal security of the believer. When he was asked to state his opinion plainly regarding such questions as the part which man plays in his own conversion, whether natural man can co-operate with or resist the overture of God, whether man is capable of exercising saving faith on his own initiative, his answer tended always to be equivocal. Sometimes his equivocation may have been unintentional, resulting from circular reasoning from which he could not escape because his doctrine of the total spiritual ineptitude of man was unclear. He admitted freely that it was sometimes *expedient* (his word) to remain silent as to his position rather than to utter a falsehood about it.[2] But he seems not to have recognized that while silence may be proper in the *absence* of a request for a clear statement, it is not proper in the *presence* of such a request. In the latter situation, silence is tantamount to a declaration of error by default.

Arminius held that man had free will for the initiation of repentance and faith. Yet when asked why some men exercised this freedom by responding and others by refusing the overtures of God, he replied in effect,

"It is the grace of God working in them that makes them respond."

"Then why does not the grace of God act to make all men respond?"

"Because the grace of God is directed only towards those who God sees will respond."

And so we end up with the conclusion that the grace of God which brings a response is exercised to bring a response, and that it brings a response because this is why it is exercised. All men can respond, but only some do. Why only some?

"Because God enables them to by his grace."

"Why does He not then enable all men to respond?"

"Because He extends his grace only to those He knows will do so."

"Then what makes the difference between men?"

"The difference is in their responsiveness."

"How does this difference come about?"

"It comes about because God's grace enables those who do respond to respond."

"On what is God's selective enabling based?"

"On foreseen responsiveness in the objects of his grace."

The discussion becomes never-ending and there is no way to break out of it. Calvin's answer to this same problem obviates this circularity by preventing it in the first place and thus allows forward linear progression with very fruitful consequences. Admittedly his answer is irrational in the sense that it is beyond human reason to understand what predetermines God's good pleasure. The rationale of this good pleasure is secret (Deut. 29:29). Yet the fact of his good pleasure is revealed in the New Testament (Eph. 1:5), and if we in faith start with this as the reason why some men are chosen, instead of seeking to base God's choice on some good quality resident in man himself, we break the circle which plagues Arminians and Lutherans and open the way for progress by extension of logical argument. Thereafter discussion becomes generative of entirely new understanding, and theological refinement is possible.

---

2. Carl Bangs, *Arminius*, p. 269.

For one thing we can now begin with the knowledge that all men are *equally* sinful and hopelessly lost. From this we move forward to a number of related doctrines, not the least important of which is that saving faith is not something that man contributes himself but must be an integral part of the atoning benefit of Christ's sacrifice. Like salvation, repentance and faith are gifts of God. We do not need to argue this logically; we need only to read Scripture with our eyes open. The logic is apparent once we have accepted revelation. Similarly it follows that if a man is not saved by exercising his own faith he cannot be lost by ceasing to exercise it. Again this is not merely a logical extension without Scripture to support it, for Scripture tells us plainly that Election means God's choice of the individual and not the individual's choice of God (John 15:16); and God is not a man that He should change his mind (Num. 23:19).

As we have already noted, Arminians have evaded the question of eternal security by a process of deception in the use of words. They agree that believers never lose their salvation. But when asked, "Why not?" they reply, "Because a man loses his salvation only when his faith fails." He thus becomes *de facto* an unbeliever and satisfies the condition of the statement that a man who is actually a believer is one who by definition still enjoys his salvation.

Thus it came about that there developed two factions within the Reformed Movement, one of which tended to be rigidly correct and sound in doctrine but accusatory and lacking in charity, while the other became illogical and unorthodox, yielding to the ever-present humanistic tendencies of a non-Christian world, but broader-minded, more conciliatory, more humane—and in many ways more successful in terms of evangelism and missionary effort. To wed the two theologies seems the most desirable thing in order to preserve the truth without destroying charitableness, brotherly love, and missionary zeal. But human nature being what it is, common sense and humanism inevitably overweigh strict faithfulness to Pauline theology. The tension between these two streams of developing doctrine may in the end prove to be essential for the preservation of both truth and charity.

What the history of the Arminian conflict demonstrates is that while the broader-minded, less precise, and more open-ended interpretation of the elective purposes and methods of God may soften the stark realities of man's need and his relationship to God as a sinner under judgment, the Calvinist position retains a certain clarity of formulation which in the long run is far more fruitful as a guide to thought and action not only in spiritual matters but in almost all areas of man's cultural and social life as well. The inner conflicts inherent in Arminianism which invite debilitating uncertainty are replaced by a redeeming measure of integration and assurance of both mind and heart which is liberating and energizing.

Meanwhile, the Roman Catholics also struggled with the question of the security of the believer and came to a conclusion which is quite different from either the Arminian or the Calvinistic position. Their starting point was different in one very important respect. They believed that baptism is a divinely ordained yet magical rite, efficacious in its effect whether performed by a believer or an unbeliever. In some mystical way a change is wrought in the spiritual status of the baptized individual, a change which is essential for the operation of divine grace. This change is permanent and proof against all subsequent sin, even against those which are mortal in nature. Baptism does not in itself constitute salvation but it opens the way. Once performed it need not and indeed cannot ever be repeated. Venial sins do not undo this fundamental change, and penitence (for lesser sins) and penance (for grosser offences) are sufficient to restore the baptized individual to God's favour even after a life of almost total indifference.[3] Venial sins leave the individual in the position of being able of his own free will to recover himself into a state of favour with God; mortal sin destroys this possibility, requiring that God Himself must then act sovereignly on the individual's behalf to effect restoration. Penance is required, measured by the extent of the offence. Then the sufferings of Christ act by way of compensation.

It is difficult to describe precisely what baptism accomplishes, but it comes near to establishing a kind of "security," since its effect is not destroyed by venial sins. The relationship which it guarantees between the soul and God is a kind of sealing such as Paul speaks of in Ephesians 1:13, 14 and 4:30. Or to use another simile, it is a divinely implanted seed which retains an inerasable character (1 John 3:9). As a rite administered at the very beginning, a divine imprint is set upon the soul so that it preserves throughout life the possibility of salvation at the last. Venial sins do not erase this imprint though they can make the individual very sick. Mortal sins render the individual dead, the imprint being no longer of any effect, so that he cannot recover *himself* by any means. He has lost all "principle of vitality."[4] But God can raise the dead, and therefore there is hope. This principle of vitality seems to be somewhat analogous to the capacity for believing which, Arminius held, has by the grace of God been preserved in every man despite the Fall. It does not represent the actual exercise of faith but only the capacity to exercise faith which the grace of God can act upon.

It is difficult to define in terms of conventional Protestant dogmatic theology what the nature of this permanent change in the soul of the baptized individual really is. It may in fact be dangerous to attempt a definition in such terms. Though we are fully aware of these dangers, it may still be

---

3. See G. C. Berkouwer, *Studies in Dogmatics: Faith and Perseverance*, pp. 48 f.
4. "Sin" in *A Catholic Dictionary*, p. 777.

helpful to view this change as somewhat analogous to opening up the windows of the conscience towards God. Without this magical rite, the conscience is dead towards God and the individual is unable to respond to his grace. Once the window is opened, however, the individual thereafter is always aware of, or can of himself respond to, the grace of God in spite of the venial sins which he commits daily. Penitence is quite within his power and is normally all that is required to keep his soul open to the grace of God. Mortal sins, however, have the effect of closing the window so that while the conscience remains as a faculty, the soul has lost the power of exercising it towards God. Nevertheless God may still by his grace reopen the window so that the mortal sinner may yet recover himself by penitence and penance. If he should refuse to respond to God's overtures, the window remains closed permanently and he can look forward only to eternal punishment in the world to come.

The man whose sins are only venial will reach the end of his life secure in the hope of heaven but not yet entirely prepared to enter without embarrassment into the presence of God. For this man, purgatory is designed to perfect in the next world that which was begun in this. Purgatory is not reprobation or punishment, but joyful preparation. It will be joyful because the sinner who has experienced the grace of God will desire earnestly to be freed of all his unwanted failings and made fit to stand unashamed in the presence of God.

Thus baptism, which is in Roman Catholicism equated with regeneration, is not unlike a kind of potential security for the believer. Without this mystical change in the soul brought about by baptism, the destiny of the individual is dark and hopeless indeed; with it, the destiny of the believer holds promise of fulfillment so long as he continues throughout life to cooperate with the grace of God.

Lutherans never held to this kind of continuance, though when Luther spoke of man's passive aptitude for saving faith he seems to have been approaching the same idea. Roman Catholic doctrine taught that while baptized man has no assured security, he does have a stamp of God upon him that can never be eradicated entirely though it can be rendered ineffective. It cannot be reimprinted. The stamp is in fact indelible.

The Roman Catholic doctrine therefore views baptism as a divinely appointed rite by which a permanent change is effected that can *never* be undone. Even the baptized individual who dies in mortal sin is still in a relationship to God which is different from that of the unbaptized. He does not simply revert to the position of the unbaptized individual, but he places himself in far greater jeopardy by having once tasted but cast away the grace of God. However one defines the term *security* in this context, this much at least can be said: the baptismal imprint cannot be undone. It may therefore be a great gain—but it may be an even greater penalty.

By contrast the Lutherans held that a believer could fall away totally to such an extent as to have need of being regenerated all over again, thus experiencing a second justification.[5] But the Lutherans did accept the distinction between venial and mortal sins and quoted 1 John 5:16: "[There is] a sin not unto death . . . [and] there is a sin unto death." Of the sin unto death John wrote: "I do not say that he shall pray for it." Such a passage is believed quite sufficient to support the distinction between what is venial and what is mortal sin.

Now Lutherans saw saving faith as a gracious gift from God, not something which springs out of the heart of natural man. They therefore distinguished between the capacity to exercise saving faith and actually doing so. A baby has a capacity for language but due to circumstances (deafness caused by disease, for example) the child may never actually employ it; similarly the individual though retaining a capacity for the exercise of faith may, due to the disease of sin, never actually do so.

By contrast, Arminius saw saving faith as something which man must always be able by nature to exercise for otherwise God could not fairly demand it of him. He argued that God would not command man to do what he has not ability to perform. Thus, since it is the individual's own exercise of faith that secures his salvation, it is clear that subsequent loss of this faith must result in the forfeit of salvation. Yet Arminius seems to have felt that this must be a rare occurrence. While by a certain "sleight of hand" he was able to commit himself in writing to the statement that the believer is eternally secure, he really meant only that mortal sin and saving faith cannot co-exist.

Calvin dealt with venial and mortal sin in the life of the believer in his usual decisive way. He said of believers that all their sins must be counted as venial because there is now no condemnation to them that are in Christ Jesus (Rom. 8:1). Thus the believer cannot commit mortal sin and lose his salvation. Nevertheless, he said, in the sight of God all sins are mortal for "the soul that sinneth, it shall die" (Ezek. 18:4). For the believer mortal sins are now venial only, because the Lord Jesus Christ has already suffered the fatal consequences of them in the believer's place.

And thus emerged three distinct theologies out of the debate surrounding the question of eternal security. Today, the final Point of Calvinism might better be restated as the *Preservation* of the Saints rather than Perseverance, for this is really what is involved.

Now we have noted that Calvin was accused of depending upon logic rather than upon Scripture to establish his position on eternal security. In a sense the accusation was just. He applied his logic directly to Scripture it-

---

5. Berkouwer, *Faith and Perseverance*, p. 64.

self. He presented the clear statements of the Word of God on the subject and drew the conclusion that if a particular individual was thus elected to salvation for no reason other than that it was God's good pleasure, the salvation of that individual could not possibly fail to be realized. The essential ingredient of the believer's security lay not in his own power to persevere but in the intention of the Father to present to the Son as gifts all those for whom the Son had paid the full purchase price. Calvin's argument was therefore logical but the premises were not arrived at philosophically. The premises were matters entirely of revelation.

The statement of the Lord Himself, "My Father who gave them to Me," (John 10:29) is the starting point. The fact that we are the gift of the Father to the Son, a circumstance that implies we are in some special way God's possession even before we come to the Son, is constantly reaffirmed by the Lord Himself. It seems to be the starting point of his special concern in what is truly the "Lord's Prayer" in John 17 (especially v. 6). And that we are gifts of the Father to the Son is repeated again and again in John's Gospel: 6:37, 44, 65; 10:28, 29; 17:2, 6, 9, 11, 12, 24; and in many other places. No giver can make a gift of that which is not already his to give. And is it conceivable that God can give to the Son such a present unless it is given in perpetuity? Jesus said: "This is the Father's will [the Greek here is the strong word *thelēma*, meaning *intention*] who has sent Me, that of all whom He hath given Me, I should *lose* nothing but should raise it up again at the last day" (John 6:39).

It is important to observe the care which Paul takes to underscore the fact that we are not saved by *our* faith but *by Christ's faithfulness*. It is well known to Greek scholars that the word *pistis* (πίστις) has a dual meaning: *faith* or *faithfulness.** The point is an important one. If we are saved by our faith it is obvious that we might lose that faith and with it our salvation. But Scripture does not say we are saved by our faith even though we constantly presume this to be so. The Word of God is remarkably explicit on the matter, though the fact has tended to be blurred by most of our translations.

For example, note Galatians 2:20: "I am crucified with Christ: nevertheless, I live; yet not I, but Christ liveth in me: and the life which I now live in the flesh, I live by the faith of the Son of God, who loved me, and gave Himself for me." It is necessary to look at this passage with care in order to

---

*Bultmann has this to say about the word: "In accordance with the Greek feeling for language, πίστις can denote not only the confidence one has but also the confidence one enjoys, i.e., *trustworthiness* . . . . Concretely πίστις means the *guarantee* which creates the possibility of trust, that which may be relied on, or the assurance of reliability . . . . This leads on the one side to the sense of *certainty, trustworthiness*, on the other to that of "means of proof" . . . . In particular πίστις denotes the reliability of persons, *faithfulness.*" (*Theological Dictionary of the New Testament*, Vol. VI, p. 177)

establish the point we are making so that it may be recognized in many other parts of Scripture. The words that need close scrutiny are, "I live by the faith of the Son of God." The reason we need to pause in reading these words is that habit of thought prompts us to read them as though Scripture were really saying, "I live by faith in the Son of God." In point of fact Paul is saying that we do not live by faith *in* the Son of God but by the faith *of* the Son of God. And if we remember that the word rendered "faith" may just as properly be translated "faithfulness," then we see that our life is not dependent upon our faith in Christ but upon Christ's faithfulness.*

This particular truth is underscored by Paul in many places. Thus in Galatians 2:16 he wrote: "Knowing that a man is not justified by the works of the law, but through [Greek *dia*, followed by the genitive] the faithfulness *of* Jesus Christ, even we have believed in Jesus Christ, that we might be justified by means of [Greek *ek*, followed by the genitive] the faithfulness *of* Christ." And again in Galatians 3:22: "The Scripture hath concluded all under sin, that the promise through [Greek *ek*, followed by the genitive] the faithfulness *of* Jesus Christ might be given to them that believe." In each case it is the faithfulness of Jesus Christ and not the perseverance of the believer which is the basis of his eternal security.

The New Testament is full of this principle. Note that in Romans 3:22 the righteousness of God which is imputed to us is not described as being the result of our faith in Jesus Christ. Rather, the correct rendering is: "The righteousness of God which is through *[dia]* the faithfulness *of* Him . . .," that is, through his faithfulness. And then again in Philippians 3:8, 9: "Yea doubtless, and I count all things but loss for the excellency of the knowledge of Christ Jesus my Lord . . . [that I may] be found in Him, not having mine own righteousness, which is of the law, but that which is through *[dia]* the faithfulness *of* Christ, the righteousness which is of God founded upon faith." We have customarily read these familiar passages as though they were speaking about *our* faith *in* Jesus Christ. Although many translations have not followed the lead provided by the King James Version and have interpreted the words as "in Jesus Christ," a number of modern versions have

---

*The Greek at this point is as follows: ἐν πίστει ζῶ τῇ τοῦ υἱοῦ τοῦ θεοῦ. By way of comment it may be said that ἐν followed by what is called an instrumental dative is to be rendered "by means of." The rest of the phrase is correctly rendered, "the faithfulness of the Son of God." On this matter see Dana and Mantey, *A Manual of Grammar of the Greek New Testament* (Toronto: Macmillan, 1955), section 122. Any Greek grammar will serve to elucidate the matter. An excellent New Testament example is to be found in Rev. 6:8: "And power was given unto them . . . to kill *by means of* the sword and hunger and death and the beasts of the earth."

been faithful to the original, especially those which set out to be as literal as possible.*

Any translation which is unfamiliar may seem contrived at first, but it is surely comforting to know that even when our faith does fail us, his faithfulness stands firm. As Paul wrote to Timothy (2 Tim. 2:13): "If we believe not, yet He abideth faithful: He cannot deny Himself." Thus we are kept by the power of God through his faithfulness unto salvation (1 Peter 1:5), for He is able to save to the very end *(eis to panteles)* them that come unto God by Him (Heb. 7:25).

Jesus Christ is in fact both the *author* and the *finisher* of our faith (Heb. 12:2). The anointing which we have received *abides* in us (1 John 2:27), for we are sanctified by the offering of the body of Christ *once for all* (Heb. 10:10) and in the sight of God perfected *forever* (Heb. 10:14). When Paul says that nothing can separate us from the love of God which is in Christ Jesus our Lord (Rom. 8:38, 39), he exhausts the English language to make this security comprehensive: nothing on earth or in heaven, nothing in life or in death, nothing past, or present, or future. Thus he could say with absolute assurance, "He that hath begun a good work in you will perform it [i.e., carry it through] until the day of Jesus Christ" (Phil. 1:6). The same assurance inspired the Lord's people in the Old Testament also: "I know that, whatsoever God doeth, it shall be for ever: nothing can be put to it, nor anything taken from it: and God doeth it, that men should fear before Him" (Eccles. 3:14).

Not one of these assurances depends in any way upon the constancy of man, or upon his own inner resources of obedience or courage or loyalty or anything that is his. Our security lies outside of ourselves, solely in the faithfulness of the Lord our Saviour and in the unchangeableness of God's purposes in numbering us among his elect. We were his choice (John 15:16), not He ours. In this lies our security.

What then do we do with those passages which seem to imply that we may lose our salvation by falling from grace (Gal. 5:4), having our names taken out of the Book of Life as a consequence (Rev. 22:19)? Are we indeed called upon to work out our *own* salvation in this sense (Phil. 2:12) and to endure to the end if we can (Matt. 24:13) by not committing some unpardonable sin (Heb. 6:4-6) and thus becoming a castaway (1 Cor. 9:27)?

---

*Among those versions which have remained true to the original Greek may be listed: the *Berkeley Version*, Wesley's version under the title *Explanatory Notes on the New Testament*, Ferrar Fenton's *The Holy Bible in Modern English*, the *Concordant Version*, which has attempted a faithfulness to the original at the cost of some smoothness in its composition, Young's *Literal Translation of the Bible*, and an interlinear version published by the Watchtower Bible and Tract Society (an agency of the Jehovah's Witnesses Movement).

What happens when a child of God does disobey—and who doesn't? Is there punishment for the disobedient? If so, in what sense is there now therefore no condemnation to them that are in Christ Jesus (Rom. 8:1), or does this apply only to those who "walk not after the flesh but after the Spirit"?

This qualifying statement has for centuries troubled those who believe that the Lord once for all made a full, perfect, and sufficient sacrifice for our sins. If He died for my sins, must I also pay the penalty of disobedience whenever my life is displeasing in his sight? Or am I truly forgiven already, wholly freed from the penalty of all that I have done not in accordance with his will, and of all that I do daily, and of all that I shall yet do? Am I indeed covered by a blanket of pardon that is so comprehensive that I am no longer regarded as a sinner before the Lord but as righteous, not because of what I am in practice but because of what He did on my behalf when He offered Himself in my place? I am convinced that there *is* now no condemnation any more to them that are in Christ Jesus, and that this declaration is unconditional.

As for the rest of this verse as it appears in the King James Version ("to them . . . that walk not after the flesh, but after the Spirit"), it is almost universally agreed by scholars that it has been introduced into the text by mistake. The following modern versions bear this out: *New English Bible, New International Version, New American Standard Version, Revised Standard Version, New American Bible, Jerusalem Bible,* Rotherham's *Emphasized Bible,* Williams' translation, Smith and Goodspeed, Barclay, and the translation by Wuest. This is a case where the eye of the copyist long ago was momentarily distracted to the same sentence in Romans 8:4b and copied it by mistake—a process known as dittography. It almost certainly does not belong in the original text. The assurance of no condemnation is unqualifed: "There is therefore now no condemnation to them that are in Christ Jesus."

In that case there cannot possibly be any *penalty* for disobedience. What often seems to be the consequence of disobedience and therefore is assumed to be penalty, coming as a painful or distressing occasion for rebuke, *is not punishment but chastening.* The Lord, in his graciousness, sometimes allows the expected consequences of our disobedience to trouble us for our good in order that we may be corrected thereby and more nearly conformed to his will. "Whom the Lord loveth He chasteneth, and scourgeth every son whom He receiveth" (Heb. 12:6). But there is no penal aspect in such a sequence of events; it is only an exhibition of his concern for our well-being. Indeed very often there is not even this much of a consequence, our own repentance being quite sufficient for his purposes. In a true sense, the more immediately the correction comes, the more concerned may we judge our heavenly Father to be about us. He is anxious that we should not damage ourselves by our disobedience for we are his beloved children.

But because our awareness of this loving concern is so often dimmed, we need to keep reminding ourselves that judgment really is past. We have already been forgiven all our trespasses (Eph. 4:32). Notice how forgiveness is spoken of here in the past tense: "As God for Christ's sake *hath forgiven* you." Or in Colossians 2:13: *"Having forgiven* you all trespasses."

Now it is sometimes argued that we are forgiven our offences only after we have committed them. But the truth of the matter is that the Lord Jesus Christ took these offences upon Himself long before we were even born. "[He] bore our sins in his own body on the tree" (1 Peter 2:24). The penalty of these offences, though they were not yet committed, was paid there and then. That judgment is past. When troubles come our way and we feel we can see their connection with our own disobedience, we should remind ourselves that we are not being punished but being chastened now in order that we not be condemned with the world later on. As Paul says, "When we are judged, we are chastened of the Lord, that we should not be condemned with the world" (1 Cor. 11:32). It is in this sense that judgment begins at the House of God (1 Peter 4:17). The word translated "judged" in 1 Corinthians 11:32 is the Greek *krino*, a word which means simply "to assess" without any necessary connotation of whether such assessment is favourable or unfavourable. The same applies to the word translated "judgment" in 1 Peter 4:17. The word translated "condemned" in 1 Corinthians is formed from the same basic root but it is compounded with the prefix *kata-*, which means *down*, thus fixing the sense of condemnation upon the word. It is important to note these different meanings, for many passages in which the word *krino* occurs are used to support views which go far beyond the original text. Such, for instance, is the common remark, "Oh, we mustn't judge!" as though we ought never to evaluate the work of anyone even when such an evaluation is essential before considering him for some particular appointment.* Scripture does not require us to be deliberately naive. We are called upon to be charitable but not at the expense of surrendering good judgment. Assessment in this sense is proper if we are to act responsibly, but condemnation *(kata-krino)* is another matter.

---

*Human nature being what it is, it is all too easy for us to begin with honest assessment only to slip into uncharitable condemnation. I believe that this is what the Lord had in mind in Matthew 7:1 when He advised the Pharisees against making any kind of *moral* assessment, warning them that they would receive the same kind of unfavourable assessment if they made a practice of doing this to others. Everyone has to make judgments; life requires it. But our judgment must be righteous judgment (John 7:24), that is, *fair* judgment. The making of fair judgments is commanded here just as plainly as the command not to make unfair judgments is given in Matthew 7:1. The two passages have to be taken together. The Greek for the word *judge (krino)* is the same in both cases. It was probably impossible for the Pharisees, by their very training, to make any such fair assessment of the moral behaviour of their fellow men.

In 1 Corinthians 11:31 we read: "If we would judge ourselves, we should not be judged." Here the first word *judge* is *dia-krinō* (not merely *krinō*, nor yet *kata-krinō*, but *dia-krinō*), which means to examine critically, to keep a critical eye on our own behaviour. Then if we take action to correct what we find undesirable in ourselves we shall not need to be assessed by God and chastened. We are in a position, with the help of the Holy Spirit, to correct our own faults in a measure by mortifying the deeds of the body, for example; and when we undertake to do this faithfully there is no need for the Lord to impose his chastening upon us. But whether we do anticipate his chastening or not, the end result is the same: what we experience is correction not condemnation.

In short, for the child of God such correctives are not penalties but remedies. We are no longer in a Court of Law before an outraged Judge, but in a family circle before a disappointed Father. The *must* of the law has become the *should* of the family. Righteous anger is replaced by genuine disappointment. What is being endangered is not *relationship* but *fellowship*. Chastening is a privilege, not a penalty; a proof of concern, not a demonstration of anger.

It is not always possible to find exact "opposites" which will show precisely the difference in the nature of the consequences of disobedience in the life of the unbeliever and the believer. But the following tabulation may help to make this clear, especially if the words set in capitals are placed one against the other in each instance.

TRANSFORMATIONS

An offended JUDGE   becomes   a disappointed FATHER.
A forbidding COURTROOM   becomes   a warm FAMILY CIRCLE.
Strict PUNISHMENT   becomes   sympathetic CHASTENING.
Moral ANGER   becomes   parental CONCERN.
MUST, or else . . .   becomes   SHOULD, because . . .

RELATIONSHIP to God is now made real by FELLOWSHIP with God.

To recognize this shift is of profound importance to the child of God, for what was once a cause of fear on *legal* grounds has now become a cause of concern on *familial* grounds. We seek the Father's forgiveness not because we fear his wrath and the consequent severing of relationship as though we had lost our membership in his family, but because we become aware of his disappointment and the consequent loss of fellowship. Confession ensures the restoration of this sense of fellowship. It is forgiveness in this context that we are seeking, forgiveness for having disappointed Him even as we seek forgiveness from our friends when we disappoint them. Forgiveness in the legal sense is not at issue here; that is already a *fait accompli*. Yet although we are legally forgiven we may still grieve the Lord and lose the sense of his presence and find ourselves out of fellowship with our brothers and sisters in the Lord. For the child of God, *unconfessed sin* is not the same as *unforgiven sin,* but unconfessed sin is still offensive to God because it entails a breach of fellowship. So we seek his forgiveness on this account. And when we nourish an unforgiving spirit towards another brother we endanger our fellowship at that level, too.

It is for this reason that Paul says in Colossians 3:13, "Even as Christ forgave you, so also do ye." He does not say that we are forgiven because we forgive others but rather that we forgive others because we have been forgiven. Then what are we to do with Matthew 6:12, 14, 15? Clearly we have here a different kind of forgiveness, for we are not in a position to exercise the right of judicial forgiveness; only God can forgive sins (Mark 2:7). What the Lord was calling the disciples to do, and calls us to do, is to maintain fellowship wherever possible by keeping the channels open. This is not a question of legal satisfaction but of exhibiting a forgiving spirit to maintain fellowship. When we pray, "Our Father who art in heaven" (Matt. 6:9), we are acknowledging for ourselves the unquestionable fact (if we are born again) that God is our Father. This relationship is the starting point. But what happens when we are disobedient and show no repentance towards God is that our fellowship with Him is sacrificed. And the same thing applies with respect to our brothers and sisters in the Lord. An unforgiving spirit towards them endangers the possibility of fellowship with them and is reflected inevitably in a loss of the sense of communion with our Father, for they are members of the same family and the whole family circle is strained.

When we nourish an unforgiving spirit towards another brother or sister in the Lord, we endanger our fellowship vertically and horizontally. We are called upon to forgive those that trespass against us in order to preserve or restore fellowship at both levels, with God and with his children. It is not legal forgiveness we need now but family forgiveness. "If we walk in the light as He is in the light, we have fellowship one with another, and the blood of Jesus Christ his Son cleanseth us from all sin . . . . And truly our fellowship is with the Father and with his Son Jesus Christ" (1 John 1:7 and 3). Legal forgiveness is essential for sonship, *to establish relationship* within the family of God; familial forgiveness is essential *to maintain fellowship.*

This important truth is easily lost sight of. We see a Christian in a time of suffering and imagine we can trace the effect to a supposed cause, saying to our brother, "Well, it serves you right." I have had this experience when my own brothers in the Lord have spoken with unbelievable harshness, assured in their own hearts that I was suffering the *punishment* of my own disobedience. Yet these same people in the very next breath would probably preach to the unsaved that the Lord Jesus assumed responsibility for all the sins of believers and that thenceforth there is no penalty. We have to learn to see both in our own experience and in the experience of our brethren that when calamity overtakes, neither we nor they are being punished. Sonship itself is not in question; there is not the least possibility of salvation being *lost* because of disobedience any more than there is of salvation being *won* by obedience. The seeming penalty is no penalty at all. It is allowed only as an exhibition of the Lord's loving concern. It is the chastening of a child received into the family of God forever, with whose perfecting He is graciously concerned.

But this does not mean that we are free to disobey. There *is* a penalty in a manner of speaking, but not in the legalistic sense. The penalty is loss of fellowship both with the Lord's people and with the Lord Himself.

One day we may perhaps be called upon to watch a rerun, as it were, of our lives as God has seen them, and all that we have done in self-will will be tested by a fire that will entirely consume the dross. And how we shall rejoice to see it altogether destroyed forever! We shall shed these old rags of self-righteousness with enormous relief when we see them held up for comparison with the spotless linen garment which the Lord is to provide for us and which is the true righteousness of the saints (Rev. 19:8)—and then committed to the flames.

This process of refining fire is set forth in 1 Corinthians 3:11-15: "For other foundation can no man lay than that which is laid, which is Christ Jesus. Now if any man build on this foundation gold, silver, precious stones, wood, hay, stubble; every man's work shall be made manifest: for the day shall declare it, because it shall be revealed by fire; and the fire shall try every man's work, of what sort it is. If any man's work abide which he hath built thereupon, he shall receive a reward. If any man's work shall be burned, he shall suffer loss: but he himself shall be saved; yet so as by fire."

I have known people who were fearful at the thought of coming before the Judgment Seat of Christ (Rom. 14:10 and 2 Cor. 5:10) to have their lives tested in this way. But why should we be afraid? Should we not rather rejoice at the thought that all the garbage of our daily living will be utterly consumed, leaving us only with what the Lord Himself has been able to realize of his own nature and Person in our individual lives? That will indeed be a day of great salvation!

The wonderfully reassuring thing here is that even if a man's total life work as a child of God should turn out to have been built of dead things such as wood, hay, or stubble, so that his building is wholly consumed by the flames, *yet he himself is safe* (1 Cor. 3:15). He himself is beyond destruction even though all else of his own doing should prove to be perishable.

There are a number of rather similar passages in Corinthians. Apparently the saints in that wanton city of Corinth were particularly subject to the evil influences of their pagan environment. Some indeed evidently became so corrupt that the Lord could no longer allow them to remain in the world as part of the living Body of Christ, and He took them home rather than permit them to completely poison the Church's life. It will be remembered that Ananias and Sapphira were taken suddenly home (Acts 5:5 and 10) though their offence might seem to us scarcely to warrant such a drastic penalty. But it should also be remembered that when the Body of Christ was still an infant organism, very small evils had a potentially much more serious consequence for its well-being, magnified as they were in their potency for evil by the very immaturity of the Christian church and by the fewness of its numbers. God therefore took what can best be described as "heroic measures" to preserve the purity and vitality of the Body of young believers by at once removing the corrupted organs. Ananias and Sapphira were thus immediately taken home, for at that stage of its development the Church could not sustain such corruption in its fellowship. This is rather analogous to emergency surgical intervention in the interest of the patient's life.

This swift action did not, however, constitute a revocation of personal salvation, as will be apparent by a reference to a somewhat parallel case recorded in 1 Corinthians 5:1-5 where Paul writes: "It is reported commonly that there is fornication among you, and such fornication as is not so much as named among the Gentiles, that one should have his father's wife. And ye are puffed up, and have not rather mourned, that *he who hath done this deed might be taken away from among you.* For I verily, as absent in body, but present in spirit, have judged already, as though I were present, concerning him that hath so done this deed, in the name of our Lord Jesus Christ, when ye are gathered together, and my spirit, with the power of our Lord Jesus Christ, *to deliver such an one unto Satan for the destruction of the flesh, in order that the spirit may be saved in the day of Jesus Christ."*

So here, then the Church of God had matured at least to this point, that Paul was instructing the saints on how themselves to deal with gross immorality among believers. The offender was to be publicly delivered to Satan for his removal by death. And yet Paul gave the Corinthians every assurance that although the physical life of such a disobedient child of God was thus to be forfeited his spirit was eternally secure, for he was a brother in the Lord and safe in the salvation of his spirit despite the need that his physical life be cut short. The object of this drastic step was twofold: (1) to preserve the health of the local church (1 Cor. 5:6, 7); and (2) to prevent the individual himself from a kind of spiritual reduction to near zero. Paul was not recommending a form of capital punishment by human agency but a special form of termination of life administered by Satan himself who has the power of death (Heb. 2:14). Such a drastic step, which by some has been taken to mean that the individual's behaviour might deteriorate to the point of complete loss of salvation, already demonstrates precisely the opposite. A child of God who progresses so far in his betrayal will be taken home *before* he endangers his very soul!

Such occasions were apparently not infrequent in the earliest days of the Church. But not every serious failure was a cause for such drastic surgery. Remedial action of a less dramatic nature was often possible. As John wrote: "If any man see his brother sin a sin which is not unto death, he shall ask, and He shall give him life for them that sin not unto death. There is a sin unto death: I do not say that he shall pray for *it*" (1 John 5:16). Clearly, there were alternatives in some cases, but not in all. In this light, we see at once that the reference here is not to a loss of salvation but to a situation in which disobedience has proceeded beyond the point where the offender will any longer benefit by chastening. All that remains is to take him home, in order that his spirit may be preserved. Thus Paul in Romans 8:13 warns the Roman Christians likewise: "If ye live after the flesh, ye shall die: but if ye through the Spirit do mortify the deeds of the body, ye shall live."
He is speaking here of a physical body and of physical life, not of the salvation of the soul. Gross disobedience could bring death: better to amend one's ways and live.

Moreover, while some of the actions of the saints may not have been unduly injurious to themselves, it did happen that younger Christians patterning their lives along similar lines were going much farther in departing from godliness, and endangered themselves fatally as a consequence. So Paul wrote (Rom. 14:14, 15): "I know, and am persuaded by the Lord Jesus, that there is nothing unclean of itself: but to him that esteemeth anything to be unclean, to him it is unclean. If thy brother be grieved with thy meat [i.e., with what you feel free to indulge in] then walkest thou not charitably. *Destroy not him with thy meat, for whom Christ died."* The meaning of this warning is clear enough. Behaviour which to a more mature Christian is inoffensive may appear in a different light to a weaker brother who is thereby led astray. Such a brother may turn into licence what for the stronger Christian is only an expression of liberty in the Lord, and he may so fatally corrupt his own spiritual life that the Lord will find it necessary to take him home. Thus, what we allow ourselves as being harmless in our own spiritual life may become the cause of a weaker brother's destruction.

So did Paul write also to the Corinthians in another passage (1 Cor. 8:9-11): "But take heed lest by any means this liberty of yours become a stumbling-block to them that are weak. For if any man see thee which hast knowledge sit at meat in the idol's temple, shall not the conscience of him that is weak be emboldened to eat those things which are offered to idols; and through thy knowledge shall the weaker brother perish, for whom Christ died?" The circumstance behind this warning was a commonplace one in those days. When a sacrifice was taken to any one of the pagan temples throughout the Roman Empire, it had to be the best meat obtainable. The meat was given to the priests who appear to have taken only a portion of it to lay on the altar fire to be consumed. It was their privilege to sell the rest of the meat in a kind of open market which was called the "Shambles." The money from this went into the coffers of the temple to pay its expenses. This meat, thus offered to the public at a very reasonable cost, was naturally the best meat that could be purchased, and many people took advantage of it—including, evidently, many Christians. They were not condoning the offering of sacrifices to pagan deities who were no gods at all, but merely taking advantage of an inexpensive source of good meat. But weaker brethren, only recently saved out of paganism which produced this supply of meat, not unnaturally mistook the motives which prompted Christians to buy it, perceiving only that they were thereby contributing to the maintenance of the worship of idols. Their conscience being defiled when, in spite of their doubts, they continued to follow the example of more mature Christians, the quality of their spiritual life was undermined, sometimes with fatal consequences.

If we the Lord's children see a brother behaving in this dangerous way, we are encouraged to make some effort to correct him if possible. Most of us are reluctant to do this, all too aware of our own spiritual frailty. Nevertheless James wrote (5:19, 20): "Brethren, if any of you do err from the truth, and one turn him again; let him know, that he which turneth the sinner back from the error of his way *shall save a soul from death* and shall hide a multitude of sins." Once again there is no question of personal salvation being at stake but of turning an erring brother back from a course of action which can have only fatal consequences for his life here on earth if he persists.

Peter reiterates this warning to believers among his brethren, the Jewish Christians, when he writes (2 Peter 2:1): "But there were false phophets also among the people, even as there shall be false teachers among you, who privily shall bring in destructive heresies, even denying the Lord that bought them and bringing upon themselves swift destruction." The use of the word *destruction* seems harsh but it is common in Scripture in this context. We have seen it in the passage in Romans 14:15 where we are warned to "destroy not him . . . for whom Christ died." Similarly in 1 Corinthians 3:17 Paul says, "If any man defile the temple of God, him shall God destroy; for the temple of God is holy, which temple ye are." All these passages refer not to pagans but to believers, to the saints who denying their Lord were in danger of being removed and taken home prematurely for the sake of the Body of believers whose spiritual life they endangered.

Many passages refer to this circumstance by implication; but we do not recognize them when we are reading the New Testament, for we seldom observe the circumstance itself today, now that the Church is worldwide and perhaps less endangered as to its continuance by personal disobedience of individual members. Yet such verses are everywhere to be observed. Consider Hebrews 12:9: "We have had fathers of our flesh who corrected us, and we gave them reverence: shall we not much rather be in subjection unto the Father of spirits, *and live?*"

It appears that in Corinth the Lord's people were in the habit of meeting for a kind of Communion Breakfast. Some were making it not so much a memorial of the Lord's death, which it was intended to be, as an occasion for merrymaking and indulgence in purely carnal appetite. Paul wrote to them to remind them that what they were supposed to be celebrating was the Lord's death (1 Cor. 11:23-26) and that by eating and drinking unworthily they were guilty of sacrilege. "Let a man examine himself," Paul wrote, "and so let him eat of that bread and drink of that cup. For he that eateth and drinketh unworthily, eateth and drinketh condemnation to himself, not discerning the Lord's body. For this cause many are weak and sickly among you and many sleep" (1 Cor. 11:28-30). Now, what does this last observation signify? It signifies that by their improper attitudes as the Lord's people, many were spiritually enfeebled, and many others had already been taken home by the Lord and were now asleep in Jesus.

Such sudden judgments are not limited to the New Testament. The Old Testament had witnessed the same kind of thing on a number of occasions, as will be observed by reference to Genesis 38:9, 10 (the case of Onan); Numbers 16:30-32 (the case of Korah); and 1 Chronicles 2:3 (the case of Er). But such illustrations seem to differ slightly in purpose for they were probably judgments imposed with dramatic suddenness upon men who were *not* the Lord's people. Such seems to have been the case also with Herod in Acts 12:21-23.

But all other New Testament examples cited are clearly identified as having reference to members of the household of faith and as such cannot be viewed therefore as penal in nature. They were corrective in the sense that the offenders were prevented from destroying themselves further; in the final analysis they were carried out in mercy, not in anger, their contemporaries having been encouraged to warn them of their own personal danger and to turn them back before it was too late. Even in the worst situation, where the saints are specifically called upon to commit a wilfully disobedient brother to Satan for the destruction of his body, it is still clearly said to be a measure intended to *preserve* his spirit in the day of the Lord Jesus (1 Cor. 5:5). Many passages commonly used to demonstrate that a child of God can carry his disobedience to the point of being lost really demonstrate precisely the opposite. The Lord's sudden action is not a final judgment but the emergency operation of a spiritual surgeon who quickly removes the gangrenous organ to save the patient's soul.

There is no doubt that we can and do grieve the Holy Spirit, whose presence within us secures for us our awareness of sonship in the family of God (Rom. 8:16; Gal. 4:6; Eph. 4:30), and assures us of the Lord's presence within (1 John 3:24). These are the assurances that are partially forfeited when we are disobedient, but such grieving of the Holy Spirit does not mean we surrender our actual sonship or the Lord's presence within. As David said (when he had proved himself capable of murder in consequence of his coveting Bathsheba): "Restore unto me the *joy* of thy salvation" (Ps. 51:12). And when he besought the Lord not to take away his Holy Spirit from him (v. 11), we must remember that the Old Testament saints did not enjoy the uninterrupted presence of the Holy Spirit as we do. With them, the Holy Spirit came and went. It is not until John 14:16 that the promise of his abiding presence was given. In this respect the Old Testament experience was different, as is evident from such passages as 1 Samuel 10:6-10 and 16:14; though we find a contrast in 1 Samuel 16:13.* Evidently the Lord did not deal with all Old Testament saints in the same manner, nor did He deal with them as He deals with us in this present age. What David recognized was the danger of losing his sense of *fellowship* with the Lord, not of losing his relationship; the joy of his salvation, not his salvation per se. The good works of the Lord's children are not to preserve a relationship which would otherwise be lost, but to maintain a fellowship—which is a very different thing.

Yet we are not left without responsibility, for it is our responsibility to maintain that fellowship both with the Lord and with the Lord's children. What a blessing it is that we do not have the responsibility of maintaining our relationship as members in the family of God! If we did, we would be in a constant state of being disowned and being reinstated, a most unsatisfactory kind of life to be termed "more abundant" (John 10:10).

We must see from the implications of these many references that there is a real sense in which by forsaking our walk with the Lord we may become fruitless, cut off from the vine (John 15:4). We do indeed have a responsibility to walk in the light and not to be so habitually disobedient as to fail entirely to exhibit the grace of the Lord Jesus Christ (Gal. 5:4). We are to demonstrate actively in our lives the expected fruits of our salvation (Phil. 2:12), and in times of grave persecution to remain a faithful witness to the end (Matt. 24:13), thus avoiding any danger of becoming "disapproved" in our discipleship (1 Cor. 9:27, where the Greek has *adokimos* [ἀδόκιμος], the antonym to the Greek *dokimos* (δόκιμος), which means "approved," as

---

*The reference is to David. "And the Spirit of the Lord came upon David from that day forward." Does this mean "and never left him"? If it does, David's prayer in Psalm 51:11 was heard ("Take not thy Holy Spirit from me") and the Holy Spirit never did depart from him. In this case David cannot be made an example of those who lose their salvation, as has been done by Arminians. The same would be true of Peter, who is similarly used as an example, for did not the Lord pray that his faith would *not* fail (Luke 22:32)? Clearly he had his time of serious doubt, but surely not to the point that the Lord's prayer for him was refused!

in Romans 14:18; 16:10; 2 Tim. 2:15, etc.). It is in this sense that we *save* our life, though we may be sacrificed to the world.*

We cannot leave this subject without giving some thought to two classic passages of Scripture which are considered powerful weapons in the arsenal of those who would argue against the eternal security of the believer. I have in mind Hebrews 6:1-6 and Luke 15:11-32. Let us look at the Epistle to the Hebrews first for here we read the frightening words, "It is impossible for those who were once enlightened, and have tasted of the heavenly gift, and were made partakers of the Holy Spirit . . . if they should fall away, to renew them again unto repentance."

To understand this warning we need some knowledge of the background of those to whom these words were addressed. And it is important first of all to understand what it meant to a Jew at that time to "believe in Jesus Christ." For this passage has particular reference to "the doctrine of Christ" (Heb. 6:1), or, as this would be understood by the Jewish people, "the doctrine of *the Messiah*" (the definite article being present in the original Greek).

On many occasions during the Lord's earthly ministry we learn that people who called themselves, or who are referred to as, disciples or believers not infrequently became offended at his words and walked no more with Him. It is almost certain that some of these who were once "believers" became his most bitter enemies. What then was meant by the word *believer* in such a context?

It should be realized that the identity of the Lord Jesus presented a number of real problems to the Jewish people. The Lord Himself acknowledged

---

*The question of having one's name taken out of the Book of Life (Rev. 22:19) is a difficult one to resolve. For the Lord said that whoever committed sin of any kind would have his name taken out of the Book of Life (Exod. 32:33). This implies that every man born into this world has his name *entered* in a Book of the Living (a kind of register of all viable births?) to begin with. Presumably all who die before reaching the age of accountability never have their names removed from that Book; and since the Calvinist's position is that such children dying in infancy are to be counted among the elect, Election involves a name's being indelibly inscribed in the Book of Life. Then what of those who are among the elect, and who achieve maturity by passing beyond the infant stage? Are their names indelibly inscribed? When they reach the age of accountability and are disobedient, for all become sinners (Eph. 2:3), then what happens to their names in the Book of Life? Are their names merely left inscribed because they are among the elect, even though they ought really to be removed? Or is this "accounting system" a different kind of accounting system, one that is written in the language of eternity and not in the language of time? There is nowhere in Scripture, to my knowledge, any indication that the names of the elect of God are ever removed from the Book of Life. Perhaps they were written in before the world began (Luke 10:20?), as though they formed part of the stated contract between the Father and the Son as a record of those who would be given to the Son by the Father—and for whom the Son died. Is there perhaps more than one Book of Life: one for the non-elect, from which names are expungeable, and the other for the elect, from which names are never expunged (Rev. 20:12-15)?

that the intense hatred which finally built up against Him was based in part on a genuine misunderstanding and confusion as to his identity. When Jesus on the cross said, "Father, forgive them, for they know not what they do" (Luke 23:34), it was not merely an expression of supreme charitableness; there was an element of truth in it. They did not know what they were doing. Their action was not only morally wrong, it was also a profound *mistake*. Peter, under inspiration, acknowledged this as part of the truth when he said, "And now, brethren, I realize that through ignorance ye did it, as did also your rulers" (Acts 3:17). And Paul likewise in 1 Corinthians 2:7, 8 said: "We speak the wisdom of God in a mystery, even the hidden wisdom, which God ordained before the world unto our glory; which none of the princes of this world knew: for had they known it, they would not have crucified the Lord of glory." As we have seen already, even the Jewish authorities admitted when it was too late that they had made a mistake. This prompted them to desire Pilate to make doubly sure that the tomb was sealed "lest his disciples come by night and steal Him away and say unto the people, He is risen from the dead: so the last error shall be worse than the first" (Matt. 27:64). This does not excuse them, because their real reason for having the Lord crucified was that they hated Him. Even so, it does show that coupled to their hatred of Him for personal reasons was a genuine doubt about Him on messianic grounds.

From their study of Old Testament prophecies the Jews had concluded that when the Messiah came He would free them from all their enemies (Luke 1:71). At that moment their most oppressive enemy was the Roman authority. All other oppressors except the Egyptian Pharaohs had been Semitic like themselves. The Roman oppressors were Gentiles, the lowest of all people in their estimation. The Messiah was to come as a Conquering King, setting the people free from the invaders of their land and liberating their glorious capital city, at the same time bringing healing and prosperity to the whole nation. But in the background, less distinct and less dramatic, one was to come whom they identified as the Suffering Servant, a mediator between themselves and Jehovah; one who would die for their sins (Isa. 53), die for the nation (John 11:50), being "cut off, but not for himself" (Dan. 9:26). If a single Person was to fulfill both roles, it was difficult to reconcile how the King could also be the Suffering Servant, how the one who conquered could also be the one so abused as to be scarcely recognizable (Isa. 53:2-4). It seemed impossible that one who was to lead their armies to victory and set them at the head of the nations, sitting in glory upon the throne of David *forever*, could be the one who was to be "brought as a lamb to the slaughter" (Isa. 53:7). Were there, then, really two separate Saviours: a Lamb who would "save his people from their sins" (Matt. 1:21) and a Lion who would deliver the nation from its enemies (Luke 1:71)?

The secret, of course, lay in the resurrection. But the Old Testament had attached remarkably little importance to the fact of resurrection and it was not therefore a solution the Jews were likely to look for. Indeed there are only a few intimations with respect to Messiah that the resurrection would play a vital role in his ministry. For example, Psalm 16:10 ("Thou wilt not leave my soul in hell") seems to be a reference to the Messiah; but an even less specific passage in Isaiah 53:10 ("He shall prolong his days") does not seem to have been recognized at all. Yet the resurrection of the Lord was the missing key and, as though to emphasize this in prospect, the Lord Himself increasingly made reference to the fact that after three days He would rise again. But his words were lost even upon his closest disciples, because they shared the traditional biblical wisdom of their own day. In point of fact of course, Messiah was to be both the Lamb of God and the Conquering King, fulfilling the two roles perfectly by dying as the Lamb and rising again to become the King.

When John came preaching, he was sent to prepare the people for their King and for the coming Kingdom. This was his identifiable mission. In this role the Jewish people as a whole visualized him as fulfilling the position of the forerunner of the Messiah. When he suddenly appeared in the wilderness the people were excited and full of hopeful expectation. The nation's servitude under the Roman heel would surely soon be at an end, and they flocked to hear him and to ask what they must do to qualify for a place in the victory parade. This was really their motive: not repentance and sorrow for their sins, but eagerness to be on the winning side. Evidently John himself did not at first actually know the identity of the Messiah. He heard the call to prepare the way but he had not yet any certainty as to who the Messiah was. It seems unlikely that he could have anticipated that the Messiah was none other than a relative of his, his own mother being Mary's cousin. He may in fact have had little if anything to do with Jesus since very early childhood, thirty years before. Thus as he watched day by day while the people came out of the city to hear him preach and to be ceremonially cleansed by baptism, he one day received a message from God that the *Suffering Servant* was about to come to him for public identification. Perhaps he was surprised at this since the one he was really expecting and hoping for was not a Suffering Servant but the Messiah. Yet John obediently adjusted his natural expectations and accepted the new reality. When the time came he unhesitatingly identified the One whom he had looked for as the Messiah as, in fact, the Lamb of God instead (John 1:29,36).

In later months, when John found himself in prison, he had time to reflect upon what was happening as he observed the Lord's mighty acts and saw the majesty of his Person; and he seems to have begun to wonder whether Jesus Christ might not also be the Messiah. Could Messiah and the Suffering Servant be one and the same individual?

So John sent a message to Jesus from prison: "Art thou He that should come [i.e., the Messiah] or do we look for another?" (Matt. 11:3); and the Lord sent word back to him that he should be reassured by the miracles of healing—the sight of the blind was restored, the lame were walking, the deaf were hearing, and even the dead were raised, all of which were clearly hallmarks of the Messiah according to Isaiah 35:3-6. And I think we must assume that John, like many of his contemporaries, believed on the Lord Jesus *in this sense*, even though he may have wondered why he himself was not at once set free from his imprisonment.

Meanwhile the Jewish authorities and great numbers of the common people had been struggling with the same problem, trying to make up their minds. There were all kinds of divisions among them as is clear from many passages such as John 7:43; 9:16; and 10:19. Moreover, many of the rulers "believed" also, including Nicodemus—*in this sense* (John 3:2; 12:42). One might say that this kind of faith was more like wishful thinking than firm conviction. Could this man, seemingly so meek and gentle, and often completely "retiring," really be the stuff of a Messiah who would successfully challenge the authority of Rome? Yet they were all impressed both by the regality of his presence and by his miraculous powers. Even the claims which He made for Himself were so stupendous that it seemed doubtful any ordinary man would dare to make them. Everywhere He went He was fulfilling messianic promises of healing, and the people swung back and forth between conviction and doubt, never quite able to make up their minds and dreading the consequences of making a mistake.

Preconceived ideas of what Messiah would be like proved a serious barrier to recognition for they were coloured almost entirely by ambition for power, not by any desire for holiness. The Jewish leaders genuinely imagined that they themselves would form Messiah's inner circle, but here his inner circle was composed of unlearned and ignorant men drawn almost entirely from the wrong strata of religious society.

In short, at one moment the Jewish authorities "believed" He was the Messiah and the next moment they doubted whether He could possibly be. They were both divided among themselves and within their own hearts. And, as is often the case, they were remarkably handicapped by ignorance of the Scriptures and of the circumstances surrounding the Lord's background, about which they were in a good position to be knowledgeable. Had they taken the trouble to enquire, the Temple records would have told them that Jesus was not a Galilean but a Judean from Bethlehem, and of the lineage of David through both Mary and Joseph. Yet in John 7:52 they disqualified Him by assuming He was from Galilee, and at the same time demonstrated their ignorance of the facts of history by suggesting that Galilee was the one place from which one should not expect a great prophet to arise. But in point of fact Elijah, the greatest of Israel's prophets, and Jonah, their greatest prophet to the Gentiles, were both from Galilee. Nicodemus beautifully illustrates the genuine confusion which existed in the minds of many of the Jewish religious leaders at that time.

Consequently it is very important to understand that when we are told "many of the Jews believed on Him," they were not necessarily exercising *saving faith,** faith in a personal Saviour as we commonly think of such faith, but *messianic faith*, confidence that their dreams of national liberation were about to be realized in the Person of Jesus Christ. They witnessed his miracles, and enjoyed the fruits of them. Hundreds were healed of diseases or were blessed with restored vision or hearing, and some of them recovered loved ones from the grave. Never in human history was any community so largely freed of disease as these people who lived round about Jerusalem in our Lord's time! Here was encouragement indeed to this kind of faith, and yet the One through whom these blessings came seemed constantly to fall short of their ideal by his forthright repudiation of their religious standards and of their own station and importance.

Above all, his refusal to challenge the Roman authorities while at the same time advising the Jews to pay their taxes completely baffled their sense of propriety. Could this possibly be Messiah? What had looked promising developed into a more serious situation when it appeared that it was really the authority of the Jewish leaders that was about to be overthrown. As his miracles increased in magnitude, climaxing with the raising of Lazarus and the general acclaim of the common people which followed, it was felt the time had come to settle the issue once for all. The simplest course was to turn Him over to the Romans as a captive. If He then vindicated his mes-

---

*It was possible for a Jew to express such faith that he would be accepted into the fellowship by the believers and even be baptized as a Christian, and yet that man's faith was not a *saving* faith. This seems to be true of Simon who is sometimes called Magus (being one of the Eastern Magi) and sometimes Magnus (after the Vulgate rendering of Acts 8:9). According to Acts 8:9-24 this man's profession of faith was accepted by Philip and the Christians of Samaria. And he was baptized as a believer. Whether Simon was a Jew or not, he was certainly living amongst Jews in Samaria and, like the Jews, was greatly impressed with signs and wonders. The word denoting Simon's amazement at the "signs" which accompanied Philip's ministry is the same word which is used to express the amazement of the Samaritans at Simon's sorcery. It tells us something about the nature of his "faith."

Subsequently, when Peter came to confirm the believers by the laying on of hands and when these believers experienced a special outpouring of the Holy Spirit (as was normal at that point in the Church's development), Simon at once tried to buy from Peter rights to the same power. Peter's response was immediate: "Thy money perish with thee. . . . Thou hast neither part nor lot in this matter: for thy heart is not right in the sight of God. Repent therefore of this thy wickedness. . . . For I perceive that thou art in the gall of bitterness and the bond of iniquity" (vv. 20-23). Simon's trembling response was not a turning to his God for forgiveness, but an entreating of Peter to act on his behalf. It seems almost certain from those circumstances that though Simon had faith, it was not a *saving* faith. He had the same kind of faith that many of the Lord's earlier followers had who later turned entirely against Him. The writer of Hebrews 10:39 may well have had this in mind when he wrote, "Not of them who draw back unto perdition; but of them that believe to the saving of the soul."

siahship by some mighty act leading to Rome's destruction, there would be no question as to his identity, and their own position would be secure. If He allowed Himself to be taken and shamed before his own disciples and before the nation, the claims He had been making would clearly be invalidated, *especially if they could get Him crucified.* Any other kind of death might turn Him into a martyr and make a hero of Him. Crucifixion would demonstrate publicly that He was not merely repudiated of men but cursed of God (Gal. 3:13) and therefore totally disqualified as Messiah.

And it worked out as the Jewish authorities planned. He was seized by the Romans, disgraced by public trial, mercilessly abused by a mob of soldiers —and all this entirely without the slightest resistance. His presentation before the people by Pilate, shamed, disfigured, ridiculed, and apparently helpless, must have struck the people like a thunderbolt. The greater our expectations, the more devastating is the shattering of them. Even his own circle of personal friends was demoralized in utter amazement at the sudden turn of events. Their faith in Him as the promised Messiah collapsed.

After the "tragedy" was all over, the two disciples on the way to Emmaus summed up the general feeling of all the disciples when they said, "We trusted that it had been He which should redeem Israel" (Luke 24:21). *This* was their faith, and it had been shattered by events. Pragmatic Peter said simply, "I go a fishing" (John 21:3); and his companions in disillusionment said, "We also go with thee." It was the end of a dream.

It is true that the Jewish authorities had engineered it all, and they had achieved his repudiation, which was precisely what they intended. Yet there are indications that they were as disappointed in the success of their own plans as the common people were disappointed in the failure of theirs. The common people really had believed Jesus was truly the Messiah, and when He had ridden into Jerusalem in a manner precisely fulfilling the predictions of Zechariah 9:9, their excitement had been intense. "All the world" seemed to have gone with Him (John 12:19), and no doubt the Romans were as disturbed by it all as were the religious authorities themselves, though for a different reason.

We know only too well the rest of the seeming tragedy and the unforeseen triumph which followed the resurrection. But though his triumph was public enough in the sense that thousands of Jews became *true* believers in Him as the Lamb and were wonderfully saved, yet it was not a public triumph in a national sense, for Israel remained officially unconvinced of his identity as Messiah. Pride would not allow them to admit their appalling error publicly, though there were undoubtedly great numbers among the officials who had witnessed his miracles and had joined in the general acclaim only to find their hopes dashed in the events of the crucifixion. These now witnessed the joy and exultation of thousands whose faith had suddenly been re-established and who were turning their world upside down, daily flooding the Temple precincts with their manifestations of joy. Yet the hated Romans were still there, still masters of the land, still exacting from them onerous taxes and many demeaning services. What did it all signify? Meanwhile, though the disciples were telling the people that the old sacrificial system was at an end, the religious authorities had repaired or replaced the rent veil of the Temple, and the whole elaborate system had once again been restored and was going on exactly as before.

How was it all to be reconciled? Was this man really the Messiah or not? And their daily disputations and arguments, which apparently continued for years until the Romans finally destroyed the city and the Temple in A.D. 70, left many of the Jews half-believing, half-doubting, never certain of their own position, still having no personal faith in the Lord Jesus as Saviour. Their "doctrine" was not about a Saviour at all, but about a Messiah; it was "a doctrine of the Messiah" (Heb. 6:1) which absorbed their attention, and it did not pertain to the matter of personal salvation for the individual (Heb. 6:9).

Whoever wrote the Epistle to the Hebrews addressed himself to this problem. "Therefore," he wrote, "leaving the question relating to the doctrine about the Messiah, let us go on to perfection of repentance from dead works and of faith towards God," that is, of *saving faith*. It was quite possible for these half-believers to stop short, even after many of them had personally experienced the wonders of the Lord's active ministry among them by being themselves healed, a ministry which was a foretaste of what would happen when the Kingdom of God was finally established, a demonstration of "the powers of the age to come" (Heb. 6:5). As persecution began to cull their ranks and many were called upon to suffer the consequences of premature defiance of Roman authority, these one-time messianic believers, persisting in their half-faith by returning to the Temple sacrifices and separating themselves from true believers in Jerusalem, had in effect rejoined the screaming crowds who had demanded the Lord's crucifixion in the first place. They were crucifying the Lord a second time (Heb. 6:6). Such Jewish "believers," while saying they believed the Lord Jesus to be the Messiah after all, yet resorted once again to the old sacrificial system and thus demonstrated their lack of any saving faith and of any true comprehension of the role the Lord Jesus had played as the Lamb of God. It was these who were now by this Epistle being warned not to make this fatal mistake but to abandon the old sacrificial system altogether and to cast themselves upon the Lord alone for their personal salvation. This is the burden of verses 9-12: "Beloved, we are persuaded better things of you, and *things that accompany salvation* [i.e., not just messianic promises], though we thus speak. For God is not unrighteous to forget your work and labour of love which ye have showed toward his name, in that ye have ministered to the saints and do minister. And we desire that every one of you do show the same diligence to the full assurance of hope to the end: that ye be not slothful but followers of them who through faith and patience inherit the promises."

And the alternative? In the nature of the case there is only one alternative—"a certain fearful looking for judgment." If after experiencing all these things and concluding that the Lord is truly Israel's Messiah, they should now refuse this work as a personal Saviour also, there simply remains no more sacrifice for sins (Heb. 10:26), and they are hopelessly lost. There is no other destiny except certain judgment (Heb. 10:27). Messianic faith is in vain unless they also have a saving faith.

This is the background of this ominous passage which has caused so many saints to tremble, needlessly fearing that their salvation might be in jeopardy. In actual fact a passage such as this one, having specific reference to Hebrew "believers" rather than to Gentiles, and specifically addressing itself to a rather unique and soon to be ended situation, cannot be safely applied with the same force outside of the circumstances which occasioned its writing. It belongs to us now as an essential part of the Word of God to complete our understanding of a particular situation, but it must be read and understood in the context of its intention. It has to be remembered that the Jewish people of that day expressed two rather different kinds of faith, faith in a national Messiah and faith in a personal Saviour. Mary rejoiced in God her *personal* Saviour (Luke 1:47) while Zacharias rejoiced in a *national* Saviour (Luke 1:71). John in prison undoubtedly recognized the fulfillment of Isaiah 53. What he needed to be assured about was the fulfillment of Isaiah 35. The disciples, and Peter in particular, saw the Lord as the Messiah: "Thou art the Messiah" (Matt. 16:13-16, 21, 22). Of this they were sure at that time. The Jewish authorities were not so sure: "Art thou then the Messiah?" (Mark 14:61). We must therefore distinguish between the faith which had messiahship as its object and the more personal faith which had as its object the work of the Suffering Servant. The messianic issue was constantly to the fore in everyone's mind as witnessed, for example, by the events of John 4:25-42, where the nub of the controversy was not, "Is this man a Saviour?" but, "Is this indeed the Messiah?" (v. 42). And this was the object of the faith expressed in verses 39-41.

On the way to Emmaus this truth comes out very clearly when the two travellers so specifically express their shattered hope that Jesus might have been the national Messiah, "He who should have redeemed Israel" (Luke 24:21). The Lord had responded by saying, "Ought not the Messiah to have suffered these things before entering into his glory?" (Luke 24:26). Perhaps because they did not recognize their need of a personal Saviour, a need which required that one should suffer death in their place, what happened to Messiah was totally beyond them. They were still missing the key, his bodily resurrection. Reconciling what seemed to be two mutually exclusive roles, that of the Lamb and that of the Conquering King, was the basic problem facing every Israelite. Even the prophets themselves had the same problem (1 Peter 1:9-11): "Receiving the objective of your faith, even the salvation of your souls. Of which salvation the prophets have enquired and searched diligently, who prophesied of the grace that should come unto you: searching what, or what manner of time the Spirit of Christ which was in them did signify, when it testified *beforehand the sufferings of Messiah, and the glory which should follow.*" Paul's concern when preaching to the Jewish people was to provide a key to this reconciliation (Acts 17:3): "Opening and alleging that Messiah must needs have suffered, and risen again from the dead; and that this Jesus, whom I preach unto you, is Messiah." It is all of a piece; a believer in Israel was not necessarily a believer in the sense in which we use the term today, yet in many cases there were true believers in the terms of reference under which the Lord presented Himself to them as the hope of Israel. Yet this was only half of the belief that was essential to personal salvation, and the Epistle to the Hebrews was concerned with providing the grounds for encouraging that faith to progress to perfection. Such half-believers were unsaved, and those who went part way and turned back were not fit for the Kingdom of God (Luke 9:62). This seems clearly to be the explanation of the seeds which fell by the wayside and at first responded with enthusiasm, as many of the Jews did, but afterwards were offended or frightened away. John puts the matter thus: "If they *had* been of us, they would have continued with us" (1 John 2:19). They did not persevere to the end, and they were not saved.

I believe we witness even today something analogous. There are many whose lives are chaotic, powerless, and meaningless. We present to them a Lord who will straighten everything out, and in their desperation they are at once encouraged to look to Him for help. The question of a personal Saviour from the *penalty* of sin never enters this kind of Gospel message. It is not "look to the Saviour for forgiveness and restoration to the family of God whom you have outraged by your disobedience" but "take Him on board as the perfect Captain and make your life a success." This message offers a kind of "Gentile Messiah" rather than a personal Saviour; accordingly, the initial response results in a marvellous sense of relief. But later, things don't work out precisely as anticipated and "the sow that was washed turns back to its wallowing" (2 Peter 2:22). It happens again and again. It is a tragedy. The true child of God has quite another experience. We, too, get dirty and need cleansing daily, a fact which implies in some measure a return to our former wallowings. But there is this vital difference, as the Lord said to Peter, " 'If I wash thee not, thou hast no part with Me.' Simon Peter saith unto Him, 'Lord, not my feet only, but also my hands and my head.' Jesus saith unto him, 'He that is washed needeth not save to wash his feet, but is every whit clean: and ye are clean' " (John 13:8-10). The all-over washing we receive in Him is "once for all"; it is only that our daily walk soils our feet. Only our feet need cleansing every day if we walk in his fellowship unbrokenly. For the rest, we are clean in his sight—*forever*, in this sense eternally sanctified (Heb. 10:14). It is important today, as it was when the Epistle to the Hebrews was written, not to make the mistake of presenting the Saviour to be accepted as Lord before we have presented the Lord to be accepted as Saviour.

The second famous passage is the story of the Prodigal Son (Luke 15:11-32). And this requires but little comment if careful attention is paid to the precise wording. The key here becomes apparent as soon as we ask, What was the son's estimate of his own position relative to his father when he was in "the far country"? He was still a son, his father was still his father. In the depths of his anguish he said to himself, "How many hired servants of *my* father have bread enough and to spare, and I perish with hunger! I will arise and go to *my* father and will say unto him, Father, I have sinned against heaven and before thee, and am no more worthy to be called thy son . . . ."

Note that he did not say, "I am no more worthy *to be* thy son," but, "I am no more worthy *to be called* thy son." Not for one moment did he question his own sonship, not for one moment did he imagine that his relationship had been severed. What had suffered was fellowship, not relationship. Even his self-righteous brother who had remained at home recognized this continuing relationship: "As soon as this *thy son* was come, which hath devoured thy living with harlots, thou hast killed for him the fatted calf." When the father rejoiced at the return of his prodigal son and said, "This my son was dead, and is alive again; he was lost, and is found," he cannot surely have meant what we often bend this to mean, for the son himself had assurance of the continued relationship before he began his return journey. Once redeemed, always redeemed—this is the position reflected in both the Old Testament and the New. As Isaiah 44:22 puts it: "I have blotted out, as a thick cloud, thy transgressions, and, as a cloud, thy sins: return unto Me; for I have redeemed thee." The last phrase here assures us that although we may have wandered away our redemption is a completed fact. We are not invited to return *in order that* we may be redeemed but because we have already been redeemed once for all.

What a wonderful assurance such security of sonship brings to us his often wayward children! Once saved, always saved. Praise God!

So there they are: the Five Points, the five great asseverations of the Pauline-Augustinian-Calvinistic system of Reformed Faith which together constitute a satisfying, defensible, coherent, and thoroughly biblical confession that is realistic with respect to man's powers, position, and need, and honouring to God in its unqualified adherence to the principle of sovereign grace.

We have now to see how this sovereign grace of God was, and will be worked out in the life of the nation Israel, and in the personal life of every individual who is called to be a member of God's blameless family.

PART THREE

The Implications for Daily Life

INTRODUCTION

In this part there are four chapters which may seem out of place to those who are familiar with the contents and format of most studies of Calvinism. It is not usual to insert chapters which really deal more with personal life and experience into a volume that is otherwise strictly theological in argument. But I think it is a mistake to divorce theology from experience in this way.

The first chapter is titled "The Comfort of Calvinism" and to my mind there is tremendous comfort in knowing that God is sovereign, that He is our loving heavenly Father and we are his children, accepted in the Lord.

It is to our practical advantage to explore how the sovereignty of God is worked out in the daily relationships of life, and not merely how God deals with history in a somewhat impersonal, wholly objective manner, as though we were not part of the stream of it ourselves.

And there are some very satisfying answers to some very practical problems. Some of these answers become almost obvious and self-evident once we have distinguished between certain terms commonly used in Scripture which have all too frequently been treated as mere synonyms. I have in mind such terms as the *ways of God* and the *works of God, the wishes of God* and *the will of God, righteousness and wickedness* as opposed to *good and evil,* and *fruits* as opposed to *works,* to name only a few. I think it will become apparent, or at least I hope it will, that there are real differences between these terms as employed in Scripture, although we commonly use them imprecisely and so surrender certain insights which might otherwise have been gained by reading the Word of God more carefully.

If the reader should feel that this particular section of the volume is really out of place in a serious theological study, I hope he will nevertheless resist the temptation to skip through to Part IV, which returns to a more usual theological approach. For although Part III is a departure to some extent, it deals with a very essential facet of the whole problem of God's sovereignty in the affairs of men, especially as it relates to personal life.

My own experience has in many ways been a complete departure from what most of the Lord's children expect of life, but well over forty years of living and walking with the Lord in spite of life's vicissitudes have taught me that the certainty of God's sovereign grace, and all that ensues from this certainty, can be the most *saving* faith that a man can have.

11

THE COMFORT OF CALVINISM

In his *Systematic Theology* Charles Hodge wrote: "The whole course of history is represented [in Scripture] as the development of the plan and purposes of God; and yet human history is little else than the history of sin."[1] Can we equate the existence of sin and its consequences with the plan and purpose of God? Is *this* what God originally intended, or has the plan gone wrong?

How sadly true it is that human history, and personal history for each one of us, has been little else than the history of sin. And although we are constantly reminded of this sad circumstance, we still insist that we believe God is in control of every situation, and our Calvinistic theology demands that this be so; and yet we behave by our worrying as though the success or failure of our lives in fulfilling the will of God is dependent upon ourselves. We have no great difficulty in publicly acknowledging with thankfulness the sovereignty of God in our successes and times of good fortune, but when things go badly with us and especially when it is clearly our own fault, we do not even privately thank the Lord for the consequences.

Not that we should thank the Lord for our having failed; but if what we have been saying has any validity, then should we not say, "Thank You, Lord," for the consequences that God allows to arise out of our disobedience, even when these consequences have all the appearance of punishment? We must surely see from Scripture that these consequential events are not punishments but blessings, evidences of our heavenly Father's concern for our good. Only if this is so can we honestly say that *"all things* work together for good" (Rom. 8:28). It is true that this is conditional for the passage goes on to say "to them that love God." Now our love of God is not necessarily reflected in our obedience even though it ought to be. Obedience may be a demonstration to others of something, just as disobedience is. Our love of God is not really dependent on either obedience or disobedience. It is dependent upon the Holy Spirit (Rom. 5:5) who creates it within us. Obe-

---

1. Vol. I, p. 544.

dience arises out of love thus created; it is not the cause of that love, but the consequence of it. The Lord did not say, "If you keep my commandments, you love Me," but, "If you love Me, keep my commandments" (John 14:15). That is the goal, the desirable thing: the hope that our lives will reflect the state of our hearts. But our actions often belie our love for the Lord; yet they are a contradiction not a denial of that love, for that love remains because it originates in God, not ourselves. It is ourselves we hate when we are disobedient, not God that we hate! We love God as a response to his love, not because we are obedient but because He first loved us (1 John 4:19). We often disobey those whom we love! Romans 8:28 is really an assurance that all things do indeed work together for good to them who have been called into this relationship of reciprocal love. This assurance is not based upon the extent to which our behaviour truly reflects that love. For whose behaviour ever does? Things work together for good not because we are good but *because God is sovereign* and He loves us.

So we do disobey, and all too frequently. Our personal lives, like human history, are records of sinful behaviour. Israel's history was a similar record, and yet the Old Testament is a story of the superintending providence of God who constantly brought good out of evil in the life of this elect nation, just as He constantly brings good out of evil in the lives of his elect children today. But more than this—and here is the almost unbelievable thing about this record—God not only overrules all the circumstances attendant upon his children's disobedience so that they turn out for good, but He often ordains those very disobediences! He not merely foresees them and plans ahead to compensate for them by his gracious providence; He predetermines that they shall be performed!

If one needs a single good example, it is significantly to be found in the most dreadful act of human violence and hatred that man has ever committed: the crucifixion of the Lord Jesus Christ. That this was not merely foreseen by the Father, but *predetermined* (Acts 2:23) and *determined before to be done* (Acts 4:27, 28) is stated categorically in the clearest possible terms:

> Him, being delivered by the determinate counsel and foreknowledge of God, ye have taken, and by wicked hands have crucified and slain (Acts 2:23).

> For of a truth against thy holy child Jesus, whom Thou hast anointed, both Herod, and Pontius Pilate, with the Gentiles, and the people of Israel, were gathered together, for to do whatsoever thy hand and thy counsel determined before to be done (Acts 4:27, 28).

Many of us find a profound intellectual satisfaction in the grand truths of Calvinism with their emphasis upon the sovereignty of God, and yet we often fail to find real comfort when we are in trouble. We simply do not apply what we know to what we daily experience of the vicissitudes of life. We have the answers in our heads but do not relate them to the questions in our hearts. We lack the ability or the faith or the will to apply what we *know* to serve as a monitor of what we *feel.* Our knowledge is too objective and our faith is too small.

Now surely, one of the most comforting things about any faith in the absolute sovereignty of the grace of God ought to be the assurance we derive from that faith that God is still on the throne even in our most dismal defeats and that the clouds we so much dread are waiting to pour only showers of blessing on our head. Our lives are so full of stupidities, unwisdoms, ineptitudes, and plain selfishness and confusion of motive that it would be wonderful indeed if we could be fully and once-for-all persuaded that the same grace which overwhelmed us when we were sinful *sinners* and which called us into God's blameless family is still operating when we are sinful *saints!* If only we could grasp the fact that the whole of life is of a piece in this respect, that even when we walk in the shadows of our own disobedience, it is nevertheless God who has appointed the shadows! And if we once understand that He does not merely *ordain* our blessings and *allow* our difficulties but ordains both blessings and difficulties alike, then we are in a position to view the shadow as protection and not as a threat. What an extraordinary thing it would be to bask in the shadow as we bask in the sunshine! Yet this is what the New Testament invites us to do. As Paul says, "In everything give thanks" (1 Thess. 5:18).

This seems reasonable enough if the tribulations are not due to our own disobedience. But most of our tribulation seems to be of our own engineering.

When it is *not* our fault we may not find it hard at all. "Martyrdom" can actually be quite rewarding! It is when the martyrdom takes on the appearance of punishment that it becomes burdensome. And our lives are such that we tend to live in the expectation of punishment, even while we are boldly preaching to others that there is now no condemnation to them that are in Christ Jesus (Rom. 8:1). Our public preaching is correct; our private practice is not.

What is implicit in many New Testament passages on this question of the sovereignty of God in appointing our circumstances is explicit to a remarkable degree in the Old Testament. And here it appears most obviously in connection with the dismal record of Israel's failures. Being a faithful account of man's selfishness and pride worked out on a national scale, the history of Israel is full of illustrations of the fact that God not merely overrules our mistakes *but often even ordains them.*

Before proceeding to demonstrate this from Scripture it is important to underscore the fact that it is the acts themselves which He ordains, not the motivations behind them. Since human life is so full of such acts it is not perhaps surprising that the Old Testament contains many more explicit statements about the sovereignty of God in actions that were culpable than it does about his sovereignty in actions that were meritorious. Of course, revelation is needed to make this point, and without this revelation we would probably not be aware of the truth. We can well imagine that God overrules our mistakes and makes them turn out for good, but what these many passages of Scripture reveal is that He not merely *overrules* these mistakes, nor merely *allows* them, but often *ordains* them. Can it really be that our mistakes are part of his plan?

While God is sovereign, He does not always exercise his sovereignty in all matters and upon every occasion. Sometimes He permits what He might otherwise forbid. He thus exercises the sovereignty of his will in two different ways: absolutely overruling the will of man where it does not conform to his own intention or design, but permitting it to express itself where nonconformity to his own intention is of no consequence or is more acceptable than the alternative use of compulsion. What is of consequence to his own intention is known only to God, and it is therefore often not possible for man to know with certainty whether his actions are free or hedged about by the the divine overruling.

We thus have two forms of divine willing—that which represents God's *intention* and is therefore predetermined for man and cannot be evaded, and that which is his *permissive will* and is not imposed upon man's activities even when man does things which God would prefer he not do. On the one hand, man is therefore providentially and sovereignly appointed to certain actions which form an essential part of the plan of God for his creation, and on the other, man is encouraged or invited, but not sovereignly overruled, to actions which do *not* play an essential part in the plan of God for his creation. There is, in short, a divine intention and a divine inclination, a sovereign will and a permissive will, a requirement and a preference, an election and a predilection, a decree and a desire, a command and a request, a must and a should, a will and a wish.

It is as though God had a master plan that runs like a river through history, sweeping along all in its channel compellingly towards a foreordained goal. Outside of this current along each bank are many things which may or may not be done, and which, whether done or not, in no way check or even assist the current flow. God's master plan thus proceeds towards its fulfillment willy-nilly, forming the current of the divine intention, decreed and unchangeable. In short, what He predetermined has been, is being, and will be done infallibly. This river is formed of his intentions, his sovereign acts, his requirements, his elections, his decrees, his commands, his musts, and his will.

Along the bank are his inclinations, permissions, preferences, desires, requests, shoulds, and wishes. Here He permits man that measure of freedom of action with which He may be gladdened or saddened. But in no way does this measure of freedom modify or interfere with the movement of his purposes towards their appointed end.

What God *intends*, He decrees; what God *permits*, He has foreseen. And thus by a combination of foreordination and foreknowledge, his will remains sovereign, while man retains sufficient freedom to be held accountable—always for his motive, but sometimes for his actions as well.

Let us look into the situation as it is reflected in Israel's history in the Old Testament. The Word of God is full of unexpected insights, and it is when we learn to accept these unexpected things that we make the most significant progress in our understanding of the Lord's dealings with his people.

For the somewhat restricted purposes of this brief survey we shall attempt a review of Israel's history only so far as it illustrates the sovereignty of God in relation to human frailty and sinfulness. The remarkable thing is how explicitly this truth is set forth in the Word of God. Even where man's intentions are manifestly wicked and not merely misguided, there we find the Lord saying most explicitly, "This thing is of Me." And the more wicked such actions are, the more explicit and emphatic is the statement of divine responsibility for the consequences likely to be. What must be borne in mind always is that action and motive have to be kept apart in making moral judgments. We assume a good deed has a worthy motive and an evil deed an unworthy motive. This is a naive judgment. Many good deeds are performed for entirely unworthy reasons, and sometimes evil deeds are necessary in the course of events (like the judicial taking of life, for example) but the motives are not unworthy. The surgeon who amputates a gangrenous leg is performing an evil operation but not a sinful one. Whether an act is good or evil depends upon immediate (historical) circumstance; whether an act is sinful or righteous depends upon eternal (moral) circumstance. Good and evil are not the same as righteous and sinful. God does evil (Job 2:10; Isa. 45:7; Lam. 3:38; Amos 3:6; etc.) but never sin. Man may do good deeds but they may have to be judged sinful in the light of eternity (Matt. 7:22, 23). It is extremely important to recognize these fundamental differences. We are invited to taste and see that the Lord is good (Ps. 34:8) but never that the Lord is righteous—that would be to tempt the Lord. And this we are expressly forbidden to do (Matt. 4:7).

Now Israel's story begins with the preferring of Jacob over Esau, and with God's decision that although Jacob was not really the first-born (Gen. 25:25, 26), he was to enjoy the rights and privileges of primogeniture when he reached maturity. This decision was a sovereign decision taken by God without respect to any merit that Jacob might acquire and in plain contradiction of the actual order of birth (Rom. 9:11, 12). How was this predetermination in the divine plan brought to pass? And why did not God overrule at the time of parturition, so that Jacob was *actually* born before Esau? Would this not have been a better way to achieve his purposes since no deception or trickery would ever have been involved later?

We do not know the answer to this, but we do know that as a consequence of the birth order that actually occurred, Jacob later fulfilled the will of God only by taking advantage of his brother's more carnal nature, what the world might call Esau's earthiness (Gen. 25:27-34), and by using the grossest form of deception (with his mother's connivance) upon his aging and nearly blind father (Gen. 27:1-33). By the first he secured the right to the status of first-born, and by the second he secured parental sanction and validation of it. In the whole affair there was not one admirable thing. It was in fact shameful for a son to treat his trusting father so, and despicable that his mother should enter into the scheme and help him to pull it off. But pull it off he did. The blessing customarily reserved for the first-born, by which his privileged position was legally confirmed once for all, was "mistakenly" given to Jacob, and once given could not be revoked. Though Esau sought with tears to have his father revoke it, his pleading was in vain (Heb. 12:17 and Gen. 27:34, 35). This wretched performance was, as we know from Romans 9:11-13, directed towards an end which was entirely in keeping with the Lord's sovereign will. Yet what an extraordinary way for God to have allowed it to be fulfilled!

One wonders how it would have been fulfilled if Jacob had been an entirely honourable man. I suppose we too sometimes undertake by equally devious means to assist the Lord in the fulfillment of his purpose. At any rate by foul means, not fair, Jacob became the founder of an elect nation. So God performs his strange work, ordaining good and evil at one and the same time (Isa. 41:23) to our dismay, bringing good out of evil, and making the sinfulness of man to praise Him while restraining that which does not (Ps. 76:10).

Jacob's family grew until he had twelve healthy but not altogether scrupulous sons to perpetuate his seed. Among them was one who was to become the saviour of his family, but only *because of* the unscrupulousness of his brothers! This exceptional individual was Joseph.

Now Joseph had become the envy of his ten older brothers because of the special attention paid to him by the aging Jacob. One day their envy was acerbated to the point that they decided to do away with him by dropping him into a pit without clothing, food, water, or shelter from the sun (Gen. 37:24). But just as they were about to leave him, an alternative plan was formulated when the chance of selling him as a slave to some passing Ishmaelite traders on the way to Egypt presented itself unexpectedly (Gen. 37:28). And so Joseph was carried away into Egypt, a stripling and a slave, mourned by his father who believed him dead.

But in Egypt God prospered Joseph exceptionally; and because of his divinely inspired wisdom regarding the bountiful harvests over which he became chief administrator, he was elevated to the position of Prime Minister (Gen. 41:39-44). The famine which Joseph had predicted was apparently everywhere in the Middle East and it was a famine specifically ordained of God (Ps. 105:16, 17). The situation in Palestine became so serious that Joseph's father sent his ten sons down into Egypt to buy enough grain to keep them alive. And so they came face to face once more with the brother whom they had planned to murder but sold into slavery instead. In due time Joseph revealed his identity to them and assured them of his forgiveness, and supplied all their needs. But the really important thing in this story is the insight which Joseph had acquired into the ways of God in dealing with his people. Once his brothers had recovered from their surprise and apprehension at finding themselves in the presence of a brother whom they had once sought to destroy, Joseph explained the circumstances of the whole course of events *from God's point of view*. Notice how explicit he is:

> Now therefore be not grieved, nor angry with yourselves . . . for God did send me before you to preserve life . . . . And God sent me before you to preserve you a posterity in the earth . . . . *So now it was not you that sent me hither but God*. . . (Gen. 45:5, 7, 8).

A little later Joseph made an extraordinary statement which reveals how clearly he understood the guiding hand of God in every circumstance, and how proper it is, when there is evidence of true repentance, that we should know that even our worst actions fall within the pattern of God's foreordination, either as part of what He intends or as part of what He permits. What He intends He decrees *shall* be done, and what He permits He foresees *will* be done; and thus by a combination of foreordination and foreknowledge God's sovereignty remains absolute. And so Joseph said to his brothers:

> But as for you, ye thought evil against me; but God meant it unto good . . . to save much people" (Gen. 50:20).

The family, once settled in Egypt, multiplied greatly in numbers and apparently acquired wealth enough to excite the envy of the native people (Ps. 105:23-25). In their prosperity Israel forgot that they were in a foreign land, and they forgot the promise made to their forefathers that they were to be singled out, placed in the Promised Land, and made a light to the Gentiles by their unique relationship to the Lord. Like so many of us when we dwell at ease, they forgot that this was not their home and that they were a special people, chosen out of the world to be separate from it in order that they might bear witness against its wickedness. So God raised up a new ruling family, and in particular the Pharaoh of the Exodus (Rom. 9:17, 18), under whom Israel was to rediscover that they were indeed a people apart. Under this tyrannical but vacillating man Israel was to be welded into a nation conscious of itself, a nation that was to "be born at once" (Isa. 66:8) when they made the greatest escape in history.

It is necessary to underscore that the Pharaoh of the Exodus was a vacillating man, for it seems from the record as though he was almost willing, after the slightest display of God's miraculous power, to let Israel go without a struggle. It is as though at the end of each day as catastrophe fell upon the land, Pharaoh was quite ready to let them go. But then overnight he suddenly discovered in himself new resolve which he had not anticipated the night before, so that in the morning he revoked the permission of the previous day and threatened Israel with even greater debasement. Every day new calamities overtook him and weakened his resolve. Every night he recovered himself and strengthened his resolve by morning. What Pharaoh did not know was that the energy of the new resolves did not arise from within himself but from God. When Romans 9:18 tells us that God hardened Pharaoh's heart, it seems that we are to understand that God energized him (the word is a quite appropriate rendering in view of its basic meaning) in his original resolution. God was determined that when Israel went out, the circumstances should be so exceptional that they would never forget them. And in order to do this, Pharaoh had to be given such powers of resistance to the demands of the people for their freedom that the people would be brought almost to despair. Only by this means would their Exodus remain indelibly imprinted in their memory. And yet, in spite of the fact that we know by revelation how Pharaoh gathered the resolve he needed to resist God's determination that his people should be set free, we also know that this same Pharaoh was punished for his resistance by being overwhelmed in the Red Sea, a circumstance intelligible only when the action itself is separated from the motive which prompted it. Pharaoh's motive was evil; his action was entirely according to the intention of God. This beautifully illustrates the fact that the sin of the world is not that it does not *do* the will of God but that it does not *choose* the will of God.

And so Israel embarked on the Exodus, which was so crucial an event in their history that it has literally marked their "birthday" and has been annually remembered by them as such ever since. No other event, not even the entry into the Promised Land, has held such a treasured place in their collective memory. To them it marks "the beginning."

They crossed the wilderness with many reminders of the Lord's special care for them all and so found themselves on the threshold of their new home. Spies were sent ahead who came back with tremendous reports of the prosperity they could expect to enjoy, but also of the resistance with which they would meet. However, the people were also assured that strong resolution would carry them through.

And then their courage failed them. They dared not trust the God who had brought them thus far and go on to possess their possessions. Cowardice or lack of faith—it is all the same really—resulted in their return to the wilderness when they might have crossed Jordan into a land flowing with milk and honey whose fruitfulness had been so dramatically demonstrated to them by the bunch of grapes which it required two men to carry (Num. 13:23)! Here they wandered about for another forty years, until every adult who had reached the Promised Land but had turned back (save only Joshua and Caleb) was laid to rest with his fathers, never having tasted of the blessings which had been promised. When a new generation had replaced the old, the people once again found themselves on the threshold, and this time ready to go in and possess the land. It is only later that we are told why God predetermined that there should be this long delay of forty years.

We know now that in this interval the political situation in Egypt deteriorated to such an extent that the Promised Land, which had been united and strongly fortified as a province of Egypt, gradually slipped out of Egypt's control. Its original strength in unity was dissolved by the rise of petty kings and chiefs, and by internal dissent and squabbling among its princes. In Egypt the Pharaohs seem largely to have lost interest in maintaining tight control, and the result was that Israel was enabled, when the time came, to enter the land and capture it piecemeal. The enemy presented no united front against them.

Nevertheless we are told specifically that God did not allow Israel too easy a victory even then, in order that they might not become prematurely at ease themselves. Not all the petty kings and princes yielded at once. Here and there resistance was stiff indeed. Thus in Joshua 11:20 we read: "It was of the Lord to harden their hearts that they should come up against Israel in battle, in order that He might destroy them utterly." There was a real danger that too easy a submission would have led to alliances fatal to Israel's divinely appointed development. Thus it is recorded in Judges 2:20-23 that the Lord sometimes deliberately withheld total victory, saying, "I also will not henceforth drive out any more from before thee of the nations which Joshua left when he died; that through them I may prove Israel."

Moreover, the land might have become so depopulated that wild beasts would have multiplied out of hand and threatened the sparse settlement which Israel could effect while their numbers were still comparatively few. And so in Exodus 23:29 the Lord said: "I will not drive them out from before thee in one year, lest the land become desolate and the beasts of the field multiply against thee." Clearly God was still sovereign and knew what was best.

Whenever we find ourselves encouraged by circumstances to go forward only to discover difficulties in the path, we should not be surprised if some of them, like the river Jordan in Israel's case, are miraculously dried up as our feet touch the waters. But we should not presume that there will be no testing of faith by the opposition of the enemy merely because we have received a clear signal to go forward. It is a striking thing, as we know now, that it was only because Jordan *was* in flood (Josh. 3:15) that the river was so providentially backed up by the undercutting of its banks some miles upstream. For this flooding evidently started a landslide to form an artificial dam which caused the waters to back up in "a heap" (Josh. 3:13, 16). This lasted just long enough for the children of Israel to pass dry-shod over the Jordan and thus appear with distressing suddenness on the other side, precisely at a time when the opposing enemy waiting for them felt it least likely they would cross. So it comes about that God converts obstacles into bridges, for He is in charge also of the *timing* of events in our lives, a fact which often accounts for a large measure of the element of miracle in our walk with the Lord. No doubt the Israelites were surprised a little at the resistance they met here and there. They must have felt that if the Lord had brought them out of Egypt in order to give them the Promised Land, He would simply hand it to them without loss of life or severe struggle.

What the Israelites did not know was that God had reasons for strengthening the hand of the enemy against them even as He had reasons for hardening Pharaoh's heart. And these reasons were not merely that He might prove them and build their character as a people, but also that He might protect them against enemies which they could not possibly know about, the wild animals of which they had no previous experience. These things are clearly written for our instruction (1 Cor. 10:11).

It might seem rather absurd to leave one kind of enemy (human ones) in order to protect against another kind of enemy (animal ones), but history shows that when a new land is suddenly depopulated by conquest, serious consequences may follow. Marco Polo in his *Travels* (Chap. XLV, p. 166) notes that this is precisely what happened in one area of Kublai Khan's Empire when the native population was so decimated that the wild animals multiplied alarmingly and it became no longer safe for human settlement. The situation in the Promised Land might well have developed in the same way. It is a parable of Christian life. With the Lord's help we can sometimes conquer certain obvious failings in our lives, only to find that we have left a vacuum, like the man who swept his house of the evil demons that were in it, but did not ensure an alternative occupancy, with the result that seven times as many devils took up residence instead (Luke 11:26). Self-reformation is always in danger of just such an eventuality.

In due time judges served as governors while the nation passed through its teething pains. One of these judges was Samson, and at that time Israel's most persistent enemy was the Philistines. But, alas, Samson compromised the situation by falling in love with a Philistine woman at the very time he was supposed to be preserving Israel against their depredations. This is analogous to the Christian pastor who takes a non-Christian as a wife while seeking to preserve the separation between his people and the world. We know from the New Testament that it is contrary to the Lord's explicit instructions for any Christian to be yoked with a non-Christian in this way, and it must be particularly so in the case of a Christian leader (2 Cor. 6:14). The extraordinary thing is that this action, so completely contrary to all that we know of the Lord's dealings with us, turns out in Samson's case to have been specifically the Lord's doing.

It was natural that Manoah and his wife, Samson's parents, should have been particularly grieved by their son's actions, for they were godly people and had dedicated their son to the Lord's service. His rise to a position of leadership in Israel must have greatly rewarded them. But now it seemed as though Samson had forsaken the Lord's way entirely and betrayed both their aspirations for him and Israel's hope. But Judges 14:4 makes a surprising statement: "His father and his mother did not know that it was of the Lord, that He sought an occasion against the Philistines." And as events turned out, Samson slew more of the Philistines, and probably more important people *among* the Philistines, when he died than he had throughout his life. And all this because he fell in love with and married a Philistine woman contrary to the whole spiritual import of Israel's family life. We do not hear of any further trouble with the Philistines for another twenty years.

When in due time under Solomon Israel had peace all around, the Golden Age of their history seemed to have dawned. They were united as they had not been united hitherto. Jerusalem was beautified as their capital city, a great Temple was erected to the glory of God as a single place of worship to which all the tribes went up as one man, and an era of great personal prosperity seemed to have been ushered in. It must have appeared to many that this was the millennium towards which all their prophets had looked forward. But as soon as Solomon died a division between the north and south, between Israel and Judah, suddenly emerged, threatening to bring their great hopes to an end. Once again we are surprised to find that although this rift between Rehoboam in Judah and Jeroboam to the north was really due to pigheadedness and inexperience on Rehoboam's part (2 Chron. 10:1 ff.), it was nevertheless God's intention that it should happen. It was a fatal division within the nation, and it proved disastrous for the nation's survival. And yet in 2 Chronicles 10:15 and 11:3, 4, we have a simple summary statement of the fact that what happened was precisely according to God's foreordained plan.

Very briefly, the situation arose because the people of the northern part of the Kingdom became increasingly unwilling that the south should be the centre of everything. They wanted a greater measure of independence and they found a leader in Jeroboam, a man who had been something of a maverick in Solomon's days and had been forced to flee into Egypt as a consequence. Jeroboam was called back to the north to head a new independent party; they then arranged to meet Rehoboam to negotiate new terms of union which would give them greater autonomy. Rehoboam wisely consulted his elder statesmen and they advised him to speak peaceably to Jeroboam and to treat his demands with moderation. But Rehoboam *unwisely* followed the advice of the younger aristocracy in Judah who suggested sterner measures, including a substantial increase in taxes. Unfortunately, this was the policy which Rehoboam adopted—with fatal consequences. This is the summary background of 2 Chronicles 10:15:

> So the king [Rehoboam] hearkened not unto the people: *for the cause was of God,* that the Lord might perform his word which He spake by the hand of Ahijah the Shilonite to Jeroboam the son of Nebat.

The northern tribes rebelled and Rehoboam had no alternatives but either to lose face and do nothing about it, or go to war with them and force them to submit to his terms. This is the background of 2 Chronicles 11:2-4:

> But the word of the Lord came to Shemaiah, the man of God, saying, Speak unto Rehoboam the son of Solomon, king of Judah, and to all Israel in Judah and Benjamin, saying, Thus saith the Lord, ye shall not go up nor fight against your brethren; return every man to his house: *for this thing is done of Me.* And they obeyed the words of the Lord, and returned from going against Jeroboam.

Once again the progressive course of Israel's history was rudely disturbed, this time by the foolishness and pride of a young king who inherited a kingdom just when it had reached its highest stage of development and prosperity. Thereafter, until the time of the Captivity and Exile to Babylon, the nation virtually ceased to be an effective witness among the nations to the great God who had chosen them as a special people for this very purpose. The whole story is indeed a dismal one.

But the saddest part of all was yet to come, for when a greater than Solomon (Luke 11:31) came to heal all the breaches within the nation and to enable Israel to fulfill its mission to the world as spiritual ambassadors under the Messiah, they failed to recognize Him and crucified Him instead, thus virtually committing national suicide.

Yet even this was all part of God's determinate will in order that in their casting away, their spiritual mission might be turned over for a season to the Gentiles (Matt. 21:43) who should, in bringing forth the fruits thereof, be blessed with blessings which would have come to them through Israel had that people fulfilled its mission. Such seems to be the burden of Paul's words in Romans 11:13-31. Paul therefore concludes (vv. 32-36):

For God hath concluded them all in unbelief, that He might have mercy upon all. O the depth of the riches both of the wisdom and knowledge of God! How unsearchable are his judgments, and his ways past finding out! For who hath known the mind of the Lord? Or who hath been his counsellor? Or who hath first given to Him, and it shall be recompensed unto him again? For of Him, and through Him, and to Him, are all things: to whom be glory for ever. Amen.

As we look back over this record of the failures of God's people, we see it was not merely that God was in their victories to be praised as the Lord of all circumstances, but God was in their failures just as actively and sovereignly, performing his "strange work" as Isaiah was inspired to term it (Isa. 28:21). That their failures were reprehensible is clearly stated in Scripture and we are faced accordingly with the apparent anomaly of action that is foreordained in accordance with God's predetermination being at the same time culpable. But did God really *plan* these actions or did He merely allow them?

Sometimes the latter seems the more reasonable conclusion. And yet in the most crucial of reprehensible actions—the acquisition of the right of the first-born by Jacob, the selling of Joseph as a slave, the division of the Kingdom just when it had reached the climax of its development as a nation, and the rejection and crucifixion of the Messiah who would have fulfilled all of Israel's dreams—there can be no question as to whether these actions were decreed and foreordained or merely foreseen and permitted. They were clearly decreed.

What this extraordinary historical record shows to us, the Lord's people, is that God is just as sovereign in times of failure as in times of success, in defeat as in victory. This is a really important lesson to learn. It is not surprising that the Lord has seen fit to emphasize it in the Old Testamant, especially at certain crucial periods of Israel's history. We are so accustomed to reading success stories, and even *Christian* success stories, that we imagine God's purposes are fulfilled only, or at least *best*, during those times when our lives are "successful." But for most of us such successes are few and far between. We may have a measure of peace about our failures but it is not likely we shall derive any comfort from them; and it is almost certain that as soon as the Lord takes occasion to allow certain consequences in order that He may perfect in us that which He has begun (Phil. 1:6), we shall be tempted to view them as punishment and others will be quick to confirm our worst fears. Frankly, I find it almost impossible not to make this false estimate of what is happening. Yet in my mind I know that the dangers to our spiritual welfare from success are far greater than the dangers from failure. If God is concerned with the making of *saints* rather than the production of *executives*, then obviously He must ordain or allow far more failures than successes. Logically a highly "successful" Christian life may very well be a failure from God's point of view. We know this. We recognize it in others. We see it again and again. And yet we desire success. This is another way of saying we have more desire for the wrong kind of success, the kind of success which in God's view is failure, than we do for the kind of failure which in God's view is truly success. The secret of thus entering into God's thoughts is surely to realize very clearly why He has chosen us, and the extent to which He is sovereign over all the circumstances of our lives, both the happy and the unhappy ones. We have not yet learned the real meaning of the Lord's words in Isaiah 55:8: "For my thoughts are not your thoughts, neither are your ways my ways, saith the Lord." Perhaps it is for this reason that Paul wrote to the Corinthians (1 Cor. 1:27-29): "But God hath chosen the foolish things of the world to confound the wise; and God hath chosen the weak things of the world to confound the things that are mighty; and base things of the world, and things which are despised, hath God chosen, yea, and things which are not, to bring to nought things that are: that no flesh should glory in his presence."

12

THE GIFTS AND CALLING OF GOD

Paul uses two analogies to describe how the personal endeavours of the Lord's people are co-ordinated with the labours of others for the fulfillment of his purposes. The first analogy is the body and its members which are integrated into a viable organism, the many members acting as one body. The second is the Temple and its stones which are fitted together to form a unified structure. Paul speaks appropriately of the organs of the body as being "fitly *joined*," articulated, as a functioning whole (Eph. 4:16); and of the stones of the Temple as being "fitly *framed*" (Eph. 2:20-22), much as a carpenter speaks of framing a building.

Assembling the organs into a viable organism naturally has to be undertaken before the amalgamation of the many organisms into a larger community such as a congregation. In an analogous way, when Solomon's Temple was being built, the stones were selected and shaped at the quarry *before* they were delivered to the site. Presumably this was equally true of the timbers for the woodwork, and perhaps even the plates of precious metal that were to embellish the furnishings. In 1 Kings 6:7 we are told that "when [the Temple] was in building, it was built of stone made ready before it was brought thither: so that there was neither hammer nor axe nor any tool of iron heard in the house while it was in building."

If we take this passage as having a secondary meaning which symbolically looks forward to the building of that spiritual Temple which was to be formed in this present age as a habitation for God in the world, the description is reminiscent of what David says about the prenatal development of his own body which he speaks of as being "made in secret" (Ps. 139:15). We are indeed, as Paul puts it (1 Cor. 3:9), "God's building"; and much of the preparation of the individual stones of this spiritual Temple is done in secret, before these "stones" are brought to the site for incorporation. How does this pre-site preparation work out in life?

First of all, I think we must assume that our genetic endowment is foreordained. We are always being told that the genes we inherit are shuffled by

243

chance, randomly, without any guiding hand. The only channelling circumstance is that our parents cannot pass on to us what they do not have, and even then half of what they do have is withheld in each transaction. Who, then, guides the shuffling? God, surely. Certainly He is able. And Scripture shows that such "castings of lots" may indeed be divinely overruled as the Lord sees fit. In another connection admittedly, but in a somewhat parallel circumstance, Joshua 14:2 reads: "By lot was their inheritance as the Lord commanded." And Proverbs 16:33 says: "The lot is cast into the lap but the whole disposing thereof is of the Lord." The basic principle is clear here.

So the foundations of our character, our temperament, and our capacities are of God's choosing in so far as they are related to inheritable factors. And from Psalm 139:16 we see that subsequent foetal development is also within the compass of his oversight.

Secondly, in early life the social and cultural circumstances into which we are born are under the Lord's control and are arranged to work in conjunction with our genetic endowment to produce the kind of person suited to the role we later are to play within the Body of Christ. All this has been planned from the beginning of the world before ever we were born or even the human race existed at all. The personality we have is not an accidental byproduct of chance genetic endowment, nor of the fortuitous cultural environment which has surrounded us as we grew into adulthood. It is part and parcel of a grand design in which a sovereign and gracious God carries forward to completion the plan He had from the very beginning.

In this plan all men are probably involved in greater or lesser degree, but the elect are uniquely privileged by being able to co-operate *knowingly* and therefore with a measure of freedom. For any plan which we can enter into understandingly we are also able to enter into willingly, and God works in us not only to do his will but also to choose it (Phil. 2:13). And this is possible because, as the Lord said to his disciples (John 15:15), the elect are no longer merely servants but friends who know what their Lord is doing. Such is the prerogative of all those who were chosen to be part of the Father's household as gifts to the Son, for whom the Son covenanted to pay the price of ransom.

The extraordinary thing is that this plan was formulated before the world began. Consider the implications of the following passages.

> According as He hath chosen us in Him *before the foundation of the world* . . . having *predestinated us unto the adoption of children* by Jesus Christ to Himself, according to the good pleasure of his will, to the praise of the glory of his grace wherewith He hath made us accepted in the Beloved: in whom we have redemption by his blood, the forgiveness of sins, according to the riches of his grace (Eph. 1:4-7).

> We are bound to give thanks always to God for you brethren beloved of the Lord, because God hath *from the beginning* chosen you to salvation through sanctification of the Spirit and belief of the truth, whereunto He called you by our Gospel to the obtaining of the glory of our Lord Jesus Christ (2 Thess. 2:13, 14).

> [God] who hath saved us and called us with an holy calling, not according to our works, but according to his own purpose and grace, which was given us in Christ Jesus *before the world began* (2 Tim. 1:9).

And so also in Revelation 17:8 it seems that *"from the foundation of the world"* the names of the elect were entered in the "account book" of God, which perhaps records the names of the participants in the covenant made by the Father with the Son. And according to 1 Peter 1:19, 20 the Lamb Himself was at the same time foreordained to be our Redeemer: "[Ye were redeemed] with the precious blood of Christ, as of a Lamb without blemish and without spot: who verily was foreordained *before the foundation of the world."*

We were therefore not shaped as a mere by-product of blind forces. We were deliberately planned for, even though we were hewn out of the same lump as the non-elect, yet singled out with the divine purpose always kept strictly in view. Each of us in this sense is special by foreordination, elected to a role, a life work, and a course of life divinely adjusted to make end products out of us as God sees fit, those end products representing our "apprehension" in Christ towards which we, like Paul, are constantly being inclined by his grace (Phil. 3:12-14).

We know today that genetic endowment and prenatal influences play a crucial role in the molding of our potential. David had a remarkable measure of insight into these factors when he wrote Psalm 139:13-16:

> For Thou hast possessed my reins: Thou hast covered me in my mother's womb. I will praise Thee; for I am fearfully and wonderfully made: marvellous are thy works; and that my soul knoweth right well. My substance was not hid from Thee, when I was made in secret and curiously wrought in the lowest parts of the earth [a Hebraism for the womb]. Thine eyes did see my substance yet being unperfect; and in thy book all my members were written, which in continuance were fashioned, when as yet there was none of them.

Perhaps in this Book of which we have spoken already, there was also put down a specification for each of us, setting forth all these "givens" which were to guarantee the end result in terms of human potential.

And so we come to our physical birth already bearing the stamp of God upon us, and already in part shaped as a vessel of his design, awaiting only to be filled with his appointed content to serve predetermined functions in the House of God, in the Body of Christ.

To bring this shape to maturity, we must learn obedience by the things we experience in the process of growing up, even as our Lord Himself did (Heb. 5:8), until the time comes for us to be about our Father's business. It is the common experience of the Lord's children that after we are converted we can look back in retrospect over these pre-Christian days and discern the hand of the Lord at work here and there, monitoring the experiences of our pagan lives and ruling or overruling the circumstances of childhood and adolescence, tending all things towards the service which we later come to see as the Lord's calling for us to perform as his chosen vessel. It would seem that even the angels have a part to play in this schooling process, being sent to minister to them who *shall be* heirs of salvation when converted (Heb. 1:14).

How much thereafter of our life is by God's ordination? A very great deal. And "ordination" is the proper word to use, for did not the Lord Jesus say, "Ye have not chosen Me, but I have chosen you, and *ordained* you . . ." (John 15:16)? To what are we ordained? To bear fruit. And how? And what kind of fruit?

Let us look first of all at the *how.* We may do this by juxtaposing several passages of Scripture which form a connected thread though they are presented separately. In Ephesians 2:10 Paul wrote: "We are his workmanship, created in Christ Jesus *unto good works, which God hath before ordained that we should walk in them."* And then in Colossians 1:10 he expressed his prayerful concern for the Colossian Christians that they should "walk worthy of the Lord, unto all pleasing, *being fruitful in* every good work . . . ."

So here we have a statement to the effect that God has ordained for his children certain good works, certain duties to perform, certain responsibilities to assume, in short, a specific life work. And then is added the further requirement that we not merely perform these appointed good works but do so in such a manner that the very doing of them bears fruit. We have, then, first of all some measure of understanding of how the *gifts* of God are arranged for in the constitution of each of his children, and now we see that the *calling* is also prearranged. But what is the fruit this calling is directed towards producing?

Although we commonly assume that fruit means the "winning of souls for the Lord" and tend to judge one another's lives chiefly by this criterion, it does not seem that this is precisely what is meant in Scripture by the term *fruit.* Interestingly enough, one passage from Paul's First Epistle to the Corinthians which seems clearly to be referring to this kind of Christian activity quite specifically identifies such results as works, not fruits (1 Cor. 9:1). The most explicit statement regarding the nature of fruit is to be found in Galatians 5:22, 23, where it is spelled out in terms which show unequivocally that fruit is recognizable only in terms of the development of character, or even more specifically in the achievement of a truly *Christ-like* personality. For what are these descriptive terms but a word picture of the Lord Jesus Christ Himself? The object of the works which are foreordained that we should walk in them is to produce character, which means to exhibit the Lord Jesus Christ in us. Any other result of what we do really misses the purpose for which God called us to the doing.

It is worth noting that in Galatians 5:22 the word *fruit* is written in the singular. And this is in keeping with the fact that the Lord's character was singular, of a piece. The same truth appears in Philippians 1:11, though many translations have blurred the fact by using a plural form even though the Greek is in the singular. It will be noticed that in Galatians 5:19 Paul speaks of "the works [plural] of the flesh"; and this plurality is reflected in Isaiah 64:6 which reads, "All our righteous*nesses* are as filthy rags." Our good works and what displays of righteousness we may profess are always piecemeal. The garment of righteousness with which the Lord clothes us is seamless.

In Ephesians 5:8-11 we find that in the sense of producing Christ-like character the works of darkness are entirely unfruitful: "Now ye are light in the Lord: walk as children of light; (For the fruit of the Spirit is in all goodness and righteousness and truth), proving what is acceptable unto the Lord. And have no fellowship with the *unfruitful* works of darkness." These unfruitful works of darkness are not necessarily evil deeds in the social sense. They may be good deeds in so far as they benefit others, yet they are unfruitful to the doer because the motive of their doing is wrong. Thus we find that in the Great Judgment many will appear before the Lord and say (Matt. 7:22, 23): "Lord, Lord, have we not prophesied in thy name? And in thy name have cast out devils? And in thy name done many wonderful works?" "Then will I profess unto them," the Lord told his disciples, "I never knew you: depart from Me, ye that work iniquity." Such works have the earmarks of a certain goodness, but in terms of their effect on the doer they are evil, even as the scrupulous fulfillment of the law created a spirit in the Pharisees which was entirely inimical towards the Lord who gave them the law.

It is equally possible for Christians to do unfruitful good works, good works which are not without benefit to others, but are unfruitful in their effect upon themselves. The deed itself may be correct enough; the motive is wrong. This is why the Lord warned against judging by actions. He did not say, "By their deeds ye shall know them," but, "By their *fruits* ye shall know them" (Matt. 7:16). Paul said (1 Cor. 13:3), "Though I bestow all my goods to feed the poor . . . and have not love, it profiteth *me* nothing." It is most important to note the personal pronoun here, for it would be quite untrue to say that a starving man is not benefited when he becomes the recipient of bread at someone else's expense. It is not that the poor are without profit, it is the giver who is unprofited. Or if one wants to be even more precise, the giver is unprofited *in the sight of God.* In the sight of men he receives a reward, for men often do not see the motives, and men whose hearts are evil are often labelled as public benefactors, as doers of good.

The manifest objective in foreordained good works is that the doing of them will prove a fruitful exercise for the doer. It is thus that we are to be made perfect, not by meditation or reflection or retreat from all engagement in the affairs of the world, but by good deeds before ordained that we should walk in them. And the term *walk in them* surely signifies a life work for the Lord. Thus in Hebrews 13:20, 21 the writer prays: "Now the God of peace, that brought again from the dead our Lord Jesus, that great Shepherd of the sheep, through the blood of the everlasting covenant, make you perfect [i.e., mature you] *in every good work,* to do his will, working in you that which is pleasing in his sight, through Jesus Christ; to whom be glory for ever and ever. Amen."

So the pattern of life that will be most fruitful for the child of God will always be precisely that occupation which involves doing the work which God has before appointed for him. The reason is clear enough: we are his creation, our potential is of his making, our capacity of his design. Consequently for the appointed work we are divinely equipped with the necessary qualifications. I do not believe that the Lord ever calls any of his children to a task which they are incapable of doing. And as we observe others we have to remember that we are not sufficient judges of whether the demands of a duty or a call will be beyond the reach of the one who seems to be receiving it. Because the stones are prepared in secret, often in ways undiscovered even by ourselves until afterwards, only God knows what latent capabilities are hidden in his children; and in times of emergency people surprise us by performing magnificently where we doubted any capacity at all. Certainly Jonah can hardly have imagined himself as a successful evangelist to the heathen. Gideon was sure he was not the man to do the job he heard God calling him to do (Judg. 6:11-15). So too Moses (Exod. 4:10); and Jeremiah (Jer. 1:6, 7); and Paul (2 Cor. 12:7-9). Indeed one suspects that because self-confidence is always so dangerous, we never really ought to feel adequate for God's work; and when we do we are probably about to engage in what is either not his work at all, or his work done in the wrong way.

That every child of God has a specific work which involves both gifts and calling is clearly indicated in Scripture. We need only remind ourselves of the man in Matthew 25:14, 15 who upon a leave of absence for a while handed over to his servants the reins of government and distributed talents so that they would be equipped—*"to every man according to his individual ability."* Mark has a similar account (13:34) in which a certain man "left his house and gave authority to his servants and *to every man his work."* In these two parables we have it stated by implication that to every man talents are given and to every man is given a work which is specifically his. Peter tells us (1 Peter 4:10) that "every man has received *a* gift." There is no definite article in the original, a circumstance which has the effect of strengthening the implications of universality. We are simply being assured that every one of the Lord's children (for this letter is specifically addressed to the Lord's children) does have a gift.

It is impossible to conceive of God's plan, thought out in eternity and guaranteed at such a cost, failing to ensure not only an appropriate work for each of those who are to engage in it, but also appropriate qualifications. And as a reflection of the wisdom of God, the perfecting of each individual involved in the plan is to be secured by fitting his capacity to the work he has to do. When any man or woman consciously works at full capacity in the sense of using his abilities with maximum effectiveness, that individual is likely to derive the greatest possible personal satisfaction, and will be maturing most effectively. This is God's way. And it is almost certainly true, as Augustine said, that the child of God is physically immortal until his appointed work is done. Indeed, this may be the intent of Paul's observation regarding David when he said, "After he had served his own generation, he fell asleep" (Acts 13:36).

It is Paul who was inspired to make it very clear that the position which any child of God occupies within the Body of Christ is in no sense accidental; it is a divinely appointed position effectively realized by the Holy Spirit. Paul spent a whole chapter on the matter (1 Cor. 12:12-31), epitomizing what I have been saying above with the words, "Now hath God set the members *every one of them* in the Body, as it hath pleased Him" (v. 18).

So there we have in effect the gifts and the calling which are both of God, and which "are without repentance" (Rom. 11:29), without anything tentative about them, without any possibility of his changing his mind about them. The gifts are secured to us by providential overruling of our genetic heritage whereby we are equipped constitutionally to fulfill some specific role to which we are elected—for Election is not only to salvation. I believe that Peter is speaking of Election in this sense when he says (2 Peter 1:10): "Wherefore, brethren, give diligence to make your calling and election sure," and then it follows naturally, as Peter goes on to say, that "if ye do these things, ye shall never fail" (so the Greek). For how could we possibly fail if we are fulfilling the role which God has called us to fill, and using the talents with which He has endowed us?

The calling, the circumstances in which our lot is cast, are providentially of his overruling. Should these circumstances become difficult and we be under the impression that we could do better elsewhere, nevertheless, we should not be too ready to move away. The casting of our lot is truly in

God's hands. "As God hath distributed *to every man*, as the Lord hath called *every one*, so let him walk . . . . Let every man abide in the same calling wherein he is called" (1 Cor. 7:17, 20).

This is a principle we overlook rather easily and its denial in practice contributes greatly to the instability of many young Christians, an instability which they euphemistically mistake for flexibility. John the Baptist's advice seems to have paralleled that of Paul, when he admonished those who came to him seeking baptism and new instructions for life to go on in their calling (Luke 3:10-14), seeking only to fulfill their roles with greater faithfulness.

The difference between the life thus fulfilled, and the seemingly unfulfilled life of the one whom, because of gross disobedience, God removes prematurely to prevent further damage, is one of those secret things which belong only to Him (Deut. 29:29). We shall perhaps know the answer in heaven—or we may by then simply have lost all interest in the question. Possibly even the life thus unfulfilled is not so much a life unfulfilled as it is a cup reduced in size, the full filling of which is commensurate to its smaller volume. It seems almost certain that there will be some "small children" in heaven and some "young men" and some "aged" saints. Why not also some "cherubs"? All will be *perfect*—but at different stages of spiritual maturity. The Lord was perfect in the cradle (why else could He have been worshipped?), perfect as He grew through childhood, and perfect in mature manhood. At no stage was He imperfect. He did always and only those things which pleased his Father (John 8:29). It is no sign of imperfection to find in heaven that individuals have achieved different stages of development. The rosebud may be as perfect in its form as the full bloom is perfect in its maturity.

The different callings we have make distinctions among us because they are callings within the context of the world where we live out our daily lives. It is not entirely improper to recognize such differences. We attach more honour to one who can lead and give meaningful direction to the labours of many others—and rightly so. For only a few either want to assume responsibility of this kind, or are able to do so with success. The market place attaches a higher value to that which is less common but important to a greater number of people, and our Christian calling operates within this framework of values. Yet the born leader is just that—a *born* leader. The accomplished musician is gifted, talented, use whatever term you will. These things are indeed gifts or talents, and whatever term we use it is likely to reflect what the Bible says about gifts and talents and callings, all of which are of God.

The credit or discredit which attaches to the gifts or talents or callings we have is not really in the gifts or talents or callings themselves but in the use we make of them, or even more importantly, in the motives behind these uses. Luther was perfectly right when he said, "Who sweeps the floor as unto the Lord makes both that and the action fine." The floor and the action alike! Often the action is good enough but not the motive, and the use to which we put our talent may conceal the truth that we are really ministering to our own ego, displaying our talents rather than investing them in the service of the Lord. At such times we need to remind ourselves of what Paul said in 1 Corinthians 4:7: "Who maketh thee to differ from another? And what hast thou that thou didst not receive? Now if thou didst receive it, why dost thou glory as if thou hadst not received it?" Why, indeed!

But what a comfort to know that our lot is cast by the Lord; our gifts are of his appointing, and our life work planned way back there in eternity! If we could only rest assured of this in times of delay, or defeat, or uncertainty. Such assurance does not lead to inaction; it leads to freedom of action with the right kind of confidence. Any kind of confidence other than that based securely upon the sovereignty of the grace of God is misplaced. Isaiah said (26:12): "Lord, Thou wilt ordain peace for us: for Thou hast wrought all our works in us." Amen! The two, faith in his sovereignty and peace of mind, go together.

13

PUNISHMENT OR CHASTENING?

The perfecting of a saint takes a lifetime. When the individual has matured—and the word *perfection* in the Greek seems to have this connotation—that individual may be said to have apprehended that for which he is apprehended in Christ Jesus (Phil. 3:12). Or to put this in more colloquial terms, when the individual has realized the level of development in Christ which the Father has seen as the maximum potential in keeping with opportunity, endowment, and experience, then that individual is mature. And I suspect that that individual is also ready to go home to heaven.

When the Lord Jesus Christ was mature in this sense (Heb. 5:8, 9) He was ready to go home to glory, and if He had chosen He need never have come down again from the Mount of Transfiguration (Luke 9:28-36). Hebrews 12:2 tells us, however, that "instead of" (so the Greek)* entering into this joy that was at that moment open to Him, He turned back, came down from the Mount and set his face like a flint to go to Jerusalem, there to despise the shame and endure crucifixion. He made that choice because it was a choice that He was free to make. He was not made as we are made but with the potential for endless life (Heb. 7:16); like Adam before he sinned, He was not subject to death and need *never* have died. He had been made perfect (i.e., mature) by the things which He had experienced and was ready to enter into heaven by transformation without tasting death at all. That this is possible even for mortal man is clear from 1 Corinthians 15:51. For Paul is saying in this passage that when the Lord returns there will be a number of his children who will pass into glory without the experience of dying. As he wrote: "Behold, I show you a mystery: We shall not all sleep, but we shall all be changed, in a moment, in the twinkling of an eye, at the last trump: for the trumpet shall sound, and the dead shall be raised incorruptible, and we shall be changed" (1 Cor. 15:51, 52). In that tremendous

---

*The use of ἀντί followed by the genitive clearly indicates this meaning.

moment, the dead in Christ will be raised, and the living will be transformed.

It may be that Enoch was transformed and taken home without experiencing death (Heb. 11:5) because in some extraordinary way he had, in a manner of speaking, prematurely matured so that his time of graduation came unexpectedly. For he had this testimony, that he pleased God. It is difficult to know whether anyone else ever has really achieved such complete maturity, except the Lord Jesus Himself (John 8:29); and if not, how to reconcile this failure with the sovereignty of God's grace. It seems very doubtful if the majority of us who are the Lord's children do ever achieve our maximum potential as God sees it for each of us individually in Christ. Perhaps such maturing is part of God's *desiring* rather than part of his *willing*? I suppose this means that in some way we are all taken home when we have reached our potential and when allowing us to remain would not serve to mature us any further. For the great majority of us, it must be that we fall short of what God would like, but that cannot come as any surprise to Him. God's sovereignty is matched by his omniscience, and all his plans must be based upon his sure foreknowledge of what will be.

We are in a quandary here for if the child of God is taken home only when God sees the maturing process has gone as far as it can, are we to assume that there is a built-in potential that is probably almost never realized? Is this then a thwarting of the will of God?

Perhaps the problem is with the word *mature*. Could it be that maturity is not perfection in the sense of having achieved maximum potential for good but in the sense of having achieved *perfect hatred of sin*? Many older Christians experience a growing despair at the apparent lack of progress towards purity of heart that they once dreamed of in their earlier walk with the Lord. But it is possible that such despair may itself be a matter for rejoicing, because it could signify not so much a greater measure of failure to achieve holiness of life in the commonly accepted sense, but a greater measure of awareness of *un*-holiness. The truth is that the closer we are to the Lord the more clearly we begin to see ourselves for what we really are. The brighter the light, the deeper the shadows and the more likely are we to see the dirt. In our house, when the sun shines right down the hall in the evening, we suddenly become aware of the cobwebs festooning the ceiling—one of the penalties of living in the country, where spiders abound! Throughout the day these cobwebs don't show and we are apt to be quite happy with the general state of our housekeeping. This is a parable from life and is reflected in John 3:19: "Men loved darkness rather than light because their deeds were evil."

Progress towards maturity is not to be measured by victory over the sins we are aware of, but by hatred of the sins which we had overlooked and which we now see all too clearly. The nearer we come to the Lord, the more sinful we shall undoubtedly feel ourselves to be. When we hate sin with a perfect hatred, then it may be we are ready to be taken into the presence of the King, for to hate sin perfectly is to have our *love* made perfect also (1 John 4:17). In a sense this would suggest that the darkest period of our lives may well be just before the dawn: "He turneth the shadow of death into the morning" (Amos 5:8).

Now if the Lord chastens his loved ones in order to complete this perfecting process, how does He carry out this chastening? He uses the world. In Psalm 23:4 David wrote: *"Thy rod and thy staff they comfort me."* We read the words *rod* and *staff* as though the rod were a magic wand to smooth out our path when we run into roadblocks, and the staff a kind of shepherd's crook to haul us out of pits we fall into when we have wandered out of the way. But how does the rest of Scripture view these "comforting" rods and staffs?

Well, consider Isaiah 10:5 as a case in point. Isaiah is here warning Israel of the fate that awaits them at the hands of the Assyrians, who are about to descend on their land to lay it waste and carry them into captivity. Here are the Lord's words written by Isaiah under inspiration: "O Assyrian, the *rod of mine anger*, and the *staff in their hand is mine indignation.*" Here, then, are God's rod and staff in one aspect. Israel was both to be punished in anger and chastened in concern. The many in the nation who had no true "membership" in God's commonwealth would perish in the massacres which were to accompany the country's devastation at the hands of the Assyrians or would die languishing in Assyria as captives. The remnant of the Lord's people still faithful but caught up in the fate of the nation as a whole would in many cases no doubt also die in Assyria and Babylonia like their countrymen, but not in despair. What was to be punishment for the many would be chastening for the few. The rod and staff were to perform both offices. Above all, Israel would be permanently purged of any temptation towards the kind of idolatry to which their forefathers had constantly fallen prey while they were in the Promised Land. Seventy years later their children would return to Palestine and never again revert to the worship of idols, even after their worship of the Lord God of their fathers had decayed to a mere formality.

When the Lord promised to David a son who would establish his kingdom gloriously and finally build the Temple which David had dreamed of building, the Lord said to David (2 Sam. 7:14, 15): "I will be his father and he shall be my son. If he commit iniquity, I will chasten him with *the rod of men* and with the stripes of the children of men; but my mercy shall not depart away from him . . . ." *Men* are the Lord's rod.

As the day of Israel's captivity drew near, the part that the worldly nations around them were to play in their chastening became more and more explicit. Thus in Isaiah 7:20 the prophet warned Israel: "In the same day shall the Lord shave *with a razor that is hired*, namely, by them beyond the river, by the king of Assyria, the head and hair of the feet and it shall consume the beard." Note that the Lord was to do this shaving and it was to be total, and furthermore that He would hire a razor (the Assyrians and the Babylonians) as his barber. Then again in Jeremiah 47:6, 7: "O thou sword of the Lord, how long will it be ere thou be quiet? Put up thyself into thy scabbard, rest, and be still. How can it be quiet, seeing the Lord hath given it a charge against Ashkelon, and against the sea shore?" Here, then, the razor has become a sword. One always thinks of the "sword of the Lord" as being a pure Excalibur in the hand of God, perhaps even the Word of God itself. But here we find it to be nothing else than a line of oriental monarchs who were about as ruthless as the world had ever seen up to that time. History tells us that these Babylonian and Assyrian Emperors sometimes beheaded virtually every conquered male who could possibly bear arms, and piled up the heads in huge pyramids outside the devastated cities as a warning to any inhabitants who might have escaped their wrath. Were these men really the "sword of the Lord"? Apparently they were—"appointed of God."

But what was to be punishment for the many was still only to be correction for those who remained faithful in Israel. And Habakkuk 1:12 seems to have been penned by and for this remnant: "Art Thou not from everlasting, O Lord my God, mine Holy One? We shall not die. O Lord, Thou hast ordained them for judgment; and, O mighty God, Thou hast ordained them for correction." So here we have a single agency in the hands of God used to *punish* the faithless in Israel but to *correct* the faithful. Superficially it must have seemed at the time that all were being treated alike. But it was not really so, and we have to assume that the saints were actually experiencing as chastening what the wicked were at the same time experiencing as punishment. Such a conviction would surely be a tremendous comfort to those who found themselves sharing the national calamity. To the many it was an evil; to the few it was a good.

When calamity overtakes a community there must surely be always this fundamental difference in response to the circumstances; for to the one, catastrophe is either meaningless or is seen as a punishment, whereas by the other it may be seen for what it is—chastening. Our response to these two alternative interpretations of events is bound to be different. If we see catastrophe as punishment, we are made bitter or craven; if we see it as chastening, we may look heavenward and be comforted. To ensure the latter, two things must be believed: first, God knows what He is about and is sovereign, and the men of the world who are the source of our grief are his servants; and secondly, God is our Father, and acts towards us only in loving concern and for our good. What destroys the faith of the many may

confirm the faith of the few. One has to use the word *may* in these propositions because we are so slow to believe and trust, and we understand so little of the Lord's ways with us.

Yet no chastening seems pleasant at the time (Heb. 12:11); if it did, it
could not be serving its intended purpose! So we naturally cry out against
it. Although David must certainly have known that the chastening of the
Lord was for his own good and absolutely necessary, yet in Psalm 17:13, 14
he prayed: "Arise O Lord . . . deliver my soul from the wicked, which is
thy sword: from men which art *thy hand,* O Lord, from men of the world,
who have their portion in this life." And it appears that one day the tables
will perhaps be turned and Israel will become the rod in God's hand to punish the nations who are the rod in God's hand today chastening Israel's children. As Jeremiah 51:20 put it: "Thou [Israel] art my *battle-axe* and
weapons of war: for with thee will I break in pieces the nations, and with
thee will I destroy kingdoms."

Meanwhile, the saints are chastened and the rest are punished; and in
both cases God in his sovereignty uses men as his weapons, as his *sword,* his
razor, his *battle-axe,* his *rod,* and his *staff.* And sometimes He uses the
saints to chasten one another.

When we are chastened by the world we are apt to see it as a form of persecution. In our conceit we may imagine that this persecution comes because the world finds our "righteousness" offensive. But in point of fact it
may be because it is the Lord who is displeased with us, with our *un*righteousness, and determines that it must be corrected. When our friends, our
brothers and sisters in the Lord, are chastened we may very well be tempted
to mistake it for punishment. We are terribly confused in our thinking
about these things. But what a tremendously comforting thing it is to remind ourselves when "the boss" comes down hard on us (even if we deserve
it) that this same boss is the Lord's rod or staff which is really intended to
comfort us, to chasten us, not for our hurt but for our good. Rightly understood, such persecution ought to be a source of thankfulness, not com-
plaint. A life lived in such a spirit would make it somewhat easier for us to
fulfill Paul's injunction: "In every thing give thanks: for this is the will of
God in Christ Jesus concerning you" (1 Thess. 5:18).

Yet how difficult it is to be thankful when we are troubled in this way.
And the difficulty almost always stems from our inability to grasp the fact
once for all that "there is therefore now no condemnation to them that are
in Christ Jesus" (Rom. 8:1). Penalty has become merely consequence, and
even this consequence may not ensue unless the Lord sees that it will serve a
purpose for good. The consequence which follows upon our failures does
not have the nature of penalty but rather of occasion for concerned action
on God's part. The consequence is not penal consequence but loving concern. The element of condemnation is missing entirely, not because a sinful

action is no longer sinful, but because the aspect of sinfulness has been removed by being laid upon the Lord Jesus Christ on Calvary. The penal aspect has been dealt with once for all, and what remains is an occasion which God may or may not decide to make use of for our good.

How wonderful it is that in John 15:15 the Lord says: "Henceforth I call you not servants; for the servant knoweth not what his lord doeth: but I have called you friends; for all things that I have heard of my Father, I have made known unto you"! What does this mean? Well, first of all, it means that the Lord's children have had their status changed from that of servant to friend. All men are servants of God by reason of their being his creatures (Ps. 119:91). They are like hired men, and have their allotment of life as the hired man has his term of employment. Job 14:6 acknowledges this fact thus: "Turn from him [from man] that he may rest, till he shall accomplish as a hireling his day." Men fulfill God's will by his overruling of the circumstances of their lives. They are not as a rule aware of this unless it is specifically revealed to them. Under normal circumstances they do not do his will consciously, knowing what it is. There is no deliberate desire to please the Lord. On the other hand, it is the prerogative of *friends* to act knowingly, and only actions knowingly performed are meritorious, for it is the motivation that is rewarded. The servants who merely did what they were commanded to do were in this sense "unprofitable" (Luke 17:10).

Paul spoke of having a *commission* to preach and he said: "Yea, woe is me if I don't preach the Gospel" (1 Cor. 9:16). But then he added, "If I do this thing *willingly*, I have a reward" (v. 17). He says that necessity was laid upon him; and yet he could rise above the fact of necessity and choose to do what was laid upon him by compulsion, thus converting it from a compelled to a voluntary act, and receive accordingly the reward of consciously pleasing his Lord. The secret of his statement is in the words, "If I do this thing willingly, I have a reward." And he could do it willingly only if he could do it knowingly; and he could do it knowingly only if his relationship to the Lord was not merely that of a servant but of a friend, for the servant doesn't know what his lord is up to.

There is a beautiful illustration of this principle in the case of Abraham. In Genesis 18:17 the Lord said: "Shall I hide from Abraham the thing that I do?" And the answer, in effect, was, "No, I will make it known to him." And why to Abraham? Because according to 2 Chronicles 20:7 and James 2:23, Abraham was in a special sense a *"friend* of God."

Now the mind of God is revealed in what He does, whereas the heart of God is revealed in the *way* He does it. The distinction between ways and works is an important one. Psalm 103:7 tells us that "the Lord made known his *ways* unto Moses, his *acts* unto the children of Israel." This is not merely a poetic play upon words. The difference is reaffirmed in Hebrews 3:9, 10:

"Your fathers tempted Me, proved Me, and saw my *works* forty years. Wherefore I was grieved with that generation and said, They do always err in their hearts; and they have not known my *ways."* Putting these two passages together we can see that while the children of Israel observed the Lord's doings for forty years, they entirely misunderstood the reasons why the Lord did them; his motivations were hidden from them. It was otherwise with Moses. Moses saw not only his work but his way. Indeed, Moses had prayed that this might be so (Exod. 33:13) when he said to the Lord; "Now therefore, I pray Thee, if I have found grace in thy sight, show me now thy way, that I may know Thee, that I may find grace in thy sight."

When in Isaiah 55:8 the Lord says, "My thoughts are not your thoughts, neither are your ways my ways," He is not talking about his works, but about the *why* and *how* of his doing them. It is not the prerogative of the servant to question his master about his reasons for doing the things that he does, but it is the privilege of a friend to have these reasons explained to him, unasked. In so far as we need to know God's reasons, they form an essential part of revelation, but they are not set forth in such a way that the casual reader can easily satisfy mere curiosity. Revealing his will to us as friends, He is able to communicate what He is about and thus to invite us to enter by choice and willingly into his plan and purpose. We are then in the position to undertake voluntarily what the Lord may nevertheless have predetermined we are to do willy-nilly. A predetermined act voluntarily undertaken becomes thereby a free act, and acts performed freely and willingly are the only acts worthy of reward. The man who does an evil act willingly is also worthy of reward, namely, to be punished. In neither case is it the deed itself that counts in the moral balance of things, but the motive which prompted the doing of it. It is not the works themselves but the ways in which they are done that matter in the Judgment. Many kindnesses that we perform are marred by the way in which we perform them, and we recognize even an outwardly kind act as morally unworthy if the motive is self-serving. Is God any less of a judge of our ways than we are of one another's? God works in the world that they do his will; He works in his children that they not only do but also will his will (Phil. 2:13). Thus, by being elevated to the position of friends, we are also in a position to know what the Lord is doing.

Now it is a great comfort for the child of God to be assured that the man of the world who opposes him in his business life, or rewards him with evil in his social life, or prevents his worship or disrupts his study or intrudes into his time of meditation in his spiritual life, is a servant of God—while he himself is a child of the King! Suppose in all our daily relations with men of the world we were to walk always in the light of this knowledge. What a difference it would make! To know that the grace of God is sovereign is not a cold, hard-nosed, and calculating view of theology. It is a reflection of the truth of the Word of God, an essential part of the total implication of the Gospel of salvation by faith without works of merit.

When we hope to find a parking place and somebody gets there first, when we rush to get in line for some bargains in the world's market place and they are all sold out just before our part of the queue reaches the counter, when the piece of cake on the plate we had our eye on as we moved along the line is taken by the diner just ahead of us, when we are by-passed for a position we felt so important to us and so right for us, when a house we longed to own is sold only a few days before we can meet the financial or other requirement, when a person we don't respect is credited by others for a work we did at some cost to ourselves, when. . . . We could go on indefinitely. Life seems so full of daily disappointments and little injustices. The epitaph of life for so many is summed up in the one word *Almost*.

For the Lord's child, the worker is more important than the work, the effect is more important than the event, the objective than the means, the motive than the deed. If only we could trust our sovereign Father and his grace, we would allow Him to mold our character without so much disappointment and rebellion on our part. And in the rat race of business life, what a marvellous thing to live daily secure in the knowledge that "promotion cometh neither from the east, nor the west, nor from the south. But God is the judge: He putteth down one, and setteth up another" (Ps. 75:6, 7). This fact gives force to 1 Peter 5:6, 7: "Humble yourselves therefore under the mighty hand of God that He may advance you [so the Greek] in due time: casting all your anxiety upon Him; for He is concerned about you."

The fundamental hindrance to this maturing process is the self which must have its way. This self has to be put to death. It is to be put to death by crucifixion. The crucifixion of our *self* in this pilgrimage is not without its parallels to the crucifixion of the Lord. The Lord invites us to take up our cross and follow Him (Mark 8:34), and He has repeated this invitation on several occasions in the Gospels. Glibly we decide to surrender ourselves to Him, expecting a joyously fulfilled experience to result, and anticipating all kinds of fruits in the commonly accepted meaning of this word. But what happens?

What happens is that, if we really mean business, the Lord takes us at our word and begins the ordeal of crucifixion, *using the world as executioner!* We are often surprisingly willing, in some particular area of our life, to "take up our cross" provided that we are permitted to conduct the execution ourselves and in our own way. But there is no way a man can crucify himself! There is on record a case of an individual who tried it. He managed to nail his feet and, extraordinary though it seems, he even succeeded in nailing one hand. But then he was in trouble, for there was no way that he could, now single-handed, nail the other hand! In the end, after some hours of agony he was released by friends and is believed to have survived.

Crucifixion has to be done by someone else. It is a terribly painful, prolonged, and shameful death. In the olden days it seems to have been a rule that once a man had taken up the crossbar, his fate was sealed. The prisoner was reprievable, I believe, until he performed this symbolic act and started on the journey to the place of execution. It is almost certain that the condemned man did not, and probably could not, carry the whole cross. The upright was normally left in place on some prominent knoll at a decent distance from the city, ready for its victim. The condemned man was required to carry only the cross bar (it was called *patibulum* in Latin), and when he arrived at the site his outstretched arms were fastened to it, and it was then hauled up and secured in place. His feet were tied or nailed and the body rested on a small peg or *sedile* between his legs to support some of his weight. Although initially this *sedile* must have afforded enormous relief, in the end it contributed to the prolonging of the agony by extending survival time significantly. Some men and women are known to have survived for days in this awful position, and one case of survival for nine days is on record.

According to Alfred Edersheim, it was customary once the man had picked up the crossbar for the crowd to heap upon the condemned prisoner every imaginable insult and abuse short of actual physical assault. It was, manifestly, a most awful form of slow death. It is said that men sometimes had their eyes plucked out by birds, being quite unable to defend themselves. Some had limbs torn off by wild beasts at night. In such a position the victim was utterly helpless and exposed, and during the hours of darkness would be entirely alone.

And *this* is what the Lord was inviting us to expose ourselves to when He said we too must take up the crossbar and walk towards the execution of self, if we would really come after Him. Crucifixion is something that is done *to* us; it is not something that we do to ourselves. We can only initiate it by picking up the crossbar, that is, by a completely honest determination, which is undoubtedly what the Lord meant when He said, "Take up your cross." The rest is done to us by the world—and even by our friends.

This crucifixion is a *daily* process (Luke 9:23). It is a *slow* process, something that takes years. It is a *passive* process that we are called upon to endure, not a process that we are called upon to engineer. Paul said, "I *am crucified* with Christ," not, "I crucify myself" (Gal. 2:20). It is a *reciprocal* process whereby, as Paul put it in Galatians 6:14, "the world is crucified unto me and I unto the world," for the separation tends to be increasingly mutual.

But perhaps the most painful part of all is that those nearest and dearest to us are often called upon to play a role in the process. The wounds that the Lord felt most keenly were inflicted by his friends (Zech. 13:6), and He warned his disciples that they too would experience the same kind of injury.

But whatever the circumstances, it is comforting to know that we are always in his care and that He is always in charge. "And I heard as it were the voice of a great multitude . . . saying: Alleluia: for the Lord God omnipotent reigneth!" (Rev. 19:6). It was *martyrs* who exulted thus!

14

SOVEREIGNTY AND RESPONSIBILITY

In this chapter I am concerned to establish that there is a significant difference in meaning between the words *evil* and *sin,* a difference which profoundly affects the implications of a number of passages of Scripture of great importance to a correct understanding of the basis of divine judgment and human responsibility.

In ordinary conversation, we commonly equate evil and sin and employ the words more or less interchangeably. But in doing so we effectively conceal a distinction between the words as employed in Scripture, thereby creating problems in interpretation which are then resolved only by the very unsatisfactory method of assuming that the text cannot possibly mean what it says. When we learn that God does evil, appoints evil, intends evil, purposes evil, and even creates evil, we seem to be left with no alternative but to explain such passages away. And this we must do, of course, if evil and sin mean the same thing, for we cannot suppose that God is the author of sin. Indeed, we know He is not, for He refuses to listen to those who sin (Isa. 59:2; John 9:31).

Thus we seem to be forced to make a distinction between the two words. But as soon as we decide that this is proper, we come across passages where the supposed distinction is ignored! Thus Habbakuk 1:13 reads, "Thou art of purer eyes than to behold evil and canst not look on iniquity [i.e., sin]." Is this a case of repetition for the sake of emphasis in which evil and sin are synonymous terms, or do we have two separate statements used by the Holy Spirit to drive home the point that God cannot countenance either evil or sin?

Now this problem in the use of terms applies not only in the matter of evil and sin but in the matter of their opposites, goodness and righteousness. Are these also to be distinguished, or are they likewise synonymous terms used indiscriminately?

An examination of many key passages in the New Testament suggests that a real distinction does exist. In the Old Testament the issue is far less clear. But the reason for this may be that the Old Testament is a study of religious experience rather than of the underlying theology which accounts for that experience. It is in the New Testament that the theology of Christian experience becomes explicit, pre-eminently in Paul's Epistles. And it is therefore that we find in the New Testament a certain precision of language that is largely lacking in the Old Testament.

In common parlance we are not precise in our use of many words. The context of the conversation conveys our meaning as a rule, or it may happen that precision of meaning is not important. Thus we may speak of a good man or a righteous man, but we do not stop to consider whether a man may be good who tells a lie to save a friend. During the war under Nazi pressure not a few Christians faced this as a very practical problem. They were being good, but were they righteous? By the same token, when we speak of an evil man or a sinful man, we assume there is essentially no difference, and often we are perfectly right. But yet we know that there are some evil things that must be done which are nevertheless not wicked—like the amputation of a leg in an emergency. An evil act may or may not be sinful, though a sinful act is almost always an evil one. The two facets of a single deed can often be separated by the discerning mind.

It is indeed difficult to distinguish evil and wickedness, and goodness and righteousness, *in the abstract*. One must consider these words in their context. When man does evil it is usually sinful; when God does evil it cannot possibly be. Clearly the words as used in Scripture are to be distinguished.

The best lexicographers of the Greek (Kittel, Thayer, Liddell and Scott, etc.) have not altogether clarified the situation, and the reader is left to struggle with the problem for himself. There are indeed difficulties, for virtually every "rule" is broken distressingly often.

It is possible that the basic difference from a biblical point of view is that evil and goodness are ethical in character and temporal in effect whereas, by contrast, sin and righteousness are moral in character and eternal in consequence. Evil and goodness apply to relationships between man and man, "horizontal" in bearing and "historical" in effect, whereas sin and righteousness are identified with relationships between man and God, "vertical" in their connection and everlasting in consequence. The former, moreover, relate chiefly to what we *do*, the latter to what we *are*. These contrasts are set forth as in the chart on the following page.

In the light of these distinctions between what is wicked and what is only evil and therefore between what is culpable and what is only unfortunate, let us look at what Scripture has to say on the subject and then see if there are general principles that will serve to illuminate satisfyingly the relationship between the sovereignty of God and human responsibility. The issue is not merely an academic one; it relates to our sense of the rightness of things, and if God is truly righteous and omnipotent, it is surely proper to expect that in all his ways He will not merely act justly but will be *seen* to act so.

	EVIL & GOODNESS	SIN & RIGHTEOUSNESS
CHARACTER	ETHICAL	MORAL
EFFECT	TEMPORAL	ETERNAL
RELATIONSHIP	HORIZONTAL AND MAN-TO-MAN	VERTICAL AND MAN-TO-GOD
CONSEQUENCE	HISTORICAL	EVERLASTING
RELATIVE TO	WHAT WE DO	WHAT WE ARE

When the wicked are fulfilling the purposes of God, how can they justly be held accountable? Not every evil deed is foreordained, for not every evil deed forms part of the predeterminate counsel of God, but it must surely be by his permission. We do know from Scripture that some evil deeds are foreordained, like the selling of Joseph or the crucifixion of our Lord, and that in spite of their predetermination those who performed them were nevertheless held accountable. What kind of justice is it that holds men accountable for an evil deed which it has been foreordained they shall perform? It seems that Paul, when speaking to the Christians in Rome, had been asked this very question, "Who then is morally accountable?" Or as he put it in Romans 9:19: "Thou wilt say then unto me, Why doth He yet find fault? For who has resisted his will?" On what basis will any man be judged accountable if the sovereignty of God really extends this far?

We have no great problem in understanding the justice of holding men accountable for evil deeds which are performed as *free* expressions of their own will. Because such actions are humanly initiated, they are in a sense doubly culpable. They are culpable because of the evil they entail, and they are culpable because of the wicked intention which lies behind them. And there is thus an important difference between what is evil and what is wicked. For there are many evil acts which must be performed in society but which are performed normally by people whose intentions are good. The executioner who carries out the sentence of a judge, whose judgment is fitting and is directed towards the good of society, is carrying out an evil act with good intention, for it is undoubtedly an evil thing that a man's life should have to be cut short; yet it may, if it is truly fitting, also be a righteous act. It is an evil thing that a surgeon should have to remove a gangrenous foot and leave a man lame for life, and yet his intention is morally correct if he honestly believes it is the best treatment. An evil deed need not have any aspect of wickedness about it. The amputation of a man's leg is an unfortunate evil but it does not per se involve any moral impropriety that would convert it into a wicked act.

This is not a novel truth. It has been talked about by philosophers probably since man first began to think in abstract terms. But is it simply an abstract idea, interesting but not of practical importance? Or is it an important truth essential to an understanding of what is said in Scripture in connection with good and evil, righteousness and wickedness, reward and punishment? Let us look at some passages which give us very firm guidance in this matter and which provide some amazingly satisfying answers.

First of all, it is very clear that while God can never be accused of committing wickedness, He is often expressly declared to be the author of evil. Because of our confusion in the use of these two words, *evil* and *wickedness*, such a blanket statement may well be very disturbing to one who has not examined the matter in the light of the Word of God. Yet, that God does evil is stated so frequently and so unequivocally in Scripture that it is remarkable how few commentators have taken this matter into account except to explain it away. What can one do with such a plain statement as the following? In Isaiah 45:7 it is written: "I form the light, and create darkness: I make peace, and create evil. I the Lord do all these things."

Now in the Scofield Bible there is a footnote at this point which correctly explains that the Hebrew word *ra'*, translated "evil" in Isaiah 45:7, is elsewhere translated "sorrow," "wretchedness," "calamities," but never translated *sin*. God created evil only in the sense that He made sorrow, wretchedness, and calamities, which are assuredly among the fruits of sin but not to be equated with sin, for many evils (earthquakes, for example) have nothing to do with sin. I believe this is a perfectly fair statement of the case as far as it goes, and yet I feel it glosses over a most important aspect of God's sovereignty.

The story of Job suggests that evil does not always come as the direct result of sin. I am not suggesting that Job was not a sinner, for all men are sinners, and Job must be counted as one of them. But the story of Job as set forth in Scripture seems clearly to go out of its way to establish the fact that the calamities that came upon him were not directly the consequence of his unrighteousness nor even of someone else's. They came from Satan, *by God's permission.*

The first chapter presents the background of the scenario. Job is pictured as performing faithfully what was required of him as head of his household in a time antecedent to the establishment of the Mosaic ritual and of the building of the Temple. He offered sacrifices for his family and himself in a way which I believe we must assume was divinely ordered in those early days; and in Job 1:8 we read the Lord's extraordinary testimony to Satan regarding Job's moral stature, thus confirming strongly his introduction in verse 1 as a man "perfect and upright and one that feared God and eschewed evil." So the Lord said to Satan, "Hast thou considered my servant Job, that there is none like him in the earth, a perfect and an upright man, one that feareth God and escheweth evil?" This was God's judgment of the man.

Nevertheless, because of certain circumstances which are revealed to us in Job 1:9-12, of which Job himself was evidently not aware, a series of terrible calamities fell suddenly upon him and devastated him. Job was neither rebellious nor embittered, but it was quite otherwise with his wife who saw herself reduced to ruin on his account. So she said to Job (2:9): "Dost thou *still* retain thine integrity? Curse God and die." It is interesting to note that even in his utter wretchedness he retained his integrity and his wife observed it with surprise. How could he be so docile? God had unfairly demolished him; why should he want to live any longer? Let him simply curse God to his face and be struck dead. . . .

But Job answered (v. 10): "Thou speakest as one of the foolish women speaketh. What? Shall we receive good at the hand of God, and shall we not receive evil?" And then the writer added significantly: "In all this did not Job sin with his lips."

Shall we not receive evil from the hand of God? What an extraordinary statement to make! And Job is immediately exonerated from any suspicion of foolishness or impropriety for having said it. Clearly then, we may here observe a case of evil originating with the Lord for purposes quite other than the punishment of a man's wickedness. Moreover, we have a somewhat parallel circumstance in the New Testament in the case of the man born blind. In John 9:1 ff. we read: "As Jesus passed by, He saw a man who was blind from his birth. And his disciples asked Him, saying, Master, who did sin, this man or his parents, that he was born blind? Jesus answered, Neither hath this man sinned nor his parents: but that the works of God should be made manifest in him."

Here is a case of a manifest evil, blindness from birth, that was not traceable, in this instance, either to the man's own sin or to the sin of his parents. Clearly it was not the Lord's intention to have us suppose that neither the man nor his parents were sinners. In the context the Lord plainly intended his disciples to understand rather that this particular instance of blindness from birth was not directly attributable to human wickedness but was in the strictest sense purely an act of God. It was an evil that God had appointed for a very special purpose. It was not a penalty. It is difficult to know what language the Lord could have used beyond what He did to make this any clearer. And we must conclude, I think, that not all wretchedness or sorrow or calamity is the direct fruit of sin—even though in a sinless world such evils ought never to be necessary, for the exhibition of the glory of God would not need this kind of demonstration.

In Lamentations 3:38 Jeremiah asks a question: "Out of the mouth of the most High proceedeth not evil and good?" This is put in the form of a question in the original because Jeremiah is really asking, "Do not both evil and good proceed out of the mouth of the most High?" And clearly the implied answer is, "Yes, indeed."

In Amos 3:6 it is asked, "Shall there be evil in a city and God hath not done it?" It is hardly sufficient to say that evils come about everywhere and always because of human wickedness in city life, though this is undoubtedly *a* truth. But is it really *the* truth of this utterance? Would, then, the text not have to say rather that God had permitted it than that He had actually *done* it?

The Hebrew word *'asah* rendered "done" in this passage is a word which may mean "doing" or "making" (nearly two thousand times), or it may mean "appointing." The former is by far the more frequent rendering in the King James Version. But even if one should seek to escape the implications of Amos 3:6 by opting for the alternative rendering of "appointing," we still have to acknowledge that God is the initiator who makes the appointment.

Certainly in Jeremiah 36:3 the *purpose* of God was to do evil, and the same seems clearly to be implied in Judges 2:15; Isaiah 31:2; Ezekiel 6:10; Amos 9:4; and Micah 1:12. That God "brought evil" upon men is very frequently asserted without apology: Joshua 23:15; 2 Samuel 17:14; 1 Kings 9:9; 14:10; 21:21; 2 Kings 6:33; 22:16; 2 Chronicles 7:22; 34:24; Nehemiah 13:18; Job 42:11; Jeremiah 4:6; 6:19; 11:11, 23; 18:8; 19:3, 15; 23:12; 32:42; 35:17; 36:31; 42:17; 44:2; Ezekiel 5:16; 14:22; and so forth. And it is clear that here the evil is a consequence of wickedness, an appointed punishment. But I believe it is only by a strained form of exegesis that we can say the same of Job's case or of the man born blind. And we therefore have to recognize that evil is not always punishment. When man initiates evil it is often sinful and punishable, whereas when God initiates evil it never is.

Evil may in fact be good, seen in the long view, whereas wickedness can never be righteousness no matter how long a view we take. The selling of Joseph is a case in point, for it was an evil in the sense of being Joseph's misfortune at the time, but in the end it turned out for his brothers' good (Gen. 45:5)—but only because Joseph bore the penalty in his own person, and God vindicated him by raising him up, as it were, from the dead. It is indeed God's prerogative to do both evil and good together (Isa. 41:23), and

Isaiah presents this circumstance as a challenge that could not be met by false gods.

It is clear therefore that evil per se is not to be equated with sin, and that God has every right to ordain evil as well as good in the working out of his purpose, even as He has the right to make one vessel unto honour and another unto dishonour for the same reason (Rom. 9:21). And the difference does not lie in the clay itself out of which they are made, for both are made "of the same lump." And the evils that sometimes beset us are no more a just desert of our sins than the blessings which fall to our lot are necessarily the reward of our righteousness.

Then what is it that is punishable in the one who is chosen to be an agent in the working out of some evil cause divinely ordained? Many performed evil deeds in response to the Lord's direct ordination, yet they were punished. But not all were punished; some were even rewarded! Since it is the motive that determines whether an act is punishable or meritorious, such evil actions may sometimes be worthy of reward even as the executioner receives his wages. Indeed, we are likely to reward him well, because he is doing a task that is hateful to ordinary people. Will God then condemn those who similarly perform an evil deed essential to the fulfillment of his purposes simply because the deed itself is evil of necessity? And will He necessarily reward a good deed done under the same conditions?

But what if a man takes pleasure in performing the evil deed? Obviously that is an entirely different matter. It is not the deed that is punished, but the spirit in which the deed is carried out: it is the *heart* that makes guilty, not the *hand*. Although the purposes of God are thus carried forward, yet the agent now becomes accountable, not for the deed itself but for the pleasure he experienced in giving free expression to his own inclination to injure a fellow man. The hands of those who crucified the Lord Jesus Christ (Acts 2:23) were wicked not because they crucified the Lord, for this was in express fulfillment of the Father's predetermined plan. They were wicked because they had a wrong reason, a wrong motive, a sinful intention in what they did. They did it because they hated Him without a cause (John 15:25), not because they clearly understood that it was God's will that He be crucified. And this therefore provides us with a paramount instance in which the sinfulness of the world does not lie in the fact that it thwarts the will of God by not doing it, but in the fact that it does not *choose* the will of God. It is the motive, not the deed, that is culpable.

There is a beautiful illustration of this principle to be found in Isaiah 10:5-12, one verse of which we have already considered. But now let us look carefully at the whole passage, omitting for brevity only verses 9 and 10.

> O Assyrian, the *rod of mine anger*, and the staff in their hand is mine indignation. *I will send him* against an hypocritical nation, and against the people of my wrath will I give him a charge, to take the spoil, to take the prey, and to tread them down like the mire of the streets. Howbeit *he meaneth not so*, neither doth his heart think so; but it is in his heart to destroy and cut off nations not a few. For he saith, "Are not my princes as good as kings? . . . Shall I not, as I have done unto Samaria and her idols, so do to Jerusalem and her idols?" Wherefore it shall come to pass that when the Lord hath performed his whole work upon Mount Zion and on Jerusalem, *I will punish the fruit of the stout heart of the king* of Assyria and the glory of his high looks. (my emphasis)

Four salient points stand out in this remarkable passage, which is a behind-the-scenes revelation of history as seen from God's point of view. First of all, as we have already noted, the Assyrian was God's servant, his rod and his staff (v. 5). Secondly, he was sent by God to fulfill God's will, which in this case was to perform an evil work upon Jerusalem and the people of Judea, to devastate their city and their land, to slaughter many of their people, and to carry away their wealth and the precious furnishings of Solomon's Temple (v. 6). Thirdly, the King of Assyria clearly had no conscious intention of fulfilling the will of God. In his own heart he was prompted entirely by self-serving motives. He did not for one moment consider the possibility that he was acting under divine compulsion. Though his *actions* originated with God, his *intentions* originated entirely in his own mind (v. 7). And finally, he was to be punished, not for his deeds but for the fruit of his proud heart, that is to say, for the motivation which sent him forth to descend upon Judea like a wolf upon the fold (v. 12).

Here then we have a perfect example of the dual perspective of historic events. There is no doubt that we shall see many things in an entirely new light when we see them in eternity from God's point of view. Even now as we look back at the Lord's dealings with ourselves we are aware that some things, taken at the time as incomprehensible disappointments or even tragedies of a sort, have nevertheless turned out for good, even as Joseph's experience did. We begin to discern in retrospect that some who opposed us to our temporary discomfort, and intending our hurt, were actually serving the Lord's purposes. Though they acted as the Lord's rod and staff, they were in the final analysis sent to be a source of correction and improvement, not for our confounding.

But what is an evil, performed according to the Lord's intention, becomes a wickedness when the motive is not in accordance with that intention. Thus we may have the strange situation where a deed is rewarded but the motive is punished. For even such actions as have been conducted (albeit unknowingly) according to the Lord's will may be rewarded. The servant who knows not what his lord does is nevertheless worthy of his wages (John 15:15; Luke 10:7). God is no man's debtor. When the Lord borrowed Peter's boat to teach the crowds of people who pressed too closely against Him along the shore, He respected the fact that Peter made his living as a fisherman, and rewarded him with more fish than he could possibly have caught in the interval (Luke 5:4-6)!

Now sometimes both the reward for the work and the punishment for the motive are carried out by like powers, one therefore fulfilling one purpose and the other another purpose, in a system of checks and balances under the Lord's sovereign control. Thus in Ezekiel 29:18-20 we are told:

> Son of man, Nebuchadrezzar king of Babylon caused his army *to serve a great service* against Tyre: every head was made bald, and every shoulder was peeled: *yet had he no wages*, nor his army, for Tyre, for the service he had served against it. Therefore thus saith the Lord God; Behold, I will give the land of Egypt unto Nebuchadrezzar king of Babylon; and he shall take her multitude, and take her spoil, and take her prey; and *it shall be the wages for his army*. I have given him the land of Egypt for his labour wherewith he served against it, *because they wrought for me*, saith the Lord God. (my emphasis throughout)

Comment is hardly necessary here. The message is clear. So God's checks and balances keep wickedness curbed or punished, while service is rewarded at one and the same time. What is punished is the intent, which Scripture refers to as the "fruit" of a man's doings, reflected by the effect upon the man himself either restraining or confirming in him the bent of his life, the way of his heart. The man who exults afterwards in the revenge he has obtained by punishing his enemy, reveals why he punished his enemy. The father who mourns afterwards, having punished his son, reveals why he punished his son. The act in either case may be very similar, but the effect upon the doer makes all the difference. This seems to be why in Jeremiah 21:14, where the troubles which were to come upon Judea and Jerusalem were in prospect, the Lord said, "I will punish you according to the fruit of your doings."

In more personal terms, Jeremiah (32:19) repeats this warning: "Great in counsel, and mighty in work: for thine eyes are open upon all the ways of the sons of men: to give every one according to his ways, and according to the fruit of his doings." And lest any man should suppose himself immune, Jeremiah (17:9, 10) issues that familiar warning: "The heart is deceitful above all things, and desperately wicked: who can know it? I the Lord search the heart, I try the reins, even to give every man according to his ways, and according to the fruit of his doings." Alas, man's intentions are sometimes great but his work is small; or his intentions are "small" but his work is great. In either case the judgment of God is stamped above all on man's *ways* rather than his works, upon the fruit of his doings rather than upon those doings themselves.

So we have a basic principle here, that evil is not necessarily wickedness, for God Himself does evil, appoints it, intends it, or even creates it where his purposes demand. But with man evil is all too often wickedness also; so frequently is this the case that we have mistakenly equated the two words. When evils are performed by man as a direct result of God's command, they bring no penalty unless the doer takes delight in the harm that is done. In this case he is punished for his intention but not for the deed; he may in fact be rewarded for an evil deed, as Nebuchadrezzar was. If he should perform an evil that the Lord has not commanded and if he should do it with wicked intent, then in due time he will suffer for both the action and the intention, doubly condemned for a wickedness doubly offensive.

There is, of course, another side to this. The Lord's people may perform good deeds and yet the motive may be self-serving. Paul's hypothetical "un-loving" gift to feed the poor would profit them but not himself, as he openly admitted (1 Cor. 13:3). In 1 Corinthians 9:16, 17 Paul speaks of the commission he had received to preach the Gospel. Yet he disclaimed any merit in the mere fact of being a preacher. "For though I preach the Gospel, I have nothing to glory of: for necessity is laid upon me; yea, woe is unto me if I preach not the Gospel! For if I do this thing willingly, I have a reward: but if against my will, a dispensation of the Gospel is committed unto me." The secret of reward was not obedience—but *willing* obedience. It is thus quite possible to perform the Lord's will perfectly and yet not receive a reward; moreover, it is quite possible to be punished for doing it, as the Assyrian King Sennacherib was.

Sometimes the good deeds of men are involuntary, kindnesses done by accident as it were, or unknowingly. Such good deeds are good in themselves but obviously not righteous, and not being righteous they are not meritorious. Similarly, as we have seen, there will be those who will profess to have done many good deeds in the Lord's name who yet will be declared "workers of iniquity" (Matt. 7:23).

Alternatively, there are times when the intention is right but by reason of circumstances actual performance proves impossible. What of these? If intention is what is rewarded or punished, then is the actual doing important in this respect? Is not a man counted guilty merely for secret desires? Indeed, he is. Whoever looks upon a woman with lust in his heart has already committed adultery but for lack of opportunity (Matt. 5:28),* even as coveting is stealing but for lack of opportunity, and hating is murder (1 John

---

*The Greek γυνή (*gunē:* woman) in this case almost certainly has the common meaning of the "wife of another." See Oepke, in Kittel, *Theological Dictionary of the New Testament*, Vol. I, p. 776.

3:15). The fact that no actual killing has been committed is not important in the judgment of the individual, though it obviously is in the social context. Thus the Jewish people slew the Lord by hating Him—and then crucified Him. Thus the King James Version rightly renders the Greek of Acts 5:30 as "slew and hanged [Him] on a tree" (in that order), and similarly Acts 10:39. This is a profound truth. Moreover, it was a normal practice with the Jews to slay first before crucifying as will be seen by reference to many related passages of Scripture such as Joshua 10:26 and Matthew 23:34. They hated the Lord long before the crucifixion, and their hatred was potential murder awaiting only the proper opportunity.

But again, the reverse is also true. A kindness fully intended is counted with God as actually done and rewarded as such. The best example is seen in David's desire to build the Temple. So firm was his resolve to build that he set the process in operation and began the preparation and assembly of the needed materials long before the Temple construction was begun. Yet because he was a man of war (1 Chron. 28:3), the Lord would not allow the desire of his heart to be fulfilled in the actual building of it. When the day finally came to consecrate the House of God of which David had dreamed, his son Solomon said to the people (1 Kings 8:17-19): "It was in the heart of David my father to build an house for the name of the Lord God of Israel. But the Lord said unto David my father, Whereas it was in thine heart to build an house unto my name *thou didst well* that it was in thine heart. Nevertheless, thou shalt not build the house; but thy son that shall come forth out of thy loins, he shall build the house unto my name." So David did well, just as much as the faithful servant in Luke 19:17 who was commended for having actually "done well."

Paul states this as a general principle. Thus in 2 Corinthians 8:12 he writes: "If there be first a willing mind, it is accepted according to what a man hath, and not according to what he hath not." The widow who cast in two mites which was everything that she had (after all, she might have put in only *one* of them) had in fact given more than all the rest who cast in a mere pittance of their abundance (Luke 21:2).

How statisfying this all is! How appropriate! The only necessity is that we assume that God is precise in his revelation and that He requires us to distinguish between things that differ: between intention and deed, and therefore between wickedness and evil. Paul recognizes the difference between goodness and righteousness when he points out the simple truth that in a time of emergency a man will more readily give up his life for a *good* man than for a *righteous* one! Goodness in man is appealing; righteousness is forbidding. In Romans 5:7 he writes: "Scarcely for a righteous man will one die: yet peradventure for a good man some would even dare to die." It is true!

A good deed has primarily a historical significance on a horizontal plane and on a short-term basis, as between man and man. A righteous act has a vertical dimension with ultimate reference to God and to eternity. It was against Bathsheba and Uriah her husband that David did an *evil* thing (Ps. 51:4), whereas the unrighteousness of his act was essentially against God. It was in this sense he could speak of it as being "against Thee, and Thee only. . . ."

There is something cold and harsh about righteousness when it has reference to relationships between men. There is something warm and kind about goodness. A good man can lie to save a friend and thereby confirm our sense of goodness in his nature. There is a real difference between these two terms, as there is between evil and wickedness.

So we seem to have a partial solution to a troublesome problem in the minds of many people. The wicked are punished even when their evil acts fulfill the will of God and are performed under his direction. The Lord's children are fully rewarded even when all they have accomplished is but a pitiful fragment of their earnest desire. What they have longed to do, as David longed to build the Temple, they may never be permitted to see done; yet there is no doubt that when God sees that their longing is pure and holy, it will be counted as though fulfilled. The "if only" of all worldly aspirations that fail to be realized becomes the "well done!" of all spiritual aspirations that failed only because of circumstances. Perhaps in heaven we shall be surprised to find many greatly rewarded who seemed in fact never to have achieved anything, while those who stand unrewarded in God's Judgment will undoubtedly find themselves in no position to quarrel with that assessment when they realize that God is not a judge of action but a judge of intention.

Here then we begin to discern the meeting place of divine sovereignty and human responsibility, of Predestination and reward.

PART FOUR

Election and Evangelism

INTRODUCTION

Three questions commonly arise in the minds of all those who earnestly desire to see their unsaved friends and relatives brought to a saving knowledge of the Lord Jesus Christ. Let us examine these three questions and see if there are satisfactory answers to be found in Scripture itself.

The first question is: *Why Preach at All?* If Election guarantees the salvation of all that are predestined to be saved, why should we be bothered with evangelism, personal or missionary? What possible difference can it make whether we speak to men or not?

Assuming that we do feel a call to evangelize, the second question is: *What to Preach?* Since Limited Atonement seems clearly to be the intention of God in the sacrifice of the Lord Jesus Christ so that Christ died effectively only for the elect, what kind of message do we have for the unsaved individual? Since we have no way of knowing in advance whether he is among the elect or not, we have no way of knowing whether Christ died for him in particular. Can we then with sincerity say to such a one, "God loves *you*" or "Christ died for *you*"? If we cannot be personal in this way, what form is our presentation to take? What actual message do we have for the individual?

The third question is: *Should Election Be Preached?* Since many are called but only a few are chosen to be saved, is it wise to emphasize the sovereignty of the grace of God which to the non-elect might seem cause for despair? Should we not rather keep quiet on the matter of God's elective purposes? Is Predestination a proper subject for public discussion?

15

WHY PREACH?

It is important to bear in mind that we are not called to personal evangelism or to the mission field simply because we want to share with others our sense of gratitude to the Lord for what He has done for us personally in saving us. This would make all personal evangelism and all missionary activity dependent upon our own feelings; and human feelings do not have the staying power to provide a solid foundation for any venture that involves both courage and sustained self-sacrifice, the rewards of which may never be seen on this side of the grave. When, as almost inevitably happens at times, we reach a low in our spiritual life, we also lose much of our sense of thankfulness. Gratitude is not strong enough to inspire us to any kind of missionary activity.

The call to personal evangelism and to all missionary activity rests upon the fact that we are *commanded* to go.

> Jesus came and spake unto them, saying, All power is given unto Me in heaven and in earth. *Go ye therefore* and make disciples of all nations, baptizing them in the name of the Father, and of the Son, and of the Holy Spirit; teaching them to observe all things whatsoever I have commanded you: and lo, I am with you always, even unto the end of the world. Amen. (Matt. 28:18-20)

We are not invited to preach the Gospel only at certain times which seem propitious or in certain places which look more promising, though there is no doubt that we are called to be wise as serpents and harmless as doves (Matt. 10:16). We are encouraged to be always ready to sow the seed. "In the morning sow thy seed, and in the evening withhold not thy hand: for thou knowest not whether shall prosper either this or that, or whether both alike shall be good" (Eccles. 11:6). In writing to Timothy Paul said, "Preach the Word; be instant in season, out of season" (2 Tim. 4:2). The Greek behind this exhortation is interesting. To "be instant" is a translation of a Greek word which has a number of meanings all tending in the same direction. These are "to stand by," "to be at hand," "to be pressing," "to be urgent," "to be earnest." The ideas of eagerness, seriousness, constancy, and preparedness are all wrapped up in the Greek verb *ephistēmi* (ἐφίστημι). The Greek which lies behind the words "in season, out of season" is perhaps more literally rendered "timely" and "untimely" (*eukairōs* and *akairōs*: εὐκαίρως and ἀκαίρως). In spite of our reasonings which would justify delay, the occasion being inappropriate, it is doubtful if the Holy Spirit could have used any two other words which would more clearly set forth the principle that we are not to be guided by our *feelings* as to the appropriateness or otherwise of the moment. There are undoubtedly times when we should remain silent, even as the Lord Jesus upon certain occasions did not allow men to give their testimony (e.g., Mark 7:36). The secret must surely be that we are to commune with the Lord continuously, seeking his instructions moment by moment so that we shall neither default nor presume.

The message is to be presented when the Lord directs, even if there is every evidence that it will not be accepted. In Ezekiel 2:7 the Lord said to the prophet, "And thou shalt speak my words unto them whether they will hear or whether they will forbear." And later Ezekiel receives further instructions in this regard, explaining to him more clearly why he was to present a message even when there was no possibility of its being accepted. Thus in Ezekiel 3:18, 19 the Lord said: "When I say unto the wicked, thou shalt surely die; and thou givest him not warning, nor speakest to warn the wicked from his wicked way, to save his life; the same wicked man shall die in his iniquity; *but his blood will I require at thine hand.* Yet if thou warn the wicked, and he turn not from his wickedness, nor from his wicked way, he shall die in his iniquity, *but thou hast delivered thy soul.*"

The principle here is a very important one. We have one responsibility: when occasion is offered, we must warn men of their position before God. If we fail to do this we are disobedient. We pay the price of that disobedience in a loss of the sense of fellowship with our Father and the Lord Jesus Christ, and with one another. Obedience to the command to speak to our friends of the Lord is the best guarantee of spiritual growth and of enjoyment of fellowship with the Lord. Yet such obedience is not essential for the fulfillment of God's purposes in Election, for He is sovereign. This is not why we are called to share our faith, as though without this active ministry the hands of the Lord would be tied. It is a privilege which the Lord allows (1 Thess. 2:4).

But there is another equally important point which emerges from these passages of Scripture and that is that the message we present serves a double purpose. To those who are elect it means the breath of life; to those who are not elect, whom God has merely allowed to go their own way by their own choice, it is a sentence of death. As Paul said to the Corinthians: "To the one we are the savour of death unto death; and to the other the savour of life unto life" (2 Cor. 2:16). And Paul asks, appropriately, "And who is sufficient for these things?" For we stand in the presence of the inscrutable will of God whose ways are not our ways but who will in the end demonstrate without doubt that He has done all things well. Isaiah 55:8-11 instructs us:

> My thoughts are not your thoughts, neither are your ways my ways, saith the Lord. For as the heavens are higher than the earth, so are my ways higher than your ways, and my thoughts than your thoughts. For as the rain cometh down, and the snow from heaven, and returneth not thither but watereth the earth, and maketh it bring forth and bud that it may give seed to the sower and bread to the eater: so shall my Word be that goeth forth out of my mouth: it shall not return unto Me void, but it shall accomplish that which I please, and it shall prosper in the thing whereto I sent it.

We do not know in any given case why we are sent to someone or someone is brought to us, whether it is to be, in a nutshell, "for blessing or for cursing," but we do know from this passage that when we use the Word of God we are obeying his command faithfully, we are absolving ourselves from the responsibility of that man's decision, and we can rest assured that it is not a purposeless undertaking. God's Word will accomplish that whereto He sends it through us.

We thus demonstrate the justice of God when men are condemned because, of their own free will, they have refused his offer of salvation; and we demonstrate his grace when men, who would otherwise refuse, accept his salvation because He gives them the power to do so. What God uses in both cases, to leave without excuse on the one hand and to save on the other hand, is his own Word. The message that will in the end bring life is not man's rationalization as exhibited in his theology, nor his intuitive understanding as set forth in his poetry, nor even the persuasive power of the eloquence by which he succeeds in captivating his hearers. The message is the Word of God, the "seed" (Luke 8:11). It is this that is germinated: "Being born again, not of corruptible seed, but of incorruptible, by the Word of God, which liveth and abideth forever" (1 Peter 1:23). And again, "So then, faith cometh by hearing and hearing by the Word of God" (Rom. 10:17). And once again, "Of his own will begat He us with the Word of truth" (James 1:18).

It is of fundamental importance to recognize that God's ultimate weapon is his own Word and not man's. The eloquence of the speaker, his powers of persuasion, and the sophistication of his techniques are really beside the point. It is not that God ignores these things: it is rather that He does not *need* them. He may be pleased to use them, but men are wonderfully saved without any of these means. The unreached derelict victimized by alcohol may stumble upon a tract through which God speaks to his soul, and he is born again without direct human intervention. There is a case, I believe, of a body of believers formed on an unevangelized Pacific island as a result of a single loose page blown from a Bible held in the hand of a missionary travelling by sea to another place.

The Word of God has extraordinary power. Some years ago I knew of an Anglican minister who did not know the Lord but served in a small Welsh mining community where a number of his less educated parishioners were the Lord's children and knew it. This minister at the time was something of a dilettante in spiritual matters and did not even consider it worthwhile preaching a sermon at every service. On one occasion he planned to forego the sermon but at the last moment, when the time arrived in the service for him to preach, he casually decided to say a few words on the text, "What think ye of Christ?"

He went up to the pulpit and started a random discourse for which he hand undertaken no preparation whatever. But while he was speaking, somehow it dawned upon him that he had to answer this question himself personally. And in some extraordinary way the light went on in his own mind and heart as he searched for words. He hesitated—then stood silently for a moment as the truth suddenly flooded his soul. Someone in the back of the church, a miner who for all his lack of education knew more of the Lord than the minister did, stood up and said in a loud voice, "Alleluia! The Parson's saved!" And he was! So here we have a case of a man saved by his own preaching of the Word of God.

In evangelism it is not that God is *dependent* upon us who already know the Lord; rather it is that our growth is dependent upon our obedience to evangelize, and God does not give commands to us which are without purpose. When our ministry occasionally succeeds in bearing fruit unto everlasting life, we can only say with Paul that "we were *allowed of God* to be put in trust with the Gospel" (1 Thess. 2:4).

There is yet another reason for personal evangelism even though we know that very few will respond favourably. The fact is that there is no other way for those very few who by grace are to respond except somebody in some direct or indirect way provide them with the occasion. The same message which is rejected by the unsaved is the means whereby the elect are brought into salvation. Elect and non-elect are indistinguishable as targets until the parting of the ways. Romans 9:21 tells us that vessels of honour and of dishonour are fashioned out of the same material. And as Paul said to the Ephesians (2:3), we all shared in times past the same kind of life, "fulfilling the desires of the flesh and of the mind; and were by nature the children of wrath, *even as others.*" The same message must therefore be presented to the elect and the non-elect alike, though the response will be exactly opposite. Under normal circumstances, in spite of our special concern for particular individuals, we can never know whether we are addressing ourselves to one who is yet to be born again or to one whom God will permit to go his own way. Only once in Scripture did a man actually know that the unsaved man to whom he was called to minister the Gospel was numbered among God's elect. In Acts 9:10-15 Ananias was sent to open the eyes of a man who was "a chosen vessel" to bear the Lord's name before the Gentiles.

It is not improper, even by standards of human judgment, that a man should be warned that if he goes on in his own way he must come into judgment. But having given men free will in the first place, the Judge is not obligated to direct that warning personally to the individual. Although such warning makes his condemnation doubly sure because the man personally warned is wholly without excuse, nevertheless, something is revealed of the Judge's character when we learn that at least He desired that the wicked should be forewarned. Even in this giving of warning there is thus an element of the grace of God displayed. At the same time it is quite fitting that we who are commanded to warn men should assume some responsibility for our negligence when we fail to do so. But when we do personally evangelize our fellow men, we are in a sense rewarded, whether our message is rejected or accepted, though we are apt to think of reward as resulting only from acceptance.

Some years ago I had occasion to see a beautiful illustration of how an apparently futile argument can bring wholly unexpected results. One of our young people with whom I had been dealing for four years, and who was yet unsaved, climbed on the streetcar at the limits of the north end of our city to make the long trip (about eight miles) downtown to a place of summer employment. On the streetcar it happened that there was another young person who loved to argue but seemed totally impervious to the Lord's claims and quite unaware of his own need of a Saviour. He fancied himself something of a sophisticated philosopher. My friend sat down beside him, and at once got into an argument with him about the way of salvation, though my friend himself had yet no assurance of his own salvation. Apparently the argument continued unabated until they both got off the streetcar half an hour later and went their own different ways to work.

At the end of the day, in the providence of God, both men caught the same streetcar back to the north end of the city and found seats side by side! In view of the enormous numbers of people coming out of work at that time in the evening, this was an unusual circumstance indeed. Needless to say, they picked up their former argument immediately.

That evening, after supper, my friend phoned me and said, "I'd like to come over and see you. I think I know what you've been trying to tell me." And within half an hour we went for a walk together and there was no doubt about it. He knew the Lord. He was rejoicing in a new life. What had happened on the streetcar was that the argument, while serving no such purpose in the mind and heart of the other young man, had nevertheless in his *own* heart and mind clarified his position so that he was in effect evangelized by his own words. It is tremendously rewarding to know that this young man went forward in the Lord and is now a revered minister of the Gospel of Jesus Christ. As to his opponent, as far as I know he was never convinced.

Those who have engaged in such personal work will bear ample testimony to the fact that even violent opposition can be rewarding, because it draws us so much closer to the Lord. We "fill up his sufferings" (Col. 1:24). We grow by exercise and learn how to deal with certain kinds of response, and there is a strange joy in being repudiated for Christ's sake. Our sense of oneness with the Lord is greatly enhanced and a new element of spiritual adventure is introduced into life.

Obedience to the commission of Matthew 28 bears its own unexpected reward. And exercise increases ability. But we are undoubtedly faint-hearted and of little faith. Let us admit before the Lord what we know in our hearts to be true, that it is not always doctrine that dulls our sense of mission but fear of the faces of men.

16

WHAT TO PREACH

It is difficult to be convincing when speaking to someone personally about the Lord if, in the interest of truth, it is improper to speak with assurance about the love of God for him as an individual. What precisely does one say? Congregational evangelism presents fewer problems, for there is an element of remoteness vis-à-vis the individual that resolves the difficulty. Yet even here it seems more telling to be able to preach the Gospel without consciously having to avoid such phrases as "Christ died for *you.*" And what does one do when the situation is intensified by personal confrontation in a question period afterwards, or when talking privately to a friend?

It is noteworthy, I think, that among all the records of sermons or fragments of sermons in the New Testament (exclusive of the Lord's), such personal statements as "God loves you" or "Christ died for you" are not to be found. These sermons were never impersonal; neither were they ever so formulated as to compromise the absolute truth. The New Testament will be found to contain sermon materials in the following places: Peter's sermons—Acts 2:14 ff.; 3:12-26; 4:9-12; 5:29-32; and 10:34-43; Paul's sermons—Acts 13:16-42; 17:22-32; and 22:1-21; and Stephen's sermon—Acts 7:2-53.

It has been argued that we do not find expressions like "God loves you" because such a personal way of speaking as we currently employ in evangelism was not then in vogue. This is not strictly true, however. In the institution of the Lord's Supper, Jesus said, "This is my body which is given *for you,*" and "This cup is the new covenant in my blood, which is shed *for you*" (Luke 22:19, 20). It is true that the "you" in both these passages is in the plural not the singular form, but it is equally certain that the Lord Jesus was directing his words to each one of the individuals present when He spoke. It is important to remember that Judas had already left the circle of those thus addressed (John 13:30), for it was not until after supper was over that the memorial was instituted (1 Cor. 11:25). Were it not for Paul's inspired statement in his letter to the Corinthians which tells us that these words were spoken after and not before supper, we could not be sure that Judas was excluded. If Judas had still been present, the Lord's inclusive address to his disciples (when He spoke of his sacrifice as being applicable to them all without discrimination) would have been inappropriate. Here Scripture has thus been marvellously hedged about. Jesus was able to say "which is shed for you [plural]" because all who were then present to whom He addressed his words were chosen vessels of his grace. The distinction between the disciples and Judas is underscored with the characteristic precision of Scripture when we are told that during the first part of the meal Jesus washed the feet of all the disciples, including Judas, whom He however set apart by himself, though He did not identify him when He said (John 13:10): "He that is washed needeth not save to wash his feet but is every whit clean: and ye are clean but not all." And John makes this comment (v. 11): "For He knew who should betray Him, on which account He said, Ye are not all clean."

The details of the Last Supper are elucidated by Alfred Edersheim in his *Life and Times of Jesus the Messiah*, where will be found reconciliation of the details given in the Gospels which at times appear to be in conflict.[1] A.T. Robertson in his *Harmony of the Gospels* orders the various portions of the biblical text in the four Gospels and in 1 Corinthians in a way that very nicely dovetails with Edersheim's commentary.[2] Certainly there is no justification here for arguing that the Lord Jesus addressed those who were elect to salvation and one who was not in the same direct and personal way. He did not say to Judas, "which is shed for *you*"; for Judas was not present when He made this statement.

One of the most common criticisms of those who hold the Augustinian-Calvinist position is that their theology of Limited Atonement tends to weaken the incentive to evangelism. I believe it would be better to say that the cause of any lack of zeal we may have lies more deeply than in our theology. The fact is that many of us lack courage when it comes to personal evangelism, and we find it convenient to cover our timidity by pleading a certain confusion as to the form of our message when we are brought face to face with the individual. But if we cannot sincerely say to an unsaved friend, "Jesus died for you," because we cannot know that it is true, are we then left without any message at all that could honestly be termed "Good News"—that is, the *Gospel?*

Manifestly the answer is, No! We are not left without any message for the individual. The message for the individual is both a general one and a par-

---

1. Vol. II, pp. 504-509.
2. Pp. 193-96 (sections 147, 148).

ticular one. First, that "this is a true saying and worthy of all acceptation, that Christ Jesus came into the world to save *sinners*" (1 Tim. 1:15): this is the general truth. And secondly, the particular truth is: "Whosoever will, let him take of the water of life freely" (Rev. 22:17); "Behold, I stand at the door and knock; if any man hear my voice, and open the door, I will come in to him" (Rev. 3:20). Such open invitations *to the individual* are characteristic of God's Word to man in both the Old Testament and the New: "Ho! everyone that thirsteth! Come ye to the waters, and he that hath no money, come ye . . ." (Isa. 55:1). It is a personal invitation (Luke 14:17). This invitation is to *come*. "Come unto Me, all ye that labour and are heavy laden, and I will give you rest" (Matt. 11:28). The message that we are to take to the individual is personal, addressed to *him* who hears and not merely *them* who hear: "Verily, verily, I say unto you, he that heareth my word and believes on Him that sent Me hath everlasting life" (John 5:24).

In Reformed theological circles there has been considerable discussion about the difficulty of knowing precisely what is to be *offered* when the Gospel is preached. In the *Canons of Dort* (III-IV. 14) it is stated that "faith is therefore to be considered as the gift of God, not on account of its being offered by God to man, to be accepted or rejected at his pleasure, but because it is in reality *conferred* upon him . . . ." What then is it that we are offering when we preach the Gospel? Herman Hoeksema proposes that according to the Canons it is not *grace*, but Christ that is offered.[3] And in order to separate these two clearly, he points out that in the Latin text of the Canons it is not said that we offer Christ but that we "present" Christ. That is to say, Christ is presented, displayed in the Gospel. This presentation is held by Hoeksema to be objective and descriptive in character. It cannot mean that God is giving an invitation, for He gives a true invitation only to the elect. The command to believe and be converted is proper, but it is general, addressed to all men. In a word, preaching appears in a slightly different light. It is no longer invitation but *declaration*.

The justification for presenting such a declaration is that if the hearer is among the elect he will receive the message as a personal invitation, and will respond in a God-ordained way. Because this is God's ordained way of leaving the non-elect without excuse and of saving the elect, it will not be necessary to preach "with the enticing words of man's wisdom" (1 Cor. 2:4). Here the word *enticing* in the Greek means, literally, "persuasiveness." Paul in this passage also underscores the fact that in order to be fruitful the Word of God cannot merely be parroted but must be presented "in demonstration of the Spirit and of power." So two things are required: (1) that we remain very close to the words of Scripture, presenting them "in the Spirit'" and (2) that God be pleased to germinate the seed thus sown. If, on the other hand,

---

3. Quoted in G. C. Berkouwer, *Studies in Dogmatics: Divine Election*, p. 222.

the hearer is not among the elect, he will not be deceived, for he will not even hear the message with his inner ear, no matter how persuasive we are. He will neither receive nor understand. He gains nothing by the encounter, but in the Judgment the Judge may justly say, "You were invited, but you did not hear the invitation because you did not want to hear it." Hereby is the justice of God exhibited. The grace of God in electing and bringing to salvation does not conflict with the wonderful truth that whosoever will may come, for it is the hearing of the truth that makes the Election of God effectual. It is the hearing of the truth that guarantees that whosoever may, will come. And in the hearing of this we may play a part by being allowed of God to proclaim the Gospel (1 Thess. 2:4).

But there is no doubt that if persuasiveness is left in our hands we are likely to try to reinforce persuasion by polishing our techniques. And so the emphasis inevitably comes to rest upon the method rather than upon the message itself. By contrast, if persuasion is entirely in God's hands through the Holy Spirit alone, then we are more apt to be driven to our knees in preparation for a fruitful ministry of evangelism whether congregational or personal. But having adopted the more appropriate emphasis of being on our knees, we ought not to hold back from engagement within the world by retreating behind the all too familiar excuse for inaction, "We must pray about it." There is a time for prayer, but there is a time when prayer is no longer an appropriate exercise if it becomes a substitute for confrontation. The Lord once said to Moses, "Wherefore criest thou unto Me? Speak unto the children of Israel that they go forward" (Exod. 14:15).

It must always be borne in mind that there is no difference between the Gospel preached to those who are not among the elect and those who are—assuming that both are yet unsaved. The message is precisely the same for both parties. We are commanded to proclaim the message, not to attempt an assessment of the suitability of the individual to whom we address it. Nor are we to neglect anyone simply because he seems an unlikely prospect, for God often delights to confound our best judgments. The most hostile and antagonistic individuals (like Paul before his conversion) are often chosen vessels. And remember that the gestation period with some is much longer than with others.

I have friends whom I have worked with for years, who never fail to attend any seminars I hold or lecture series I give, who are ready and willing at any time to talk freely about their need of salvation without hostility or brashness, and yet who admit frankly, "I am not a Christian." They seem no nearer to the Lord today than after our first serious discussion some eighteen years ago. Such people seem to be "ever learning and never able to come to the knowledge of the truth" (2 Tim. 3:7). If ever there was proof of the fact that the time of coming to birth is in the Lord's hands and not ours, it is in such cases as these. On the other hand, others, upon a very first meeting, may turn seriously at some point in the conversation and say simply and openly, "Help me in." And they mean it; and they are wonderfully saved.

I remember being in a room with about sixty young people from seventeen to twenty-one years of age. I had been talking with one of them who was already a child of God, and I quoted Revelation 3:20 at one point in the conversation as an illustration of how simple the passage from death unto life can sometimes be. Being born again requires almost no explicit theological understanding. About ten minutes later, a young girl who had a beautiful singing voice came up to me and said very quietly, "You know when you said just now, 'Behold, I stand at the door and knock; if any man will open I will come in,' well, I overheard that and . . . I did . . . and He did!" And her face showed that marvellous glow of the newborn in Christ. Later that afternoon when it was time to close our meeting, I asked her to pray. She prayed for the first time but without hesitation, and I shall never forget the atmosphere created by that short prayer. What a miracle this is! And how can one possibly account for the immediacy of some conversions when others seem to be postponed for years and years? It cannot be our earnestness, nor even the skill with which we handle the Word of God. It is plainly and simply a matter of the sovereignty of God's grace. Only God can germinate the seed, but we are invited to be busy sowing it.

Why then do we have so much difficulty knowing how to approach our unsaved friends? Perhaps if we had followed faithfully the exhortation of Paul's Epistles and left the matter of germination entirely in God's hands, while we trained ourselves rather as successful sowers of the seed, the problem would never have arisen. But when we depart from Calvinism with its emphasis upon the sovereignty of God's grace and the total helplessness of man, we tend to constitute ourselves not merely sowers but germinators, with the power to give life. And this we simply cannot do.

We are merely to make sure that we are in the Lord's way and that our seed is pure and good, unmixed with other seed (Lev. 19:19) that will be incompatible with it—even though these other seeds may appear to make the sowing easier. To be saved, a man does not need to know the theology of salvation, only the facts of its possibility through the sacrifice of the Lord Jesus Christ. Some men are curious and like to have a measure of understanding in order to clear away supposed difficulties, but there is no need to attempt the clearing away of difficulties that have not been raised. A man has only to recognize his own personal need and to be assured that that need can be met in the Lord Jesus Christ. Indeed if a man does recognize his need of a Saviour, there is a sense in which he is already among the elect, for no man discovers he is dead unless God has first germinated life within him. Yet the gestation period may be distressingly prolonged and great patience is required.

The "formula" for salvation is not set forth in Scripture in a single pattern. In some cases we are told that it is enough that a man simply call upon the Lord (Rom. 10:13). There is surely a minimum of theology here! I was talking with one friend about four years ago, sitting quietly beside an open fire. He was not a Christian but the Lord was certainly dealing with him. A few days later he told me that as he sat there that evening he suddenly said in his heart, "Lord, save me!" And the Lord did indeed, that very night— though we did not know it at the time. A few weeks later he was involved in a terrible car accident and totally paralyzed from the neck down. He still is. But his witness since that accident has been truly remarkable, as his hospital nurses and friends testify unhesitatingly. There is no bitterness and no looking back. Though his old way of life was totally destroyed, a new life has replaced it. It is wonderful what the Lord can do!

The Calvinist, acknowledging the true spiritual deadness of the unsaved individual, knows only too well that no man can come unto the Lord unless the Father draws him. No man will believe unto salvation unless he is resurrected from his spiritual deadness and made alive and granted saving faith. It is not our concern to ask, "Is this man elected to be a member of God's blameless family?" It is rather our privilege to tell him what is possible because of what the Lord has done to save sinners, and, as far as we are able, to do this using the words of Scripture. Thus a seed may be planted. Whether it germinates or not is beyond our responsibility. But if it does germinate by the power of God, then indeed our responsibility is enormously extended. It becomes our privilege and duty to water it, cultivate it, nourish it, and protect it until it has developed to a point where the fellowship of others in a more general way will ensure its continued growth. So much then for *our* responsibility in the matter.

But the question may still be asked, How can God command men to do things, to repent, for example, knowing that obedience is quite impossible for man in his fallen state? Is it reasonable that God should make such demands and then condemn the individual for not meeting them? It is a perfectly proper question, and there is a perfectly statisfactory answer to it. *God's commands are not an expression of his expectations but of his requirements.* As Thomas Boston in his justly famous book, *Human Nature in Its Fourfold State* (p. 164), has rightly put it, it is man's duty to repent of his sins because God has commanded him to do so. And God's command, *not man's ability*, is the measure of man's duty.

Of this important truth Scripture supplies innumerable illustrations. Just the simple command to "repent," repeated again and again in Scripture (cf. Matt. 3:2; 4:17; Acts 2:38; 3:19; 8:22; 17:30; Rev. 2:5; and so forth), is given with a full realization that man as a fallen creature cannot obey this command unless God in his mercy first of all undoes some of the spiritual damage of the Fall. Where salvation is the end in view, repentance is a divine gift, not a natural capacity of man (cf. Ps. 80:3, 19; Jer. 24:7; 31:18, 19; Lam. 5:21; Acts 5:31; 11:18; 2 Tim. 2:25). As Romans 2:4 assures us, it is the goodness of God, not the goodness of man, that leads to repentance. In spite of his command to do so, we do not turn ourselves to God unless He first turns us. Even in such a basic thing as repentance, God's command is not predicated on man's assumed capability of obedience but is an expression of what God requires of man.

Many such commands are set forth in Scripture. Declared to be God's requirement rather than his expectation, these commands are then followed by an assurance to the effect that He Himself will make the obedience possible. Without such enabling there is never any fulfillment of the command. Thus in Ezekiel 18:31 God's command is set forth: "Cast away from you all your transgressions whereby ye have transgressed; and make you a new heart and a new spirit." But the fulfillment of this requirement was to be realized only when God Himself acted sovereignly and without waiting for man's co-operation, as set forth in Ezekiel 36:25, 26: "I will sprinkle clean water upon you, and ye shall be clean . . . . A new heart also *will I give you*, and a new spirit *will I put within you*." Similarly, Israel was commanded: "Circumcise therefore the foreskin of your heart" (Deut. 10:16); but this was never achieved by anyone until the Lord Himself stepped in and performed it for him. "And the Lord thy God will circumcise thine heart . . . that thou mayest live" (Deut. 30:6).

Isaiah 45:22 records the familiar words, "Look unto Me, and be ye saved." But how can the blind look unto Him until they have first received their sight? We turn *to* the Lord only when we are turned *by* the Lord. Psalm 80:3 reads: "Turn us again, O God, and cause thy face to shine; and we shall be saved." So also we are commanded to love God (Matt. 22:37) but we love only after He has first loved us (1 John 4:19). We are told that if we will only open our hearts to his knocking, He will come in and fulfill both Himself and us (Rev. 3:20); but we learn from the example of Lydia "whose heart the Lord had opened" (Acts 16:14) that such opening is made possible only by the Lord. The fact is that we simply do not hear his knocking any more than a corpse in a coffin hears the mourners who bewail his passing. We are told that if we but call upon his name we shall be saved (Rom. 10:13), but Psalm 80:18, 19 makes it clear that we shall never call unless we are first made alive by his grace: "Quicken us, and we will call upon thy name. Turn us again, O Lord God of hosts, cause thy face to shine; and we shall be saved." A man must be alive before he can exercise saving faith (John 11:26: "Whosoever liveth and believeth in Me shall never die"—*liveth* and *believeth*, in that order.

The Lord Jesus Christ graciously gave the invitation, "Come unto Me, all ye that labour" (Matt. 11:28); and yet the same Lord said, "All that the

Father giveth Me shall come to Me. . . . No man cometh unto Me, except the Father which hath sent Me draw him" (John 6:37, 44). Consequently, so long as the Father does not open a man's ears to hear the call he simply cannot respond. How can any man respond to a call which by nature he is not attuned to hear? As Jesus said, "Ye will not come to Me, that ye might have life" (John 5:40). And why not? "Ye therefore hear not, because ye are not of God" (John 8:47). We thus see that many invitations to salvation are set forth in Scripture in such a way as to express a command that simply states God's requirement of man, if he is to be saved. But such commands manifestly do not represent his expectations, for in every case Scripture goes on to say that God Himself must intervene in order to make obedience to the command possible.

One reason why we view this as unfair is that we fail to realize that man unsaved is truly spiritually dead, and the dead are both unseeing and unhearing. It is a mistake to suppose that men actually do hear the voice of the Lord and honestly desire to respond affirmatively but are somehow unable to do so, as though they were actually willing but not allowed. No man is ever denied what he wishes in this respect. Whosoever will, may. But the natural man, like the wholly untuned radio, "receiveth not the things of the Spirit of God . . . neither can he . . ." (1 Cor. 2:14). This is a total impossibility until his ear is opened by the Lord, an opening which is an act of pure grace. God must tune him before he will receive the message.

Men hear *sounds* but do not recognize the significance of them. The message of the Gospel is a noise, not a communication, until God tunes the set of man's heart. The distinction between noise and message—or more scripturally, between sound and voice—is illustrated quite often in the Word of God. God speaks to a child of his but all the bystanders hear only a sound like thunder. What is a message to one is strange and disturbing and unintelligible to the rest. This happened when the Father spoke to his Son (John 12:29) and those who stood by said, "It thundered," while others supposed an angel had spoken to Him. For the words were not addressed to them personally. At the time of Paul's conversion a similar thing happened (Acts 9:7), though the King James Version has masked the circumstances somewhat by rendering the Greek word for sound *(phōnē)* as "voice." Acts 22:9 and 26:14 show that what his companions really heard was only the sound: they did not hear the message. Only to Saul did the sound appear as a voice articulating words which brought conviction to his soul.

I think the Gospel, which when clearly presented is to the believer so meaningful, is virtually meaningless to the unbeliever unless communicated to him by the Holy Spirit. People who have been spoken to plainly and clearly on many occasions, without apparently being influenced in any way, often say later on, when they have been born anew, "Why didn't you tell me before?" I have one friend of keen intelligence and mature mind who was shown the way of salvation in a manner so plain and straightforward that it is impossible to believe the message did not get through to his mind. Yet after he was very beautifully saved some months later, he explained that on the previous occasion the truth, which he now grasped perfectly, had not penetrated his thinking at all and had made no sense to him whatever. He himself marvelled that he had not been able to see it or understand it when it was first presented to him. Experience constantly reaffirms that natural man is simply not tuned in to receive spiritual truth, no matter how clearly it is stated. To the child of God rejoicing in his salvation, the meaning of the command to repent and believe seems self-evident. To the unbeliever it has no meaning whatever. Yet it is God's requirement, and it must be obeyed, if man is to be saved. And when it is obeyed man *is* saved. The crucial factor in this equation is obedience. There is no unfairness on God's part in giving the command—because there is no other appointed way.

When the rich young ruler (Luke 18:18-23) asked the Lord what he must do to earn eternal life, the Lord in complete fairness told him that if he would earn eternal life he must keep the commandments. The principle is well established in Scripture. It is stated categorically in the Old Testament (Lev. 18:5; Ezek. 20:11) and repeated several times in the New (Luke 10:27, 28; Rom. 10:5; and Gal. 3:12). If a man does indeed keep the Ten Commandments he will indeed earn eternal life: "The man that doeth them *shall live.*"

This had to be true. Any man who never once broke any of the commandments of God, who was never disobedient in any smallest way, who always and without fail did only those things which pleased the Father in heaven (John 8:29), would be worthy of eternal life and would always enjoy it. Thus the Lord Jesus Christ, having throughout his human life preserved his faultlessness in the sight of God, thereby became free to surrender that blameless life as a substitute for sinners. But the catch for all natural-born men is that partial fulfillment is not good enough. Only 100 percent fulfillment will do; for as James 2:10 has put it, "Whosoever shall keep the whole law, and yet offend in one point, he is guilty of all." It is indeed a case of all or nothing. And the Lord, in dealing with the young man to whom He was especially drawn by his earnestness, had to send him away saddened. For he had suddenly recognized that eternal life was quite unattainable to him on the terms he had supposed. Yet the promise itself of eternal life earned by good works was a perfectly genuine one. And so is the promise of eternal life to all who will believe in the Lord Jesus Christ as Saviour, or who will call upon the name of the Lord, or will take of the water of life freely, or will open the heart's door to the Lord, or will simply come to Him for refuge and rest. All of these are genuine offers, yet equally impossible of attainment, apart from the grace of God.

How ever the offer is presented, it is perfectly genuine. We can without hesitation make such invitations in just such clear and simple form: Christ died for sinners. We need not use such a misleading appeal as "Christ died for you"; but if we wish to be entirely personal it is quite proper to say, "If you will call upon the name of the Lord," or, "If you will open your heart to the Lord," or, "If you will accept Him as your Saviour." For an affirmative response to any of these will bring assurance of salvation. But we ought not to use such a misleading appeal as "Christ died for you" because we cannot apply this to *any* man indiscriminately unless we know he is to be counted among the elect, a knowledge which we surely cannot have with certainty. But presented in any other way, the invitation itself is open. Whosoever will may come. And we have every assurance that whosoever is enabled of God will indeed come. In the meantime we have many alternative forms of invitation which are entirely scriptural and in no way compromise the truth.

Thomas Boston stated the case effectively when he wrote:

> Upon very good grounds may we, at the command of God who raiseth the dead, go to their graves and cry in his name, "Awake, thou that sleepest, and arise from the dead, and Christ shall give thee light" (Eph. 5:14). And seeing that the elect are not to be known and distinguished from others before conversion, as the sun shines on the blind man's face and rain falls on the rocks as well as on the fruitful plains, so we preach Christ to all and shoot the arrow at a venture, which God Himself directs as He sees fit.[4]

But there still remains one aspect of the presentation of the Gospel which troubles many people. This is the apparent exclusiveness of the love God. If God does not love everyone indiscriminately, what then is his attitude towards those who are not the objects of his love? Does He hate them? Even to ask the question seems improper and out of harmony altogether with our concept of the nature of God. Yet we have a few passages of Scripture which seem to state in no uncertain terms that God does hate some of his creatures.

One of these passages is Hosea 9:15, which reads: "All their wickedness is in Gilgal: for there I hated them. For the wickedness of their doings I will drive them out of my house, I will love them no more." There seems to be justification here for the complete turnabout in God's attitude towards his people. But even so, the idea of hatred seems repugnant. The classic passage which has caused no end of discussion is to be found in Malachi 1:2, 3, where the crucial words, which have been quoted in Paul's Epistle to the Romans (9:13), are these: "Jacob have I loved, but Esau have I hated."

To say that the word *hate (miseō)* does not mean in this instance what we mean by the word *hate* is an evasion which will not do, for both the word *hate* and the word for *love* in this verse are the routine words used for

---

4. Thomas Boston, *Human Nature in Its Fourfold State*, p. 164.

human and divine love and hate elsewhere in Scripture. Indeed, the word *love* in this passage is the strongest of the Greek words for *love* in certain respects, and one must assume from its apposition in this sentence that the word *hate* must signify an attitude of equal intensity. The word *hate* is the word used in John 15:25, "They hated Me without a cause," a hate which was strong enough, when humanly expressed, to lead to murder. The word *love* is the word which appears in John 3:16.

All attempts to soften such a passage must inevitably appear to those who seek to attribute gross injustice to God as being no explanation at all but merely an effort to "explain away." Nevertheless, we cannot but struggle with the problem and try to find some temporary resting place for our thoughts until a better understanding emerges in God's own time.

I have personally come to wonder whether perhaps there might be a clue in the fact that God is declared in Scripture not merely to love but to *be* love itself, whereas, even more importantly in the present context, while He is declared to hate, He is never said to *be* hate. The difference may appear at first to be inconsequential but it seems to indicate that hatred is not simply the antithesis of love. In some mystical way love emanates out of God, originates with Him. He is the source of it. He does not just express love, but He is love. By contrast none of this can be applied to hate. It will be helpful perhaps to think for a moment of love and hate analogously as light and darkness, two terms which are used in Scripture in a remarkably parallel way.

Scripture tells us that God is not only love, but that He is also light. This affirmation is reinforced by telling us also that "in Him is no darkness at all" (1 John 1:5). Now darkness is not simply the antithesis of light. It is rather the absence of light. It is not something that is "there" but the result of something which is not there. Light emanates from God but darkness does not, for there is no darkness in Him. In the very nature of the case light and darkness cannot co-exist. Where there is light darkness is banished; where there is darkness there is no light.

Would it be true, then, to say that hate is not something which emanates from God, but something which is the consequence of the withholding of love? If we wish to understand how God could love Jacob and hate Esau, perhaps we first have to ask whether the explanation lies not in God at all but in Jacob and Esau themselves, and of course in every man for whom Jacob and Esau stand in this situation.

When we speak of God's love for ourselves as something which we experience in our daily lives, is the reality of which we speak evidence of some kind of response in our own souls rather than something which exists in the heart of God? Perhaps we could return to the analogy of light for a moment. When the power flows freely through a light bulb, the glow itself is proof of a vital connection with the power source, though the glow is not in the power source but in the lamp. If the switch is turned off, the glow is no longer apparent; but the power may still be as available at the source as it ever was. The darkness of the lamp results from a disconnection, a broken relationship, not a power failure.

Analogously, the love of God, would then be a true expression of his power, even as the glow of the lamp is proof of the reality of the power source. If there is another lamp in the room that for some reason is not alight, the darkness of that lamp does not originate from the source of the light in the other lamp. The darkness is inherent so long as the lamp is disconnected from the source of power. The difference in the relationship between the two lamps and the source of power is what makes the one experience light and warmth and the other darkness and cold. The power source itself is the same in both cases.

Now all men without exception at some point in their lives switch off the connection and leave themselves in darkness. But in the matter of salvation, the One who is the source of power Himself, for reasons known only to Himself, undertakes to turn on the switch of some but not of others. The result is the sudden creation of light in some and the continuance of darkness in others. The love which flows through to the elect and lightens them does not reach the others but permits them to continue in darkness. Perhaps the only way to describe the relationship of the latter is by saying it is opposite to that of the former. If love characterizes the first relationship, hate must characterize the second. Since in both cases the situation is an all-or-nothing situation, we must speak of light or darkness, life or death, love or hate. The three alternatives (darkness, death, hate) are not positive emanations but withdrawals, fatal disconnections.

So when we read in Scripture of divine hatred it seems necessary that we not consider it as an active principle, vindictive in its nature and destructive in its expression. It is simply that no light goes on, no life results, no love is experienced. Darkness overwhelms the soul, and death—and hatred. As the love of God is without the sentimental element of human mercy, so the hatred of God is without the vindictive quality of human hostility.

However, we would not make the mistake of saying that the power of God and the love of God are to be equated. What we are suggesting is that God's power is expressed most completely in the form of love. In a real sense the power of God which is witnessed in the creation (Rom. 1:20) will always be, to the child of God, an expression of his love, and accordingly, the absence of his power in the life of any man must be an expression of his hate.

The analogy we have proposed is oddly appropriate in certain ways to those passages of Scripture which speak of men's hearts being darkened (Rom. 1:21; Eph. 4:18). We are told that at one point in the earth's history God commanded the light to shine to dispel darkness (2 Cor. 4:6). The same principle is to be observed in 1 Peter 2:9. Light brings with it life and warmth; darkness entails cold and death. Moreover, here and there in the New Testament are sentences in the original Greek which, if they are construed literally, have an extraordinarily modern ring to them apropos of this analogy. For example, Ephesians 3:7 has the phrase, "by the effectual working of his power," which in the most literal translation could very properly read as "by the energy of his dynamo" (κατὰ τὴν ἐνέργειαν τῆς δυνάμεως αὐτοῦ). This is almost a transliteration of the original.

The light of the lamp, our lamp, is what we experience as love; the darkness of the other lamp is what that lamp experiences as hate. The power at the source remains unchanged, and is actually capable of producing *only* light. The difference in the end result for the two lamps stems from the connection or disconnection with the power source. The man in fellowship with God experiences God's love; the man who is cut off experiences God's hate. Jacob and Esau represent the two kinds of people who experience God in two opposite ways. Of the first, everything in his own life tends to reinforce his view that God loves him, whereas, of the other, everything in life supports the view that God hates him. The actual attitude of God to the latter must surely be one of pity or anger, both of which reactions are possible without any hatred; but effectively it must appear to him as the opposite of love.

We are tending increasingly to ignore the other side of God's love towards his creatures. Sermons more and more emphasize the love of God to the exclusion of his justice, and to speak of God's hate is completely unacceptable to our sensitive ears. Yet there is one passage of Scripture which ought to be introduced before we leave this subject.

In 2 Chronicles 19:2 we have a revealing statement made by a godly prophet named Jehu. Under divine guidance this prophet was called upon to rebuke a misguided king, Jehoshaphat, for not hating a wicked king, Ahab. "Jehu, the son of Hanani, the seer, went to meet Jehoshaphat, and said to the king, 'Shouldest thou help the ungodly and love them that hate the Lord?' Therefore is wrath upon thee from the Lord."

Here we have a man not merely rebuked but condemned for loving one of his fellow men. Would he thus be condemned if he were doing that which by popular fancy it is believed the Lord Himself always does? If God rebuked Jehoshaphat and held him accountable for loving a wicked man like Ahab, can we suppose that God loved this wicked man Ahab? Is it not more likely that with God neutrality is impossible? When the Lord said, "I wish that thou wert either hot or cold. So then, because thou art lukewarm, and neither hot nor cold, I am disgusted with you" (Rev. 3:15, 16), was He not saying in effect just this, that neutrality is impossible?

The solution I am offering is not wholly satisfactory by any means but it might help towards a satisfactory solution by the further questions it poses.

As Lord Wardour put it in speaking of one of his own tentative ideas over a century ago: "It may yet, by opening out fresh views, contribute light to minds of greater precision who may thus be enabled to hit upon the exact truth."

Our Gospel is tending increasingly to be "another Gospel" and not the Gospel of our Lord and Saviour Jesus Christ. We have presumed to improve upon revelation by modifying it to suit our enlightened sense of what is proper for man's new self-esteem. The supposed inherent kindness of the human heart is not to be offended by any reference to God's anger and hatred of man's sinful nature. We take care not to outrage our listeners by drawing attention to man's bondage and Total Depravity. We picture God as even more sentimental than man now is. After years of subjection to an increasingly unreal tinsel civilization man has almost wholly destroyed his ability to distinguish between sentiment and sentimentality. We present a God whose lack of discrimination is even greater than our own, whose willingness to compromise is broader than ours, and whose indifference to justice is similar to fallen man's.

But what does it do to man's inner being when he re-creates his God in a form even less admirable than himself? Such worship cannot but debase him. He learns to worship something less than himself and destroys the very thing which makes him human—the power to exercise righteous indignation and the ability to make moral judgments, even about his own behaviour.

The message we have is indeed good news, but it is good news to the penitent, to the lost, to the defeated and fearful, to the poor in spirit. The message is that Christ Jesus came into the world to save sinners, to save his people from their sins, to save the lost, to heal the broken in spirit, and to satisfy those who long after righteousness. The message is not for the healthy but for the sick, not for the righteous but for the unrighteous. That there is not one righteous man alive is an undeniable truth, but until a man admits his need he might just as well be counted among the healthy, the righteous, the strong in spirit—for whom Christ's offer of mercy and forgiveness and healing and grace is simply irrelevant. Men must be made aware of their sinfulness; men must be awakened to their need of a personal saviour and then presented with that Saviour in the Person of the Lord Jesus Christ.

This is evangelism, whether personal or congregational. The theology of it all is not always a necessary or even an appropriate part of evangelism. Just when and where and how the wonderful truth which underlies the Gospel, the rationale of the plan of salvation, is to be presented is the third problem to which we now turn.

17

WHEN TO PREACH ELECTION

A troublesome question still remains. There is no doubt that the teaching of the truth of Election usually causes offence to those who have been brought up to believe that it is up to man to decide for himself whether he will become a Christian or not. We do not like to be told that the choice is not ours, even when the fact is plainly stated in Scripture (John 15:16). For a long time we have lived with the idea that man is able to make this choice and is therefore responsible for doing so. It is the basic assumption of modern mass evangelism, and in the view of many people the object of such evangelism is to persuade men to exercise this freedom of choice to their own eternal benefit.

When it is pointed out that the implication of hundreds of passages of Scripture, familiar to most Christians and non-Christians alike, demonstrates clearly that this view is not a strictly biblical one, there is consternation. One English Calvinist put the matter succinctly when he suggested that Arminianism is a "common sense" faith, whereas the Gospel as elucidated by Paul is clearly a matter of revelation. It only mildly offends man's sense of his own worth to have to admit that he cannot be saved without God's help provided that he is left with the freedom of choosing to co-operate voluntarily. What offends so powerfully is the discovery that such freedom of co-operation simply does not exist. Man is truly in spiritual bondage in this matter and has no power to assist in the process of his own salvation. It is this that causes offence: it is this that necessitated revelation.

Point out to people that we are not born again to become the children of God by the will of man (John 1:13); that it is of God's own will and not ours that we are so reborn (James 1:18); that "it is not of him that willeth, nor of him that runneth, but of God that showeth mercy" (Rom. 9:16); that repentance is granted to us and is not a contribution we make of ourselves (Rom. 2:4), and the same must be said of the exercise of saving faith which is nothing less than a gift of God (1 Cor. 3:5; Eph. 2:8; Phil. 1:29; etc.); that it is God and not we ourselves who opens our hearts to the entrance of the Lord within (Acts 16:14 and Rev. 3:7, which precedes Rev. 3:20!)—point all this out and suddenly we meet with strong reaction even among those who are the Lord's children. "What possible good can be done," they ask, "by presenting such a restrictive Gospel with so offensive an element of exclusiveness? People will only be discouraged."

Many Christians are personally offended because they feel they are being reduced to mere puppets in the hands of an austere sovereign, even if that sovereignty is a sovereignty of grace. So they see it as a dangerous doctrine to proclaim publicly and are convinced that it will cause more offence than heart hunger. People will be turned away rather than be drawn to the Lord. Yet the truth of the matter is that none will be drawn to the Lord unless they are drawn by the Father, and this will happen only if they are elect. In today's liberal climate of theological opinion these commonly voiced objections are taken by many of the Lord's people as perfectly valid because they seem so obviously correct.

A great number of believers who are otherwise well acquainted with their Bibles are strangely unaware of the fact that Election is unequivocally maintained throughout the Old and the New Testaments, and nowhere more clearly so than in the Gospel of John. Yet here, if anywhere in the Word of God, people feel confident that the universality of God's love is set forth in a way that seems to exclude any idea of a selective process. This universality of redeeming love is generally claimed to be exemplified more clearly in John's Gospel than in any other part of Scripture; and yet examination of this Gospel with even a half-open mind will quickly show that the truth is quite otherwise.

Within the very first fourteen verses we find the fact of divine Election and human inability set forth unequivocally, when we are told that the power to become a child of God is not based on the will of man or the will of the flesh, or upon blood relationship, but solely upon the will of God. In chapter six of this Gospel we seem to have a turning point in the Lord's teaching on this matter. For here He deliberately set out to underscore the fact that while the invitation to "Come" is broadcast to all men, only those will come, *or can come*, whom the Father has enabled to respond because of their Election. When the Lord said (John 6:44): "No man can come to Me, except the Father which hath sent Me draw him," He touched a very sensitive place in the hearts of of his listeners. And we read in verse 60 that "many therefore of his disciples, when they had heard this, said, 'This is a hard saying: who can hear it?' "

They were offended indeed! So what did Jesus do? Did He begin to soften his message, to tone down the incisiveness of his words? By no means! He very deliberately repeated what He had said, "Therefore said I unto you, that no man can come unto Me, except it were given unto him of my Father" (v. 65). And as might be expected, the record tells us that "from that time many of his disciples went back and walked no more with Him" (v. 66).

These disciples were in effect his "school." Every rabbi of note gathered about himself a school of followers who were called disciples. In modern parlance they might be called a man's congregation. But unlike many modern pastors who withdraw their words as soon as they find they are causing offence, the Lord would not compromise. And the next three verses of this passage are a beautiful demonstration of what faithfulness to the truth can mean to men whom God has elected to salvation. As Jesus sadly watched these disciples turn away from following Him, He said to the Twelve, "Will ye also go away?" Then Simon Peter answered Him, "Lord, to whom shall we go? Thou hast the words of eternal life. And we believe and are sure that Thou art the Christ, the Son of the living God." How this magnificent confession must have warmed the heart of the Lord!

I know a minister who, having over a number of years been presented with the biblical truth about Election, gradually began to see the consequences of it in terms of his own congregation which was indeed like the mixed multitude that went up out of Egypt when Israel was "born" as a people of God. He saw many of this mixed multitude taking offence whenever this truth was broached and began to fear for them lest they should detach themselves and leave the congregation, with the result that the church's finances would of course be seriously endangered, as well as his own reputation as an agreeable, sympathetic, and broad-minded man. Little by little he began to turn from the Word of God and one day said with strong emphasis, "If teaching doctrine is going to split my congregation, I'll never preach doctrine again."

What did this resolve really signify? What *is* "doctrine"? Doctrine is teaching, instruction; and biblical doctrine is teaching what the Bible says—not parts of what the Bible says, but the whole counsel of God, and especially the Gospel which is not a common sense matter but something which has been revealed because it is not compatible with man's ordinary thinking. And so, alas, we have here a minister of the Gospel who finally determines in his own heart and promises publicly that he will never again teach what the Bible teaches about the true nature of man, about the true meaning of the Gospel, and about the real significance of the sovereign grace of God. One wonders how long the Church of God can remain a force in the world when its pastors depart so far from following the pattern set by the great Shepherd of our souls, the Lord Jesus Christ.

But when *does* one meet the issue of Election head on and proclaim it unequivocally as an essential part of the truth of the Gospel? And *how* does one present it, for it must be presented gently and wisely—though firmly and without apology. Perhaps the place for every minister of the Gospel to start is with an examination, in the light of Scripture, of the real nature of man's fallen spiritual condition as an unsaved sinner. Traditional Calvinism is surely right to begin with the Total Depravity of man, and not as the Arminians do with man's presumed capacity to exercise saving faith of himself. Such a capacity, they have held, is what God foresees and makes the basis of Election. But this is to place man in the position of being able to co-operate with God, indeed of being needed by God in a co-operative capacity before his salvation can be effected. In a very real sense man becomes his own saviour, though not without God's help. By contrast, the biblical view of man is correctly represented by the term *Total Spiritual Inability*, and with this as a starting point it is most reasonable to pass on to the question of why God should be interested in man at all. And from this we move naturally to ask, If man's salvation is wholly dependent upon the will of God, on what basis did God then decide to save certain individuals but not others? There is a logic to the ordering of the questions in the whole Calvinist position and above all it is a system so deeply rooted in Scripture that it can legitimately be identified with the Gospel itself. Calvinism *is* the Gospel and to teach Calvinism is in fact to preach the Gospel.

Certainly Scripture itself is full of the fact of the sovereign grace of God in salvation and God clearly had not such fears, as we have, in presenting it openly and in a very real sense *dogmatically*. It is questionable whether a dogmatic theology which is not Calvinistic is truly Christian. It is more nearly a baptized humanism which in the long run confirms in man his natural belief in his own powers to save himself. And the modern emphasis upon experience with its neglect of doctrine is merely substituting baptized psychology for the former baptized humanism. Today, unhappily, it is believers who are promoting this substitution for the Gospel.

Now the opinion of the great Christian warriors in the past nineteen hundred years has been remarkably consistent in this that they have never questioned the propriety or the need of openly proclaiming the sovereignty of God's grace. Certainly Paul's Epistles make no apology, nor does Peter, and as we have seen, John's Gospel is equally unequivocal in the matter.

Augustine was forthright indeed. In his *De Bono Perseveratiae* ("On the Gift of Perseverance") he held that the preaching of the Gospel and the preaching of Predestination were but two aspects of the same message (Chap. 36). He is most explicit regarding this matter. In his correspondence with two of his contemporaries, Prosper and Hilary, written about 428/9 A.D., he acknowledges (in Chap. 38) that people are saying that since the doctrine of Predestination clearly implies that some will receive the Word and will obey and will come into the faith and persevere in it, while others "are lingering in the delight of their sins," and since in both cases God has so predestinated that they should, then there is no point in stirring people up by encouragement or rebuke. What people will do, they are predestinated to do. If one is predestinated to be chosen though as yet still unsaved he will receive the necessary grace to believe in any case, and therefore won't need exhortation. If, on the other hand, a man is predestinated to be rejected he will not receive the strength to obey the Gospel and threatenings will serve no purpose.

To this, Augustine replies:

> Although these things are true, they ought not to deter us from confessing the grace of God—that is, the grace which is not given to us on account of our merits—or from confessing the predestination of the saints in accordance therewith, even as we are not deterred from admitting God's foreknowledge even though one should thus speak to the people concerning it and say, "Whether you are now living righteously or unrighteously you are what you are as the Lord has foreknown what you would be, either good if He has foreknown you as good, or bad if He has foreknown you as bad."

> For if on the hearing of this some should be turned to torpour and slothfulness, and from striving should go headlong into lust after their own desires, is it therefore to be counted that what has been said about the foreknowledge of God is false? If God has foreknown that they will be good, will they not be good whatever the depth of evil in which they *now* engage? And if He has foreknown them for evil, will they not be evil whatever goodness may *now* be discerned in them?

> There was a man in our monastery, who, when the brethren rebuked him for doing some things that ought not to be done, and for not doing some things that ought to be done, replied, "Whatever I may now be, I shall be such as God has foreknown that I will be." And this man certainly both said what was true and was not profited by this truth for good, but so far made way in evil as to desert the society of the monastery and to become a dog returned to his vomits; nevertheless it is uncertain what he is yet to become. For the sake of souls of this kind, then, is the truth which is spoken about God's foreknowledge either to be denied or to be kept back at such times, for instance, when if it is not spoken other errors are incurred?

This is a complex statement in its sentence structure, yet it reveals clearly enough that the same issue that is being brought forward today troubled men of those days. There is little new under the sun. The basic problem is whether the abuse of the truth should encourage us to prefer error. Will not error be a greater evil in the long run? And so in his Chapter 40 Augustine says plainly:

> Therefore let the truth be spoken, especially when any question requires us to declare it; and let them receive it who are able, lest perchance while we are silent on account of those who cannot receive it, those who are able to receive the truth whereby falsehood may be avoided, be not only defrauded of the truth but be taken captive by falsehood.

Here in a sense is the crux of the matter. What is the best *long-term* policy? Those who are able to receive this truth will be greatly benefited by it and will grow in their understanding. If they are denied this truth, for the sake of those who cannot receive it, the loss to them will be greater in the end than the harm done to those on account of whom it is mistakenly withheld. Balanced in the scales of ultimate good, the benefit to those who will receive it is so much greater than any harm done to those who refuse it that the truth of God must undoubtedly be proclaimed even if there is some danger in so doing.

But Augustine then suggests that we must be wise as serpents and harmless as doves, having due respect to the circumstances of the moment. The Lord said, "I have yet many things to say unto you, but ye cannot bear them now" (John 16:12). And Paul wrote: "I could not speak unto you as unto spiritual, but as unto carnal, even as unto babes in Christ. I have fed you with milk and not meat, for hitherto ye were not able to bear it, neither yet indeed now are ye able" (1 Cor. 3:1, 2). But he recognized that if those able to bear these more profound truths are given them, it is almost inevitable that those who are not able will also receive them in the process. So the problem is stated by Augustine with characteristic clarity: "When a truth is of such a nature that he who cannot receive it is made worse by our *speaking* it, but he who can receive it is made worse by our *keeping silence* concerning it, what do we think is to be done?" And he answers: "Must we not speak the truth, that he who can receive it may receive it, rather than keep silence, so that not only neither may receive it but even he who is more understanding will himself be made worse."

So there is his solution. Weigh in the balance what will cause the greatest harm: to deny a truth to one able to bear it and be greatly profited thereby, merely to prevent further harm to one who is already injured by ignorance of the truth, or alternatively, to do such good to the understanding of the one able to bear it that it outweighs the harm done to the one without understanding. And if it is a matter of permanently benefiting the saved while possibly causing temporary harm to the unsaved, our first responsibility must be to the saved. If there is a choice of doing good to the one or the other, the saved or the unsaved, and it is not possible to do good to both at the same time, we must follow Paul's injunction to do good as far as possible to all men, but "especially unto them who are of the household of faith" (Gal. 6:10).

Luther, who drew much of his early inspiration from Augustine, was equally certain that God did not intend the truth of Predestination and Election to be buried in secrecy. He said to Erasmus on one occasion:

> Where, alas! are your fear and reverence of the Deity when you roundly declare that this branch of truth which He has revealed from heaven is, at best, useless and unnecessary to be known. What! shall the glorious Creator be taught by you his creature, what is fit to be preached and what to be suppressed? Is the adorable God so very defective in wisdom and prudence as not to know till you instruct Him what would be useful and

305 When to Preach Election 305

what pernicious? Or could not He whose understanding is infinite, foresee, previous to his revelation of this doctrine, what would be the consequence of his revealing it until these consequences were pointed out by you? You cannot dare to say this![1]

Luther then quotes certain very pointed and relevant statements made by Paul, and observes:

The Apostle did not write this to have it stifled among a few persons and buried in a corner, but wrote it to the Christians in Rome which was, in effect, to bring this doctrine upon the stage of the whole world, stamping a universal imprimatur upon it and publishing it to believers at large throughout the earth.[2]

Luther went on: "You, Erasmus, object that 'if these things are so, who will endeavour to amend his life?' I answer, Without the Holy Spirit no man can amend his life to purpose. . . . Reformation is but varnished hypocrisy unless it proceeds from grace.?" In his treatise *On the Bondage of the Will* (XXIV) Luther says to Erasmus in much the same vein: " ' Who (you say) will believe that he is loved of God?' I answer, No man will believe it! No man can! But the elect shall believe it; the rest will perish without believing it. . . ." So Luther concludes: "The truths therefore respecting predestination *in all its branches* [my emphasis] should be taught and published, they, no less than the other mysteries of Christian doctrine, being proper objects of faith on the part of God's people."[3]

Luther's contemporary, Martin Bucer, entirely shared his views regarding the preaching of this doctrine to which they both subscribed with equal vigour. In his *Commentary on Ephesians* Bucer wrote: "There are some who affirm that election is not to be mentioned publicly to the people. But they judge wrongly. . . . Take away the remembrance and consideration of our election, and then, good God! what weapons would be left to us wherewith to resist the temptations of Satan?" To both men the Election of God was a very practical doctrine. To this I can only respond out of my own experience, Amen! I look back upon many occasions when the knowledge that the Lord Jesus Christ had chosen me and not I Him carried me through experiences too painful to think about today. This grand truth was—and is—the anchor of my soul. And I think considering the enormous influence on the Church of God of John's Gospel, of Paul's Epistles, of Augustine's writings, of Luther's works, of Calvin's *Institutes*, of Bucer, and a host of others, the fear that this truth is dangerous and will lessen the impact of the Gospel in the world is clearly without any foundation whatever.

---

1. Quoted in Jerome Zanchius, *Absolute Predestination*, p. 97.
2. Ibid.
3. Ibid., p. 100.

From a "common sense" point of view it would seem that it must be detrimental, but the wisdom of God is wiser than men, and the emphasis of Scripture should clearly be the emphasis of our preaching and teaching.

Even Melancthon, one of the less dogmatic of the Reformers, in his work entitled *The Common Places* (Chap. 1) treats of free will and Predestination by first of all establishing that it is both a necessary and a useful doctrine in many ways, both to be asserted and believed. He goes so far as to say: "A right fear of God and a true confidence in Him can be learned more assuredly from no other source than from the doctrine of predestination."[4] He then turns to Scripture and quotes many passages demonstrating the absolute sovereignty of God—statements in the Old Testament from Genesis, Kings, Proverbs, and others, besides many in the New Testament.

Calvin, by his example, clearly believed this doctrine was to be preached and not merely believed. In a tract entitled *The Eternal Predestination of God*, which he published in 1552 in reply to certain criticisms of his openness in declaring his faith, he wrote:

> I would in the first place entreat my readers carefully to bear in mind the admonition which I offer [in the *Institutes*]: that this great subject is not as many imagine a mere thorny disputation, nor a speculation which wearies the minds of men without any profit; but a solid discussion eminently adapted to the service of the godly, because it builds us up soundly in the faith, trains us to humility, and lifts us up into an admiration of the unbounded goodness of God towards us, while it elevates us to praise this goodness in our highest strains.
>
> For there is not a more effectual means of building up faith than the giving of our open ears to the election of God, which the Holy Spirit seals upon our heart while we hear, showing us that it stands in the eternal and immutable goodwill of God towards us; and that, therefore, it cannot be moved or altered by any storms of the world, by any assaults of Satan, by any changes, or by any fluctuations or weaknesses of the flesh. For our salvation is then sure to us when we find the *cause* of it in the breast of God. Thus when we lay hold of life in Christ made manifest to our faith, the same faith being still our leader and guide, our sight is permitted to penetrate much farther, and see from what *source* that life appeared.
>
> Our confidence of salvation is rooted in Christ, and rests upon the promises of the Gospel. But it is no weak prop to our confidence when we are brought to believe in Christ, to hear that all was originally *given* to us of God, and that we were as much ordained to faith in Christ before the foundation of the world as we were chosen to the inheritance of eternal life in Christ.[5] (emphasis mine)

John Owen (1616-1683), as J.I. Packer observed, did not deal with the issue at length but made it clear that preaching the Gospel is not a matter of

---

4. Ibid., pp. 117, 118.
5. Quoted in Fred H. Klooster, *Calvin's Doctrine of Predestination*, p. 12.

telling a congregation that God has set his love on each of them and that Christ died to save each of them, for these assertions biblically understood would imply that they all will be infallibly saved; and this cannot be known to be true. The knowledge of being the object of God's eternal love and Christ's redeeming death belongs to the individual's assurance, which in the nature of the case cannot precede faith's saving exercise; it is to be inferred from the fact that one has *already* believed, not proposed as a reason why one should believe.[6] The point is an important one.

In his book *Evangelism and the Sovereignty of God* (pp. 28, 29), Packer emphasizes the dangers of supposing that a man can decide for himself whether to become the Lord's child or not, and, as a corollary of such a decision-making process, that our responsibility is to be as persuasive as possible. As he points out, such a philosophy of evangelism can come dangerously close to a form of brainwashing. To act thus is "to assume the office of the Holy Spirit," to exalt ourselves as the agents of the new birth. Subsequently he describes how this form of evangelism degrades the Gospel into something that is not "good news" at all because it is false. In our zeal to provoke a sense of sin and unworthiness as an appropriate basis for repentance, we tend to remind people of their past failures. But the danger is that while such tactics make people feel uncomfortable, the reason for this discomfort is awareness of disappointment in themselves rather than of outrage and offence on the part of God. We should indeed be ashamed of ourselves, but the fact of God's anger is the really crucial issue in the matter. As Packer put it:

> The bad conscience of the natural man is not at all the same thing as conviction of sin. . . . It is not conviction of sin just to feel miserable about yourself and your failures and your inadequacies in meeting life's demands. Nor would it be saving faith if a man in that condition called on the Lord Jesus Christ just to soothe him, and cheer him up, and make him feel confident again. Nor should we be preaching the Gospel if all that we did was to present Christ in terms of man's felt wants. ("Are you happy? Are you satisfied? Do you want peace of mind? Do you feel you have failed? Are you fed up with yourself? Do you want a friend? Then come to Christ; He will meet your every need"—as if the Lord Jesus Christ were to be thought of as a fairy godmother, or a super-psychiatrist.) No: we have to go deeper than this. . . . To preach Christ means to set Him forth as the One who, through his cross, sets men right with God again.[7]

Amen! Such a spurious Gospel as we hear so often preached today under the guise of successful evangelism leads to unreal conversions, the kind of conversion experiences which William James, the famous psychologist of an earlier generation, wrote about as occurring among unbelievers all over the

6. J. I. Packer, *Sword and Trowel*, p. 11, col. c.
7. J. I. Packer, *Evangelism and the Sovereignty of God*, p. 60.

world and throughout history. It is psychological rather than spiritual, and so long as it is initiated humanly this is all it can ever be. The best defense against such ersatz forms of conversion is an absolute faithfulness in the preaching of Election and the sovereign grace of God. In our present disturbed social milieu the need for such faithfulness is greater than ever, and to suppose that falsehood is safer than the truth in such a crucial matter as Election is surely absurd in the extreme.

C.H. Spurgeon (1843-1892), who was perhaps the greatest evangelist in the Calvinistic tradition that England has ever seen, ministered for thirty-two years in his famous Metropolitan Tabernacle of London from 1859 to 1891. His congregation grew to 6,000 members; the church records show 14,692 registered conversions. His evangelistic ministry greatly inspired D. L. Moody, who once observed, "Everything he ever said, I read. My eyes feast on him. If God can use Mr. Spurgeon why should He not use the rest of us?"[8]

In his *Autobiography*, Spurgeon expresses his conviction:

> I have my own private opinion that there is no such thing as preaching Christ and Him crucified unless we preach what is nowadays called Calvinism. It is a nickname to call it Calvinism; Calvinism is the Gospel and nothing else. I do not believe we can preach the Gospel . . . unless we preach the sovereignty of God in his dispensation of grace; nor unless we exalt the electing, unchangeable, eternal, immutable, conquering love of Jehovah; nor do I think we can preach the Gospel unless we base it upon the special and particular redemption of his elect and chosen people which Christ wrought out upon the cross; nor can I comprehend the Gospel which allows saints to fall away after they are called.[9]

Benjamin B. Warfield (1851-1921) in one of his *Biblical and Theological Studies* ("On Predestination") wrote:

> The biblical writers are as far as possible from obscuring the doctrine of election because of any seemingly unpleasant corollaries that flow from it. On the contrary, they expressly draw the corollaries which have often been so designated, and make them part of their explicit teaching. Their doctrine of election, they are free to tell us for example, does certainly involve a corresponding doctrine of *preterition* (i.e., of the omission of those not elect).[10]

J. I. Packer has many wise and well-stated things to say on this issue. He would argue indeed that

---

8. Quoted in *Spurgeon's Sermon Notes*, ed. David O. Fuller, p. 8.

9. Vol. I, chap. XVI, p. 172. Quoted in J. I. Packer, Introductory Essay in John Owen, *Death of Death*, p. 10n.

10. Benjamin B. Warfield, *Biblical and Theological Studies*, p. 327.

. . . so far from making evangelism pointless, the sovereignty of God in grace is the one thing that prevents evangelism from being pointless. For it creates the possibility—indeed, the certainty—that evangelism will be fruitful. Were it not for the sovereign grace of God, evangelism would be the most futile and useless enterprise that the world has ever seen. . . . Regarded as a human enterprise evangelism is a hopeless task.[11]

No wonder the Arminian preacher has to exhaust the techniques of persuasion to attract men's attention, believing as he does that it is up to him to generate conviction and up to the hearer himself to respond to the things spoken. The task is literally one of raising the spiritually dead, but only God has this power. Augustine was perfectly right when he said, "We must preach, we must reprove, we must pray, because they to whom grace is given will hear and act accordingly, though they to whom grace is not given will do neither."[12]

And though Augustine rightly said that some of the Lord's people are not yet ready to receive the deeper things of God, he also held firmly to the principle that the harm done by withholding this doctrine from the Lord's people is far greater than the danger of exposing the unregenerate to it. If a choice must be made, Election must be taught—for God has most certainly not concealed it in Scripture.

In the final analysis it appears that we have but three choices. We may remain silent altogether; we may preach a Gospel which is really no gospel at all if it assumes that man is capable of responding and making affirmative decisions which Scripture shows clearly he is not able to make, being spiritually dead; or we may preach the truth as it has been committed to us in Scripture, frankly declaring the sovereign and irresistible grace of God as the only hope for man. In the light of man's total spiritual ineptitude this is the only Gospel there really is.

---

11. Packer, *Evangelism* pp. 106, 109.
12. *On the Gift of Perseverance*, XIV.

PART FIVE

The Future of the Non-Elect

INTRODUCTION

A word of special introduction is called for in presenting the following study. It is a subject bristling with problems. Anyone who embarks upon such a discussion exposes himself to all kinds of misunderstandings.

I am reluctant to include this addendum because it has to be so speculative. It seems to me that the fate of the unsaved is not clearly revealed in Scripture, and has been greatly confused by centuries of imaginative thinking in a way that is probably detrimental to our understanding and may be a gross misrepresentation of the mind of God. For reasons which will be considered briefly later, the art of the Middle Ages became increasingly grotesque whenever its subject matter was the fate of the wicked. We find it difficult to escape from this cultural heritage.

So the problem of the future of the non-elect and how this is to be reconciled with the justice of God persists. And it seems proper in any book which deals with the sovereignty of God's grace to make at least some attempt to sort these matters out a little bit even at the grave risk of being entirely misunderstood.

When I first became a Christian nearly forty-five years ago, I was enormously helped by a dear saint of God whose concern for my spiritual growth made her a veritable "mother in the Lord" to my soul. She had, at that time, found her thinking greatly stimulated by the writings of Andrew Jukes. Among his works which she had acquired was one by the title *The Restitution of All Things.* This volume presented a form of Universalism which attracted her and she asked me to read it and share my reactions with her. This I did. I found it stirred my thinking and aroused my interest in the possible fate of the unsaved for the first time. I had known the Lord for only about eighteen months, so it was perhaps not surprising that I had not previously given the matter much thought.

I visited a number of secondhand bookstores, and soon found other works which pursued equally unorthodox lines of thought on the subject. One of these was Farrar's *Eternal Hope.* This I did not feel happy about, though the level of my Christian thinking was admittedly far from informed

313

or sophisticated. However, I then searched for and found a copy of *Mercy and Judgment* by the same author, a volume which still left me unsatisfied because of some of the author's presuppositions regarding the inspiration of Scripture which I felt were inadequate.

Shortly after this, I picked up a copy of Hanson's *Universalism in the First Five Hundred Years of the Christian Church*, but in my poorly informed state of development I had a feeling I should view his data with caution, since I had no way of checking whether the extensive quotations he had extracted from the early Church Fathers were accurate and not out of context. But I did begin to feel that there were some valid arguments for questioning the deeply entrenched doctrine of everlasting punishment.

I soon added other works to a growing collection of volumes on the subject, some of them for and some against, one of which struck me with particular force because of the gentleness and spiritual tone that pervaded the author's arguments against everlasting punishment. This was Samuel Cox's *Salvator Mundi*. I have now some fourteen works on the subject and, thanks to the same dear child of God, I have also a complete set of the works of the Early Church Fathers in the Scribner thirty-eight volume edition under the titles *Ante-Nicene*, *Nicene*, and *Post-Nicene Fathers*. All these have been much studied, and I must admit that my personal views have swung back and forth somewhat over the years, resting today in the not altogether satisfactory position of being undecided in the matter.

There are, however, certain things about which I am fully persuaded. First, that the Lord is sovereign, gracious, and altogether just. He cannot allow sin to go unpunished. There is no salvation outside of Christ, nor any chance of escaping the penalty of our sins once we pass out of this life. The issue is not whether there is to be punishment, but whether punishment is to be endless. Outside of Christ there is no forgiveness in the hereafter (Matt. 12:32), but if punishment is to fit a temporal offence, the question is whether it needs to be interminable.

Secondly, when we come to glory and our understanding is enlarged beyond measure in the presence of the Lord, we shall undoubtedly say with exultation, "He hath done all things well!"

Thirdly, our sense of time will be different, and we may well have a new understanding of what *eternity* really means.

Fourthly, we shall probably see very clearly the true significance of many facets of biblical truth which are beyond our comprehension at the present. We shall gain a new spiritual perspective which may well provide an entirely new understanding of many passages of Scripture which we take for granted we already understand well enough.

And lastly, I am tending towards the view that a firm answer may not yet be possible, because God does not intend us to know in this life what we do not need to know. We know only that those who are not yet saved are already under condemnation (John 3:18). For those who are saved, judgment is already past (Rom. 8:1). Those who are already condemned are not condemned because God willed their unbelief, but because He decided to allow them to have their own way. As C. S. Lewis put it so effectively in *The Great Divorce* (p. 69):

> There are only two kinds of people in the end: those who say to God, "Thy will be done," and those to whom God says, "*Thy* will be done." All that are in hell choose the latter. Without that self-choice there could be no hell. No soul that seriously and consciously desires joy will ever miss it.

It is not difficult to see that a strong conviction that the lost are not lost forever might be harmful for those to whom the Lord has committed the preaching of the Gospel, unless there is at the same time some compensating reinforcement of their view of the terrors of being lost. Though we are not willing to admit it, all too many of us who know the Lord are comparatively unmoved by any conscious awareness of the fate of the unsaved. We are not sufficiently concerned to seek to pluck them out of the fire even though we pay lip service to a belief in everlasting punishment. There is little doubt that assurance of the ultimate safety of our unsaved loved ones would make us even more careless than we are already. It seems to me improbable that the precise nature of the future of the unsaved will be revealed to us on this side of the grave, since such a revelation could not serve a purpose sufficiently good to compensate for the evil that might be done. It might seem that we would be in a better position to vindicate the justice of God before those who challenge it, but experience shows that the people who challenge the justice of God are not really seeking answers but only seeking confirmation of their rejection of Him.

The following study must accordingly be accepted in the spirit in which it is presented, with a full awareness of the bias I have which, though far from fixed, nevertheless tends towards a somewhat more hopeful view than is current today in some segments of the evangelical community. For the reader who is interested in looking into some of the more extended works that deal with the matter, which I have myself examined with care, the following list may be useful. The order is alphabetical rather than an indication of my preferences.

Atkinson, Basil F. C. *Life and Immortality* (pb). Published privately ; no date (c. 1970).

Brabant, F. H. *Time and Eternity in Christian Thought* (Brampton Lectures, 1936). London: Longmans Green, 1937.

Brown, J. H. *Eternity: Is It a Biblical Idea?* London: Clarke & Co., 1926.

Campbell, Alexander, and Skinner, Dolphus. *Debate on Everlasting Punishment.* Utica, NY: Restoration Reprint Library reissue, 1840.

Charles, R. H. *Eschatology: Hebrew, Jewish, and Christian.* 2nd edition. London: A. & C. Black, 1913.

Cox, Samuel. *Salvator Mundi: or Is Christ the Saviour of All Men?* 3rd edition. London: Kegan Paul, 1878.

Farrar, F. W. *Eternal Hope* (five sermons preached in Westminster Abbey 1877). New York: Dutton, 1878.

————. *Mercy and Judgment.* London: Macmillan, 1881.

Finlayson, R. A. *God's Light on Man's Destiny* (pb). Edinburgh: Knox Press, no date.

Hanson, J. W. *Universalism: The Prevailing Doctrine of the Christian Church During Its First Five Hundred Years.* Boston: Universalist Publishing House, 1899.

Jukes, Andrew. *The Second Death and Restoration of All Things* (pb). 14th edition. London: Longmans Green, 1891 (reprint 1955).

Knock, A. E. Numerous pamphlets (some of 100 pages or more), all in support of a form of limited punishment and final restoration. Los Angeles: Concordant.

Torrance, T. F. *Space, Time, and Incarnation.* Oxford: University Press, 1969.

Vernon, S. M. *Probation and Punishment: A Rational and Scriptural View of the Future State of the Wicked.* New York: Ketcham, 1886.

Welch, C. H. *The Reconciliation of All Things* (pb). Surrey, England: Berean Publishing Trust, 1960(?).

18

THE NATURE OF THE PROBLEM

It would seem almost sacrilegious to suggest that we are sometimes called upon to justify God before men. We normally think only of man being justified before God. But Scripture itself recognizes the propriety of the alternative (Luke 7:29; Rom. 3:4), and seen in its proper light it is altogether appropriate to make the attempt in certain circumstances.

The world has two basic quarrels with the Calvinist position. First, that it is unjust of God to choose to save so few at the expense of so many who remain unsaved; and secondly, that the penalty imposed upon the unsaved is disproportionate, endless punishment being inflicted upon those whose offences are incurred in time. So we must look at these two aspects of the problem which seem superficially to signify a measure of failure in the purposes of God, and a measure of injustice resulting from that failure. On two counts, therefore, it seems that some attempt ought to be made to justify the ways of God with men.

I propose to deal with the second issue first, although clearly the first issue has precedence in terms of cause and effect, for if all were elected to salvation instead of only a few, there would be no second issue to deal with.

It is a commonly accepted principle of justice all over the world and in all ages that the magnitude of the offence is related to the dignity of the one against whom the offence is committed.

An offence against a wild animal (say, for example, an ape) is not normally punishable by law, least of all in a society where apes are simply part of the landscape, provided they are not a protected species. In our own culture an offence against a domesticated animal may be punishable, but chiefly because the animal belongs to someone rather than because of its own animal rights. Cruelty to a household pet is more likely to bring a penalty because by association it has been credited with a certain element of "personality." An offence against a beggar in the street may be frowned upon though officially overlooked in some societies, but not in a society with a social conscience. An offence against a neighbour is almost certain to demand an equivalent penalty, and an offence against the Mayor of a city demands an even more severe penalty since it is in effect an offence against the whole community for whom the Mayor stands as a representative. The assassination of a President of a country is likely to bring a national outcry, for he in turn stands as a figurehead of every citizen in the land.

Thus the same offensive action has a different weight of seriousness depending not upon the action itself, nor even upon the status of the doer (though this, too, becomes a factor in the case), but upon the offended party. The greater the accumulated dignity of the offended person, the more serious is the offence likely to be considered and the more severe the penalty.

When a man offends God, the offence is qualitatively maximized to infinity, for the honour of God is infinite. Such an offence is an offence against the Creator Himself and against all his creatures as well, for his honour is in a measure wrapped up in them all. Thus no greater offence is conceivable.

But is the magnitude of the offence in such a case to be measured in terms of quantity or in terms of quality? And is the punishment therefore to be severe by being protracted or by being intense? Are we to fit the punishment to the crime by making the punishment long in order to avoid making it violent, by substituting extensiveness for intensiveness?

It is sometimes argued that the injustice of everlasting punishment for a temporal offence is only an apparent injustice, since the offence is against the infinite majesty of God and must accordingly itself be of infinite magnitude. But in answer to this we have to ask whether this is merely substituting quantity for quality by assuming that length of punishment is necessary to match the severity of the crime.

Of course, we have come to this in our society. We prescribe capital punishment for murder with intent in certain cases, but then we seem to do all in our power to commute this violent punishment to life imprisonment, so substituting twenty years of bearable suffering for perhaps fifteen seconds of mortal wounding (death by hanging, electrocution, firing squad, or even beheading). We at least recognize by this policy the unwritten principle that what is brief and very intense may be balanced by what is long and much milder. Taking these two factors like the sides of a rectangle, we mark out two rectangles of equal area as it were, one standing on end like a vertical column where the depth is great and the width is short, and the other like a flat rectangle where the depth is slight but the width very long. When the two areas are approximately equal, we feel satisfied we have an approximate equivalent of justice.

If it should be asked, "Why do we substitute the long for the deep?" the answer is probably that we are cowards. We pretend to be guided by humane motives, but we are not prepared to face the further question whether life imprisonment really is more humane. There are recent cases of condemned men who, given the choice, preferred the moment of intensity and almost instant death to the long, slow agony of destruction by incarceration for a lifetime. Meanwhile, recognizing that a lifetime of incarceration is an awful thing, we introduce various moderating devices such as parole after so many years of good behaviour. The principle is not unjust, for good behaviour in such a situation may indicate some genuine measure of reform, and for the reformed character the penalty of incarceration may in fact be a greater penalty, and increasingly more painful as reformation proceeds. Thus by a certain logical extension, we see that if a man improves in character for one reason or another, what remains of his sentence becomes effectively more of a penalty, until it would become unfairly extended if his reformation were to be complete. What formerly was justice now becomes increasingly unjust. This may be the justification for amnesty.

Such self-reformation never will be complete of course, but it may happen that the grace of God regenerates the heart of the convicted man and it would then seem entirely appropriate to shorten the penalty as a matter of simple justice, since what remains of the penalty to be fulfilled will be felt so much more keenly. But of course justice is never administered perfectly, since the judge, the society, and the guilty individual are all imperfect still.

It is clear, however, that the demand for endless punishment for a temporal offence cannot be justified merely on the grounds that the offence has been against an infinite Majesty. It may well be that the quality of the punishment is, in any event, much more significant than the quantity of it. Indeed the word *eternal* may have little if anything to do with quantity at all. Eternal life is eternal because it is "otherly," that is, it has *depth* of a spiritual nature as its fundamental character, and not because it has length (John 10:10)—though length is certainly part of its essential character as John 10:28 seems to indicate. Eternal life is fundamentally a new *quality* of life. We shall return to this question later, for much hinges on the Hebrew and Greek words which lie behind the scriptural concept of eternity. That endlessness is *part* of the meaning is not to be questioned, though it is doubtful if the concept of endlessness is the underlying idea intended in either the Hebrew or the Greek words, or was even conceived by the Jewish mind, or by the Greek.

It is much more likely that the basic idea was one of indefiniteness, of *unknown* length, without defined boundaries, or alternatively of inconceivable magnitude. The idea of unlimited duration was probably absent. Indefinite, not infinite, would seem the most comprehensive meaning when applied to *time*, inconceivable in magnitude rather than infinite when applied to *size*, otherworldly rather than this-worldly when applied to spiritual things. The Eternal God may mean the God who exists outside of time, otherworldly, belonging within a spiritual order, inconceivable in these senses. As eternal life means another *kind* of life, inconceivable until it is experienced, so perhaps eternal punishment is another kind of punishment: inconceivable until it is experienced.

It is also necessary to consider that the status of the offending party does have some bearing on the magnitude of his offence. A child may commit the same crime as an adult with the same consequences to society, but we do not judge the same penalty to be appropriate in each case. Many who die unsaved must clearly die with a different status in this sense, some dying greatly privileged, some dying young, some dying without ever hearing the Gospel, but all equally unsaved. Yet if the penalty is unending punishment, whether the punishment is many stripes or few, it is effectively the same punishment for all because of its endlessness. One cannot rationally introduce the idea of a harsher or a milder punishment if both are interminable. For the factor which makes all such forms of punishment so awful is the hopelessness of the situation.

Viktor Frankl, the notable Viennese psychiatrist who survived a German concentration camp, wrote this:

> Life in a concentration camp [was so uncertain] that it could be called a "provisional existence." . . . We can add to this by defining it as "provisional existence of unknown extent."
>
> A man who could not see the end of his provisional existence was not able to aim at an ultimate goal in life. He ceased to live for the future . . . .[1]

Such a man lived only NOW and the NOW was for ever, experientially. Luther was surely right in describing eternity as *the always now.* So Augustine likewise saw the eternity of God as an ever-nowness. Frankl wrote subsequently:

> In camp a small time unit, a day for example, filled with hourly tortures and fatigue, appeared endless. A longer time unit, perhaps a week, seemed to pass very quickly. My comrades agreed when I said that a day lasted longer than a week.[2]

So we have to rethink what the word *eternal* really means in any given context in Scripture. Dean Farrar held that punishment is everlasting in effect, but limited in duration. He might perhaps have suggested with equal force that punishment is everlasting in experience also, psychologically that is, but limited in reality. Punishment there surely must be, even if it is a form of remorse and self-inflicted. A moral universe without sanctions when its laws are disobeyed would be a chaos not a cosmos.

So we have somehow to justify God in the New Testament sense and before the world, when men question the justice of his balancing of accounts. We must not deny what the New Testament certainly reveals; we need only

---

1. *Man's Search for Meaning,* p. 111.
2. Ibid., p. 112.

to think the problem through again and see if the passage of time and the controversies of the past have put us in any better position to understand what Scripture is actually saying on the subject. It may not be possible to provide an altogether satisfactory answer, but the issue has to be squarely faced anew in every generation, until some kind of understanding is achieved which will enable us to answer those who accuse God of injustice, and to do this without compromising the plan of salvation.

Because of the difficulties that the present concept of everlasting punishment introduces for even the most faithful of God's children, we have a tendency to shun the matter or to fear to challenge the orthodoxy which we have inherited lest we should find ourselves excommunicated. That previous ages were satisfied with their view of the endless torments of the unsaved is not in itself a proof that they were right but only that their conscience had not become as acute as ours in certain areas of life, even as they often seemed to have been little concerned with injustices done to those who could not defend themselves or with certain then current social iniquities such as slavery, for example. This, then, is one of the matters we must look into a little more closely if this study of the issues of Calvinism is to be at all complete.

Now the other question is why so few are called to salvation while so many are allowed to go their own chosen way to perdition. Is any plan which involves so much suffering by so many really justified for the sake of the happiness of so few? And the answer must take into account the possibility, implicit in what has been said already, that if the word *eternal* has a qualitative rather than a quantitative meaning, the disparity in numbers which is itself a quantitative factor may not be so crucial, and the answer may thus appear in a somewhat different light. Even if this should be so, the fact still remains that the many appear to suffer for the benefit of the few. For certainly it seems clear that the whole plan is justified ultimately only by the happiness of the few that are saved, and this is achieved at the expense of the unhappiness of those that are lost. This seems to be true even if the lost are in some way released from their unhappiness in the end.

Perhaps Dean Farrar was right to speak of the "Larger Hope," that the Lord may have a more complete victory, that God will truly one day be all in all. But the problem still remains whether such a created order has been fairly designed when the many in some measure suffer for the few. Of Farrar's conclusion, I think it must be said that his presuppositions were of doubtful validity. He placed a higher value upon human reason than is justified, and one cannot agree with his lower estimate of the inspiration of Scripture. Human reason cannot guide us safely here because we have no knowledge of what life is for the unsaved beyond the grave, apart from revelation. And that revelation is not explicit enough for us to draw any firm and precise conclusions. We have certainties indeed with respect to the future of the elect, but we do not have the same kind of certainties with respect to the future of the non-elect.

Men like Shedd, Hodge, Warfield, and other theological giants of past years have questioned whether Scripture actually intends to leave us with the idea that *few* are saved and *many* are lost. The classic passage which at once comes to mind in this connection is Luke 13:23, 24. But this is a question asked by the disciples, not actually a statement made categorically by the Lord. "Then said one unto Him, Lord, are there few that be saved? And He said unto them, Strive to enter in at the strait gate: for many, I say unto you, will seek to enter in, and shall not be able." The answer of the Lord would seem to be a tacit acceptance of the questioner's supposition, and certainly experience seems to confirm the fewness of the saved. Moreover, the Lord's words, "Fear not, little flock; it is your Father's good pleasure to give you the kingdom" (Luke 12:32), reinforce the impression of the paucity of numbers. Again, in Matthew 7:13 f. the Lord said: "Enter in at the strait gate; for wide is the gate and broad is the way that leadeth to destruction, and many there be which go in thereat. For strait is the gate and narrow is the way that leadeth to life, and few there be that find it." And then in Matthew 20:16 and 22:14 the Lord repeats the words, "Many are called, but few are chosen."

With such passages before us, how then does it come about that profound theologians can speak as though *few* does not mean few, and *many* does not mean many? They do it by the simple device of arguing that we need not assume that the few who are old enough to choose the narrow way are the only ones who enter heaven. Many enter without reaching the age of choice, infants all over the world and since the world began.[3] These must therefore be included among the redeemed, and to their number Shedd*

---

3.   Benjamin B. Warfield, *Biblical and Theological Studies*, pp. 334 f.

---

*In his *Dogmatic Theology*, Shedd has this to say: "The electing mercy of God reaches to the heathen. It is not the doctrine of the Church that the entire mass of pagans, without exception, have gone down to endless impenitence and death. That some unevangelized men are saved, in the present life, by an extraordinary exercise of redeeming grace in Christ, has been the hope and belief of Christendom. It was the hope and belief of the older Calvinists, as it is of the later" (Vol. II, pp. 706 f.).

The *Westminster Confession* (X.3), after saying that "elect infants dying in infancy are regenerated and saved by Christ through the Spirit, who worketh when and where and how He pleaseth," adds, "so also are all other elect persons [regenerated and saved by Christ through the Spirit] who are incapable of being outwardly called by the ministry of the Word." This is taken to mean not merely that insane and imbecile individuals have hope of redemption, but also that many in the heathen world are also chosen for redemption by some means other than the exercise of saving faith as we understand it.

would add the heathen who would have believed had the Gospel been preached to them.

In his *Reformed Doctrine of Predestination* (p. 145), Loraine Boettner argues that probably 50 percent of all human beings born will be redeemed by this route.

> If it is true that all those who die in infancy, in heathen as in Christian lands, are saved, then more than half of the human race even up to the present time has been among the elect.

Calvin took the position that a child who dies in infancy is as elect as the adult who is converted. The Lord thus has, as it were, two modes of assuring salvation. This may well be true, yet one wonders if it is not rather a subterfuge than a satisfying answer to the problem. Can it really be termed a victory for the Lord when the soldiers in this warfare are saved only by being removed from ever encountering the enemy while they are still too young to have arrived at the battlefront?

Warfield quotes, with approval, the words of William Temple who, in 1913, wrote: "The earth will in all probability be habitable for myriads of years yet. If Christianity is the final religion, the Church is still in its infancy. Two thousand years are as two days."[4] The implication here is that in time the Church will cover the earth; but what then of the Lord's words, "When the Son of man cometh, shall He find faith on the earth?" (Luke 18:8)? And is this poor exhausted earth still good for thousands of years yet? And furthermore, is Warfield correct when he expresses the hope that the Church will act as leaven "for good"[5] when leaven is consistently used in the New Testament and in rabbinical literature as a symbol of an evil, corrupting influence? Should we not rather expect to see the pervasive evil of godlessness bringing all society into decay until the Lord returns to put things to rights again?

But even if we add the disadvantaged heathen as Shedd proposes, we are still far short of a total victory and must suppose that at the very least perhaps one-fifth of the world's population is still lost. Indeed, must it not be admitted that even if one single soul is lost for eternity, the plan has been a failure, the cost has been too high? Did not the shepherd rejoice more over the one lost sheep that was found again even though the ninety-nine were safe (Matt. 18:13)? And what then if He had not found that lost sheep— that one lone creature that was not in the fold? Would the shepherd ever have ceased to grieve? How can we then suppose that the salvation even of a majority of God's creatures will be sufficient to cover the cost of the re-

---

4. Ibid., p. 347.
5. Ibid., p. 348.

mainder who are not returned to the fold? In the political arena a majority won is victory enough, but can this ever be true in the moral arena?

Dostoyevsky in his *The Brothers Karamazov* has one of the brothers, Ivan, recounting to his younger brother, Alyosha, the story of a well-educated Russian mother (this was about 1825 or so) who battered her infant daughter mercilessly and then locked her in the bathroom. But when the little child still did not cry out against her abuse, the mother became so enraged that she rushed into the bathroom and filled the child's mouth with her own excrement, and cast her on the floor in a corner. The child lay there, beating the floor with her tiny fist in her torment as she tried to empty the filth out of her mouth and call for her mother's mercy. And Ivan asks poignantly:

> Tell me yourself, I challenge you—answer. Imagine that you are creating a fabric of human destiny with the object of making men happy in the end, giving them peace and rest at last, but that it was essential and inevitable to torture to death only *one* tiny creature—that baby beating its breast with its fist for instance—and to found that edifice on its unavenged tears, would you consent to be the architect on those conditions? Tell me, and tell me the truth.
> "No, I wouldn't consent," said Alyosha softly.

Admittedly the illustration is not truly a parallel in so far as the staging of the situation is concerned, but the same principle is involved. Could one, *humanly* speaking, recommend a plan that introduced upon the scene billions of souls destined to live forever in happiness at the end, if it involved even one of them in everlasting torment as a consequence? Yet again it is very important to underscore the word *humanly*. For what do we really know about the nature of time in eternity? And there is always the possibility, remote though it may be, that the sufferings of the wicked might bring even to themselves a measure of joy fully compensating at the last. Even if, which also seems unlikely, the time spent by these billions in happiness were to pass psychologically very slowly whereas the time spent by the ones in torment were to pass psychologically very quickly, yet if both are to last for ever the situation is not really eased, the circumstance is not really mitigated in any way.

There seems no way to escape the dilemma except possibly by linking the factor of endlessness (if this is indeed the crucial factor) to the *effect* of the sentence rather than to the sentence itself, or by making punishment serve not merely as the wages of evil but also as a means of correction until no more punishment is required. Let us examine some of the alternatives that men have proposed as they struggled with this truly difficult problem. These alternatives are not new; the Church Fathers looked at them all and for the most part ended up with some kind of everlasting torment. Yet there have always been a few men, truly devoted to the Lord and resting their soul securely in his salvation and holding absolutely to the inspiration of Scripture, who have found some of these alternatives still viable and more attractive than the current orthodoxy of many evangelical people today.

Perhaps we shall yet find some tentative resting place which fully honours the Word of God and might even explain why the fewness of the elect was an essential element of God's over-all plan for his creation.

19

FOUR ALTERNATIVE SOLUTIONS

There are perhaps only five alternative views regarding the future of the unsaved. The first of these five is not really a candidate and has not been countenanced by Christians because it is simply a denial of any future whatsoever for either the saved or the unsaved. But it is an alternative. It is well exemplified in a statement made by Bertrand Russell, who may be taken as representative of a very large number of thoughtful and intelligent people today sharing his dismal philosophy of human destiny. Essentially, these people hold that we are like the beasts that perish, reabsorbed at death into the material universe of physics and chemistry as though we had never been. Personal existence results from an accidental coming together of electrochemical forces that have no permanent significance. In 1938 Lord Russell was quoted as saying:

> Man is the product of causes which had no prevision of the end they were achieving: his origin, his growth, his hopes and fears, his loves and beliefs, are but the outcome of an accidental collocation of atoms, No fire, no heroism, no intensity of thought or feeling, can preserve an individual life beyond the grave: all the noonday brightness of human genius, is destined to extinction in the vast death of the solar system, and the whole temple of man's achievement must inevitably be buried beneath the debris of a universe in ruins—all these things, if not quite beyond dispute are yet so nearly certain that no philosophy which rejects them can hope to stand.[1]

Such an answer to the problem appears to many people today to be the only, the simplest, and the most rational answer; but it is in fact none of these things. The prospect of absolute personal annihilation may be faced with some equanimity in youth where it is too remote to matter, and so is applied to others but not to ourselves. But later years bring second thoughts for most people, and this kind of annihilation becomes infinitely sad to contemplate. There is no doubt that the acceptance of such a fate is not the sign of a free healthy spirit but of a diseased one. God has set eternity in the

---

1. Quoted in J. W. N. Sullivan, *The Limitations of Science*, p. 175.

heart of man. In every culture and apparently throughout history it has been normal for man to assume that he has some continuance beyond the grave. This modern view of annihilation is a symptom of the malaise of our society.

So we really have only four alternatives that require consideration at the end of such a study as this:

1. Annihilation of the unsaved.

2. Universalism—in which all are saved and none are punished.

3. Punishment of the unsaved which will one day terminate in restoration to fellowship with God.

4. Everlasting punishment and unbroken banishment from the presence of God.

Let us examine these briefly and then compare the consequences of each as they reflect upon the justice of God.*

1. ANNIHILATION OF THE UNSAVED

There are a number of passages of Scripture which it is claimed support the concept of annihilation, but at least some of these passages, *taken in their context*, do not really seem to warrant such an interpretation. Among them are the following:

> The light of the wicked shall be put out, and the spark of his fire shall not shine (Job 18:5). *(This suggests that his "substance" is to be utterly consumed, not even a spark remaining alive.)*

> The wicked shall perish, and the enemies of the Lord shall be as the fat of lambs: they shall consume; into smoke shall they consume away . . . . The transgressors shall be destroyed together; the end of the wicked shall be cut off (Ps. 37:20, 38).

> When the wicked spring as the grass, and when all the workers of iniquity do flourish; it is that they shall be destroyed forever (Ps. 92:7).

> As the whirlwind passeth, so is the wicked no more (Prov. 10:25).

---

*Throughout the following section a number of passages of Scripture are listed which are claimed by supporters of various alternative views. In many cases these passages have already been dealt with and analyzed to show that they need not, and probably should not, be interpreted at their face value since the words employed often have important alternative meanings. It may therefore prove disconcerting to the reader to find such passages now quoted in support of a position which it has been previously suggested they cannot be used to support. This is inevitable, of course, because these verses *are* used in support of these alternative views by certain classes of people. We have therefore adopted the policy of putting in brackets after each passage a reference to the pages in this volume where the more probable meaning is dealt with at some length. It will be seen that these references relate chiefly to alternative renderings of such words as *saved, all, world, willing,* etc.

Behold, all they that were incensed against Thee shall be ashamed and confounded: they shall be as nothing; and they that strive with Thee shall perish. Thou shalt seek them . . . even them that contend with Thee: they that war against Thee shall be as nothing, and as a thing of nought (Isa. 41:11, 12).

All they that know thee among the people shall be astonished at thee: thou shalt be a terror, and never shalt thou be any more (Ezek. 28:19).

For the day of the Lord is near upon all the heathen: as thou hast done, it shall be done unto thee: thy reward shall return upon thine own head. For as ye have drunk upon my holy mountain, so shall all the heathen drink continually, yea, they shall drink, and they shall swallow down, and they shall be as though they had not been (Obad. 15, 16)

Behold the day cometh, that thou shalt burn as an oven; and all the proud, yea, all that do wickedly, shall be stubble: and the day that cometh shall burn them up, saith the Lord of hosts, that it shall leave them neither root nor branch (Mal. 4:1).

The Lord Jesus shall be revealed from heaven with his mighty angels, in flaming fire taking vengeance on them that know not God, and that obey not the Gospel of our Lord Jesus Christ: who shall be punished with everlasting destruction from the presence of the Lord . . . (2 Thess. 1:7-9).

If we sin wilfully after that we have received the knowledge of the truth, there remaineth no more sacrifice for sins, but a certain fearful looking for of judgment and fiery indignation, which shall devour the adversaries (Heb. 10:26, 27).

I think the most recent presentation of this view is found in a small but effectively written work by the well-known evangelical Basil F. C. Atkinson, an English writer who has been described as a modern Matthew Henry. His argument is formulated entirely by an appeal to Scripture and he holds that in this context death *means* death and destruction *means* destruction. The second death (Rev. 20:14; 21:8) is a total cessation of life. Daniel 12:2 seems to speak of the first death, a natural death followed by a sleep in the dust, awaiting resurrection to judgment. The second death will not be a sleep but an annihilation. While the fires of Gehenna are indeed unquenchable, such fires can burn out when there is nothing left to consume. They did in the Valley of Hinnom, the garbage dump outside the city walls of Jerusalem; the fires which were intended to consume the refuse did burn out, historically, once there was no more dumping of garbage after the city had been deserted at the time of the Captivity in Babylon. Similarly the burning of the Lord which was to fall upon Israel's folds and flocks and orchards as a punishment was unquenchable in the sense that it was inescapable. Nevertheless, it too died out when the land was deserted. Sodom and Gomorrah suffered the vengeance of "eternal fire" (Jude 7), but it seems likely that this fire burned itself out in hours, if not in minutes. The effect was everlasting, for Sodom and Gomorrah disappeared. Even if they were to be rediscovered and rebuilt, the old Sodom and Gomorrah so perished as to be still (1978) undiscovered, for all the searching that has been undertaken.

According to this view, the fire of hell is not to correct but to consume. When its consuming is wholly complete, death itself will cease to be a reality, thus fulfilling in an unexpected way 2 Timothy 1:10, in which the Lord Jesus Christ is said (prophetically) to have "abolished death." As a fire goes out when nothing remains to keep it alive, so death is abolished when there are no dead left, for the fire will consume them until the place thereof knoweth them no more. One might borrow John Owen's famous title and apply it in a new context, calling this "the death of death." It is not necessary, as some critics of this view have argued, that annihilation be instantaneous at the time of Judgment; the stubble that is consumed and the refuse that is burned take time to burn, but they are finally destroyed. The end result is not immediate destruction but final destruction, which is essentially the argument of the annihilationists.

The annihilation of the wicked at least frees the universe from the dualism of two hostile kingdoms co-existing for ever and ever, even if they do so with a great gulf fixed between them. If it is true that few are chosen and many are lost, the kingdom of darkness would be larger than the kingdom of light; and its annihilation would have at least this advantage, that the victory of the Lord Jesus Christ would ultimately be unchallenged. Continued co-existence, on the other hand, even if the kingdom of darkness is very small, indeed if it were only one single individual, would still demonstrate an incomplete victory—and in a sense an incomplete victory is really no victory at all.

In the new heavens and the new earth of 2 Peter 3:13 which are to be created "wherein dwelleth righteousness," would this not require that evil be permanently eliminated? Indeed the annihilationists argue that either there must be restitution of all things or the wicked must be completely consumed. Many earnest Christian people of evangelical persuasion believe that they are driven by the plain sense of Scripture to one or the other of these two alternatives. There have always been a few earnest spirits, from the earliest times to the present, persuaded that the Scriptures tend towards the annihilationist view. By removing the wicked altogether, it is felt that a passage such as 1 Corinthians 15:28 is more likely to be fulfilled completely, when God will become all in all and every remaining knee in the universe will bow before the Lord Jesus Christ to the glory of the Father.

Although the concept of annihilation may ease the problem of final complete victory, it does seem to make the creation of so many billions of individuals purposeless. Yet a naturalist might argue that such an apparent waste of life is not without parallels in Nature as a whole. It is pointed out that when a codfish lays several million eggs, only a few of these eggs (some authorities say only two or three) are believed to develop into adults to perpetuate the species. It is held that in some way the millions that do not develop provide a special chemical environment for the favoured survivors without which they would not reach maturity.

The analogy is a harsh one indeed, for we are not speaking here of mere animals but of living human beings who are indeed perishing, but surely not perishing according to the Creator's design as we may suppose is true in the case of cod spawn. The problem of numerical imbalance remains. G. C. Berkouwer in his *Divine Election* (p. 207) struggles with this problem of numerical imbalance and points out that Herman Hoeksema has actually gone so far as to suggest that it was necessary for these enormous numbers of people to be rejected from the Kingdom. He does not hesitate to say that God "had to" adopt this plan. Hoeksema proposes that the rejected "are in a sense the price, the ransom, which God pays for the higher glory of his children." According to this view, He could not do otherwise for there was no other possibility for Him. The price had to be paid. Such a bald statement strikes the mind as wholly unacceptable. And yet as we have already seen, it may not be altogether irrational. It seems that God did indeed have to reject some. And by rejection is not meant that God elected them to reprobation but rather that He did not elect them to salvation. To save all men would involve overruling the free choice of all, since man by nature universally rejects God's offer of salvation. But to overrule the free choice of all men is to invalidate the plan to allow man freedom of choice to begin with, and thus to reduce him to the status of puppet. Alternatively, to save none at all would rob the creation of any point. If none are to be saved, it were better not to create man and allow him to make a free choice. God had no alternative but to elect some and not to elect the rest. But whether we can go so far as to say with Hoeksema that the loss of the many is intended as a benefit to the few is another matter, even though it may seem to be a logical necessity.

It is also important to realize that death is not necessarily a curse. It comes to many as a relief. Indeed God seems to have ordained death for *fallen* man, not for unfallen man, and did so not as a penalty but as a remedy. Adam and Eve were cast out of the Garden specifically to *prevent* their eating of the Tree of Life and so living on forever as corrupted, sinful people. We may gather from this that unending life in a sinful condition was, at least in this world, an unthinkable alternative to dying, and the action taken to secure against such a contingency was, if we look carefully at Genesis 3:22-24, undertaken with great urgency. The Lord "drove them out" and stationed an angel at the gate of the Garden whose flaming sword (the instrument of death) turned *every way*, specifically to guard the way to the Tree of Life: death was therefore inescapable. The circumstance has been seized upon by some annihilationists to support the argument that annihilation is at least vastly to be preferred to unending continuance in a sinful condition.

Such, then, is the first alternative, and such are some of the problems it poses, and some of the answers it is believed to provide, and some of the possible reasons which may make it a not altogether absurd solution to what is admittedly a profound problem. However, there is one strong argument against it which has been stated effectively by R. A. Killen. He wrote recently: "The wicked will not be annihilated by the second death as judgment for their sins any more than Christ was annihilated when He paid the penalty for our sins."[2]

2. UNIVERSALISM

The term *Universalist* may be applied to two classes of people. There are those who believe that there is no punishment at all. It is assumed that everyone will be automatically forgiven by a benevolent Creator who is loving towards all his creatures and has already made adequate provision for their forgiveness in the sacrifice of his Son who died effectively for the sins of all men.* And then there is a second class of persons who believe that for all who die unregenerate there will be a period of punishment *that is corrective rather than punitive.* When these have paid "the last farthing" they will be released from the place of punishment and brought back into fellowship with God.

We propose to deal separately with these two broad classifications, but there are certain key passages of Scripture which are claimed by both parties as proof texts in support of their position. Such a key passage is Colossians 1:20: "And having made peace through the blood of his cross, by Him to reconcile all things unto Himself, by Him, I say, whether they be things in earth or things in heaven." What is here intended by the word *reconciliation* is held to be plainly established by the following verse (21), which reads: "And you [the saints at Colossae] that were once alienated and enemies in your mind by wicked works, even now [Greek *nuni*] hath He reconciled . . . ." Like the saints who are *already* reconciled, the rest of the universe will also be reconciled. Indeed as 2 Corinthians 5:19 says: "God was in Christ, reconciling the world unto Himself, not imputing their

---

2. "Eternal State and Death" in *Wycliffe Encyclopedia*, ed. C. F. Pfeiffer, Vol. I, p. 553.

---

*For the sake of simplicity in this brief presentation, the theological views of Karl Barth which bear on this issue, in which he comes very close to a Universalism of this type, are not discussed. Nor is the word *universal* to be confused with the use made of it by Reformed theologians to describe what amounts to Unlimited Atonement.

trepasses unto them." And so also John 3:17: "God sent not his Son into the world to condemn the world, but that the world through Him might be saved." To this might be added 1 John 4:14: "And we have seen and do testify that the Father sent the Son to be the Saviour of the world."

There are a number of passages which Universalists of this first class commonly take literally in order to prove their thesis:

> Therefore as by the offence of one, judgment came upon all men to condemnation, even so by the righteousness of one, the free gift came upon all men unto justification of life (Rom. 5:18).

> For God hath concluded them all in unbelief that He might have mercy upon all (Rom. 11:32).

> For to this end Christ both died, and rose, and lived again, that He might be Lord both of the dead and the living (Rom. 14:9).

> As in Adam all die, so in Christ shall all be made alive . . . . that God may be all in all (1 Cor. 15:22, 28).

> That in the dispensation of the fullness of time, He might gather together in one all things in Christ, both which are in heaven and which are in earth, even in Him (Eph. 1:10).

> [God] will have all men to be saved, and to come to the knowledge of the truth . . . . [Jesus Christ] gave Himself a ransom for all, to be testified in due time (1 Tim. 2:4, 6). *(Cf. pp. 162ff.)*

> For therefore we both labour and suffer reproach, because we trust in the living God, who is the Saviour of all men, especially of those that believe (1 Tim. 4:10). *(Cf. p. 166.)*

> He Himself likewise [was partaker of flesh and blood] that through death He might destroy him that had the power of death, that is, the devil (Heb. 2:14).

> He is the propitiation for our sins: and not for ours only, but also for the sins of the whole world (1 John 2:2). *(Cf. pp. 172ff.)*

Now Universalists who foresee no judgment whatever make two basic assumptions. The first is that God is more concerned with exhibiting his benevolence than demonstrating his justice, and the second is that man is essentially good and by nature wants to amend his ways, given the opportunity. He will only have to have his faults pointed out to him in the Judgment to repent immediately and turn from his wickedness and live.

Universalists hold that since God loves all men equally and gave his Son to die for their sins, He cannot conceivably display any vindictiveness or demand that man should also bear the penalty for offending Him. He is so filled with benevolence that He will forgive and dismiss all charges. One reproachful look will be sufficient to break down the recalcitrant, even as the Lord turned and looked at Peter. Men will weep bitterly for their sins and this repentance will validate the Atonement already made for them.

Such a view derives from a very inadequate conception of the disastrous effects of the Fall upon human nature. The assumption is made that man is still essentially good at heart and will feel perfectly comfortable in the presence of an absolutely holy God, no matter how wicked one has been during life. It is taken for granted that despite the testimony of history and personal experience, creatures who all their adult lives have been selfish and rebellious against what they know to be right will suddenly be entirely different.kinds of people, capable of contributing to the well-being of a perfect society (heaven) as soon as they are placed in the position of being able to do or be or have whatever they like without restraints of any kind—which of course is their concept of heaven. The possibility that everyone else will also be making precisely the same plans for personal self-satisfaction does not strike such people as any hindrance to the creation of an ideal society.

As to the nature of God, He is seen as a benevolent Father who is never angry at sin or seriously concerned in any way with our failings, which are all perfectly excusable. He will simply forgive. But as Albertus Pieters long ago pointed out, forgiveness is a much more difficult thing from God's point of view than it is from man's point of view.

Disobedience always requires sanctions. Unless there is a penalty for disobedience, obedience becomes a matter of total indifference.* If any law can be broken with impunity, it is an unnecessary law and should be abolished. Sin and penalty are riveted together, or sin is not sin but merely a harmless alternative. But we live in an ordered universe, a *cosmos*, which has been designed with two governing systems of law, one of which we call *natural* (or physical) and the other *moral* (or spiritual). It is difficult for us who are normally far more aware of these natural laws to realize that there really is another balancing system of laws which are of even greater significance because they are eternal and unbreakable, and not merely temporal and variable.

We know by experience that disobeying natural laws involves penalties, but to a surprising degree the consequences are not always fatal. We lose our balance and tumble to our hurt, but we may completely recover. To fall in respect to the spiritual order is a far more serious matter, however, because it is fatal. The penalty of falling over may be a wound which will heal: the penalty of sin is death. In this second world order there are no small slips that are comparatively harmless corresponding to the physical order. The temporal penalty in the natural context becomes an eternal one in the spiritual context.

---

*A. W. Pink wisely observed, "Precept without penalty is simply advice, or at most a request; and rewards without punishments are nothing but inducements" (*Gleanings from Scripture: Man's Total Depravity*, p. 306).

We observe this fundamental distinction in the fact of miracle. Whenever it pleases Him, God can superimpose on the natural order another set of laws, not hitherto known to us, which we call miracle. The Bible is filled with such instances, as for example when both the Lord Jesus *and Peter* walked on the water. But we do not have any evidence whatever of the suspension of a single principle altering the terms upon which the moral order of the universe is based. It is clear therefore that the moral order is far more exacting and immutable than the natural order. The moral law evidently cannot be "bent"; it is unadjustable. This implies that it is also far more fundamental, and any tampering with it would be more disastrous for the whole universe than would upsetting the cohesive bonds within the atom or removing gravitational forces, for example. The universe would cease to exist as a system of order, and this apparently would apply equally in the physical world as in the spiritual world. But we give little thought in daily life to the consequences of our moral failures.

The set of laws which we commonly suppose we can violate with least danger are the laws which in actual fact exact the most lasting and inescapable penalties. There are several reasons for the little respect which we pay to this awesome fact. One is that breaking the moral laws of the universe as a rule imposes a slow-acting penalty. In the physical order, if we step blithely over the edge of a cliff we are likely to pay the penalty a few seconds later. In the moral order it may be years before we *experience* any rebuff. "The mills of God grind slowly, yet they grind exceeding small," as Longfellow said in his poem "Retribution."

In the physical order it appears that with God all things are possible (Matt. 19:26), or to put it slightly differently, an almost infinite variety of adjustments can be made. But in the moral order no such flexibility exists. There are many things that even God is constitutionally unable to do—even if He wanted to. Of course *if* He wanted to do some of these things, He would not be God. God cannot lie, for example (Titus 1:2; Heb. 6:18). God cannot countenance iniquity (Hab. 1:13). Man can do these things, but God cannot. It looks as though God should be able, if He wishes, to dismiss man's disobedience and rebellion as of little consequence. He would then seem to be magnifying his benevolence by simply forgiving anyone who regrets his sin and admits his faults. But it is necessary to bear in mind that men may be sorry for entirely the wrong reasons. Sorrow is not always "godly" sorrow (2 Cor. 7:10); it may be remorse which is only a form of self-commiseration when it is discovered that things have not worked out as expected. This is not godly sorrow for sin but disappointment over failure where one had anticipated success. Such forms of repentance accomplish nothing towards the reformation of character; they only bear witness to the crumbling of false hopes. In Judas' case it led to suicide (Matt. 27:3-5), which is an illustration of "the sorrow of the world," a sorrow that, as

2 Corinthians 7:10 also points out, "worketh death." P. Carnegie Simpson in his book *The Fact of Christ* has observed that there is really no comparison between forgiveness in human relationships and the forgiveness of God. "Forgiveness is to man the plainest of duties; to God it is the profoundest of problems."[3] The reason for this fundamental difference in the two situations is that we are not responsible for sustaining either the physical or the moral fabric of the universe. When we overlook faults in one another, the fabric of the universe is not fatally disturbed. With God the situation is quite otherwise. If He should deliberately set aside these laws, the universe would collapse.

Pieters speaks of the "oughtness" of things and points out rightly that if God arbitrarily forgave He would destroy his own creation entirely in its most important constituent. To do this just once would be fatal, let alone to do it for millions of human beings who have merely repented when they realized they had "backed the wrong horse." It is no answer to say that the sinner has repented, for what is there about repentance that cancels the oughtness of the penalty? The criminal who maims an innocent man for life cannot compensate merely by repenting and saying, "I'm sorry," no matter how sincere he is.

To preserve the moral fabric of the universe there must be penalty. That is why God sent his Son into the world, that the whole moral fabric might be preserved, while yet providing a proper basis for the remission of sins. The only basis for such remission is that the Lord Jesus Christ bore the penalty in his own Person. But if any individual rejects this sole solution to the problem of forgiveness, then there is no other substitute penalty available. He must pay the penalty himself. Having rejected the only ground for forgiveness which preserves the moral order, there is nothing left for the guilty party except "a certain fearful looking for judgment" (Heb. 10:27). The word rendered *fearful* in this passage means, more literally, "terrible." The penalty for disregarding the natural laws of the universe is severe enough; the penalty for disregarding the moral laws of this universe is terrible—always.

Pieters wrote: "Some people think that because a man ought to forgive another man freely if he repents, therefore God ought to do the same." But the context is entirely different. Man is not responsible for maintaining the fabric of the moral universe; God is. We can forgive offences when others repent, and we should, because we have similarly offended. But we are both penitents in this context, and forgiveness means little more than agreeing to make allowance for one another. We cannot really forgive in such a way as to cancel the offence from the record as though it had never occurred. Only God can *forgive* in such a way that the order of the universe remains

---

3. Quoted in Albertus Pieters, *Divine Lord and Saviour*, p. 117.

intact—and He does so only because He Himself in the Person of his Son, the Lord Jesus Christ, paid the penalty required to preserve that moral fabric.

At the same time, how could there be any reward unless there is also punishment? The one is inconceivable without the other. To reward one above another is to inflict punishment on the other by lesser reward; and if *all* are equally rewarded, *none* are rewarded at all. One cannot plead for a universal amnesty and at the same time promise reward for good behaviour, for the concept of good behaviour implies a difference between individuals which a universal amnesty would ignore. Universalism which is based on the assumption of a general spirit of bonhomie in which both God and man equally disregard the issues of righteousness and sin is not really a promise of happiness for everyone but a denial of any absolute values of any kind, a heaven that is a moral vacuum and without character. Such a heaven would be meaningless and worse than earthly existence where, for all its tragedies, there are at least recognizable values because there are differences in reward.

Now a subterfuge which is often appealed to by evangelists who are anything but Universalists in their eschatology is to try to separate the sinner from his sin. The same principle has been adopted by Universalists who deny punishment. The idea is that God loves everyone equally and that what He hates is only their sin, which He views as something divorced from their persons. If He loves everyone but everyone is a sinner, then we must assume that the sinner is the object of his love while only the sinner's sin is the object of his displeasure. This looks like a neat arrangement, but is it really so?

In actual fact this arrangement creates an impossible situation whether it is a principle applied to punishment or reward. For when the wicked are punished we have to suppose that they stand aside as spectators watching some kind of substance which represents their sinfulness being punished while they themselves are in no way injured. If this were the case, then obviously the rich man in Luke 16:24 should not have asked Lazarus to cool *his* tongue but some kind of impersonal something which was outside of himself and associated only with the evils for which that tongue was responsible. But this is not what he actually did; he was himself tormented. It is impossible to conceive of the punishment of a man's sin without the man's suffering the punishment himself, for it is impossible to separate the sinner from his sin. It follows inevitably that God cannot at one and the same time love the sinner and hate his sin. If He loves the sinner it can only be because the sinner has been separated, that is, *absolved*, from his sin.

And what has been said of the punishment of the sinner manifestly applies with equal force to the rewarding of the saint. It is difficult to see how the redeemed could stand back and watch while his good deeds are rewarded without relation to himself as a person. In what objective sense would the reward be presented? We cannot ask, "To *whom?*" If we ask, "To *what* is the reward presented?" are we asking a meaningful question?

Surprisingly enough, Universalism creates more problems than does annihilation. For one thing our sense of justice is more severely damaged. Annihilation is at least a penalty, and though annihilation seems far more severe, the *penalty* of the penalty of annihilation is far less than the penalty of Universalism. For as we have seen, bland forgiveness is tantamount to throwing away the operating principle which governs the universe. Moreover, annihilation might be considered a more merciful form of judgment than unending torment. If there must be judgment, and one has the choice of unending torment or annihilation, there is little doubt which would be objectively preferable. Universalism cuts the Gordian knot by eliminating judgment, but only at the cost of destroying the whole—including the concept of reward.

We find ourselves on the horns of a dilemma, saving the benevolence of God (by a universal amnesty) at the expense of his integrity, or saving the justice of God (by annihilation of the wicked) at the expense of his wisdom and foresight—for surely to have created untold millions for extinction does challenge the worthiness of the original plan.

3. LIMITED PUNISHMENT

The classic passage which seems difficult to interpret in any way other than by assuming a limited period of punishment followed by release is found in Matthew 5:25, 26:

> Agree with thine adversary quickly, while thou art in the way with him; lest at any time the adversary deliver thee to the judge, and the judge deliver thee to the officer, and thou be cast into prison. Verily I say unto thee, thou shalt by no means come out thence, till thou hast paid the uttermost farthing.

Less unequivocal but with similar implications is Luke 12:46-48:

> The lord of that servant will come in a day when he looketh not for him, in an hour when he is not aware [i.e., not expecting], and will cut him in sunder and will appoint him his portion with the unbelievers. And that servant, which knew his lord's will and prepared not, neither did according to his will, shall be beaten with many stripes. But he that knew not, and did commit things worthy of stripes, shall be beaten with few stripes. For unto whomsoever much is given, of him shall much be required; and to whom men have committed much, of him they will demand the more.

There are significant parallelisms between these two warnings. The time of salvation, of escape from punishment for debts, is *now*. "Now is the day of salvation" (2 Cor. 6:2), and to delay is to run the risk of being caught in debt and unable to pay, and suddenly cast into prison. Once one is delivered to the judge, the consequences are inevitable. There is no question of amnesty.

Moreover, the penalty is suited to the measure of guilt. Transposing the story into the terms of the present discussion, we note that those who have heard the Gospel and rejected it would appear to be in a more serious position than those who have not heard it (Luke 12:48). There is an adjustment of penalty under the analogy of many or few stripes, a circumstance of particular importance since the number of stripes allowed as a maximum by law was only forty. Forty stripes must have been frightful torment and seemingly endless, since the guilty man appears to have been almost cut to pieces. Clearly, twenty stripes would not only be a less terrible punishment but it would also be shorter—and five stripes even shorter still. To speak of eternal punishment makes this kind of analogy inappropriate. There is the implied assurance that while there can be no shortening of the term it is not interminable, since the offending party by implication is to be released when he has paid the uttermost farthing.

The only alternative is to assume that in both parables the Lord was confining Himself to warnings about civil disobedience and the probable consequences. The Jewish people were at this time particularly grieved by the petty regulations imposed upon them daily by the Romans. These regulations involved such demeaning tasks as being forced to carry the baggage of a soldier whenever the soldier either could not manage it alone or did not feel disposed to do so. The assistance of any Jew could be demanded, and he was required by law to walk one mile. There were many aggravating taxes, the worst feature of which was that they were imposed in order to enable the aggravators to continue their aggravations! Small civil disobediences must have been frequent, a constant source of friction and ill-feeling between the oppressors and the oppressed. Both sides became exasperated finally to the point of open warfare. But was this really the intent of the Lord's words? It seems unlikely in either passage.

We thus have here some potential evidence of a more moderate view of future punishment than is commonly supposed to be reflected in many other passages. Yet the passages used to support everlasting torment are both very specific and very numerous, if we are reading them correctly. It would seem that these two passages hardly carry sufficient weight against so many with contrary implications, but they cannot be ignored. One way to resolve the apparent conflict would be to attach to the more numerous passages a different meaning by reinterpreting the significance of such words as *ever, everlasting, eternal,* and *eternity.*

But it seems difficult to justify the correction of so many passages to bring them into line with such a small number that appear to contradict them. It has often been said that the "plain reader" could not help but conclude from a study of the New Testament that the punishment of the unsaved is to be eternal in the sense of endless. And although certain versions have attempted by a retranslation of these four crucial words to give a different colour to the statements in which they occur, the impression remains that only by a form of special pleading can the alternative sense be maintained. The Church as a whole has remained uneasy about admitting such an alternative even though almost every child of God would welcome it if it could be clearly established. It is not merely a kind of natural bias which favours a form of vindicative punishment that creates this resistance, nor is it only long-established habit of thought, though both these factors may play a part. There is some intuitive feeling that to introduce hope of release is to remove much of the sanction of the demand which God makes upon his creatures for obedience. Yet many thoughtful people feel that any kind of obedience which results from fear of the consequences is not the kind of obedience God is seeking.

We might also argue from what we know of the justice of God and his expressed "delight" with the sons of men (Prov. 8:31) even in their rebellious state, that there would be no element of vindictiveness, of penalty imposed without benefit to the offender. Just as we recognize levels of responsibility for misconduct, depending upon the privileges of the offender, and adjust our system of penalties accordingly as Luke 12:46-48 clearly indicates, will not God do the same? But how can He do so if that awful equalizer of punishment, endlessness, is applied to all indiscriminately?* Few stripes or many stripes become meaningless terms. And it seems rather unnecessary for the Lord to have said anything about coming out thence (Matt. 5:26) if no such final release from prison was either contemplated or possible.

It has been suggested that the rich man who called across the great gulf to Lazarus (Luke 16:22-24) had already experienced some measure of change for the better in his own heart. Did he not, perhaps for the first time, show some concern for his brothers that they should be warned (vv. 27, 28)? It does suggest the emergence of some very slight improvement of character. Is it so very unlikely that the torments of hell, in addition to being punitive, should also be in some measure corrective?

In our culture we do not have much faith in corrective punishment, but in some respects we may be exceptional in this. The Russian people, for example, seem to be very differently constituted. Under conditions of suffering that we find appalling, such as are described by Solzhenitsyn, the Russian

---

*According to A. T. Schofield, in a paper before the Victoria Institute in London, "Endless time was never a part of the Jewish figurative teaching in the Talmud concerning Gehenna (which was the Valley of Hinnom). It always included the hope of exit after a longer or shorter period" ("Time and Eternity," *Transactions of Victoria Institute*, LIX:289).

spirit is frequently neither embittered nor hardened but only *chastened*. Perhaps we do not punish severely enough. The more we try to alleviate the aspect of *penalty* in our prisons, the more rebellious our prisoners seem to become. A good friend of mine in the United States once said to me, "I believe when we punish a child we must make the punishment severe enough to bring real tears. Unless the child weeps, he seems to harden his heart and simply becomes more rebellious." Perhaps this is the secret. We have been heading in the wrong direction. And perhaps the torments of hell, however they are induced, whether by self-accusation or by other means, are not intended to embitter but to chasten. The spirit must not be merely rebuked, it must be broken. "A broken and a contrite heart, O God, Thou wilt not despise" (Ps. 51:17).

The fire, then, would be both to consume and to purge. Even in Nature there are many circumstances in which fire achieves both purposes at once: the dross being flammable is consumed and removed, and the gold is refined. It may not be without significance that fire, not frost, is the agent of God's chastening because, although both can be equally painful and under certain conditions of test almost indistinguishable, only fire can both purge and refine at one and the same time.

This, of course, looks like the classic Purgatory. But such is not the case. Purgatory was for the redeemed in Roman Catholic view, for those not completely sanctified when they died and who needed this extra cleansing to prepare them for heaven. The believer is only partially covered by the Lord's sacrifice and is therefore called upon to endure some of the penalty himself, the penalty of unconfessed sins which must be atoned for in Purgatory. The heathen were not candidates for Purgatory but for hell, from which there was no hope of release.

But the view we are considering is not this at all. What we are speaking of here is the punishment of those who have rejected the Lord's sacrifice altogether. These must pay the *whole* price themselves, and will not come out thence till the penalty is paid in full.

But could it be that as one by one these tormented but purified souls come to the end, they like the Prodigal Son arrive once more in the Father's presence as spiritually innocent, not born again but purged of the effects of the Fall and ready to begin a new process of development in *spiritual* life? It would not be necessary to assume that the fires of hell have completely neutralized the individual's prior development during life. An individual with the intellectual capacity of an Einstein would retain those capacities, the purging process relating only to spiritual and not intellectual development. For there is no reason to suppose that death will destroy the trained mind of the sinner any more than it will destroy the trained mind of the saint. Perhaps finally the sinner will be willing to bow his knee and acknowledge Jesus Christ not as *Saviour*, but as *Lord*, to the glory of the

Father (Phil 2:10, 11). When the last sinner has paid the full penalty and been cleansed by fire, then God could become "all in all" (1 Cor. 15:28) and the last enemy *death* will be abolished (1 Cor. 15:26), since there will be no more creatures separated from the Creator.

Would it be altogether improper to suppose that, in the process of purification or perhaps in the process of re-education and rebuilding, the Lord's people will have a work to do, these returned prodigals becoming their spiritual charges? There might well be a divine matching in such a process, the simple caring for the simple and the more sophisticated for the more sophisticated. Each prodigal will then be an appropriate charge of a child of God whose personal history has best fitted him or her to foster that particular individual.

There are passages of Scripture which might be taken to support such a view. For example, in Isaiah 49:8-10 the following words are addressed to the saints:

> Thus saith the Lord, in an acceptable time have I heard thee, and in a day of salvation have I helped thee: and I will preserve thee, and give thee for a covenant of the people, to establish the earth, to cause to inherit the desolate heritages [RSV has here "to apportion the desolate heritages"]; that thou mayest say to the prisoners, Go forth; to them that are in darkness, Show yourselves. They shall feed in the ways, and their pastures shall be in all high places. They shall not hunger nor thirst; neither shall the heat nor the sun smite them: for He that hath mercy on them shall lead them, even by the springs of water shall He guide them.

Similarly in Isaiah 57:15, 16 we find the words:

> For thus saith the high and lofty One that inhabiteth eternity, whose name is Holy; I dwell in the high and holy place with him that is of a contrite and humble spirit, to revive the spirit of the humble, and to revive the heart of the contrite ones. For I will not contend for ever, neither will I be always angry: for the spirit should fail before Me, and the souls which I have made.

It almost seems as though the Lord was aware of the possibility of the destruction of the soul in despair, and would not have it so. We do not have here the sense of an angry Judge who is vindictive, but a Judge whose perfect justice is nevertheless not without a strain of mercy. Is it possible then that the Lord through the saints will thus make known to principalities and powers in heavenly places the wisdom of God according to his eternal purpose which He purposed in Christ Jesus our Lord (Eph. 3:10, 11)?

But, of course, this is far beyond what Berkouwer calls the "boundaries" of Scripture as presently understood, and must be treated with great caution until (and *if*) God confirms or repudiates it by fresh illumination on the matter from some hitherto unsuspectedly relevant portion of his Word. For the Word of God continually expands our understanding and is in turn broadened in its relevance as we bring forth out of its treasures things new and old (Matt. 13:52).

One of the most godly of the early Greek Fathers was a man named Origen (c. 185-254), who, as far as we know at the present time, was probably the first Christian to write a commentary on any extended portion of Scripture. He was also one of the first to set forth any form of systematic theology. He was a most prolific writer and the number of works credited to him ranges from six thousand reported by Epiphanius, two thousand by Pamphilus, to eight hundred reported by Jerome. The decline in reported numbers may reflect the progressive loss of manuscripts. One of his most important works is titled *De Principiis*.

Origen addressed himself to the present issue in *De Principiis* (III. vi. 3) as follows:

> I am of the opinion that the expression by which God is said to be "all in all" means that He is "all" in each individual person. Now He will be "all" in each individual in this way: when everything that any rational understanding, cleansed from the dregs of any sort of vice, and with every cloud of wickedness completely swept away, can either feel, or understand, or think, will be wholly God; and when it will no longer behold or retain anything other than God, but when God will be the measure and standard of all its movements; then God will be "all," for there will no longer be any distinction between good and evil, since evil nowhere exists; for God is all things, and to Him no evil is near: nor will there be any longer a desire to eat from the tree of the knowledge of good and evil, on the part of him who is always in the possession of good, and to whom God is all.
>
> So then, when the end has been restored to the beginning, and the termination of things compared with their commencement, that condition of things will be re-established in which rational nature was placed, when it had no need to eat of the tree of good and evil; so that when all feeling of wickedness has been removed, and the individual has been purified and cleansed, He who alone is the one good God becomes to him "all" and that not in the case of a few individuals, or of a considerable number, but He Himself is "all in *all*." And when death shall no longer anywhere exist, nor the sting of death, nor any evil at all, then verily God will be all in all.

Admittedly, Origen tended to be speculative, but his devotion and scholarship were unquestionable and he remained for twenty-eight years the head of the Catechetical School in Alexandria. His father was martyred in 202, during the persecution of Septimius Severus, and Origen wishing to follow his father was prevented from doing so only when his mother took all his clothes and hid them! We thus have the interesting situation in which a young man in the heroic devotion of his spirit was willing to throw away his life, but not his dignity. At any rate, it is clear that the problem of the final destiny of the non-elect troubled the more thoughtful in the Church of God then as it still does today.

So we have yet to consider the final alternative. It is the alternative which has always seemed to reassert itself in the end. One reason perhaps is that those who adopt any one of the other three alternative views have in the long run tended to depart steadily from the faith. Yet these alternatives may not have been the *cause* of their departure but a *symptom* of a certain attitude of mind which places more confidence in common sense than in revelation. In his book *Probation and Punishment* (p. 273), S. M. Vernon, without specifying which kind of Universalism he is referring to, quotes an anonymous writer, with approval, as follows:

> The history of Universalism shows that it began in this country [USA] with an acceptance of orthodoxy on all points but that of the eternity of future punishment, and that gradually it proceeded to reject the deity of Christ, the Trinity, vicarious atonement, and the entire evangelical scheme. Is it wise to leap into a gulf until we know how deep it is?

The warning is one we do well to heed, yet not perhaps to the extent of being entirely discouraged from constantly re-examining the issue, for there are surely yet many things to be discovered from the Word of God. And it could be, after all, that the everlastingness of punishment belongs to its effects, not its duration, as Dean Farrar suggested.

4. EVERLASTING PUNISHMENT

The great majority of Christian readers have to depend upon a *translation* of the New Testament, being unable to follow the original Greek. Merely to set forth the many passages of Scripture in which the concept of everlasting punishment is predicated on the use of such words as *ever, everlasting,* and *eternal,* all of which are translations of the original Greek word *aiōn* in some form or another, serves no useful purpose, since the meaning of this word *aiōn* is still a matter of dispute among scholars. To refer to these translations begs the issue, for these translations reflect a theological bias and it is possible that they may not have genuinely captured the intent of the original. All the translations that have achieved general acceptance whether in English, French, German, Spanish, Dutch, Latin, or any other Indo-European language (with the exception of Greek, of course), have assumed that the pejorative words in the original convey the idea of everlastingness.

To make the assumption of everlasting punishment is natural enough because the same qualifying term is used for *life*. The saddest thing about life is its transitoriness. Indeed, since all things seem to grow old and die, permanence becomes a virtue in itself in most cases. Not to die seems naturally to be an essential characteristic of any ideal existence anyway. So whatever the nature of the life that the Lord promises, it must at least have endlessness or it is not ideal at all. A more perfect kind of life that is nevertheless transitory would be far from ideal. Endlessness is a *sine qua non*. When the Old Testament speaks of God as eternal, commentators have often pointed out that the writer's object was to comfort the reader with the assurance that while man is like the grass of the field in the brevity of his existence, God remains. God is always there. It is not so much that God has endless existence as it is that He abides unchanged (Heb. 13:8) through all the changing scenes of personal life and human history.

When the word *eternal* is applied to life in the same sense that it is applied to the being of God, we must surely have something much more in mind than simply its everlastingness. While it is essential that such a life should not be transitory, it is even more important that it should have the right quality and depth to distinguish it from the shallowness of our present life. The Lord's promise that it would be life abundant (John 10:10) seems to outweigh the implications made elsewhere that it will never end. It is perhaps our preoccupation with length rather than depth that makes us equate the word *eternal* with endlessness. All our lifetime we live in fear of death, so that it seems essential in our view that eternal life should be endless, and undoubtedly it is. We need only remind ourselves of the Lord's words, "He that liveth and believeth in Me shall never die" (John 11:26). But mere continuance cannot be the chief characteristic of the life which is in Christ Jesus. Indeed, continuance may not be the *essence* but the *result* of the quality of that life. So long as it is perfect it is endless. Endlessness inheres in its perfection, not its perfection in it endlessness. What is perfect in the sight of God is imperishable. It is not perfect because it is imperishable, but imperishable because it is perfect. It is only the imperfect that must be perishable in the very nature of things from God's point of view.

We ought to expect, therefore, that if a single word is used to describe life and punishment, this single word must have two different meanings, since the two modes of existence are fundamentally different. We cannot properly speak of eternal life and eternal punishment if the word in both cases has the same value, for what is perfect cannot be equated even antithetically with what is imperfect.* If only one word is available *(aiōn)* and it must be applied to the being of God, to the nature of the new life in Christ, and to

---

*With reference to everlasting punishment, A. T. Schofield, in "Time and Eternity," a paper presented before the Victoria Institute of London in 1927, suggests that the idea of eternity is not duration but *changelessness*. Thus in relation to everlasting or eternal punishment the essential feature is not one of endlessness but of unchangingness. The idea will appeal to those who see such punishment as endless, for although changelessness is not to be equated with endlessness it seems to include it. On the other hand, it is conceivable that something might be changeless only while it lasts, as the note held by a violin or a trumpet or a piano. In fact it seems almost impossible to settle this issue on the basis of the meaning of the word which is normally considered to be the key. (See *Transactions of Victoria Institute*, LIX:287.)

the torments of the wicked in hell, it must of necessity have several different meanings. It is therefore a word which is coloured by the noun it qualifies, and not the reverse as we tend to assume.

A study of the Hebrew and Greek words which are often translated *ever*, *everlasting*, and so forth, tends to support the view that these translations are more in the nature of interpretations. Now the original words in the Hebrew of the Old Testament and the Greek of the New *(ólam* and *aiōn)* are undoubtedly equivalents in every way, so that the meaning of the New Testament *aiōn* must be determined not from Classical Greek usage but from the Hebrew usage of the word *'olam*. We have in certain respects a much better knowledge of the nuances of meaning in ancient Greek than we do in ancient Hebrew. But this knowledge can be misleading because the Greek of the New Testament had its meaning stamped upon it not from ancient Greek but by the Jewish scholars who somewhere around 250 B.C. undertook to make an authoritative translation of the Hebrew Scriptures into Greek. By the time of our Lord this translation had in fact achieved something of the stature of the King James Version in the English-speaking world, and it had a profound influence on the literary forms and vocabulary of the New Testament.

One of the greatest authorities on this Jewish-Greek authorized version known to us as the Septuagint was Henry B. Swete (1835-1917). He considered that the New Testament phraseology had a Hebrew rather than a Classical Greek source, the Greek of the Septuagint which clearly underlies it being a special kind of Greek created to reflect Hebrew thought transposed into a Greek tongue. The New Testament is full of Hebraisms spelled out in Greek in a way that is foreign to Classical Greek, even as many of the common Greek words received new and highly specialized meanings.

As we have noted, the Hebrew word frequently translated *everlasting* is *ólam*. It occurs approximately 420 times in the Old Testament. Of these occurrences it is translated some 350 times as *ever*, *everlasting*, and so forth (267 times as *ever*, 64 as *everlasting*, 15 as *evermore*, and less often *eternal*, *forever* or *always*, etc.). The Septuagint used the Greek *aiōn* to represent *ólam* 372 times, and employed circumlocution for the remainder. It is clear therefore that *'olam* and *aiōn* are genuine equivalents in the Scriptures. *Aiōn* is the word employed throughout the New Testament to convey the same basic concept as *'olam*. The meaning of *aiōn* in the New Testament, whether applied to life or to punishment, hinges therefore in the final analysis not upon Classical Greek usage, where we might follow either Plato or Aristotle who expounded upon its use and came to antithetical conclusions, but upon the Hebrew, where the concept of everlasting seems to be almost, if not quite, absent.

The nearest approach in Hebrew to the idea of eternity, of time stretched to infinity, is not in the Hebrew word *'olam* per se but in *'olam* followed by the compound *le* (to) and *ádh* which is approximately equivalent to the English word *beyond*. Whenever the Septuagint translators met in the Hebrew text with the compound form *ólam le 'adh*, they tended to use the intensive form of the Greek word *aiōn*, which is achieved by repeating it, a device coming through into English as for "ever and ever." Comparatively few occurrences of this Hebrew compound form appear in the text, a circumstance which appears to reflect the relative disinterest of the Jewish people in so distant a subject. The Hebrew mind was experience-oriented and very practical in its religious aspirations.

As to the precise meaning of the word *ólam*, there is still no certainty. According to Brown, Driver, and Briggs *(Hebrew and English Lexicon of the Old Testament)*, its root is dubious. Basically it appears to mean an age of indefinite length, *indefinite* but not infinite, though as a rule *long*, or "of old." In so far as a man may make a covenant to last as long as he lives, a covenant of a lifetime, so the word came to mean essentially (as far as the individual was concerned) a covenant *for ever*. But this was understood in the practical framework of a single life. It meant essentially unbreakable, not to be cancelled, perpetual in this sense. Applied to divine things it achieved an expanded meaning and has the sense of lastingness. Yet the concept of eternity does not seem to be consciously explicit in such usage. A compact lasts as long as there are two partners to it. If one of them should die, it is automatically terminated. There are many situations in the Old Testament in which for historical reasons permanence was not in view, yet the word *ólam* was used as though it were. A city which was to be utterly destroyed was to be punished *for ever*. Again we are reminded of Dean Farrar's statement that punishment might be terminated but the effects could be everlasting.

In many cases the idea of a specific period of time is clearly intended. The Book of Daniel was particularly important for its influence on later Jewish eschatology, especially in so far as it carried the promise of the coming Messiah and the Kingdom He was to establish, the Golden Age to come. Those who were to take part in this Golden Age were encouraged to look forward to the "life of the age to come," a hope which was translated in the Septuagint as *aiōnian* life; and this phrase appears in the New Testament where it is rendered into English as "eternal life." If a distinction is allowed between the words *eternal* and *everlasting*, such life is more accurately termed eternal than everlasting, for eternal is more qualitative, and is nearer to the original than is everlasting which places the emphasis upon quantity. It is perhaps significant that in Matthew 25:46, which employs the same word *aiōn* twice, first with reference to punishment and then with reference to life, the King James Version has nevertheless made a distinction by rendering this passage thus: "And these shall go away into *everlasting* punishment but the righteous into life *eternal*." In many modern translations Matthew 25:46 is not translated this way, the word *eternal* being used in both connections. One has the feeling that translators are shying away from the word *everlasting*. According to the concordance the *Revised Standard Version* has not employed the word in the New Testament at all.

In their rendering of Matthew 25:46 it seems the translators of the King James Version made a distinction between punishment and life, applying to the first a quantity (everlasting) but to the second a quality (eternal). Consciously or unconsciously many people feel happier with the word *eternal*, simply because it avoids placing the emphasis on the time element. But by adopting the word *everlasting* instead of the word *eternal* in Matthew 25:46 an effort seems to have been made to lay emphasis on the lastingness of punishment as though to distinguish it from the quality of life. This shows in a small way how differently we tend to view the two destinies, yet very few people reading this passage are aware of this inconsistency.

In the non-canonical books the word *olam* is often used with a clearly limited meaning even in connection with life. Thus in Enoch 10:10 we read of certain rebellious men whose vain hope was to enjoy "eternal life," which is then spelled out more specifically as being life for five hundred years. In the same chapter a man who is to be punished "forever" (v. 5) is, in verse 12, more specifically to be punished for a period equivalent to seventy generations. In Enoch 14:5 this is spelled out as being "for all the days of the world."

Now the same uncertainties meet us when we examine the Greek equivalent *aiōn*.[4] Classical Greek usage doesn't help us. Commonly the Greeks distinguished between *aiōn* and *kronos* by saying that *kronos* was "time" as such, whereas *aiōn* was "a fragment of time." However, Plato disagreed and deliberately reversed the two meanings, holding that *aiōn* meant timelessness, eternity in which there were no divisions into days or weeks or years, while *kronos* was divisible into measurable units. As a matter of fact Plato elaborated his understanding of the word *aiōn* by saying that it stood for three ideas: (1) timelessness; (2) what is unchanging; and (3) what is perfect. But then Aristotle came along and said that the opposite was true: *kronos* was the abstract concept *time*, whereas *aiōn* was a fragment, that is, *a* time.

The translators of the Septuagint do not seem to have been guided at all by any such refined distinctions. And in the New Testament under the inspiration of the Holy Spirit, the two were sometimes combined, as in Romans 16:25, 2 Timothy 1:9, and Titus 1:2, where we read of "the ages of time," which is rendered into English as "before the world began." One has the feeling that what is intended is a sense of the dim and distant past, but there is little or no precision in the use of these terms that would justify

---

4. *Theological Dictionary of the New Testament*, Vol. I, pp. 197 f.

dogmatism. The general sense when such phrases are applied to the future seems to be much the same: time stretched-out indeed, but not necessarily endless.

As Hermann Sasse of Erlangen points out in his treatment of *aiōn* in Kittel's *Theological Dictionary of the New Testament*, the use of reduplication merges the idea of a fragment of time "into that of a long but limited stretch of time. . . . At this point we are confronted by the remarkable fact that in the Bible the same word *aiōn* is used to indicate two things which are antithetical, namely, the eternity of God and the duration [transitoriness] of the world."[5]

That the word often has a clearly defined sense of restricted time is amply demonstrated by its use with such prepositions as *before* and *during*, by qualifying words such as *the former, this, the future*, and by phrases such as "the end of the age(s)," and so on. Indeed, there are many verses in which the word *aiōn* cannot mean "eternity." For example, the mystery of the Church was not hidden from *eternity* (Eph. 3:9), nor have the prophets been speaking since *eternity* (Luke 1:70), nor can one suppose that a man who had just received his sight would say, "Since *eternity* was it not heard that any man opened the eyes of one born blind" (John 9:32). In each case the intention is clearly not "eternity," but "within the memory of man" or "for a very long time" or simply "since the world began." On the basis of such references quite elaborate schemes of *ages* have been devised by various commentators, each age being viewed as distinct and having a beginning and an ending, some of which are already past and at least one of which is yet to come, equated with the millennium.

It is not unnatural with such flexibility of meaning that the word should sometimes appear to be used in a contradictory way. In the apocryphal *Testament of Issachar*, the phrase *hypnos aiōnios* is translated as "an eternal sleep" from which nevertheless the sleepers are to be awakened in due course.[6] If when referring to the past the word *aiōn* cannot really mean *everlasting*, it appears unwise to assume it does when referring to the future, even though it seems obviously to do so when we find it used to qualify life in Christ or the nature of God Himself.

But if the meaning is not one of quantity but quality, the situation is clarified in that the time element may not be the writer's concern. That God is everlasting is certainly true but if his existence is to be described solely in those terms, the Hebrew needs some form of expression other than merely the use of the word *'olam*, and correspondingly the Greek needs some word other than *aiōn*. It may be that the New Testament writers wanted chiefly to emphasize the essential difference between the tentative and unsatisfactory

5. Ibid., p. 202.
6. *New International Dictionary of New Testament Theology*, Vol. I, p. 442.

nature of this life on one hand, and the quality of the life that is in Christ Jesus on the other. Accordingly, following Jewish interpretations of the Old Testament prophets, especially Daniel, these New Testament writers associated the life in Christ with the life of the Messianic age to come and thus adopted the same terminology as used in the Book of Daniel—*aiōnian* life, which we have translated "eternal life."

In many ways these ancient people, both Jews and Gentiles, thought more deeply than we commonly do about the nature of existence in the world to come, and about the being of God in relation to the passage of time. Though Augustine stood at the intellectual pinnacle of his age, his wonderful thoughts on these matters were not entirely without precedent. Although that age seemed barbarous enough, it was by no means an intellectual vacuum. The Jewish philosophers like Philo often came quite close to a position similar to that adopted today regarding the nature of time as we now have begun to understand it. But Augustine's conception of the eternity of God is certainly remarkable enough in present light. He wrote for example *(Confessions,* XI. 13):

> Thy years stand together at the same time . . . nor are some pushed aside by those that follow, for they pass not. . . . Thy years are one Day and thy Day is not like our sequence of days but is Today. . . . Thy Today is eternity.

What eternity means with respect to the being of God is not unendingness so much as "now-ness," what Luther termed *totum simul,* "the whole at once," or "total immediacy."[7] What we experience as now and, furthermore, is experienced without hope of future change, is to all intents and purposes experienced as *unending.* Although such matters are certainly beyond our comprehension, we must surely suppose that God does not experience the present with any consciousness of an ending to it. It is this absence of consciousness of the end that seems to be the nearest we can get to eternity. Yet in times of intense suffering which in anticipation we know *will* come to an end, there may at the time be no conscious hope of an end so that it becomes unbearably endless while it lasts. The present is then all that we experience and since we carry the present with us there is no conscious passage of time and suffering becomes timeless. To all intents and purposes it becomes unending. Perhaps in some such direction as this we must go if we are to understand in any meaningful way what eternal punishment really means. And the more severe the punishment, the more endless is must appear to be.

If the word *'olam* determines the meaning of the word *aiōn* in the New Testament, we may note only that it has apparently a basic meaning of

---

7. T. F. Torrance, *Space, Time, and Incarnation,* p. 34.

"hiddenness," which when applied to the passage of time means only undefined as to its length. Perhaps the word *eternal* is to be preferred to the word *everlasting* because it leaves us a little more free of the connotation of endlessness as its chief characteristic. Whether 'olam and aiōn mean everlasting is a matter which we cannot determine with certainty. When the Hebrew le 'adh is appended to the word 'olam we probably come very close to the idea of time so extended as to reach beyond any conception of its magnitude. Remembering that the Septuagint translators adopted the policy of rendering this Hebraism into Greek form as "unto the ages of ages," a phrase which comes into our English versions as "for ever and ever," we can suppose only that the mind of the Spirit is conveying to us that punishment is just as lasting as the Hebrew 'olam le 'adh suggests to our minds—awful enough, whether everlasting or not, and beyond conceiving.

20

THE CONTINUING DILEMMA

We have considered the pros and cons of four alternative views of the destiny of the unsaved. The first (annihilation) seems unsatisfactory because although it recognizes the justice of punishment, it leaves unexplained why creaturely existence should be given to an enormous number of individuals who are simply to be eliminated as though they had never existed. Total annihilation by an act of God seems a more ruthless form of punishment than even endless torment that is self-imposed.

The second alternative (Universalism) essentially ignores the problem of justice entirely, and from a Christian point of view is quite unacceptable.

The third alternative, limited punishment, in the dual role of vindication of the law and correction of the lawbreaker, makes much more sense, yet still presents problems until we can be sure that the meaning of the words translated *eternal, eternity,* and so forth, has been unequivocally established one way or the other.

Finally, the alternative of everlasting torment, though our versions almost without exception favour it, seems somehow to challenge the justice of God and the wisdom of his original purpose. Yet the other alternatives in one way or another do not seem to have commended themselves to the Church of God throughout the centuries. Is it likely that for all these centuries we have been holding a false view in this matter?

In summary, then, it may be said that almost all the arguments against either annihilation or any kind of restoration tend to be vitiated by poor understanding of what is being rejected. First of all, with the exception of the Universalist view, none of those who argue for these other alternatives would question the certainty of punishment for sin. Judgment leads to condemnation, and the penalty imposed is commensurate with the offence. Annihilationists like Basil Atkinson simply argue that men suffer for their sins to the point of extinction. By this means hell is made in some ways an even more awful reality than is suggested by everlasting punishment, which is at least a form of personal survival.

Those who see the penalty as a sentence to be served out until the last farthing has been paid do not hold, as some critics imply, that the absence of saving faith still makes the position of the condemned quite hopeless. The advocates of limited penalty would not deny that the man condemned to hell dies in unbelief and therefore cannot be saved *on the ground of faith*. They would argue rather that whereas faith saves from the penalty of sins, these are not saved from the penalty of sins but suffer that penalty themselves. Their ultimate release is not an escape from the penalty but the payment of full satisfaction. Nor is saving faith applicable to them when they are released; such faith would be too late.

One argument against annihilation which is often raised is that the "soul" is inherently immortal, though Scripture says otherwise (1 Cor. 15:53, 54). The soul is only *contingently* immortal, as sustained by God. The Lord alone had the power of life within Himself. Even unfallen Adam's immortality was contingent upon God. Immortality of the soul is Greek invention, not biblical revelation. Luther considered the doctrine of the immortality of the soul as the last of the five cardinal errors of the papal church.[1]

The issue, in short, is not, Will the unbelieving be punished? but Will they be punished for ever and ever? If so, the universe will never be free of the presence of evil and the Lord's victory will never be truly complete. As Augustus H. Strong sums up the situation:

> In any treatment of the subject of eternal punishment we must remember that false doctrine is often a reaction from the unscriptural and repulsive over-statements of Christian apologists. We freely concede: (1) that future punishment does not necessarily consist of physical torments, it may be wholly internal and spiritual; (2) that the pain and suffering of the future are not necessarily due to positive applications by God, they may result entirely from the soul's sense of loss and from the accusations of conscience; and (3) that eternal punishment does not necessarily involve endless successions of suffering, for since God's eternity is not mere endlessness we may not forever be subject to the law of time.[2]

To this I can say, Amen! And add only that probably one of the most awful features of hell, and one least often acknowledged in the literature, is the fact of isolation.* The individual will not merely be separated from God

1. Basil F. C. Atkinson, *Life and Immortality*, p. iii.
2. *Systematic Theology*, p. 1035.

---

*It is significant that far more attention is being paid by psychiatrists today to the factor of isolation as a cause of human sickness. Deprivation of company has turned out to be one of the most distressing punishments a prisoner can be subjected to, and there are moves to have it internationally outlawed as an inhumane form of torture. Harry Stack Sullivan (a renowned psychotherapeutic clinical psychiatrist regarded by some to be second only to Freud) observed that "absolute isolation would be equal to death." The most awful of all isolations is to be cut off from God, which probably entails being also cut off from all other human beings. In this case it has to be viewed as a self-imposed torture.

but from all other men. There will be no company to commiserate with. As C. S. Lewis put it, "There are no personal relationships in hell."

Perhaps there we have to let the matter rest, having seemingly exhausted the means of elucidation at our disposal. The reader will undoubtedly sense my own leaning towards the third alternative, but I must confess that I am by no means confident that such a hopeful alternative is justifed in the light of our Lord's own awful warnings.

PART SIX

**Summing Up
Synergism: The Fatal Leaven**

21

THE LEAVEN OF SYNERGISM

Throughout the centuries since God covenanted to save man through the sacrifice of his Son, Jesus Christ, whereby He provided a full, perfect, and sufficient satisfaction for our sins, one aberration of the Gospel has recurrently threatened the truth. It is the view that man must make some contribution himself in securing his salvation. It is not the size of this contribution that is the important factor, but *the necessity of it.*

It is as though healing is promised to a terminally ill patient if only he will prepare himself in some way, or yield himself, or present himself at his own expense before the physician. The Roman Catholic Church holds strongly to the view that some self-preparation is essential, usually in the form of a willingness to make amends for wrongs done, or to effect some self-correction in order to merit the grace of God. The Lutherans place the emphasis on the necessity of man's willingness to accept God's salvation. Modern evangelism calls upon men to "make an active decision" as though to pick up the phone and arrange an appointment. Or the patient is invited at least to unlock the door before the physician can make this call and heal him. This door is locked on the inside and can be unlocked only by the patient.

But there is no question of the patient's healing himself. On this there is a wide measure of unanimity. He does need the Saviour; but he is not considered to be without any ability to assist in some way, or at least to co-operate in the healing process, though the measure of his co-operation may amount to no more than that he allow the physician to visit his soul.

Whatever form the human contribution takes, it always means that salvation is a co-operative activity. Salvation is not a God-*only* process, but a God-*and* process. This working together is termed *Synergism*. Such Synergism was a religious philosophy with humanistic overtones even in Old Testament times, and it has been in evidence in every generation. It is man's demand not to be considered impotent. Man admits his sickness, but he is unwilling to admit his death.

Theologically, Synergism is fatal to any sound Christian soteriology, for it is a denial of man's total bondage in sin and a claim to some remaining will to absolute good. By and large, the Greek Fathers were always content to place the grace of God and the free will of man side by side, and as a consequence, the Greek Catholic Church early assumed a synergistic position. The Roman Catholic Church followed suit—though somewhat more slowly. Since the Council of Trent it has held dogmatically that man prepares himself and disposes his own heart to receive the grace of justification.[1]

The Reformation was a total break with this almost universal teaching, a recovery of a truly monergistic doctrine of salvation, a *Solus Deus* position. But like all other revivals of the truth of the Gospel, it soon began to be plagued by those who demanded that allowance be made for man's autonomy if he was not to be a mere puppet, some tiny admission of spiritual competence, some small part which man might be called upon to play, as a sound basis for exhortation in preaching the Gospel and as an incentive to those striving after holiness.

Luther himself was wholly committed to a *God only* position. Unregenerate man is spiritually dead, not perfectly well as Pelagius held, nor merely sick as Arminius held, but completely dead as Calvin held. We have already traced briefly the gradual leavening of Luther's position by the synergistic tendencies of those who followed him (pp. 59-64). This fatal return to the heresy of all ages was, in Germany, largely the result of one man, Melancthon (1497-1560).

It was this godly and gentle man whose humanistic influence introduced once again the corrupting stream into Lutheran theology, where it took the seemingly harmless form of attributing to man nothing of a positive nature but only a non-resistance to the overtures of God without which the Holy Spirit is unable to make the grace of God effectual unto salvation. Luther was aware of this tendency from its first reappearance among his disciples and spoke out strongly against it. He said (in *Table Talk*, under the heading "Of Free Will"):

> Some allege that the Holy Spirit works not in those that resist Him but only in such as are willing and give consent thereto, whence it follows that free will is a cause and helper of faith; and consequently the Holy Ghost does not work alone through the word, but that our will does something therein.
> But *I say it is not so; the will of man works not at all* in his conversion and justification . . . . It is a matter on which the Holy Spirit works (as a potter makes a pot out of clay), equally in those that are averse and remiss as in St. Paul. But after the Holy Spirit has wrought in the wills of such resistants, then He also manages that the will be consenting thereto.[2]

---

1. Louis Berkof, *History of Christian Thought*, p. 146.
2. Quoted in W. G. T. Shedd, *Dogmatic Theology*, Vol. II, p. 474.

Luther agreed that Melancthon seemed to be asking very little when he proposed that we grant only man's non-resistance as his contribution. But Luther warned that this "very little" was more dangerous than the "very much" that the Pelagians demanded when they argued that man was wholly capable of meriting the grace of God, for it had the appearance of a relatively harmless concession whereas in fact it was a fatal one. For those who support it are teaching that "we are able to obtain righteousness and grace by that 'very little.' " The Pelagians struck Luther as being more forthright. He saw Melancthon's apparently mild concession as the more dangerous because it was less patent. The very violence of his diatribe against Erasmus in his famous work on *The Bondage of the Will* stemmed from the subtlety of this synergistic position. And in this connection Luther wrote:

> These [Pelagians] assert that it is not a "certain little something" in us by which we obtain grace, but we obtain it by whole, full, perfect, great and many efforts and works. Our adversaries [the followers of Melancthon], however, declare that it is a mere trifle and practically nothing at all by which we merit grace.[3]

And here, as Luther saw it, was the danger. It is no longer the Gospel of the sovereign grace of God that we are proclaiming, but the delusion of the sovereignty of man who in the final analysis holds the trump card. It is not a Gospel of revelation but a Gospel of common sense, for why would God command men to repent or yield to the overtures of the Holy Spirit if man did not of his own have freedom of will to do so?

In the Western Church the drift to Synergism was slower than in the East. At the Council of Orange (A.D. 529) it had been agreed that "God does not wait for man's decision."[4] But at the Council of Trent (1545-63) the synergistic view was officially written into the theology of the Roman Catholic Church, it there being agreed that man's will is a decisive factor. Berkhof says: "In the days of the Reformation the monergism of the Reformers was opposed by the Roman Catholic Church with greater vehemence than any other doctrine."[5] Indeed it may very well have been the major reason for the calling of the Council of Trent in the first place.

The Reformation was nothing less than the purging out of this synergistic tendency. And yet so strongly entrenched in human nature is its basic philosophy that within fifty years it was, as we have seen, once again embraced by the Lutheran community, and the terms of surrender were couched virtually in the words of Melancthon. Melancthon held that conversion is the result of the combined action of three causes: (1) the truth of God; (2) the

---

3. Quoted in Ewald M. Plass, *What Luther Says: An Anthology*, Vol. I, p. 346.
4. G. C. Berkouwer, *Studies in Dogmatics: Divine Election*, p. 31.
5. Berkhof, *History of Christian Thought*, p. 146.

Holy Spirit; and (3) the will of man. He made a *facultas* out of a mere *capacitas*, an active ability for grace out of a passive aptitude for the reception of it.[6] And so after over five hundred pages of debate and discussion of the issue, the *Formula of Concord* finally confesses: "Towards this work [of grace] the will of the person who is to be converted does nothing but *only lets God work in him* [my emphasis] until he is converted."[7]

Meanwhile Arminius, assuming this active ability on the part of the unregenerate man, argued that the basis of Predestination to Election was God's foreknowledge of those who would exercise this capacity responsively. And by this heresy he left a similar community of misguided followers both in Holland and, even more seriously, in England and the New World, who, holding the synergistic view, formed a further major division of the Church of God. Methodism, and out of Methodism a number of other denominational bodies, cultivated the error which has largely inspired modern evangelistic methods. Such human techniques of persuasion are held to be in line with God's appointed method of reaching the unregenerate. Thus man usurps the convicting role of the Holy Spirit of God.

The consequences of these "persuasive techniques" in the free world are yet to become fully apparent. Already we see a great resurgence of religious enthusiasm, but if we look at the staying power of these thousands of decisions for the Lord it has to be admitted that the picture they often present a few months after "conversion" suggests there may be something seriously amiss with the method of evangelism, if not perhaps even more seriously with the theology which has inspired the method.

Karl Barth in a small volume entitled *God in Action*, sometimes referred to as his "Little Dogmatics," elaborates on this issue. To him Monergism is the keystone to any stand by the Church against the secular authority because it places the outcome of events squarely in the hands of God. As soon as we begin to say "God *and,*" man becomes increasingly important as the decision maker and God decreasingly so. In due time God is reduced almost to the position of assistant or even bystander. The battle becomes not the Lord's but man's. When the world comes in like a flood to overwhelm the Church as Hitler's world did, man finds himself alone in his weakness and no longer able to meet the challenge. In 1934 Barth said to an English audience:

> I'm sure that everyone of you is horrified [i.e., by what was happening to the Christian Church in Germany], and says in his heart: I thank God that I am not a German Christian! I assure you that it will be the end of your road, too. It has its beginning with "Christian *life*" and ends in paganism.

---

6. Augustus Strong, *Systematic Theology*, p. 816.
7. *Book of Concord*, p. 539.

For, if you once admit "not only God but I also," and if your heart is with the latter—and friends, that's where you have it—there's no stopping it . . . .

Let me warn you now. If you start with God and . . . you are opening the doors to every demon. And the charge which I raise against you, I lay before you in the words of Anselm: *Tu non considerasti, quandi ponderis sit peccatum!* You have failed to consider the weight of sin. And that is the sin: that man takes himself so very seriously.[8]

This seemingly small concession to which Luther refers always has had the effect of opening the way to a flood of error that effectively neutralizes Paul's Gospel of salvation by faith without works. As W. G. T. Shedd observed:

The position of partial ability or synergism comes to the same result with that of full ability [i.e., Pelagianism] so far as divine independence and sovereignty are concerned. For it is this decision of the sinner to contribute his quota, to "do his part" in the transaction, which conditions the result. It is indeed true, upon this theory, that if God does not assent, the act of faith is impossible. But it is equally true that if the sinner does not assist, the act of faith is impossible. Neither party alone and by himself can originate faith in Christ's atonement. God is as dependent in this respect as man.[9]

G. C. Berkouwer wrote in a similar vein: "This theme of synthesis [between God's grace and man's power of decision] runs like a red thread through the history of the doctrine of election. It is the theme of harmony, of co-operation."[10] And it is a poison, fatal to the Gospel. It is a heresy that slowly undermines all the implications of the truth of the sovereign grace of God. Warfield refers to it as

the evil leaven of synergism, by which God is robbed of his glory and man is encouraged to attribute to some power, some act, some initiative of his own, his participation in that salvation which has come to him from pure grace . . . . Any intrusion of any human merit, or act, or disposition, or power, as ground or cause or occasion, into the process of divine salvation—whether in the way of power to resist or ability to improve grace, or the employment of grace already received—is a breach with Calvin.[11]

And a breach with Calvin in this respect is a breach with Augustine and, more importantly, a breach with Paul. In short, the difference between a monergistic and a synergistic faith, between a *God only* and a *God and*

---

8. *God in Action*, pp. 137 f.

9. *Dogmatic Theology*, Vol. II, p. 472.

10. *Divine Election*, p. 29.

11. Benjamin B. Warfield, *Calvin as a Theologian and Calvinism Today*, pp. 16,

Gospel, is nothing less than the difference between the Gospel of our Lord and Saviour Jesus Christ on the one hand, and all other religious systems of belief, whether pagan or so-called Christian, on the other. There are basically only two alternatives. If man contributes any essential part towards his salvation, he effectively becomes his own saviour, even if that contribution takes no more concrete form than that of merely allowing God to act by non-resistance.

There is here a clear point of demarcation. It is all of God or it is no good news at all. If man is free to resist, God is not free to act, for He is bound by man's freedom. If God is to be free to act, man must be bound by the will of God. There can be nothing harmful in such a bondage, since perfect freedom by definition is perfect obedience to perfect law, and "the law of the Lord is perfect" (Ps. 19:7). In the perfect order which is yet to come there can never be any conflict of wills since God's will and man's will are to be one, and both are therefore to be entirely free. But in a fallen world, God's grace must be irresistible or man's will can remain forever opposed to God, and the will of the creature overrides the will of the Creator.

In truth there is no "Gospel" that is not entirely rooted in the sovereignty of God's grace in salvation, which is the sum and substance of Calvinism. And I venture to say that it must be not merely a three-point or a four-point Calvinism, but a *five*-point Calvinism. To depart from this is to surrender the whole by giving it a logical incoherence which makes it indefensible whether from Scripture or by reason. The crucial issue is the sovereignty of God's grace in the most absolute sense, a pure unabashed Monergism.

The only defence against Synergism is an unqualified Calvinism ascribing all the glory to God by insisting upon the total spiritual impotence of man, an Election based solely upon the good pleasure of God, an Atonement intended only for the elect though sufficient for all men, a grace that can neither be resisted nor earned, and a security for the believer that is as permanent as God Himself.

If such a system creates some problems because of the limitations of our comprehension, the problems it creates are not nearly as serious as the problems of another kind created by the alternatives which in fact destroy the Gospel altogether by dishonouring the sacrifice of the Lord Jesus Christ both as to its sufficiency and its efficacy.

BIBLIOGRAPHY

Aquinas, Thomas. *An Introduction to Saint Thomas Aquinas.* Edited by Anton C. Pegis. New York: Modern Library, Random House, 1948.

Atkinson, Basil F. C. *Life and Immortality.* Published privately; no date.

Augustine. In *Nicene and Post-Nicene Fathers.* New York: Christian Literature Co., 1887 (First Series).
Anti-Pelagian Writings: On Marriage. Volume V.
Enchiridion. Volume III.
On Grace and Free Will. Volume V.
On Rebuke and Grace. Volume V.
On the Gift of Perseverance. Volume V.
On the Predestination of the Saints. Volume V.
On the Spirit and the Letter. Volume V.

Bangs, Carl. *Arminius.* Nashville: Abingdon Press, 1971.

Barth, Karl. *God in Action.* New York: Round Table Press, 1963.

Berkhof, Louis. *History of Christian Thought.* London: Banner of Truth, 1975.

_____. *Systematic Theology.* Grand Rapids: Eerdmans, 1969.

Berkouwer, G. C. *Studies in Dogmatics: Divine Election.* Translated by Hugo Bekker. Grand Rapids: Eerdmans, 1960.

_____. *Studies in Dogmatics: Faith and Perseverance.* Translated by Robert D. Knudsen. Grand Rapids, Eerdmans, 1958.

Boettner, Loraine. *The Reformed Doctrine of Predestination.* Philadelphia: Presbyterian and Reformed, 1975.

Boston, Thomas. *Human Nature in Its Fourfold State.* London: Religious Tract Society, 1720.

Browne, E. Harold. *An Exposition of the Thirty-Nine Articles.* London: Parker & Son, 1860.

Butterfield, Herbert, *Christianity and History,* London, Bell & Sons, 1950.

Calvin, John. *Institutes of the Christian Religion.* Edited by John T. McNeill. Philadelphia: Westminster Press, 1960.

_____. *The Pastoral Epistles.* Translated by Pringle. 1948.

Chadwick, Henry. *The Early Church.* New York: Penguin Books, 1967.

Cunningham, William. *Historical Theology.* London: Banner of Truth, 1969 reprint.

Dabney, Robert L. *Discussions: Evangelical and Theological.* London: Banner of Truth, 1967 reprint.

_____. *Lectures in Systematic Theology.* Grand Rapids: Zondervan, 1972 reprint.

Edersheim, Alfred. *The Life and Times of Jesus the Messiah.* 2nd edition. New York: E. R. Herrick, 1886.

Frankl, Viktor. *Man's Search for Meaning.* New York: Pocket Books, 1973.

Gromacki, Robert Glenn. *The Virgin Birth: Doctrine of Deity.* Nashville: Thomas Nelson, 1974.

Hague, Dyson. *The Life and Work of John Wycliffe.* London: Church Book Room, 1935.

Hodge, Charles A. *Systematic Theology,* Grand Rapids: Eerdmans, 1973 reprint.

Killen, R. A. "Eternal State and Death." In *Wycliffe Encyclopedia.* Edited by C. F. Pfeiffer et al. Chicago: Moody Press, 1975. Volume I, p. 553.

Klooster, Fred H. *Calvin's Doctrine of Predestination.* Monograph Series III. Grand Rapids: Calvin Theological Seminary, 1961.

Lewis, C. S. *The Great Divorce.* New York: Macmillan, 1966.

McGiffert, A. C. *A History of Christian Thought.* New York: Scribner's, 1933.

Meyer, Carl S. "Luther." In *New International Dictionary of the Christian Church.* Edited by J. D. Douglas. Grand Rapids: Zondervan, 1974, p. 609.

Neander, Augustus. *Church History.* Translated by J. Torrey. Edinburgh: T. & T. Clark, 1891.

Neve, J. L. *A History of Christian Thought.* Philadelphia: Muhlenberg Press, 1946.

Packer, J. I. *Evangelism and the Sovereignty of God.* Chicago: Inter-Varsity Press, 1966.

_____. Introductory Essay in John Owen, *Death of Death.* London: Banner of Truth, 1963.

_____. "The 'Old' Gospel of Calvinism vs. the 'New' Gospel of Arminianism." In *Sword and Trowel* (1969). Volume 1, no. 5, pp. 5-12.

Parker, T. H. L. *John Calvin: A Biography.* Philadelphia: Westminster Press, 1975.

Pieters, Albertus. *Divine Lord and Saviour.* London: Fleming Revell, 1949.

Pink, A. W. *Gleanings from Scripture: Man's Total Depravity.* Chicago: Moody Press, 1966.

Plass, Ewald M. *What Luther Says: An Anthology.* St. Louis: Concordia, 1959.

Polo, Marco. *Travels.* New York: Library Publications, no date.

Robertson, A. T. *A Harmony of the Gospels.* New York: Harper & Row, 1950.

Schofield, A. T. "Time and Eternity." In *Transactions of Victoria Institute* (1927). Volume LIX, p. 289.

Shedd, W. G. T. *Dogmatic Theology.* Grand Rapids: Zondervan, 1969 reprint.

Simon, Edith. *The Reformation.* In *The Great Ages of Man.* New York: Time-Life, 1966.

Spurgeon's Sermon Notes. Edited by David O. Fuller. Grand Rapids: Zondervan, 1974.

Strong, Augustus. *Systematic Theology.* Valley Forge, PA: Judson Press, 1907.

Sullivan, J. W. N. *The Limitations of Science.* New York: Pelican Books, 1938.

Torrance, T. F. *Space, Time, and Incarnation.* Oxford: University Press, 1969.

Vernon, S. M. *Probation and Punishment: A Rational and Scriptural View of the Future of the Wicked.* New York: Ketcham, 1886.

Warfield, Benjamin B. *Biblical and Theological Studies.* Edited by Samuel G. Craig. Philadelphia: Presbyterian and Reformed, 1968.

_____. *Calvin and Augustine.* Edited by Samuel G. Craig. Philadelphia: Presbyterian and Reformed, 1971.

_____. *Calvin as a Theologian and Calvinism Today.* London: Evangelical Press, reprint of 1909 edition.

Zanchius, Jerome. *Absolute Predestination.* Grand Rapids: Sovereign Grace Publications, 1971.

STANDARD REFERENCE WORKS

Book of Concord. Translated by Theodore G. Tappert. Philadelphia: Fortress Press, 1959.

A Catholic Dictionary. Edited by William E. Addis and Thomas Arnold. 11th edition. London: Virtue and Co., 1928.

New International Dictionary of New Testament Theology. Edited by Colin Brown. Grand Rapids: Zondervan, 1975.

New International Dictionary of the Christian Church. Edited by J. D. Douglas. Grand Rapids: Zondervan, 1974.

Theological Dictionary of the New Testament. Edited by G. Kittel. Grand Rapids: Eerdmans, 1972.

INDEX OF SCRIPTURE REFERENCES

2 Thessalonians

1:7-9—329
2:12—118
2:13—25, 140, 245
2:14—245

1 Timothy

1:15—122, 157, 287
2:1-6—162, 169
2:1, 2—165
2:4—165, 333
2:5—165
2:6—115, 165, 333
2:15—166
3:16—108
4:10—149, 166, 333
4:16—166
5:21—33, 132
6:10—164

2 Timothy

1:7—121
1:9—245, 348
1:10—350
1:19—140
2:13—203
2:15—214
2:19—139
2:25—123, 291
2:26—62
3:5—39
3:7—288
4:2—279
4:3—66
4:18—166

Titus

1:2—335, 348
2:11—163
2:14—150

Hebrews

1:3—150
1:14—246
2:9—115, 170, 171
2:14—209, 333
3:9, 10—258
4:15—110
5:7—108

5:8—246, 253
5:9—253
6:1—183, 214, 220
6:1-6—214
6:4—203
6:5—203, 220
6:6—203, 220
6:9—220
6:9-12—220
6:11—112
6:18—118, 335
7:16—253
7:21—183
7:25—203
8:10—97, 119
9:12—150
9:26—115
10:10—156, 203
10:14—203, 223
10:26—221, 329
10:27—221, 329, 336
10:39—218
11:3—40
11:5—254
11:25—26
11:33—97
12:2—125, 203, 253
12:6—204
12:6-11—182
12:9—109, 211
12:11—257
12:17—183, 234
13:8—345
13:20, 21—248

James

1:18—9, 145, 176, 178,
    179, 188, 281, 299
2:6—164
2:10—126, 293
2:23—258
5:15—167
5:19—211, 167
5:20—167, 211

1 Peter

1:3—176
1:5—193, 203
1:9-11—222
1:12—112
1:15—162

1:19—245
1:20—245
1:21—124
1:23—177, 178, 179,
    281
1:24—108
2:6—33, 132
2:9—150, 297
2:24—108, 150, 205
4:10—249
4:17—205
5:6—260
5:7—260
5:9—173

2 Peter

1:4—182
1:10—249
2:1—211
2:19—22, 23, 118
2:22—222
3:4-7—168
3:9—152, 166
3:13—330

1 John

1:1—108
1:3—207
1:5—295
1:7—115, 207
2:1—172
2:2—149, 172, 333
2:19—222
2:27—203
2:29—177
3:5—110, 115
3:9—177, 198
3:15—272, 273
3:16—160
3:24—212
4:2—108
4:7—177
4:9—150
4:14—149, 333
4:17—255
4:19—25, 230, 291
5:1—124, 177
5:4—177
5:16—200, 210
5:18—177
5:19—151

INDEX OF NAMES

INDEX OF SUBJECTS

381